WHISTLEBLOWING IN THE EU BANKING AND FINANCIAL SECTOR

This book provides guidance on the laws of whistleblowing in the EU banking and financial sector.

Covering all the relevant EU legislation, including the Directive on the protection of whistleblowers, the book provides insights from France, Luxembourg and Ireland alongside the relevant international, Council of Europe, and US laws. Following the adoption of the Directive on whistleblowing, the book offers the necessary understanding of the legal landscape, relevant case-law analysis, and examples stemming from EU and US jurisdictions.

Providing clarity and expert analysis in a complex area, the book is a must-read for researchers, government officials, and practitioners.

Hart Studies in Commercial and Financial Law: Volume 21

Hart Studies in Commercial and Financial Law

Series Editors: John Linarelli and Teresa Rodríguez de las Heras Ballell

This series offers a venue for publishing works on commercial law as well as on the regulation of banking and finance, and the law on insolvency and bankruptcy. It publishes works on the law on secured credit, the regulatory and transactional aspects of banking and finance, the transactional and regulatory institutions for financial markets, legal and policy aspects associated with access to commercial and consumer credit, new generation subjects having to do with the institutional architecture associated with innovation and the digital economy including works on blockchain technology, works on the relationship of law to economic growth, the harmonisation or unification of commercial law, transnational commercial law, and the global financial order. The series promotes interdisciplinary work. It publishes research on the law using the methods of empirical legal studies, behavioural economics, political economy, normative welfare economics, law and society inquiry, socio-legal studies, political theory, and historical methods. Its coverage includes international and comparative investigations of areas of law within its remit.

Volume 1: The Financialisation of the Citizen: Social and Financial Inclusion through European Private Law
Guido Comparato

Volume 2: MiFID II and Private Law: Enforcing EU Conduct of Business Rules
Federico Della Negra

Volume 3: Reforming Corporate Retail Investor Protection: Regulating to Avert Mis-Selling
Diane Bugeja

Volume 4: The Future of Commercial Law: Ways Forward for Change and Reform
Edited by Orkun Akseli and John Linarelli

Volume 5: The Cape Town Convention: A Documentary History
Anton Didenko

Volume 6: Regulating the Crypto Economy: Business Transformations and Financialisation
Iris H-Y Chiu

Volume 7: The Future of High-Cost Credit: Rethinking Payday Lending
Jodi Gardner

Volume 8: The Enforcement of EU Financial Law
Edited by Jan Crijns, Matthias Haentjens and Rijnhard Haentjens

Volume 9: International Bank Crisis Management: A Transatlantic Perspective
Marco Bodellini

Volume 10: Creditor Priority in European Bank Insolvency Law: Financial Stability and the Hierarchy of Claims
Sjur Swensen Ellingsæter

Volume 11: Chinese and Global Financial Integration through Stock Connect: A Legal Analysis
Flora Huang

Volume 12: The Governance of Macroprudential Policy: How to Build Regulatory Legitimacy Through a Social Justice Approach
Tracy C Maguze

Volume 13: A Socio-Legal Theory of Money for the Digital Commercial Society: A New Analytical Framework to Understand Cryptoassets
Israel Cedillo Lazcano

Volume 14: Venture Capital Investment and Government Incentives: Law, Regulation and Policy Design
Tamara Wilkinson

Volume 15: Regulating Primary Markets in the Capital Markets Union: Between Uniformity and Differentiation
Konstantinos Serdaris

Volume 16: Regulating Innovation in the Digital Age: A Demand-Centred Toolbox for the Data-Driven Economy
Nikita Divissenko

Volume 17: Digital Assets in Enforcement and Insolvency: Securing Creditor Access and Protecting Customer Interests in the Crypto World
Edited by Christian Koller and Matthias Lehmann

Volume 18: Transnational Mortgage Law: Reconstructing the Global Framework for Housing Finance
Guido Comparato and Irina Domurath

Volume 19: UNCITRAL Model Laws on Digital Trade: Electronic Transferable Records, Digital Identity and Trust Services
Luca G Castellani

Volume 20: Markets in Crypto-Assets Regulation: Law and Technology
Edited by Matthias Haentjens, Louise Gullifer and Ilya Kokorin

Volume 21: Whistleblowing in the EU Banking and Financial Sector: Theory and Practice
Dimitrios Kafteranis

Whistleblowing in the EU Banking and Financial Sector

Theory and Practice

Dimitrios Kafteranis

•HART•
OXFORD • LONDON • NEW YORK • NEW DELHI • SYDNEY

HART PUBLISHING
Bloomsbury Publishing Plc
Kemp House, Chawley Park, Cumnor Hill, Oxford, OX2 9PH, UK
1385 Broadway, New York, NY 10018, USA
Bloomsbury Publishing Ireland Limited, 29 Earlsfort Terrace, Dublin 2, D02 AY28, Ireland

HART PUBLISHING, the Hart/Stag logo, BLOOMSBURY and the Diana logo are trademarks of Bloomsbury Publishing Plc
First published in Great Britain 2026

1

A catalogue record for this book is available from the British Library.

A catalogue record for this book is available from the Library of Congress.

ISBN:	HB:	978-1-50997-745-1
	ePDF:	978-1-50997-746-8
	ePub:	978-1-50997-747-5

Typeset by Lumina Datamatics Ltd

For product safety related questions contact productsafety@bloomsbury.com

To find out more about our authors and books visit www.hartpublishing.co.uk. Here you will find extracts, author information, details of forthcoming events and the option to sign up for our newsletters.

To my parents, Stergios and Eleni, and to my sister, Maria-Sofia, for their love, support, and encouragement, which helped me believe in myself and pursue my dreams.

FOREWORD

It is with great pleasure and a strong sense of collegial admiration that I write this foreword to Dimitrios Kafteranis's book, which addresses one of the most pressing and conceptually rich areas of contemporary legal scholarship: whistleblower protection and its role in modern systems of governance and accountability.

I have had the privilege of knowing Dimitrios over a number of years, first through academic conferences, then in my capacity as external examiner of his doctoral thesis, and subsequently as a collaborator in research projects and publications. Throughout this time, I have come to appreciate his intellectual rigour, as well as his sustained commitment to advancing our understanding of whistleblowing as both a legal and a societal phenomenon.

As I engaged with the manuscript, I was struck not only by the depth and clarity of the legal analysis, but also by the author's ability to situate whistleblowing within a broader normative and institutional context. This is not simply a doctrinal account of legal rules and protections. Rather, it is a thoughtful exploration of the principles, tensions, and policy choices that underpin whistleblower protection across the European and international legal framework.

The book explores the complex interplay among legal frameworks, organisational cultures, and individual decision-making. It highlights the extent to which legal protections, however sophisticated, remain deeply dependent on the environments in which they operate. In doing so, it reminds us that whistleblowing is not merely a technical issue of compliance, but a fundamental component of democratic accountability and institutional integrity. As has often been observed in the literature, whistleblowers act as a form of guardians of the public interest, providing a crucial mechanism through which wrongdoing can be exposed and addressed.

One of the most compelling aspects of this work is its engagement with the interaction between different legal regimes; most notably, the relationship between freedom of expression as protected under human rights law and the compliance-oriented frameworks developed within regulatory systems. This analysis clarifies the existing legal complexities in this area of law and raises important questions about the future direction of whistleblower protection in an increasingly interconnected and regulated world.

At the same time, the book is not limited to analysing the current state of the law. It is also, implicitly and at times explicitly, a call for reflection and reform. In an era characterised by rapid technological change, growing reliance on complex organisational structures, and heightened expectations of transparency, the role of whistleblowers is more important than ever. Yet, significant challenges remain:

fear of retaliation, cultural barriers, and the limitations of existing legal frameworks continue to inhibit effective reporting. The questions that emerge are both difficult and necessary: How can legal systems better support those who come forward? How can organisations foster a culture of openness and accountability? And how can we reconcile the tension between confidentiality, loyalty, and the public interest?

The originality of the book also lies in its comparative and outward-looking perspective. By engaging with different legal systems and regulatory approaches, Dimitrios contributes to a broader and more sophisticated understanding of whistleblower protection as a global issue, shaped by shared challenges, distinct legal traditions and institutional contexts.

Overall, the analysis is both insightful and thought-provoking. This is a work that will be of considerable interest to legal scholars, practitioners, policymakers, and anyone concerned with the integrity of institutions and the rule of law.

To borrow and adapt the spirit of Constantine P Cavafy, the journey that this book invites us to undertake is indeed one 'full of adventure, full of knowledge'. I have every confidence that it will make a lasting and meaningful contribution to the field and that it will be received with the attention and recognition it so clearly deserves.

Stelios Andreadakis
Reader in Corporate and Financial Law
Brunel University of London

ACKNOWLEDGEMENTS

I want to thank all the colleagues at the University of Luxembourg, Coventry University, and others around the globe for their ideas and suggestions throughout the preparation of this book. More specifically, Dr Stelios Andreadakis has provided me with his support from the beginning of my academic journey to the present. The same applies to my colleague, Dr Aikaterini Pantazatou, for her constant support and encouragement.

CONTENTS

TABLE OF CASES

Primary Sources

CJEU Law

ECtHR Case Law

French Case Law

German Case Law

Irish Case Law

Luxembourg Case Law

Swiss Case Law

UK Case Law

US Case Law

TABLE OF LEGISLATION

Australian Legislation

Belgian Legislation

Canadian Legislation

EU Legislation

French Legislation

Irish Legislation

UK Legislation and other

UN Conventions

US Legislation

INTRODUCTION

The purpose of this book is to examine the level of protection offered by EU law to whistleblowers who report breaches of the EU's banking and financial sector legislation, assess it critically, and propose changes to enhance whistleblower protection. The scandals presented below have triggered a shift in perception and the need for whistleblowing. The protection of whistleblowers is a delicate issue, as several interests are at stake, and a fair balance should be achieved. On the one hand, there is a constant need to detect wrongdoing, enforce rules, and impose sanctions on those who violate the law. On the other hand, whistleblowers who report wrongdoing to enforce regulations and protect society often face retaliation or complex rules, leading to confusion and discouragement from reporting.

Whistleblowers are regarded as regulatory intermediaries who address the problem posed by the lack of knowledge in complex markets.[1] They are valued based on the information they provide to enhance regulatory goals.[2] Whether reporting internally or to the authorities, whistleblowers are a significant source of information and a valuable asset for maintaining market order. Eventually, there is a need to protect them and provide a strong incentive for them to come forward.

I. Introducing Whistleblowing to the Legal World

The phenomenon of whistleblowing is not new. Since humans started seeing themselves as structured societies, reporting public-interest misconduct has been recognised as an effective criminal policy tool.[3] In Ancient Athens (fourth–fifth centuries BC), citizens could report breaches of law and request prosecution, regardless of personal involvement.[4] Athenian citizens could denounce another citizen who was violating Athenian laws. These persons were widely known as 'sycophants'.[5] During the Roman Empire, the phenomenon persisted, with 'delatores'

[1] I Kampourakis, 'Whistleblowers as Regulatory Intermediaries: Instrumental and Reflexive Considerations in Decentralizing Regulation' [2020] *Regulation & Governance* 11.

[2] ibid.

[3] AD Berkowitz, CM Tusk, IJ Downes and CS David, 'Whistleblowing' (2011) 16(4) *Employee Relations Law Journal* 15, 32.

[4] HJ Wolff, 'Normenkontrolle und Gesetzesbegriff in der attischen Demokratie' (1970) extrait des Sitzungsberichte der Heidelberger Akademie der Wissenschaften, 8ff and 18ff.

[5] F Panagopoulou-Koutnatzi, *The Institution of Whistleblowing: An Ethical-Constitutional Perspective* (Sakkoulas Publications, 2016) 18ff.

allowed to bring accusations, testify, or provide information.[6] Whistleblowing was revived in the modern era by Ralph Nader.

Ralph Nader, a US political activist, first defined whistleblowing and codified the term 'whistleblower'. He defined it: 'An act of a man or woman who, believing that the public interest overrides the interest of the organisation he serves, blows the whistle that the organisation is involved in corrupt, illegal, fraudulent or harmful activity.'[7]

During Nader's period and afterwards, whistleblowing was seen as moral bravery, where individuals felt morally obliged to blow the whistle.[8] Under this perception, whistleblowing is enshrined in the rights to freedom of expression and to be informed.[9] The whistleblower was not just sharing information about wrongdoings but was also exercising their right to freedom of expression to inform the world of these wrongdoings. Their protection was necessary to exercise their right to freedom of expression. This conception of whistleblowing reflects a democratic perception.[10] Whistleblowers serve the public interest and democratic values by informing the public. However, the necessary protection was not always available. Over time, this democratic perception was replaced by a managerial view.

At the turn of the twentieth century, a global coalition against corruption began to form. The UN and other organisations adopted legal measures to combat corruption.[11] In these legal instruments, whistleblowers played a key role in addressing corruption. Whistleblowers were seen as effective anti-corruption tools, and the legislation aimed to protect them. The concept of whistleblowers as anti-corruption tools flourished, and their protection attracted the attention of legal scholars.[12] The anti-corruption role of whistleblowers emphasised a managerial view, with their importance tied to the information they reported and their protection. The democratic perception diminished, replaced by a utilitarian and instrumental view.

The managerial approach to whistleblowing has become more apparent recently.[13] Over the past two decades, whistleblowers have drawn attention from legal scholars and global citizens because of the banking and financial scandals they revealed in the US and EU. These scandals demonstrate the pivotal contribution of whistleblowing in contemporary society. Nevertheless, rather than focusing on the information disclosed and on how to protect whistleblowers effectively, the

[6] SH Rutledge, *Imperial Inquisitions: Prosecutors and Informants from Tiberius to Domitian* (Routledge 2001) 9.

[7] ibid.

[8] JC Peterson and D Farell, *Whistleblowing – Ethical and Legal Issues in Expressing Dissent* (Kendall/Hunt Publishing Company, 1986) 7.

[9] W Vanderkerchhove, 'Freedom of Expression as the "Broken Promise" of Whistleblower Protection' (2016) 10 *Revue des droits de l'homme* (online), para 28, journals.openedition.org/revdh/2680?lang=en accessed 15 May 2025.

[10] JP Foegle, 'Le lanceur d'alerte dans l'Union Européenne: démocratie, management, vulnérabilité' in M Disant and D Pollet-Panousis (eds), *Les lanceurs d'alerte* (LGDJ éd. 2017) 107–120.

[11] United Nations Convention against Corruption (adopted on 31 October 2003, entered into force 14 December 2005) GA Res 58/4 (UNCAC).

[12] Vanderkerchhove (n 9) paras 9–10.

[13] Foegle (n 10). See also Kampourakis (n 1).

focus tends to be on questioning whistleblowers' personal motives. The scandals showed that whistleblowers faced difficulties, lacked protection, and were often criticised negatively.

II. The First Coup: The Financial Crisis of 2002–2003

The 2002 US financial crisis underscored the global need for whistleblowers' protection. The 'too big to fail' motto and the 'laissez-faire' approach led to corporate failures, which in turn resulted in adverse social and financial consequences.[14] Voices of concern raised by employees of major corporations had been ignored. The abuses by corporations, such as Enron and WorldCom, ranged from accounting fraud to market manipulation. Employees lost salary and pension benefits, leading to public distrust in the government.[15]

The 2002 financial crisis led the United States to adopt the Sarbanes-Oxley Act (SOX) under the Republican administration of President George W Bush.[16] SOX had an impact, as it was one of the first laws to adopt provisions on corporate whistleblowing, providing protection. SOX's labour protections are notable given the US's 'at-will' employment doctrine, where employees have few rights upon dismissal. It was the government's response to public outcry and distrust and an effort to regulate capital markets better. Regarding whistleblowing, SOX emphasised the importance of internal reporting systems. These reporting systems resulted in corporate compliance programmes that regulate behaviour and encourage employees to report misconduct internally.

SOX's influence extended beyond the US. US corporations in the EU had to create internal reporting systems to comply with SOX's whistleblower provisions. This obligation established the first high-level contact between EU Member States

[14] D Windsor, 'Capitalism' in LM Salinger (ed), *Encyclopaedia of White-Collar and Corporate Crime*, 2nd edn (SAGE, 2013) 141. The 'too big to fail' refers to big banks, corporations and financial institutions which are, simply, too big (in terms of activities and growth) that make it impossible to fail. The 'laissez-faire' approach, supported by libertarians and conservatives, opposes market regulation, because it regards it as an abuse of power by the government and as a limit to the economic well-being of the nation.

[15] Two women became symbols of that period: Sherron Watkins and Cynthia Cooper. They raised concerns about their corporations' decisions and practices, but both were ignored. Watkins reported internally, first anonymously, but she quickly identified herself behind the letters received by the human resources, revealing fraud in Enron. Even though she had a meeting with the founder, CEO and Chairman of Enron, Kenneth Lay, she faced retaliation and lost her role as vice president. Cooper raised fraud concerns internally, but she could not stop the harm coming from the top of WorldCom. These two women, along with Coleen Rowley, gained the title of 'Person of the Year' from *Time Magazine* in 2002.

For more information, see J Morse and A Bower, 'The Party Crasher' *TIME* (2002–2003) content.time.com/time/specials/packages/article/0,28804,2019712_2019710_2019677,00.html accessed 15 May 2025.

[16] Sarbanes–Oxley Act of 2002 ('Public Company Accounting Reform and Investor Protection Act (in the Senate) and 'Corporate and Auditing Accountability, Responsibility, and Transparency Act') (Pub. L. 107–204, 116 Stat. 745, enacted July 30, 2002).

and whistleblowing in the corporate sector. Nevertheless, this unprecedented approach was not always welcomed. France's resistance to the SOX obligations was remarkable. The National Committee on Informatics and Liberties (CNIL) refused to allow US corporations to implement internal reporting schemes, characterising them as 'snitching' (*délation*, a term with a negative connotation for reporting in French-speaking environments).[17] This resistance was eventually overcome, allowing US corporations to adopt internal reporting systems. However, it showed EU Member States were not ready to accept whistleblowing, given their history.[18]

A. Second Coup: The Financial Crisis of 2009–2010

SOX failed to prevent a new crisis affecting the US and the world.[19] In 2009, the subprime mortgage crisis caused major banks and financial institutions worldwide to fail. The corporate compliance systems, which were criticised, failed to detect wrongdoing promptly. The consequences of this crisis are widely known, even to those not directly involved in banking and financial law. The recession after the 2009 financial crisis is still visible, especially in the southern EU Member States.[20] The US reacted to the 2009 financial crisis by enacting the Dodd-Frank Wall Street Reform and Consumer Protection Act of 2010.[21]

The 2009 financial crisis revealed the SOX model's shortcomings in US internal reporting, as reflected in Dodd-Frank's provisions on whistleblower channels.[22] The whistleblowing provisions of the Dodd-Frank Act mark a milestone in protection, showing a major change in the US. Most significantly, the whistleblower should report to the Securities and Exchange Commission (SEC) rather than internally if they want to be protected and, further, considered for a financial reward. While SOX promotes internal whistleblowing, Dodd-Frank requires whistleblowers to report to the SEC.[23] Internal whistleblowing is not excluded under Dodd-Frank,

[17] CNIL, Déliberation relative à une demande d'autorisation de MacDonald's France pour la mise en œuvre d'un dispositif d'intégrité professionnelle, n° 2005-110 (2005).

[18] N Lenoir, 'Les lanceurs d'alerte – Une innovation française venue d'Outre-Atlantique' (2015) 42 *La Semaine Juridique – Entreprise et Affaires* 38.

[19] RH Filler and JW Markham, 'Whistleblowers—A Case Study in The Regulatory Cycle for Financial Services' (2018) 12 *Brooklyn Journal of Corporate, Financial & Commercial Law* 337.

[20] M Luchtman and J Vervaele, 'Enforcing the Market Abuse Regime: Towards an Integrated Model of Criminal and Administrative Law Enforcement in the European Union?' (2014) 5(2) *New Journal of European Criminal Law* 196.

[21] Dodd-Frank Wall Street Reform and Consumer Protection Act (Pub. L. No. 111-203, § 929-Z, 124 Stat. 1376, 1871, 2010).

[22] The Congress's purpose, by adopting the Dodd-Frank Act, was to 'motivate those with inside knowledge to come forward and assist the Government to identify and prosecute persons who have violated securities laws and recover money for victims of financial fraud'. Senate Report n° 111-176, The Restoring American Financial Stability Act (2010) www.congress.gov/congressional-report/111th-congress/senate-report/176/1 accessed 15 May 2025.

[23] S Osborne, 'Dodd-Frank Whistleblower Provision: Determining Who Qualifies as a Whistleblower' (2017) 41 *Delaware Journal of Corporate Law* 908.

but reporting internally results in losing the mandated protection. In *Digital Realty Trust, Inc. v Somers*,[24] the Supreme Court clearly stated that a whistleblower must report to the SEC to be eligible for protection under Dodd-Frank.[25]

Justice Ruth Bader Ginsburg, writing for the Court, stated that 'Dodd-Frank's text and purpose leave no doubt'. The whistleblower should report to the SEC, demonstrating a shift from prioritising the protection of corporations and employees to protecting the integrity of capital markets, thereby focusing on reporting to the authorities. The protection of whistleblowers improved with the introduction of financial rewards and a promise of anonymity. From SOX's labour protection to Dodd-Frank's financial rewards, whistleblowers have gained more protection through financial incentives than labour law.

III. Consequences for Europe: The Case of Ireland

Europe was affected by the 2009 financial crisis, which had severe consequences for several EU Member States.[26] Ireland, Greece, Portugal, Spain, and Italy had their banking sectors almost entirely ruined by the financial crisis that began in the US. Taking Ireland as an example, the Irish banking crisis severely damaged the country's banking sector, leading to significant changes.[27] One of those was the introduction of whistleblower protection. The banking crisis highlighted the disadvantage of the country's lack of whistleblower protection.

A report for Ireland by Transparency International National Integrity Systems (NIS) in 2012 noted:

> In the context of Ireland's banking crisis, it is notable that only a small number of individuals with knowledge of serious malpractice and corporate governance failures came forward with information. Although cultural factors may have contributed to this silence, there is also substantial evidence to suggest that fear of retaliation is a significant factor inhibiting people from speaking out in the public interest.[28]

In addition, the Mahon Tribunal's final report, a public inquiry into planning corruption, emphasised the importance of whistleblowing in uncovering

[24] *Digital Realty Trust, Inc v. Somers*, n° 16-1276, 583 U.S. (2018) 12.

[25] D Kafteranis and Stelios Andreadakis, 'Internal Whistleblowing in the United States after Digital Realty Trust vs Somers: A Look from the Other Side of the Atlantic' (2025) 54(2) *Industrial Law Journal* 1–32.

[26] M Esposito, 'The European Financial Crisis – Analysis and a Novel Intervention' (2014) Harvard University scholar.harvard.edu/files/markesposito/files/eurocrisis.pdf accessed 15 May 2025.

[27] AL Centonze, 'The Irish Banking Crisis' (2014) 5(2) *Review of Business and Finance Studies* 85. See also B Clarke and N Hardiman, 'Crisis in the Irish Banking System' (2012) Geary WP2012/03, researchrepository.ucd.ie/bitstream/10197/4925/1/Clarke_and_Hardiman%2c_Crisis_in_the_Irish_banking_system._2012.pdf accessed 15 May 2025.

[28] J Devitt (ed), 'National Integrity Systems – Ireland' (2012) Transparency International, 15, www.transparency.org/files/content/pressrelease/2012_NIS_Addendum_Ireland_EN.pdf accessed 15 May 2021.

corruption and stated that whistleblower protection should be robust.[29] The Nyberg Report noted that, before the crisis, there was a lack of critical debate and analysis on the situation. Voices raising concerns about the banking sector's condition were ignored, and many hesitated to speak out, fearing sanctions.[30] Ireland aimed to pass whistleblowing laws due to concerns about its international image, beyond the influence of the banking crisis.

Strong whistleblower protection legislation enhances a country's reputation and attracts investment.[31] During the Irish banking crisis, a negative attitude towards whistleblowing prevented anyone from informing authorities or the public about the situation. The Commission of Investigation into the Banking Sector noticed:

> The minimal number of warning voices was largely ignored. Attempts by banking insiders during the period to send cautionary signals to market participants about escalating property values were dismissed as ill-informed and wrong. Doubters (the few that identified themselves as such to the Commission), in the main, grew unsure over the years when nothing seemed to go wrong. It also appears that some stayed silent in part to avoid possible sanctions. The Commission suspects, based on discussions held with a wide number of people, that there may have been a strong belief in Ireland that contrarians, non-team players, fractious observers and whistleblowers would be informally (though sometimes even publicly) sanctioned or ignored, regardless of the quality of their analysis or their place in organisations.[32]

IV. The Influence on the European Union: Changing the Rules in the Banking and Financial Sector

The 2009 financial crisis, the Dodd-Frank Act, and the banking crisis severely impacted EU Member States like Ireland, prompting the EU legislator to act. More specifically, to prevent future banking crises, the EU enacted legislation to safeguard the financial system and promote whistleblowing schemes to gather valuable information on potential wrongdoing.

[29] The Tribunal of Inquiry into Certain Planning Matters and Payments (known as Mahon Tribunal) was a public inquiry in Ireland established by the Assembly of Ireland to make investigations related to politicians' corruption. See Final Report of the Tribunal of Inquiry into Certain Planning Matters and Payments (the Mahon Tribunal), para 1.57 of ch 18, 2531. See also EB Kennedy, 'Overview: What is the Mahon Tribunal?' (2012) *The Irish Times* www.irishtimes.com/news/overview-what-is-the-mahon-tribunal-1.705457 accessed 15 May 2025.

[30] P Nyberg, 'Commission of Investigation into the Banking Sector in Ireland, (2011) merrionstreet.ie/en/news-room/releases/commission-of-investigation-into-the-banking-sector.38671.shortcut.html accessed 15 May 2025.

[31] Government Reform Unit, Department of Public Expenditure and Reform, Protected Disclosures Bill 2013 – Regulatory Impact Analysis, July 2013, 19.

[32] Report of The Commission of Investigation into The Banking Sector in Ireland, Misjudging Risk: Causes of The Systemic Banking Crisis In Ireland (2011) inquiries.oireachtas.ie/banking/evidence/misjudging-risk-causes-of-the-systemic-banking-crisis-in-ireland/ accessed 15 May 2025.

The European Banking Union, especially the Single Supervisory Mechanism (SSM), was a key development for the banking sector.[33] The European Central Bank (ECB) has extensive powers to supervise the banking sector. Along with the creation of the European Banking Union, whistleblowing provisions were introduced. The Dodd-Frank Act led to the Market Abuse Regulation (MAR), which includes robust protections for whistleblowers.[34] In an attempt to protect the integrity of financial markets, MAR contains provisions similar to those in Dodd-Frank, including clear regulations on whistleblowing and the possibility of enacting financial rewards.

Whistleblowing provisions governed the EU banking and financial sector before the adoption of the Directive on the protection of persons who report breaches of Union law (the Whistleblowing Directive). Nevertheless, new scandals at the EU level revealed that whistleblower protection has been ineffective, focusing on the reported information or the whistleblower rather than on protecting whistleblowers. Specific areas, such as tax systems closely linked to banking and finance, show how the system was inefficient at promoting and protecting whistleblowing. Over the last decade, major scandals highlighted the importance of whistleblowing, inadequate protections, and the need for deep reforms.

V. Hiding in Europe, in Luxembourg or … Everywhere

France's case was notable when such information was vital in creating the 'Lagarde list', a list of tax avoiders compiled by then-French Finance Minister Christine Lagarde. This information naming suspected tax evaders was provided by whistleblower Hervé Falciani, an employee at a major international financial institution (HSBC). It was alleged that suspected tax evaders had bank accounts in Switzerland, especially in HSBC's Private Bank (a subsidiary of HSBC).[35] Falciani cooperated with countries by providing the names of their nationals who were evading taxes at home. He left Switzerland after the HSBC scandal and has lived 'in exile' since then. In 2014, he was convicted in absentia for breaching Switzerland's bank secrecy laws and for industrial espionage.[36]

[33] European Central Bank Regulation (EU) 468/2014 of 16 April 2014 establishing the framework for cooperation within the Single Supervisory Mechanism between the European Central Bank and national competent authorities and with national designated authorities (SSM Framework Regulation) [2014] OJ L141/1.

[34] European Parliament and European Council Regulation (EU) 596/2014 of 16 April 2014 on market abuse (market abuse regulation) and repealing Directive 2003/6/EC and Commission Directives 2003/124/EC, 2003/125/EC and 2004/72/EC [2014] OJ L173/1.

[35] PR Keefe, 'The Bank Robber – The Computer Technician who Exposed a Swiss Bank's Darkest Secrets' (2016) *The New Yorker* www.newyorker.com/magazine/2016/05/30/herve-falcianis-great-swiss-bank-heist accessed 15 May 2025.

[36] Tribunal pénal fédéral, Jugement du 27 novembre 2015, Cour des affaires pénales, n° du dossier : SK.2014.46.

In November 2014, the Luxleaks scandal erupted in Luxembourg. The International Consortium of Investigative Journalists (ICIJ) published thousands of documents of PriceWaterhouseCoopers (PwC) that revealed obscure tax optimisation techniques based on tax rulings.[37] The Luxleaks case was a significant event that led to several changes in tax practices at both the national and European levels.[38] In 2015, the European Parliament decided to investigate Luxembourg's tax practices. This has led to several resolutions being passed by the Parliament, inviting the European Commission to change the existing rules on corporate tax agreements.[39]

Apart from changes and debates at the EU level, Luxembourg revised its tax ruling rules to comply with international and European standards.[40] The whistleblowers faced legal action in Luxembourg for breaching secrecy and theft. After years of adjudication, Antoine Deltour was acquitted, but Raphael Halet was condemned.[41] In Halet's case, he brought a claim before the ECtHR, alleging a violation of his right to freedom of expression. On 11 May 2021, the Strasbourg Court ruled Luxembourg did not violate Halet's right to freedom of expression, leaving him without protection.[42] On 14 February 2023, the Grand Chamber reversed the first-instance decision, ruling that Luxembourg had violated Halet's right to freedom of expression.[43]

In 2016, the Panama Papers were published by the ICIJ.[44] The documents revealed large-scale tax fraud involving EU Member States, especially the United Kingdom (before Brexit). The Panama Papers attracted public attention and that of the European Parliament. The European Parliament launched an inquiry into the Panama Papers to assess the information and propose solutions to tackle tax fraud.[45] Whistleblowers involved in the Panama Papers were never publicly named, so it is unclear whether they were protected.

[37] International Consortium of Investigative Journalists (ICIJ), 'Luxleaks Investigation' www.icij.org/investigations/luxembourg-leaks/ accessed 15 May 2025. The documents were handed to the journalist Edouard Perrin by Antoine Deltour and Raphael Halet.

[38] J Brunsden, 'LuxLeaks: Luxembourg's response to an international tax scandal' *Financial Times* (23 June 2017) www.ft.com/content/de228b90-3632-11e7-99bd-13beb0903fa3 accessed 15 May 2025.

[39] European Parliament, Resolution of 25 November 2015 on tax rulings and other measures similar in nature or effect [2015] P8_TA(2015)0408.

[40] A Irwin-Hunt, 'Luxembourg tries to shed 'tax heaven' label' *Financial Times* (15 September 2020) www.ft.com/content/ebfea57b-ce1c-4e1d-8b08-640d1a87ff99 accessed 15 May 2025.

[41] Arrêt no. 3912 du 11 Janvier 2018 concernant le pourvoi de Mr Antoine Deltour/Luxleaks, Cour de Cassation, Grand-Duché de Luxembourg andArrêt no. 3911 du 11 Janvier 2018 concernant le pourvoi de Mr Rapahaël Halet/ Luxleaks, Cour de Cassation, Grand-Duché de Luxembourg.

[42] *Halet v Luxembourg* App no 21884/18 (ECtHR, 11 May 2021).

[43] D Kafteranis and S Andreadakis, 'A New Perspective on the Protection of Whistleblowers under ECHR: Halet v Luxembourg' (2023) 68(1) *Studies in Logic, Grammar and Rhetoric* 611–27.

[44] International Consortium of Investigative Journalists (ICIJ), 'The Panama Papers: Exposing the Rogue Offshore Finance Industry' www.icij.org/investigations/panama-papers/ accessed 15 May 2025.

[45] The Greek MEP Stelios Kouloglou insisted on the need for better protection of whistleblowers in order to report wrongdoings. See also: J Garside, 'Panama Papers: European Parliament Opens Inquiry' *The Guardian* (27 September 2016) www.theguardian.com/world/2016/sep/27/panama-papers-inquiry-opens-at-european-parliament accessed 15 May 2025.

Then, in an astonishing acceleration, several dramatic cases involving financial institutions emerged across Europe. Many originated from the bravery of whistle-blowers or journalists working with them, who received no protection but suffered negative consequences. The Maltese Pilatus Bank scandal is a prime example of a journalist's bravery and the fatal consequences of her disclosures. The assassination by car bomb of Daphne Caruana Galizia, a Maltese journalist who revealed the political connections of the Pilatus Bank, which facilitated money laundering, has sustained global interest.[46]

Between 2017 and 2018, another scandal arose in the EU. The Danske Bank money laundering scandal made headlines and is considered one of the largest in the world.[47] Howard Wilkinson, a former Danske Bank manager, reported the money laundering scheme facilitated by Danske Bank. Wilkinson intended to remain anonymous, but his identity was leaked almost immediately. He testified before the Danish and European Parliaments. His career as an international banker ended when his name was implicated in the scandal.

In 2017, another international financial scandal made headlines worldwide. The scandal is known as the Paradise Papers.[48] These are leaked documents from an offshore law firm called 'Appleby' and a corporate service provider 'Estera'. The whistleblowers behind the Paradise Papers remain unnamed. The papers reveal how businessmen, celebrities, politicians, and officials used offshore jurisdictions for financial transactions.[49] Although not all named individuals were involved in criminal activity, this revealed how the global elite created an international system of tax avoidance and revenue evasion to hide their wealth offshore.

The list of scandals, though impressive, is unfortunately not exhaustive. The cases above highlight notable scandals involving EU Member States that impacted the banking and finance sector. Behind these scandals, some people knew the information but chose not to disclose it. They reported to authorities or the media but were never heard from again.[50] These scandals show that whistleblowers are vital for uncovering wrongdoings and preventing crises. However, their protection cannot be taken for granted.

[46] The chase of the bank's whistleblower Maria Efimova from Malta to Greece. See D Kafteranis, 'The Pilatus Bank Scandal: Time to Reconsider Banking Supervision, Anti-money Laundering and Whistle-blower's Protection in the EU' (2018) European Law Blog, europeanlawblog.eu/2018/12/05/the-pilatus-bank-scandal-time-to-reconsider-banking-supervision-anti-money-laundering-and-whistle-blowers-protection-in-the-eu/ accessed 15 May 2025.

[47] S Curley, 'Danske Bank: The Story of Europe's Biggest Money Laundering Scandal' *Times Malta* (23 October 2018) timesofmalta.com/articles/view/danske-bank-the-story-of-europes-biggest-money-laundering-scandal.692375 accessed 15 May 2025.

[48] R Fazzari, 'Offshore Trove Exposes Trump-Russia links and Piggy Banks of the Wealthiest 1 Percent' (International Consortium of Investigative Journalists, 5 November 2017) www.icij.org/investigations/paradise-papers/paradise-papers-exposes-donald-trump-russia-links-and-piggy-banks-of-the-wealthiest-1-percent/ accessed 15 May 2025.

[49] ibid.

[50] Some of these cases are Luxleaaks, Danske Bank, Pilatus Bank, HSBC Paris, Swissleaks, Enron, WorldCom, and the reports about the housing crisis in the US.

A. What Happened in Europe?

The scandals, public outcry, and ineffective protection of whistleblowers have led several EU countries to adopt whistleblowing legislation. Ireland adopted the Public Disclosures Act of 2014, and France adopted the Law Sapin II.[51] In addition to the efforts at the national level, the outcry that these scandals provoked, along with their European dimension, prompted the EU to react. It was clear that European institutions and regulators should have acted differently, especially in cases like Danske Bank and Pilatus Bank. At the time, asymmetry in whistleblowing protection was not justifiable given the high level of EU integration in financial and banking regulation.

Scandals revealed by whistleblowers show that poor protection in one Member State can negatively affect not only that state but also others.[52] Uneven whistleblower protection across the EU could undermine the internal market and the respect of EU rules. The European Commission stated that EU legislation is essential to enforce rules, protect the market, and establish minimum whistleblower protection standards. The European Parliament became a strong advocate for an EU legal framework to protect whistleblowers.[53] In 2017, the European Commission's public consultation found that 96 per cent of respondents supported minimum standards to protect whistleblowers.[54]

Besides the European Parliament, the Council of Europe (CoE) and the European Court of Human Rights (ECtHR) have also promoted the protection of whistleblowers. In 2004, the landmark case of *Guja v Moldova* was one of the first cases towards protecting whistleblowers in Europe.[55] The ECtHR clarified that whistleblowers are protected under Article 10 of the ECHR, safeguarding their right to freedom of expression. The ECtHR reaffirmed its case law after *Guja* and influenced the legislation and case law of states.[56] Nevertheless, their efforts were insufficient, as a European legal framework was lacking. The European Commission proposed legislation in 2018 after years of silence, and the Directive was adopted in October 2019.[57]

[51] Public Disclosures Act, n° 14 of 2014 and Law n° 2016-1691 of 6 December 2016 related to transparency, the fight against corruption and the modernisation of economic life, JORF n°0287.

[52] European Commission Staff Working Document, Impact Assessment accompanying the document of the proposal for a Directive of the European Parliament and of the Council on the protection of persons reporting on breaches of Union law [2018] COM(2018) 218 final, 3.

[53] D Kafteranis, 'The Role of the European Parliament in the Adoption of the Directive on the Protection of Whistle-blowers' (2020) 4 *Revue des affaires européennes* 903.

[54] European Commission, 'Public Consultation on Whistleblower Protection', DG Justice and Consumers [2017] ec.europa.eu/newsroom/just/item-detail.cfm?item_id=54254 accessed 15 May 2025.

[55] *Guja v Moldova*, App no 14277/04 (ECtHR, 12 February 2008).

[56] V Junod, 'Lancer l'alerte: quoi de neuf depuis 'Guja'?: (Cour eur. dr. h., 'Bucur et Toma c. Roumanie', 8 janvier 2013)' (2014) 98 *Revue trimestrielle des droits de l'homme* 459.

[57] European Council, 'Proposal for a Directive on the Protection of Persons Reporting Breaches of Union Law: Progress Report' [2019].

A matter of importance is the rationale behind adopting legislation to protect whistleblowers at the EU level.[58] The European Commission proposed legislation primarily to protect the internal market and, second, to safeguard whistleblowers. The EU's approach attributes a 'managerial' character to whistleblowing.[59] The whistleblower should be protected, as they provide information that helps detect potential wrongdoings of interest to the market, not necessarily to the public. The 'managerial' approach of the Directive on whistleblowing demonstrates a business/economic motivation for adopting the legislation.[60]

The European Commission marginalised the 'democratic' character of the whistleblower, where the employee who reports is protected for exercising the right to freedom of expression. The ECtHR upheld the 'democratic' character of whistleblowing and its case law on the protection of whistleblowers based on Article 10.[61] The whistleblower is protected because they exercise their right to free speech, not because of the information they provide to support the market's proper functioning.

While the Directive respects the right to freedom of expression, it focuses on the whistleblower's enforcement role and does not rely on the right to exercise that freedom. This need to protect whistleblowers was translated into the Whistleblowing Directive, adopted in October 2019. The Directive's provisions are added to the existing EU legal rules on banking and financial whistleblowing.

VI. Structure of the book

The main idea behind shaping this book's outline is to move from general legal background to specific issues, from historical and comparative views to urgent legal enigmas. The focus of this book is on the analysis of the Whistleblowing Directive and EU whistleblowing provisions at the banking and financial sector. Alongside this analysis, the study of international, US, and ECHR legal provisions is examined as essential to comprehend the concepts adopted by the Directive. Elements of national legislation are given by following a 'pick and choose' approach.

The book begins with a chapter on international and ECHR legal frameworks related to whistleblowing. The chapter begins by examining the international legal framework. This initial analysis of international law is essential for understanding the development of global principles on whistleblowers' protection and for exploring how international law influences European and national systems. Subsequently, the chapter examines the CoE's efforts alongside Strasbourg Court

[58] A van Waeyenberge and Z Davies, 'The Whistleblower Directive (2019/1937): A Satisfactory but Incomplete System' (2021) 12(1) *European Journal of Risk Regulation* 236, 238.

[59] Foegle (n 10).

[60] D Kafteranis, 'The Future of the Whistle-blowing Directive: Criticising its Legal Bases' (2021) 1 *Queen Mary Law Journal* 65.

[61] Foegle (n 10).

case law, which are among the earliest European whistleblowing regulations and have influenced EU and national legislation.

The analysis of US laws on whistleblowing in banking and finance serves as a global model. This is the focus of the second chapter. It is necessary to understand the US laws and identify the elements that inspired the EU. The third chapter examines the European legal framework on whistleblowing, particularly the EU sectoral provisions protecting whistleblowers in the banking and financial sectors. These provisions are part of the EU legal order and coexist with the Directive. Their analysis is crucial for understanding the rationale behind their adoption and how it relates to the Directive. The top-down approach – beginning with international laws and ending with the Directive – is crucial to observe the influence of international, US, and European laws on the Directive.

Following these three chapters, the remainder of the book examines the Directive. In the fourth chapter, the process leading to the adoption of the Directive is described, highlighting the importance of whistleblowing at the EU level in recent years and the steps taken to reach the final version. The same chapter also focuses on the legal bases of the Directive and the reasons for choosing or not choosing specific legal grounds. The subsequent chapters analyse: (1) the definition of the whistleblower, (2) the channels for disclosure and what should be reported, and (3) the protection of whistleblowers.

More specifically, the fifth chapter focuses on defining the whistleblower. Defining the whistleblower is crucial as the first step – in protecting them is understanding who falls into this category. An analysis of their characteristics – including the employer, their motives, truthfulness, and other elements that shape the individual – provides insight into the subject. The sixth chapter examines the channels for disclosure and the types of issues to report, two elements that follow from the definition. Once the whistleblower is defined, it is necessary to understand where and what to report. The issues of internal and external whistleblowing are scrutinised, along with disclosures of wrongdoing, illegality, and immorality. Finally, the whistleblower, having been defined, having reported through the appropriate channels, and having reported the correct matters, needs to be protected. Chapter seven examines their protection under labour, administrative, civil, and criminal law. Additionally, other elements of protection, such as anonymity and financial rewards, are also analysed.

1

The International Legal Framework

An Overview of International and ECHR Law

I. The Role of Legal Provisions

Whistleblowing laws vary by region and history. Recently, Europe and other areas have increasingly adopted such laws.[1] This chapter introduces the connection between whistleblowing and legal provisions, then examines international and Council of Europe (CoE) frameworks. It provides an overview of global and CoE laws before focusing on the Directive. The legal provisions discussed served as the basis for the EU Directive.[2]

The protection of whistleblowers in banking and financial scandals was uncertain. The legal provisions were either absent or not effective when adopted.[3] Scholars were sceptical about their scope and effect.[4] In research he conducted on whistleblowers' laws in Europe in 2010, Lewis concluded that 'there is not much whistle-blower protection in Europe and the legislation that exists is extremely diverse'.[5] Adopted national legal provisions were either influenced by other national (vintage) legislation, international law obligations, or other organisations' work on whistleblowing.

The international legal framework should be discussed for two reasons. First, the protection of whistleblowers has its roots in international legislation, which had been addressed on several occasions before national legislators took action. Second, the international legal framework served as an inspiration for the Directive, and the purpose is to demonstrate this influence, starting from the

[1] R Vaughn, *The Successes and Failures of Whistle-blower Laws* (Edward Elgar, 2012) 239–240

[2] Directive (EU) 2019/1937 of the European Parliament and of the Council of 23 October 2019 on the protection of persons who report breaches of Union law, [2019] OJ L395/17.

[3] Vaughn (n 1) 240.

[4] ibid.

[5] D Lewis, 'Introduction' in D Lewis (ed), *A Global Approach to Public Interest Disclosures: What Can We Learn from Existing Whistleblowing Legislation and Research?* (Edward Elgar, 2010) 2. See also W Vandekerchove, 'European Whistleblower Protection' in D Lewis (ed), *A Global Approach to Public Interest Disclosures: What Can We Learn from Existing Whistleblowing Legislation and Research?* (Edward Elgar, 2010) 15–35.

general (the international legal framework) and proceeding to the specific (the Directive). In addition, it is essential to analyse the protection of whistleblowers in the CoE and under the case law of the European Court of Human Rights (ECtHR). Their work was significant in Europe before the adoption of the Directive and has also served as an inspiration for the Directive.

II. International Legal Framework

While several international legal instruments, such as treaties, conventions, and covenants, have been adopted on human rights-related themes, none of them directly address the protection of whistleblowers. Despite this lacuna, whistle-blowing is related to the right to freedom of expression as enshrined in several international legal texts.[6] Blowing the whistle recognises the importance of free speech and the right to be informed. Whistleblowing has an intrinsic value as a human right, which allows us to tell the truth, express ourselves, and defend democratic values.[7] To that extent, whistleblowing is inherent in the right to freedom of expression without any specific relevance to it in the international legal texts on the freedom of expression.[8]

Substantive efforts and more concrete steps have been taken in the field of corruption, where the need to adopt international legal acts to combat corruption globally has provided some protection to whistleblowers.[9] Moreover, the International Labour Organisation (ILO) asks for the protection of employees who report wrongdoings.[10] Following the 2008–09 financial crisis, international institutions in banking and finance have also begun to consider whistleblowing. For instance, the Group of Twenty (G20) has produced outstanding work on the issue of whistleblowing to ensure the transparency and fairness of markets.[11] The OECD has the same goals, being a pioneer on the subject and doing meaningful work towards the protection of whistleblowers.[12] Finally, the World Bank and other international bodies are also heading in the same direction.

[6] W Vanderkerchhove, 'Freedom of Expression as the 'Broken Promise' of Whistleblower Protection' (2016) 10 *Revue des droits de l'homme* (online) 1, para 14, journals.openedition.org/revdh/2680?lang=en accessed 15 May 2025.

[7] C Tom, 'Workplace Free Speech as Human Rights' (2002) Working Paper Number 2002/10, Centre for Applied Philosophy and Public Ethics 1.

[8] Article 19 of the United Nations Universal Declaration of Human Rights.

[9] United Nations Convention against Corruption (adopted on 31 October 2003, entered into force 14 December 2005) GA Res 58/4 (UNCAC).

[10] ILO Thesaurus 2005, ilo.multites.net/default.asp accessed 15 May 2025.

[11] G20, 'Anti-Corruption Action Plan, Protection of Whistleblowers – Study on Whistleblower Protection Frameworks, Compendium of Best Practices and Guiding Principles for Legislation', (2012), www.oecd.org/corruption/48972967.pdf accessed 15 May 2025.

[12] OECD, Recommendation of the Council on Public Integrity (2017) www.oecd.org/gov/ethics/OECD-Recommendation-Public-Integrity.pdf accessed 15 May 2025.

Despite the aforementioned legal efforts, there is no concrete protection of whistleblowers as such. By presenting different international instruments, the aim is to demonstrate the role of international law in the protection of whistleblowers, its lacunae, and, in particular, to highlight the absence of a convention, treaty, or agreement on whistleblowing.[13] This is an issue that should be addressed because an international legal instrument will provide coherence and certainty regarding whistleblowers' protection.[14]

In addition, the provisions on the protection of whistleblowers under international law have inspired the development of 'international best practices' in whistleblower protection legislation.[15] These best practices are suggestions as to how to draft whistleblower legislation most effectively.[16] These best practices are inspired by the work of the United Nations (UN), the OECD and Non-Governmental Organisations (NGOs), such as Transparency International (TI). The European Union drew inspiration from these best practices when negotiating the adoption of the Directive.

A. Corruption and the United Nations: The First Steps on the International Arena

The United Nations Convention against Corruption (UNCAC) entered into force in 2005 and to date has 186 Parties.[17] Most of the countries have ratified it, demonstrating the importance of combatting corruption at both the national and international levels.[18] The economic developments of the early twenty-first century have created incentives for individuals to engage in corruption or corruption-related activities. Notably, the prevailing liberalisation policies had limited the role of the state in favour of the private sector, primarily by privatisation and contracting out. Two changes occurred as a result of this event. First, the border between the public and private sectors became blurred as the two industries became increasingly interconnected. Second, private-sector entities, in pursuit of profit, had greater incentives to engage in corruption or related activities.[19] The whistleblower

[13] The terminology may vary. International Conventions are also called treaties or covenants or statutes and so on. The substance, though, is the same: 'a merger of wills of two or more international subjects for the purpose of regulating their interests by international rules'. See A Cassese, *International Law*, 2nd edn (OUP, 2005) 170.

[14] D Kafteranis, 'The International Legal Framework on Whistle-blowers: What More Should be Done?' (2021) 19(3) *Seattle Journal for Social Justice* 729.

[15] G Ferguson, *Global Corruption – Law, Theory and Practice*, 3rd edn, vol. 1 (UVIC Press, 2018) 1014.

[16] ibid.

[17] UNCAC (n 9).

[18] R Scaturro, 'Defining Whistleblowing' (2018) IACA Research & Science 7, www.iaca.int/images/Research/Research_paper_05_Ruggero_Scaturro_final.pdf accessed 15 May 2025.

[19] Vaughn (n 1) 294.

was regarded as a powerful tool in detecting corruption.[20] Corruption flourishes when there is a low risk of being caught and, if caught, the sanction is not sufficient. By encouraging people to speak up and thus blow the whistle, there are more chances of detection. This fact, combined with strict sanctions for those who commit wrongdoings, creates an effective deterrent.

Furthermore, corruption is a power-related crime, as often governmental officials are implicated. This governmental implication distorts the market's operation, as there is a lack of transparency and trust in the government and among public and private actors.[21] The need to protect the market, especially during the liberalisation movement of the twenty-first century, was a priority, and this protection entailed the need to combat corruption coming from the government. During the neoliberal period, governments and the private sector share the same interests, notably the maximisation of profits.[22] The whistleblower was considered an essential tool in the fight against corruption, coming either from the government or from the private sector.

The UNCAC is the outcome of a process whereby the international community created a unique convention against corruption, recognising the need to take a strict stance against it at the global level. The desire for a corruption-free world has led states to implement various measures to combat corruption at every societal level.[23] One of the measures is the facilitation of disclosing information, thus whistleblowing. Whistleblowing has attracted significant attention at the international level and has become a crucial component in the fight against corruption. The discussion around this issue encompasses the need to balance the fight against corruption, freedom of expression, the privacy of information, and the loyalty of employees.[24] The purpose is to create clear standards upon which the potential whistleblowers can be based, avoiding the guesswork and uncertainty.

The UNCAC has comprehensive provisions on, among *other things*, the protection of persons reporting corruption. These persons can be characterised as whistleblowers. Article 33 of the UNCAC has the title 'Protection of reporting persons' and reads as follows:

> Each State Party shall consider incorporating into its domestic legal system appropriate measures to provide protection against any unjustified treatment for any person who reports in good faith and on reasonable grounds to the competent authorities any facts concerning offences established in accordance with this Convention.[25]

[20] P Gottschalk, *Whistleblowing – White Collar Fraud Signal Detection* (Cambridge Scholars Publishing, 2018) 83.

[21] Vaughn (n 1) 294.

[22] S Bittle and J Hébert, 'Controlling Corporate Crimes in Times of De-regulation and Re-Regulation' in M L Rorie (ed) *The Handbook of White-Collar Crime* (Wiley, 2020) 496.

[23] R Beller, 'Whistleblower Protection Legislation of the East and West: Can It Really Reduce Corporate Fraud and Improve Corporate Governance? A Study of the Successes and Failures of Whistleblower Protection Legislation in the US and China' (2011) 7 *New York University Journal of Law & Business* 873, 876–77.

[24] ibid 927.

[25] UNCAC (n 9).

The Convention, in its Article 33, invites State Parties to protect any person who decides to report one or more corruption incidents, as listed in the Convention. The person should have reasonable grounds to believe that the facts concern a corruption incident and report in good faith. It is unclear, however, whether the reasonable grounds should be subjectively or objectively determined.[26] In addition, it is often difficult to distinguish between strong suspicions and reasonable grounds. Despite the seemingly straightforward language of Article 33, the Convention fails to define important terms, as mentioned above, leaving this task to the State Parties.[27] Countries may come to different conclusions when interpreting what constitutes 'facts' or the concept of 'sufficient evidence' about the disclosure.[28]

Another problematic issue is the fact that Article 33 is a non-binding provision.[29] In 2015, the United Nations Office on Drugs and Crime issued a resource guide on good practices in the protection of reporting persons (related to the UNCAC).[30] The report recognised that significant steps have been made in a certain number of states but highlighted the need for more measures to be taken. The legal provisions should not be superficial, but they should respect more principles that will allow them to enhance the protection of reporting persons and to combat corruption. Another solution would be to establish institutions within the State Parties that would ensure corrupt entities do not misapply the law. Apart from the need to have more explicit rules on the requirements of blowing the whistle under the UNCAC, competent institutions supporting it will create uniformity and help the fight against corruption.

Article 33 of the UNCAC may be characterised as a sectoral protection of whistleblowers. The Convention focuses on reporting corruption and does not entail any other area. Whilst corruption is a significant problem in a globalised society and the market, the contribution of the UNCAC to the protection of whistleblowers is limited to this. A sectoral legal provision protects the whistleblower for a limited number of reports (here, only for corruption-related offences) and does not extend any further. Calls have been made to expand this protection to other areas by the UNCAC coalition, but this has not yet occurred.[31] Despite UNCAC's significance, it may be characterised as a small piece in the puzzle of whistleblower protection.

[26] B Fasterling and D Lewis, 'Leaks, Legislation and Freedom of Speech: How Can the Law Effectively Promote Public-Interest Whistleblowing' (2014) 153 *International Labour Review* 71, 76.

[27] K Soltes, 'Facilitating Appropriate Whistleblowing: Examining Various Approaches to What Constitutes 'Fact' to Trigger Protection under Article 33 of the United Nations Convention against Corruption' (2012) 27(4) *American University International Law Review* 925, 930.

[28] ibid. The author argues that countries should opt for the reasonable belief approach in an allegation of a protected disclosure as this is adopted by South African legislation.

[29] Fasterling and Lewis (n 26) 75–77.

[30] United Nations, Office on Drugs and Crime, 'The United Nations Convention against Corruption – Resource Guide on Good Practices in the Protection of Reporting Persons' (2015), www.unodc.org/documents/corruption/Publications/2015/15-04741_Person_Guide_eBook.pdf accessed 15 May 2025.

[31] Scaturro (n 18) 8.

B. Reasons to Adopt a UN Convention on the Protection of Whistleblowers

The UNCAC, as mentioned above, may be characterised as, to a certain extent, successful. Taking into account the success of the UNCAC, one may realise the importance of an international Convention on the protection of whistleblowers. The UNCAC has been the reference point for various regional conventions and national legislations combatting corruption.[32] In the same way, an international Convention on the protection of whistleblowers will stimulate further legal developments at the regional or national level.

An international Convention on the Protection of Whistleblowers will establish a set of rules, negotiated by the State Parties, that will serve as a reference for whistleblowers at the national level.[33] First, during the negotiation period, State Parties will have the opportunity to meet together to discuss an issue that is not only a legal but also a political, social, and cultural issue. Depending on the country or continent, whistleblowing is viewed in different ways. Taking the EU as an example, the adoption of the Directive on the protection of persons reporting breaches of Union law demonstrates a shift in perception towards whistleblowing, considering the hostility of some states, such as France and Germany, due to historical concerns (ie, the Nazi regime). Bringing together the different countries in a fruitful debate will provide the international community with a legal instrument that aims to balance various perceptions and considerations on whistleblowing.[34]

Furthermore, the Convention will clarify specific issues that are still debated around whistleblowing. It would be important, in the first place, to have a definition of the term 'whistleblower', as there has been no standard definition until now.[35] It is necessary to understand who can be characterised as a whistleblower. Other issues will also need to be clarified. For instance, the channel for disclosure is a fundamental aspect of the whistleblowing process, and it needs to be specified to whom the whistleblower should address their concerns: internally, to the authorities, or to the public. In an optimistic sense, it would be crucial to address all of the above to ensure clarity and safety for future whistleblowers, demonstrating that the international community has adopted a convention that can serve as a point of reference for their protection.

Enforcing the Convention may be a challenge, but there are ways to ensure a relatively effective enforcement.[36] One way to achieve enforcement is by obliging

[32] Council of Europe, Civil Law Convention on Corruption, (ETS No 174, 1 November 2003), Art 9.

[33] I Brownlie, *Principles of Public International Law* (OUP, 2008) 13.

[34] D Humphreys, 'The Elusive Quest for a Global Forests Convention' (2005) 14 *Review of European Community & International Environmental Law* 1, 2 (discussing the concept of commitment by the Member States).

[35] H Richard and B Peter, 'Whistleblowing and Freedom of Conscience: Towards a New Legal Analysis' (2012) Comparative Research in Law & Political Economy, Research Paper No. 1974982, 6–12.

[36] I Doron and I Apter, 'The Debate Around the Need for an International Convention on the Rights of Older Persons' (2010) 50 *The Gerontologist* 588.

countries to a mandatory report about the implementation of the Convention, in order for their compliance to be monitored and any internal debates to be more transparent. By reporting, governments will be required to engage in a constructive dialogue with the relevant international authorities that control the implementation of the Convention. Additionally, other enforcement solutions may be developed to achieve better results. For instance, the Convention may allow individual complaints to be presented to the relevant international authority, enabling them to show their problem(s) and demand a solution. The Convention may be used as a legal 'weapon' before the national courts. Arguments stemming from the Convention may be used during litigation to enhance the arguments presented by the whistleblower or by NGOs engaged in the field. Depending on the national legal system, international law may not be binding, but it will definitely influence and even convince the relevant courts to reconsider their position.

Moreover, the Convention will be a powerful advocacy tool.[37] Whistleblowing is perceived in both a positive and a negative way.[38] Its image is constantly changing, and it is challenging to argue in favour of it when the legal landscape is poor. The adoption of a Convention will provide an essential tool for advocacy groups to change the public perception of whistleblowing, ultimately transforming public opinion in a positive direction. In countries where no legislation exists for the protection of whistleblowers, the Convention will serve as a basis for putting pressure on the state to consider enacting legislation. Similarly, countries with legislation will be encouraged to review and, if necessary, modify their legislation in light of the Convention. The Convention will become a powerful tool in the right hands, helping to advocate for adequate protection of whistleblowers.

The Convention will bring about changes not only in the legal landscape but also in society and will stimulate educational reform.[39] The Council of Europe, in its report of 14 September 2014, has noticed that there are 'deeply engrained cultural attitudes which date back to social and political circumstances, such as dictatorship and/or foreign domination, under which distrust towards informers of the despised authorities was only normal'.[40] The Convention will be a tool for educating people and demonstrating that whistleblowers are, under certain circumstances, essential figures. Even in the negotiation phase, the discussions surrounding it will inform society about whistleblowers and the benefits they offer in combatting wrongdoing. Providing a debate and informing people properly about whistleblowers will create a more positive perception of them in society.[41]

[37] ibid 588.

[38] D Lewis, AJ Brown and R Moberly, 'Whistleblowing, its Importance and the State of the Research' in AJ Brown et al. (eds), *International Handbook on Whistleblowing Research* (Edward Elgar, 2014) 6–7.

[39] W Vandekerckove, T Uys, MT Rehg and AJ Brown, 'Understandings of Whistleblowing: Dilemmas of Societal Culture' in AJ Brown et al. (eds) *International Handbook on Whistleblowing Research* (Edward Elgar, 2014) 37–42.

[40] Council of Europe, Committee on Legal Affairs and Human Rights, The Protection of Whistleblowers, Doc. 12006, P Omtzigt, 14 September 2009.

[41] Vandekerckove, Uys, Rehg and Brown (n 39) 63–65.

III. The First in Europe: Council of Europe (CoE)

A. Combatting Corruption: The Work of the Council of Europe

The CoE groups 46 countries and was an early advocate of whistleblowing in Europe. Whistleblowing provisions were first introduced in response to the need to combat corruption. The term 'whistleblower' was not used in these first CoE legal instruments adopted in the fight against corruption, but in subsequent texts of the CoE concerning the protection of whistleblowers.[42] The issue of whistleblowing had been touched upon indirectly through the necessity to combat corruption.[43] The anti-corruption rationale for adopting whistleblowing protection is due to the efficiency it presents rather than the protection of human rights.[44] The international movement against corruption and the need to combat it had enabled the adoption of two conventions on corruption by the CoE. In the two Conventions adopted, the offered protection did not directly concern the persons who were alerting to a wrongdoing, but rather the persons who were informing the authorities of a criminal offence.[45]

The first is the Civil Law Convention on Corruption, adopted in 1999 and entered into force in 2003.[46] The Convention focused on the need to combat corruption, and the whistleblower is an essential tool for this fight. Article 9 provides specific protection to employees who report corruption. It states: 'Each Party shall provide in its internal law for appropriate protection against any unjustified sanction for employees who have reasonable grounds to suspect corruption and who report in good faith their suspicion to responsible persons or authorities.' Under the Civil Law Convention on Corruption, a whistleblower is defined as an employee who has reasonable grounds to believe or suspect that corruption is occurring and reports it in good faith.

The other Convention is the Criminal Law Convention on Corruption, adopted in 1999 and entered into force in 2002.[47] This Convention included provisions on the protection of witnesses and collaborators of justice. Under Article 22, each party should adopt measures to provide effective and appropriate protection for persons who report criminal offences such as bribery or trading in influence. The same protection should be offered to persons who co-operate with the investigatory or prosecutorial authorities, or who are witnesses and give testimony, in

[42] K Blay-Grabarvzyk, 'Le statut incertain des lanceurs d'alerte' in M Disant and D Pollet-Panousis (eds), *Les lanceurs d'alerte* (LGDJ éd. 2017) 124. For the term whistleblower, the CoE Recommendation CM/Rec(2014)7 is the first to use the term whistleblower.

[43] S Lamouroux, 'Moralisation de la vie publique: le Conseil de l'Europe et la lutte contre la corruption' [2013] *Constitutions* 461.

[44] W Vandekerckhove, 'Is It Freedom? The Coming About of the EU Directive on Whistleblower Protection' (2021) *Journal of Business Ethics* 1, 2.

[45] Blay-Grabarvzyk (n 42) 124.

[46] Civil Law Convention on Corruption (n 32).

[47] Council of Europe, Criminal Law Convention on Corruption, Eur. T.S. No. 173, 27 January 1999.

relation to such offences. The Convention does not categorise such persons as whistleblowers, but they are considered to perform the role of a whistleblower. These two Conventions were the first two critical steps taken by the CoE in the fight against corruption, in which whistleblowers were among the tools employed. In line with these Conventions, the CoE has produced significant work on protecting whistleblowers.

B. Moving Forward: The Way Towards the Recommendation CM/Rec(2014)7

The Committee on Legal Affairs and Human Rights prepared a report 'on the protection of whistleblowers' in 2009.[48] The rapporteur, Mr Omtzigt, analysed the legal situation of whistleblowers in the Contracting Parties and proposed to the CoE what further steps can be taken. Following this report, the Parliamentary Assembly of the CoE adopted a Recommendation and a Resolution for the protection of whistleblowers.[49] These legal texts were an invitation to the Contracting Parties to take more steps towards an adequate protection of whistleblowers. The Recommendation has emphasised the importance of whistleblowing 'as a tool to increase accountability and strengthen the fight against corruption and mismanagement'. The Resolution invited the parties to reconsider their legislation in light of the CoE's work and to consider the possibility of negotiating a convention on the protection of whistleblowers.[50]

A convention has neither been drafted nor is there one under negotiation. Nevertheless, the CoE adopted Recommendation CM/Rec(2014)7 on 30 April 2014, which is a cohesive legal text that protects individuals who report on acts and omissions in the workplace that constitute a serious threat or harm to the public interest.[51] The Recommendation was adopted by the Council of Ministers and was prepared by the European Committee on Legal Co-operation (CDCJ).[52] It is a detailed legal text analysing major elements of whistleblowers' protection.[53]

[48] Council of Europe, Committee on Legal Affairs and Human Rights, 'The Protection of whistle-blowers', Doc. 12006, 14 September 2009 assembly.coe.int/nw/xml/XRef/Xref-XML2HTML-en.asp?fileid=12302 accessed 15 May 2025.

[49] Council of Europe, Parliamentary Assembly, 17th Sitting, Recommendation 1916 (2010), 'Protection of Whistle-blowers', 29 April 2010 assembly.coe.int/nw/xml/XRef/Xref-XML2HTML-en.asp?fileid=17852&lang=en accessed 15 May 2025 and Council of Europe, Parliamentary Assembly, 17th Sitting, Resolution 1729 (2010), 'Protection of Whistle-blowers', 29 April 2010 assembly.coe.int/nw/xml/XRef/Xref-XML2HTML-en.asp?fileid=17851 accessed 15 May 2025.

[50] D Lewis, 'The Council of Europe Resolution and Recommendation on the Protection of Whistleblower' (2010) 39(4) *Industrial Law Journal* 432 and G Devers, *La Protection du Lanceur d'Alerte par la jurisprudence* (Tim Buctu ed, 2015) 38–40.

[51] Council of Europe, Recommendation CM/Rec(2014)7, 'Protection of Whistleblowers', adopted by the Committee of Ministers, 30 April 2014.

[52] Council of Europe, European Committee on Legal Co-operation, Protecting Whistleblowers, (30 April 2020) www.coe.int/en/web/cdcj/activities/protecting-whistleblowers accessed 15 May 2025.

[53] Devers (n 50) 41–43.

It defines the whistleblower, the channels for disclosure and the protection that should be afforded to the whistleblower.[54] Despite its significance, the Recommendation is still not a convention on the protection of whistleblowers.

According to the Recommendation, the whistleblower is 'any person who reports or discloses information on a threat or harm to the public interest in the context of their work-based relationship, whether it be in the public or private sector'. The Recommendation highlights the whistleblower's crucial role in fighting corruption in a democratic society. It proposes harmonising national laws for comprehensive protection, based on the national legal framework, at least including: 'violations of law and human rights, as well as risks to public health and safety and the environment'.[55] It further recommends that a special scheme should be applied to national security whistleblowers.[56]

Turning to the channels for disclosure, it suggests that reports should be addressed to the organisation, to the relevant public authorities, or to the public. Nevertheless, it does not adopt the 'three-tier' model, which implies a hierarchy among the channels;[57] on the contrary, it states that all channels should be interconnected without any given priority.[58] The appendix shows a preference for internal reporting since the whistleblower does not breach secrecy duties. The Recommendation urges Contracting Parties to promote internal whistleblowing as a sign of good corporate governance.

Furthermore, the Recommendation considers confidentiality as an essential feature of whistleblowers' protection, but it does not support anonymity. The good faith element is put under scrutiny by the Recommendation. Under Principle 22, 'the protection should not be lost solely on the basis that the individual making the report or disclosure was mistaken as to its import or that the perceived threat to the public interest has not materialised, provided he or she had reasonable grounds to believe in its accuracy'.[59] The Recommendation moves away from the good-faith element and instead favours the reasonable-grounds test. Nonetheless, under Principle 24, if the employee chooses to disregard the internal reporting system and makes a public disclosure, this may result in less protection, as 'the normative framework may recognise the legal value of an expectation to use the internal reporting system'.[60] This is a further indication of the value placed on internal whistleblowing. Ultimately, the burden of proof lies with the employer, not the employee. The employer must prove that any particular detriment experienced by the employee was not the result of the employee's whistleblowing activity.

[54] Council of Europe, Recommendation CM/Rec(2014)7 (n 51) 4.
[55] ibid para 37.
[56] ibid para 5.
[57] W Vandekerckhove, 'European Whistleblower Protection: Tiers or Tears?' in DB Lewis (ed), *A Global Approach to Public Interest Disclosure: What Can We Learn from Existing Whistleblowing Legislation and Research* (Edward Elgar, 2010) 15.
[58] Council of Europe, Recommendation CM/Rec(2014)7 (n 51) para 61.
[59] ibid para 22.
[60] ibid para 87.

The revelations of Edward Snowden have led to the adoption of new legal texts by the CoE. In 2015, Resolution 2060 was adopted by the Parliamentary Assembly.[61] This time, the focus was on protecting whistleblowers, especially those reporting on national security. The Parliamentary Assembly noted that employees of national security agencies are often excluded from protection.[62] The Assembly emphasised the need to encompass all types of employees under the term 'whistleblower' and provide them with protection.[63] It concluded that: whistleblower protection should cover employees of national security or intelligence services; asylum should be granted to whistleblowers being threatened by retaliation by their home country; and a binding legal instrument (convention) on the protection of whistleblowers should be adopted based on the Recommendation CM/Rec (2014)7.[64]

The same year, Recommendation 2073 was adopted by the Parliamentary Assembly.[65] It recalled Resolution 2060 and reiterated the need for a convention. Paragraph 3.1 emphasised the need to protect whistleblowers through a binding legal framework, possibly open to non-state parties and covering national security disclosures. From Recommendations 1916 (2010) to 2073 (2015), the Assembly repeatedly stressed the need for a convention. Despite these calls, the Committee of Ministers did not respond until 2016.

As the calls for a convention re-emerged, the Council of Ministers took action. In its response to Recommendation 2073, it highlighted the work done by the Council of Europe, the ECtHR, and other international organisations towards the protection of whistleblowers.[66] The Committee of Ministers noted that Recommendation CM/Rec(2014)7, adopted in 2014, includes principles on whistleblowers' protection, including those reporting on national security, defence, intelligence, public order, or international relations. It emphasised prioritising the promotion and implementation of this recommendation, leaving open the possibility of a future convention.

The CoE continued its work following the Committee of Ministers' refusal to draft a convention. In August 2016, the CoE issued a guide entitled: 'Protection of Whistleblowers: A Brief Guide for Implementing a National Framework.'[67] The guide, first issued in January 2015 and reprinted in August 2016, draws

[61] Council of Europe, Resolution 2060 (2015), Improving the Protection of Whistle-blowers, adopted by the Parliamentary Assembly, 23 June 2015 assembly.coe.int/nw/xml/XRef/Xref-XML2HTML-en.asp?fileid=21931&lang=en accessed 15 May 2025.

[62] Council of Europe, Recommendation CM/Rec(2014)7 (n 51) para 7.

[63] ibid para 8.

[64] ibid para 10.

[65] Council of Europe, Recommendation 2073 (2015), 'Improving the Protection of Whistle-blowers', adopted by the Parliamentary Assembly, 23 June 2015 assembly.coe.int/nw/xml/XRef/Xref-XML2HTML-EN.asp?fileid=21936&lang=EN accessed 15 May 2025.

[66] Council of Europe, 'Reply to Recommendation 2073 (2015) on Improving the Protection of Whistle-blowers', Committee of Ministers, 20 January 2016, paras 2–3, assembly.coe.int/nw/xml/XRef/Xref-XML2HTML-en.asp?fileid=22331&lang=en accessed 15 May 2025.

[67] Council of Europe, 'Protection of Whistleblowers: A Brief Guide for Implementing a National Framework', (2016) edoc.coe.int/en/fundamental-freedoms/7053-protection-of-whistleblowers-a-brief-guide-for-implementing-a-national-framework.html accessed 15 May 2025.

from Recommendation CM/Rec(2014)7 to help states develop whistleblowing laws. Its goal is to encourage them to establish a legal, institutional, and judicial framework that protects whistleblowers in law and practice. Additionally, the Congress of Local and Regional Authorities issued Resolution 444 (2019) and Recommendation 435 (2019), both accompanied by an explanatory memorandum.[68] This organ emphasised the importance of whistleblowing and examined challenges and opportunities for local and regional governments. Consequently, the proposal for a Directive on protecting whistleblowers was well received by the Parliamentary Assembly of the CoE.

C. The EU Directive's Touch: Follow the Leader

In Resolution 2300 (2019), the Parliamentary Assembly welcomed the proposal for the EU Directive and analysed its different features.[69] The Assembly insisted on the following points and invited states to comply with them. Initially, the transposition of the Directive should be completed as soon as possible, and the states of the CoE that are not EU members are particularly encouraged to comply with the Directive's rules on the protection of whistleblowers.[70] Secondly, the Assembly emphasised the need to establish a European network of independent authorities responsible for protecting whistleblowers, thereby enhancing their protection and the effectiveness of the legislation.[71] Finally, the Assembly invited Assembly members to raise awareness in national Parliaments, thereby strengthening a positive culture towards the protection of whistleblowers.[72]

On 1 October 2019, the Parliamentary Assembly adopted Recommendation 2162 (2019).[73] The Recommendation was inspired by the Report of the Committee on Legal Affairs and Human Rights, which analysed in depth the proposal for a Directive and its significance for the CoE's policies on whistleblowers' protection.[74]

[68] Council of Europe, Congress of Local and Regional Authorities, 'Report CG36(2019)14final on the Protection of Whistle-blower – Challenges and Opportunities for Local and Regional Government', 3 April 2019 rm.coe.int/the-protection-of-whistleblowers-challenges-and-opportunities-for-loca/16809312bd accessed 15 May 2025.

[69] Council of Europe, Resolution 2300 (2019), 'Improving the Protection of Whistle-blowers all over Europe', Parliamentary Assembly, 1 October 2019 assembly.coe.int/nw/xml/XRef/Xref-XML2HTML-en.asp?fileid=28150&lang=en accessed 15 May 2025.

[70] ibid paras 13.1.1 and 13.2.

[71] ibid para 13.1.2. Such an unofficial initiative has been created with the Network of European Integrity and Whistleblowing Authorities (NEIWA whistleblowingmonitor.eu/neiwa/) accessed 15 May 2025.

[72] ibid para 13.4.

[73] Council of Europe, Recommendation 2162 (2019), 'Improving the Protection of Whistle-blowers all over Europe', 1 October 2019 assembly.coe.int/nw/xml/XRef/Xref-XML2HTML-en.asp?fileid=28151&lang=en accessed 15 May 2025.

[74] Council of Europe, Committee on Legal Affairs and Human Rights, 'Report on Improving the Protection of Whistle-blowers all over Europe' Doc. 14958, 30 August 2019 assembly.coe.int/nw/xml/XRef/Xref-XML2HTML-en.asp?fileid=28096&lang=en accessed 15 May 2025.

The Recommendation highlighted the fact that a Directive will soon be voted on at the EU level, largely inspired by the Recommendation CM/Rec(2014)7 of the CoE. Based on the proposal for a Directive, the Assembly emphasised that specific policies align with the CoE, but some elements differ.[75] This fact may create a legal division between the CoE and the EU approaches. As a result, the Assembly reiterated its demand for a binding legal instrument in the form of a convention on the protection of whistleblowers.[76] Despite the Assembly's call for a convention, a refusal came again from the Committee of Ministers on 29 April 2020.

The Committee of Ministers praised the CoE's work on whistleblower protection, noting that Recommendation CM/Rec(2014)7 marks a significant international advance by providing principles to guide states in establishing legal protections for whistleblowers.[77] In addition, it underlined the importance of the guide published in 2016, which facilitates the implementation of the recommendations by national governments. Its stance towards a convention on the protection of whistleblowers has remained unchanged since 2015. The Committee of Ministers denied the need to negotiate a convention due to the complexity and the differing national approaches taken on the issue.[78] Finally, it stated that starting negotiations would be time-consuming and uncertain. Meanwhile, the Committee of Ministers urged states to implement all CoE recommendations fully and to provide technical assistance when needed.

In 2022, the European Committee on Legal Cooperation (CDCJ) of the CoE prepared an evaluation report on Recommendation CM/Rec(2014)7.[79] The report reviewed responses from 23 states on the evolution of CoE recommendations on whistleblowing, ECtHR case law, and other legal instruments, such as the Directive. It notes countries have adopted protections, but improvements are needed. EU Member States must transpose the Directive, which may conflict with CoE principles. The report suggests considering alternatives inspired by CoE principles. However, the coexistence of CoE principles, ECtHR case law, and the Directive may be inconsistent. The Court's case law differs from the more progressive Directive, which, for example, abolishes examining whistleblower motives while the Court emphasises them.

D. Concluding: The Impact of CoE on Whistleblowers' Legal Protection

Starting with the need to fight corruption, the CoE has become a key player in whistleblower protection in Europe. As a delicate issue, whistleblowing was

[75] Council of Europe, Recommendation 2162 (2019) (n 73) para 2.
[76] ibid para 3.
[77] ibid para 3.
[78] ibid para 8.
[79] A Myers, *Evaluation report on Recommendation CM/Rec(2014)7 on the protection of whistleblowers* (Council of Europe June 2022) CDCJ(2022)01rm.coe.int/cdcj-2022-01-evaluation-report-on-recommendation-cmrec-2014-7p/1680a6fee1 accessed 15 May 2025

rarely regulated by European states, but the CoE's work provided vital foundations for national laws. Its influence began with anti-corruption efforts, then led to Recommendation 2014(7), and finally supported the EU Directive. Moving from sector-specific measures to a comprehensive legal framework, the CoE's ongoing work has inspired many states and the Directive as well.

One negative point is that no Convention has been adopted, despite the efforts by the Parliamentary Assembly of the CoE. The Council of Ministers has refused to start negotiations, prioritising Recommendation 2014(7) as the primary focus for CoE Member States rather than adopting a Convention. The Directive may change ministers' stance and prompt negotiations for a Convention soon, modelled after the Directive. The coexistence of the CoE's legal framework and the Directive might prove problematic, as their respective criteria differ. This contradictory situation will be analysed below.

E. From Corruption to Freedom of Expression: The European Court of Human Rights (ECtHR)

Despite the efforts made by the CoE, the Contracting Parties were reluctant to adopt further and effective measures to protect whistleblowers. The ECtHR has played a significant role in safeguarding whistleblowers through its case law. The Strasbourg Court had previously examined 'whistleblowing' from the perspective of protecting journalistic sources, as seen in the *Goodwin* and *Fressoz and Roire* cases. Still, it had never directly addressed the protection of whistleblowers.[80]

The difference lies in the fact that journalists have a different status and enhanced protection under Article 10 of the Convention, as they are considered necessary persons to inform citizens and to criticise public power. A journalist is a public watchdog, and they should have the liberty to express themselves freely.[81] Contrary to that, the whistleblower is a worker and, as a worker, has different duties, and their freedom of expression may be limited. The Court has noted that, in order to examine whistleblower protection, the applicant must have a work-based relationship in which they are bound by the duty of loyalty, reserve, and discretion to their employer.[82]

The Court contributed to whistleblowing with its landmark decision in the *Guja v Moldova* case, in which the Grand Chamber judgment directly addressed whistleblowers' protection.[83] The Court, by adhering to the importance of Article 10 and

[80] *Christine Goodwin v UK* App no 28957/95 (ECtHR, 1 July 2002); *Fressoz and Roire v France* App no 29183/95 (ECtHR, 21 January 1999).

[81] RCA White and C Ovey, *Jacobs, White & Ovey: The European Convention on Human Rights*, 3rd edn (OUP, 2010) 432–36.

[82] *Medžlis Islamske Zajednice Brčko and Others v Bosnia and Herzegovina* App no 17224/11 (ECtHR, 27 June 2017) para 80.

[83] I Cameron, 'European Court of Human Rights: April 2007-April 2008' (2008) 14(4) *European Public Law* 468.

the freedom of expression, granted protection to the whistleblower.[84] This case was the first related to whistleblowing and, as the Court noted, 'To date, however, the Court has not had to deal with cases where a civil servant publicly disclosed internal information.'[85] The Court reaffirmed the importance of freedom of expression and its role as a supervisor of the principles that characterise a democratic society.[86] Article 10 on the freedom of expression is one of the most important articles of the Convention. The right is linked to democracy and politics and should be present in order to foster public debate. Through its case-law, the Court has given a 'constitutional' significance to this right. The Court not only protects information or ideas that are inoffensive but also those that offend and shock.[87]

The Strasbourg Court established proportionality criteria for employees' free speech in the *Guja* judgment. Mr Guja, Head of the Press Department at Moldova's Prosecutor General's Office, raised concerns about political interference, was fired, and retaliated. He brought his case to the ECtHR to determine whether Moldova violated his right to freedom of expression. The Court set six criteria for national courts to evaluate whistleblower protection under Article 10. The *Guja* case was crucial as the first to grant whistleblower protection at the European level. The Court reaffirmed its case law in subsequent cases, such as *Heinisch*, *Bucur,* and *Toma* and *Matuz*.[88]

In the *Heinisch* case, a nurse in Germany reported serious care deficiencies, but her complaints were ignored, leading her to file a criminal complaint of fraud and be fired. German courts justified her dismissal, citing disproportionate reaction and breach of loyalty. However, the Strasbourg Court, aligned with Guja principles, found that her Article 10 rights and freedom of expression were violated. In *Bucur and Toma*, a Romanian Intelligence Service employee exposed the unlawful tapping of officials via a press conference. National courts convicted him of breaching secrecy, but the Strasbourg Court ruled that Romania violated his free expression rights again under the *Guja* principles.[89]

In *Matuz v Hungary*,[90] Mr Matuz worked for Hungarian State Television as an 'editor and presenter of Night Shelter'. In 2003, a new director started making content suggestions, which were seen as censorship by him and his colleagues. Their protests failed, and in 2004, Mr Matuz published 'The Antifascist and the Hungarista – Secrets from Hungarian Television' to expose censorship, after which

[84] Convention for the Protection of Human Rights and Fundamental Freedoms (European Convention on Human Rights, as amended) (ECHR) Art 10.

[85] *Guja v Moldova* App no 14277/04 (ECtHR, 12 February 2008) para 72.

[86] D Harris, M O'Boyle, E Bates and C Buckley, *Law of the European Convention on Human Rights*, 3rd edn (OUP, 2014) 613–14.

[87] *Handyside v United Kingdom* App no 5493/72 (ECtHR, 7 December 1976) para 49.

[88] V Junod, 'Lancer l'alerte: quoi de neuf depuis 'Guja'?: (Cour eur. dr. h., 'Bucur et Toma c. Roumanie', 8 janvier 2013)' (2014) 98 *Revue trimestrielle des droits de l'homme* 459, 482.

[89] *Bucur and Toma v Romania* App no 40238/02 (ECtHR, 8 January 2013).

[90] *Matuz v Hungary* App no 73571/10 (ECtHR, 21 October 2014). See also Columbia Global Freedom of Expression, Case analysis of *Matuz v Hungary* globalfreedomofexpression.columbia.edu/cases/matuz-v-hungary/ accessed 15 May 2021.

he was fired. The Court ruled that his freedom of expression was violated, citing the Guja case, emphasising the importance of reporting channels.

Following the adoption of the Directive, the Court had to examine the case of *Halet v Luxembourg* in two decisions.[91] The Luxleaks whistleblower decisions of the Court are significant, as they are the first to be examined by the Court following the adoption of the Directive, and the first instance decision was quite contradictory. The final decision, though, confirmed that Luxembourg had violated Mr Halet's freedom of expression. Still, the Court did not modify any of its outdated criteria, such as good faith, in its reasoning.

The *Guja* case and its principles are of great importance for whistleblowers at the European level. In *Guja* and the relevant case law, the Court stated that the dismissal suffered by the applicant constituted an interference by public authorities with the right to freedom of expression.[92] Then, the ECtHR followed the 'triple test' to check whether the interference was legitimate or whether it violated the Convention. For this purpose, it examined the following three points: first, whether it was prescribed by law; second, whether it pursued a legitimate aim; and, finally, whether the interference was necessary in a democratic society.[93]

F. The 'Triple Test' of Article 10(2) ECHR

Article 10 of the Convention, like Articles 8 and 9, includes a principle (Article 10(1)) and conditions for derogation (Article 10(2)). The right to freedom of expression is broad, covering holding opinions and receiving and sharing information and ideas without state interference.[94] However, restrictions, if justified, can be imposed on the right to freedom of expression according to Article 10(2).

Every restriction upon the right to freedom of expression should be 'prescribed by law'. Any interference with Article 10 should fulfil this elementary condition.[95] This means the measure must have a legal basis in national law, and the Court should assess both its form and quality. The second part of the 'triple test' is analysing whether there is a legitimate aim, as listed in Article 10, paragraph 2, including national security, confidentiality, and the maintenance of the authority and impartiality of the judiciary.[96]

The final important part of the 'triple test' is that any interference with the freedom of expression, to the extent that it is prescribed by law and has a legitimate aim, can be justified if such interference was 'necessary in a democratic society'.[97] The Court begins by assessing if there is a 'pressing social need', considering the

[91] *Halet v. Luxembourg* App no 21884/18 (ECtHR, 14 February 2023).
[92] *Guja v Moldova* (n 85) paras 52 and 55 (citing *Vogt v Germany* 21 EHRR 205 [1996]).
[93] ibid paras 58 and 59.
[94] White and Ovey (n 81) 425–27.
[95] WA Schabas, *The European Convention on Human Rights – A Commentary* (OUP, 2015) 469.
[96] Art 10, para 2 ECHR.
[97] Schabas (n 95) 474.

interests of democratic society. Its extensive case law shows that the Strasbourg Court evaluates the proportionality of interference, taking into account factors such as the gravity, nature, and severity of the penalties.[98] This proportionality test is the same, in its essential features, as the proportionality test in Articles 8 and 9.[99]

In the *Guja* case, the Court noted that dismissing Mr Guja for leaking letters to the journal interfered with his right to freedom of expression.[100] Following its traditional reasoning, the Court continued that such an interference can constitute a breach unless it was 'prescribed by law' in pursuing 'one or more legitimate aims'. It was 'necessary in a democratic society' for the achievement of these aims.[101] Consequently, as per the wording of Article 10 ECHR (and more specifically its paragraph 2), the Court had to search the above and decide if the interference was justified or not.

First, the Court found that it is 'prescribed by law', as it believed the provisions of the Internal Regulations of the Press Department of the Prosecutor General's Office (paragraphs 1.4 and 4.11) satisfy the requirement.[102] This means that there was a legal basis in the national legal system for his dismissal, thereby ensuring foreseeability, precision, accessibility, and the avoidance of arbitrariness.[103] In continuing, the Court had to examine whether the legitimate aim was satisfied.[104] To achieve this, the Court said it should assess whether the interference was necessary in a democratic society and whether there was a proportionate relationship between the interference and its aim.

In this case on whistleblower protection, the Court relied on its case law on freedom of expression. It emphasised that 'Freedom of expression is vital for democracy and progress … this freedom has exceptions, which must be strictly interpreted. Restrictions need a convincing social need… the term 'necessary' in Article 10(2) means a 'pressing social need'… the Court decides if a 'restriction' aligns with Article 10's protection of free expression'.[105]

Furthermore, the Court reiterated that the right to freedom of expression applies to the workplace and, consequently, to civil servants.[106] However, the Court underlined that public servants have a duty of loyalty and discretion to the government because they have access to sensitive and highly confidential information.[107] The Court noted the case is unique because a public servant leaked sensitive

[98] ibid.
[99] S Greer, 'The Exceptions to Article 8 to 11 of the European Convention on Human Rights', (1997) Human Rights Files No. 15, Council of Europe Publishing 9-18.
[100] *Guja v Moldova* (n 85) para 55.
[101] ibid para 56.
[102] *Guja v Moldova* (n 85) para 58.
[103] D Voorhoof, 'Freedom of Expression under the European Human Rights System' (2010) 2 *Inter-American and European Human Rights Journal* 3, 5.
[104] *Guja v Moldova* (n 85) para 59.
[105] ibid para 69.
[106] ibid para 70.
[107] ibid para 71.

information externally. Civil servants often hold valuable internal information that interests the public. The Court was influenced by the worker's status and the anti-corruption theme, a key Council of Europe agenda item.[108]

Additionally, such individuals are often the only ones aware of workplace events. The Court cited the Council of Europe's Civil Law Convention on Corruption's Explanatory Report, which notes that 'corruption is hard to detect and investigate, and employees or colleagues are often the first to suspect something is amiss wrong'.[109] As a result, the Court affirmed that public servants can also enjoy the right to freedom of expression, under certain conditions, when they reveal information.

G. The Six Criteria Developed by the Court in the *Guja* Decision

The Strasbourg Court outlined six criteria for whistleblower protection: disclosure channel, public interest, information authenticity, whether the damage outweighs the public interest, the whistleblower's good faith, and penalties. The Court, in other cases, such as *Bucur and Toma* and *Heinisch*, has followed these criteria,[110] and they are considered established case law on the issue of whistleblowing.[111] The criteria are cumulative, and a case-by-case analysis should be conducted every time the question arises.

The first criterion set out by the Court concerns the disclosure of information: it should initially be disclosed internally or to a competent authority. If this is impossible, the information can only be disclosed to the public as an *ultima ratio*.[112] Hence, in order to decide in every case whether the imposed restriction on the right to freedom of expression was proportionate, the Court must examine whether the interested party had other effective channels for disclosure to report.

Regarding Mr Guja, the Court found that Moldovan law and the Prosecutor General's Office's internal rules did not specify a procedure. Thus, the applicant could not report internally or to a competent body, making it reasonable to disclose the information to the public.[113] The Court implies that if internal procedures and contact with authorities are unavailable, whistleblowers may notify the public.

The Court continued its analysis with the second criterion: the necessity of public interest and whether the disclosed information was in the public interest.[114]

[108] See, for instance, the Criminal Law Convention on Corruption of the Council of Europe, adopted in Strasbourg on the 27 January 1999.

[109] *Guja v Moldova* (n 85) para 72.

[110] Junod (n 88) 459–82.

[111] Schabas (n 95) 465.

[112] *Guja v Moldova* (n 85) para 73. See also *Haseldine v United Kingdom* App no 18957/91 (ECtHR, 13 May 1992).

[113] *Guja v Moldova* (n 85) para 80.

[114] ibid para 74.

The Court made the point that 'the interest which the public may have in particular information can sometimes be so strong as to override even a legally imposed duty of confidence'.[115] The Court highlighted the duty of loyalty that public servants have to respect. However, these six criteria were aimed at helping to balance the interests of all parties involved. It was also noticed that 'in a democratic society, the acts or omissions of a government must be subject to the close scrutiny not only of the legislative and judicial authorities but also of the media and public opinion'.[116]

In the *Guja* case, it was found that the public had a legitimate interest in being informed about the specific matter.[117] The published letters were vital, as they showed political authorities using their powers to influence the criminal justice system by intervening with the judicial body. The Court also emphasised that the President of the state requested greater transparency without interference, aligning with the separation of powers in a democratic state.[118] It is evident that the public interest outweighs the applicant's duty of confidentiality. What remains uncertain from the Court's reasoning is whether the prospective whistleblower should undertake this analysis beforehand and whether this test is based on an objective or subjective standard.

The concept of the public interest is not easily defined. According to Strasbourg Court case law, situations in the public interest are determined on a case-by-case basis. No exhaustive list exists; instead, it is constantly updated based on decided cases. The following situations have been characterised as falling within the concept of the public interest: the conditions of institutions which take care of elder people (to prevent abuses to this vulnerable category of citizens),[119] political influence on the judiciary,[120] abuses by the administration,[121] the interception of private communication,[122] behaviours that are contrary to the deontological standards of doctors,[123] and informing the public about the dangerous effects of microwaves.[124] The concept of public interest is interpreted on a case-by-case basis, and it is hard to be certain a priori if an issue, coming before the Court, is of public interest or not.

The following criterion is the authenticity of the information revealed.[125] The Court uses this criterion to prevent defamatory or malicious accusations. It acknowledges that freedom of expression comes with responsibilities, requiring individuals to verify the authenticity of information as much as possible. It should

[115] *Fressoz and Roire v France* App no 29183/95 (ECtHR, 21 January 1999); *Radio Twist v Slovakia* App no 62202/00 (ECtHR, 19 December 2006).
[116] *Guja v Moldova* (n 85) para 74.
[117] ibid para 88.
[118] ibid para 87.
[119] *Heinisch v Germany* App no 28274/08 (ECtHR, 21 July 2011), para 71.
[120] *Guja v Moldova* (n 85) para 88.
[121] *Bucur and Toma v Romania* (n 89) para 102.
[122] *Wojtas-Kaleta v Poland* App no 20436/02 (ECtHR, 16 July 2009), para 49.
[123] *Sosinowska v Poland* App no 10247/09 (ECtHR, 17 October 2011).
[124] *Hertel v Switzerland* App no 53440/99 (ECtHR, 25 August 1998).
[125] *Guja v Moldova* (n 85) para 75.

be noted, though, that if the authenticity of the information is contested, the Court, as it did in the *Soares* and *Gawlik* cases,[126] would rely on the evaluation of the authenticity carried out during the national proceedings. The lack of a proper analysis of this criterion makes it challenging to determine whether it is similar to the 'reasonable belief' or if it requires the information to be correct. A careful analysis of the *Bucur et Toma* case seems to put forward the concept of 'reasonable belief' rather than 'true information'.[127]

The fourth criterion established by the Court is to weigh the damage suffered by the public authority resulting from the disclosure and assess whether the damage done outweighs the public interest in the information.[128] The Court takes into account the interests and image of the public authority (or the private entity, if it concerns the private sector). Following this direction, the Court requests that national jurisdictions assess the proportionality of the information disclosed in relation to the public interest and the damage suffered by the entity in question, whether public or private. This criterion is a *stricto sensu* evaluation of proportionality.

In the *Guja* case, the Court found the letters vital to the public interest, revealing political interference in the Prosecutor's work. It stressed these issues are of public concern and citizens should not be excluded. However, it is unclear if whistleblowers should evaluate this beforehand.

Turning to the following criterion, the Court was very precise in stating that the individual should have disclosed in good faith. The bona fide whistleblower should be motivated by the public interest and believe that the information they disclosed was accurate.[129] The Court excluded whistleblowers acting in bad faith, citing personal gain or antagonism, from protection. It applied a good faith test to Mr Guja, concluding he acted in good faith despite the government's claim he hadn't used this argument before the courts.[130] It analysed the applicant's behaviour and motives, finding he aimed to fight corruption and political influence on the Prosecutor. The Court noted that he had no personal disputes with the Prosecutor General or politicians, and that he gained nothing from his disclosure.

The last criterion is related to the sanction imposed on the whistleblower and its consequences for them. The Court emphasised that this criterion is linked to the proportionality of the interference in relation to the legitimate aim pursued.[131] One may wonder if a whistleblower should be sanctioned to be considered under Court case law. So far, in all whistleblower protection cases, applicants faced sanctions for reporting. If someone reaches the Court, they have suffered negative consequences. It is thus worth questioning whether the sanctions are

[126] *Soares v Portugal* App no 79972/12 (ECtHR, 21 June 2016); *Gawlik v Liechtenstein* App no 23922/19 (ECtHR, 16 February 2021).
[127] *Bucur and Toma v Romania* (n 89) para 107.
[128] *Guja v Moldova* (n 85) para 76.
[129] ibid para 77.
[130] ibid paras 92–94.
[131] ibid para 78.

proportionate and what the negative effects are. For instance, the Court found that Mr Guja's sanction was the heaviest possible: dismissal. Although less severe sanctions could have been applied, national authorities chose dismissal, a severe penalty for employees.[132]

The Court pointed out that the heavy sanction imposed on the applicant not only had profound negative implications for his professional career, but it could also have a 'chilling effect' for future whistleblowers. In addition, the Court emphasised a contradiction from the governmental side. Although the government accused the applicant of stealing the classified letters, it then argued that these letters were considered everyday communication between state bodies.[133] For these reasons, the Court found that the severity of the sanction cannot be justified. Considering the subsequent cases of the Court, the impression is that any real and severe sanction can deter the whistleblower.

Following its extensive analysis and balancing of interests, the Court concluded that the interference was 'not necessary in a democratic society' and, as a result, Article 10 ECHR was violated.[134] In its conclusion, the Court highlighted the different rights at stake, such as the right to freedom of expression and the duty of loyalty of the civil servants, again, to give its final decision.

The Court balanced competing interests, maintaining consistency with its case law and the landmark *Guja* judgment. Its criteria inspired legislation and national courts' decisions, including the Directive on whistleblower protection and cases on whistleblower protection.[135] The Strasbourg Court's criteria have gaps and are subject to criticism. For example, the good faith of whistleblowers and the effectiveness of sanctions are hard to assess, which may discourage reporting. These six evolving criteria have both positive and problematic aspects worth examining.

H. The Dilemma: The Public and Private Sector

In its first landmark judgment, the Strasbourg Court examined a case involving a public sector worker. It initially seemed the Court only protected whistleblowers in the public sector, but this was incorrect. The *Guja* case indicates that the Court was indirectly referring to private-sector workers as well.[136] The *Heinisch* judgment established that private-sector employees can seek protection under Article 10 if their freedom of expression is violated. The applicant worked in a private elder

[132] ibid para 95.
[133] ibid para 96.
[134] ibid para 97.
[135] Commission Staff Working Document, Impact Assessment accompanying the document of the proposal for a Directive of the European Parliament and of the Council on the protection of persons reporting on breaches of Union law [2018] COM(2018) 218 final. See also A Lui and U Turksen, 'Vulnerabilities, Obstacles and Risks in Reporting Financial Crimes' in N Ryder and L Pasculli (eds), *Corruption, Integrity and the Law: Global Regulatory Challenges* (Taylor & Francis Group, 2020) 173.
[136] *Guja v Moldova* (n 85) para 70.

care institution with a contract governed by private law, which protects all workers regardless of sector. The Court distinguished between public agents, who have a duty of reserve, and private employees, who have an obligation of discretion.[137] Even though public and private workers have different duties, the protection is equally offered to both.

I. The First Corporation-Whistleblower Case: *Halet v Luxembourg*

The ECtHR protects institutional interests in reporting, primarily involving public bodies such as the Public Prosecutor's Office and the Romanian Intelligence Services. In *Heinisch*, the applicant worked for a semi-private care home for the elderly. Despite its private nature, the institution's main goal was caring for older people. Here, threats to elderly lives are in the public interest and justify reporting if the public interest outweighs institutional damage.

A question the Strasbourg Court had not yet addressed concerned private corporations, banks, and financial institutions.[138] The answer came on 11 May 2021 and 14 February 2023 in the judgments of *Halet v Luxembourg*.[139] The applicant argued before the ECtHR that Luxembourg violated his right to freedom of expression. The case centred on whether his disclosure harmed PwC more than the public's right to know. Initially, the Court found his disclosure caused significant harm to PwC, outweighing public interest. However, in the final judgment, the Court reversed this, stating Mr Halet's revelations served the public interest and outweighed the harm to PwC.

J. Is it the End: Unsuitability of the Good Faith Criterion

In the *Guja* case, good faith was crucial for determining whistleblower protection. The Court noted that denunciations motivated by personal gain or hostility do not warrant the same protection as good-faith whistleblower reports.[140] The Court is strict in applying this criterion, aiming to avoid negative implications, as evidenced by the *Langer* case. In that case, the Court found no violation of Article 10 because the whistleblower was not acting in good faith.[141]

[137] *Gormus et autres c Turquie* App no 49085/07 (ECtHR, 19 January 2016) para 50. See also JP Marguénaud and J Mouly, 'La protection européenne des salariés lanceurs d'alerte par la Cour de Cassation: un troublant exemple d'improvisation' [2016] *Recueil Dalloz* 1741.

[138] K Deckert and M Sweeney, 'Whistleblowing: National Report for France' in G Thusing and G Forst (eds), *Whistleblowing – A Comparative Study* (Springer, 2016) 145.

[139] *Halet v Luxembourg* App no 21884/18 (ECtHR, 11 May 2021). ECtHR, Grand Chamber. Case of *Halet v. Luxembourg* (n 91).

[140] *Guja v Moldova* (n 85) para 77.

[141] *Langner v Germany* App no 14464/11 (ECtHR, 17 September 2015) para 47.

Assessing good faith is complex for the Court. What if a whistleblower is driven by personal issues but reports significant public-interest wrongdoing? Why not protect such cases? For example, in *Heinisch*, the Court noted the applicant's exaggeration but found the disclosed facts valid and not a personal attack. Thus, the Court concluded the applicant acted in good faith despite her excessive reaction.[142] However, exaggeration does not necessarily indicate a lack of good faith. The Court is not drawing the line on what it considers to be exaggeration, a certain degree of excessiveness.

In the *Soares* case, the Court took a different stance. The Strasbourg Court doubted the applicant's good faith after the national court's decision. It noted that the applicant accused another employee of misusing public money but lacked evidence, basing his claims solely on rumours.[143] The Court reaffirmed the national court's finding that the applicant did not act in good faith, focusing on factual claims rather than value judgments. The serious allegations of misuse of public money required a factual basis, which the applicant failed to provide, relying only on rumours. He did not act in good faith by failing to verify the allegations' authenticity.[144] The case's approach to the good-faith criterion resembles the 'reasonable belief' test. The Court emphasises the applicant's failure to verify the authenticity of the information, not personal motives, thus failing the reasonable belief test.

In the *Aurelian Oprea v Romania* case, the good faith criterion becomes even more pronounced.[145] The applicant in question was an associate professor who had been denied his promotion on numerous occasions. He decided to expose corruption at his university by speaking to the media. The Court stated that 'the applicant's statements concerned important issues in a democratic society, about which the public had a legitimate interest in being informed'.[146] The Court focused on the protected interest, which is the public disclosure and the right of the citizens to know about this wrongdoing. Consequently, the applicant's motives become less important. In the Court's analysis, the motives of the applicant remained behind, and the requirement of good faith was minimised. The Court highlighted that '[E]ven assuming that the applicant's frustration as a result of not being promoted to a position of a professor might have been an additional motive for his actions, the Court has no reason to doubt that the applicant acted in good faith and in the belief that it was in the public interest to disclose the alleged shortcomings in his University to the public'.[147] The Court evaluates the good faith criterion as one of its six established criteria. Still, it

[142] *Heinisch v Germany* (n 119) para 85.
[143] *Soares v Portugal* (n 126) para 46.
[144] ibid. See also V Junod, 'La Liberté d'Expression du Whistleblower' (2009) 77 *Revue Trimestrielle des droits de l'homme* 238.
[145] *Aurelian Oprea v Romania* App no 12138/08 (ECtHR, 19 January 2016).
[146] ibid para 65.
[147] ibid para 71.

seems unwilling to block protection solely on this criterion, as long as the information is in the public interest.[148]

K. Who Dares to Define Public Interest?

The 'public interest' may be characterised as the most important criterion. The notion of 'public interest' is a complex concept that cannot be defined easily. This concept has been the subject of a significant debate regarding its meaning and content.[149] On its side, the ECtHR has emphasised that Article 10(2) does not allow any restriction to the freedom of expression when it comes to the 'public interest'.[150] However, this begs the question of who defines 'public interest' and how it is defined.

In a democratic society, the actions or omissions of a government should be subject not only to judicial or legislative control but also to the scrutiny of the media and the public.[151] The Court has already noticed this essential element when it defended the divulgation of important information, even though a duty of confidentiality was imposed on the whistleblower.[152] The Court has an extensive body of case law on the question of what constitutes public interest. It covers a wide range of situations. Some examples include: the care of older people, abuses by the public administration, control of private communications, behaviours that violate the deontological rules of doctors, criticism of public agents concerning a nuclear accident, and many others.[153] However, it should be noted that the factors used by the Court related to the defence of restrictions on freedom of speech, which should be necessary in a democratic society, do not clarify the meaning of the 'public interest'.[154] Actually, the public interest is treated as a factor itself.[155]

The Court stresses the importance of informing the public about issues affecting their lives. A key issue is whether private interests deserve the same consideration as public interests. For example, if only one person is involved – such as someone facing workplace sexual harassment – it raises the question of whether whistleblowing applies to private interests as well. Though the Court has not addressed

[148] See, to that extent, *Rubins v Latvia* App no 79040/12 (ECtHR, 13 January 2015), which also concerns an academic who, prior to informing the media, wrote a letter to the Rector about the revocation of his decision to merge his department. The Court focuses on the interest of the public to be informed and not on the applicant's bad faith. See also J Lewis et al., *Whistle-blowing: Law and Practice* (OUP, 2017) 18.35, wherein the comments made about *Kharlamov v Russia* App no 27447/07 (ECtHR, 8 October 2015) it is noted that the importance of protecting matters related to public interest might outweigh any obligations of good faith in the workplace.

[149] A Gordon, 'Public Interest and the Three Dimensions of Judicial Review' (2013) 64(2) *Northern Ireland Legal Quarterly* 125, 127.

[150] *Sürek v Turkey* App no 26682/95 (ECtHR, 8 July 1999), para 61.

[151] Devers (n 50) 55.

[152] *Radio Twist v Slovakia* App no 62202/00 (ECtHR, 19 December 2006).

[153] *Mamère v France* App no 12697/03 (ECtHR, 7 November 2006).

[154] D Lewis, 'Is a Public Interest Test for Workplace Whistle-blowing in Society's Interest?' (2015) 57(2) *International Journal of Law and Management* 147.

[155] ibid.

this specific case, it is believed it will follow the criteria used in the *Guja* case. The Court has a broad view of the notion of public interest, and as a result, it may offer the same level of protection.[156]

However, the concept of the public interest remains a notion that has been developed and will continue to evolve through the courts and is also highly debated in the literature.[157] A case-by-case approach clarifies this notion, highlighting the unique nature of each issue and the difficulty in defining public interest uniformly. The UK's Public Interest Disclosure Act offers an alternative, emphasising a broader focus on general interest over public interest, covering both sectors' interests.[158]

L. Thinking of the Employer

Furthermore, the Court has analysed the damage to the employer and whether the public's interest in being informed outweighs that damage. The Court examined the two elements separately, but it could have been better to analyse them uniformly.[159] The Court has to appreciate, on the one hand, the damage that the denunciation caused to the employer or the concerned public authority and, on the other hand, the interest that the public has in this information.[160] As a result, the Court has to examine the object of the denunciation and the nature of the concerned administrative authority.[161] This balancing test, though, seems to have several weaknesses.

If a disclosure reveals illegalities or wrongdoings, the question arises whether potential damage to the institution should be considered. The institution's good image is vital when it serves legitimate purposes without wrongdoing – balancing a legitimate interest with public interest. Claiming national security to justify disclosures risks allowing executive overreach. If a corporation or authority commits wrongdoing, seeking damages for disclosure suggests these may have occurred under certain conditions. This undermines democratic accountability, as institutions should be answerable to citizens.

The whistleblower is part of an accountability system that oversees institutions and serves the public by exposing potential wrongdoing that harms society, the economy, and other sectors. If wrongdoing is confirmed and the employer admits to breaching the law, the question arises: why should the potential harm caused by the whistleblower be considered? For example, if wrongdoing caused one death but resulted in massive financial losses, is there a real balance? Should courts give free rein to institutions that broke the law, even if no one died? Courts should be cautious and view the whistleblower as a vital tool for public accountability.

[156] Junod (n 144) 235.
[157] B Bozeman, *Public Values and Public Interest* (Georgetown University Press, 2007) ch 1.
[158] G Thüsing and G Forst (eds), *Whistle-blowing - A Comparative Study* (Springer Publishing, 2016) 7.
[159] Junod (n 144) 235.
[160] *Guja v Moldova* (n 85) para 76.
[161] Devers (n 50) 63.

The decision in *Halet v Luxembourg* sheds further light on the balancing of the public interest in being informed against the harm to the employer caused by the reporting.[162] This case concludes the Luxleaks saga that began in 2016. In the case, journalist Edouard Perrin and whistleblower Antoine Deltour were acquitted by the Luxembourg Cassation Court. However, Mr Halet was condemned because the information he revealed added no new insights into Luxembourg's tax agreements, already disclosed by Mr Deltour. The Luxembourg Court of Appeal ruled that Mr Halet caused greater harm to his employer, PwC, than the public's interest in the disclosed information.[163] The Luxembourg Court of Cassation confirmed the Luxembourg Court of Appeal's decision. Mr Halet then took his case to the Strasbourg Court, claiming Luxembourg violated his freedom of expression.

On 11 May 2021, the ECtHR gave its first verdict on Mr Halet's claim. The Court found no violation of his right to freedom of expression and followed the reasoning of the Luxembourg Courts.[164] While the Strasbourg Court recognised that Mr Halet's disclosures excited public opinion, they have caused more harm to PwC than the public interest in getting informed.[165] The Court argued that Mr Halet's information did not bring anything new, essential, or unknown, as the issue of Luxembourg's obscure tax practices had already been revealed by Mr Deltour, which provoked a national, international, and European debate and changes.[166] The Strasbourg Court rejected the applicant's claim that its evaluation creates novel requirements for this criterion, noting that the characterisation of new, essential and unknown information has already been part of the Court's reasoning.

In *Halet v Luxembourg*, the Court provided new developments regarding this criterion.[167] While the Court insisted that its evaluation of balancing private and public interest would not have a chilling effect on future whistleblowers, the two dissenting judges were not of the same opinion. Judges Lemmens and Pavli stated that, with this decision, they disagree with the general approach adopted by the Court about the balancing of damage.[168] The reasoning did not convince both judges of the Court, and they believe this decision would have a chilling effect on whistleblowers, as they would be discouraged from reporting because of the subjectivity and uncertainty of the concept of new, essential, and unknown information.[169] Both judges confirmed what the Court denies:, that novel requirements have been added to the general approach of *Guja* with *Halet v Luxembourg*.

[162] *Halet v Luxembourg* (n 139) paras 5–6.

[163] D Kafteranis, 'A New Perspective on the Protection of Whistle-blowers under the ECHR: *Halet v. Luxembourg*' (2020) EU Law Live 1 eulawlive.com/analysis-a-new-perspective-on-the-protection-of-whistleblowers-under-the-echr-halet-v-luxembourg-by-dimitrios-kafteranis/ accessed 15 May 2025.

[164] *Halet v Luxembourg* (n 139) paras 112–13.

[165] ibid para 108.

[166] ibid para 109.

[167] Kafteranis (n 163) 2.

[168] *Halet v Luxembourg* (n 139) paras 29–34.

[169] ibid paras 29–34

The Grand Chamber, in its verdict of 14 February 2023, overturned the previous decision by deciding that Luxembourg had violated Mr Halet's right to freedom of expression. The Court states that whistleblowers should be protected under Article 10 ECHR when they report facts of public interest (either new or repeated).[170] The tax matters at hand were of public interest, and the Court made a significant statement in that regard by protecting Mr Halet, who did not report an illegal practice or a wrongdoing but 'certain information that concerns the functioning of public authorities in a democratic society and sparks a public debate, giving rise to controversy likely to create a legitimate interest on the public's part in knowing the information in order to reach an informed opinion as to whether or not it reveals harm to the public interest'.[171]

The Court has unanswered questions, including potential harm to innocent third parties and the whistleblower's responsibility if unforeseen damages occur. It remains to be seen whether the Court will continue favouring the public interest or become more sensitive to third parties. Nonetheless, the importance of whistleblowing in reporting wrongdoing should not be diminished.

M. Authenticity: Should it be the First to be Controlled?

The Court listed six criteria but did not specify their order of examination, which can be inferred from post-*Guja* cases. The primary criterion is assessing the authenticity of information, as false information negates further review – a scenario the Court has not addressed. If the information is partly incorrect but the motives are pure, the sanctions are uncertain. Whistleblowing concerns genuine, not fabricated, information, as false information often involves defamation and undermines whistleblower protections.[172]

Moreover, the Court has affirmed that when someone exercises their right to freedom of expression, they have duties and responsibilities. When they decide to share a piece of information, they must verify, to the greatest extent possible, that it is authentic.[173] This duty is even more critical, as the whistleblower also has a duty of reserve and loyalty vis-à-vis their employer.[174] In the case of *Soares v Portugal*, the Strasbourg Court discovered that the applicant had not verified the authenticity of the information. He based his allegations solely on rumours and had no evidence to support them, which was subsequently proven by national-level

[170] *Halet v Luxembourg* (n 91) para 206.
[171] ibid para 138.
[172] When the disclosure is not a criticism in the interest of the public but rather a defamatory accusation, then the applicant cannot be protected. This was demonstrated in the *Langner v Germany* App no 14464/11 (ECtHR, 17 September 2015), where the applicant did not check the authenticity of the information even though he was in a position to do so.
[173] *Bladet Tromso nad Stensaas v Norway* App no 18957/91 (ECtHR, 20 May 1999).
[174] *Heinisch v Germany* (n 119) para 77.

investigations conducted by the authorities.[175] In addition, the national courts in the national criminal proceedings could not verify the rumours. As a result, the information the applicant gave could not be considered authentic.

This case highlights the Strasbourg Court's view of these criteria. The Court follows a case-by-case approach, assessing whether the whistleblower's information is genuine or fabricated. It relies on national courts' analysis, as it cannot verify the authenticity of the information itself. However, the Court can evaluate the submissions from the applicant and national courts to determine if they meet authenticity standards requirements.

N. Mind the Gap: Internal, Authorities, and Public Disclosures

The Court has recognised three possible channels for disclosure. The whistleblower may report internally or to the public competent authorities or make a public disclosure (informing the public directly via the internet or other platforms). The choice of public disclosure is the last solution for the whistleblower.[176] This is justified by the employees' duties of loyalty and discretion. The debate differs insofar as internal and reporting to authorities are concerned. In *Guja*, the Court did not give priority to internal or external reporting.[177] It recognised that the applicant had the possibility to either report internally or to a competent authority. Only public disclosure was subordinate to the other two forms of disclosure.[178] Even though the Court first examined the possibility of reporting internally to his employer and then to Parliament (the public authority), it did not assign a ranking to this sequence.[179]

The doubts about the priority of internal reporting over external reporting to authorities were cultivated by the decisions in *Heinisch* and *Soares*. In both cases, the Court acknowledged that a Contracting State could prescribe the priority of internal whistleblowing as a rule under its national legal framework.[180] The fact that it prioritises internal reporting over reporting to the authorities does not mean that this is the rule under Article 10 and its case law on whistleblowing. The Court noted that Contracting States have other legal obligations to fulfil, stemming from international and regional laws, and that this event enables them to grant or

[175] *Soares v Portugal* (n 126) para 47 – In this case, the applicant based his information on rumours, and he did not verify the authenticity of them before reporting. As a result, the Court concluded that he could not be granted protection, under Art 10 of the Convention, as a whistleblower.

[176] N Colneric, 'Does the Case Law of the European Court of Human Rights Show that the Convention States of the European Convention on Human Rights Must Prescribe Priority of Internal Whistleblowing as a Rule?' (2018) 6 *Soziales Recht* 232, 238.

[177] *Guja v Moldova* (n 85) para 73.

[178] Colneric (n 176) 238.

[179] The specificity with the *Guja* case is that the applicant had to report internally to his employer which happens to be the Public Prosecutor (a public authority). Despite the public authority character of his employer, the Public Prosecutor's Office is regarded as reporting internally. The option for reporting externally to a public authority is to report to the Parliament.

[180] *Heinisch v Germany* (n 119) paras 37–39 and 73–76 and *Soares v Portugal* (n 126) paras 42–43.

deny priority to internal reporting over external reporting to the authorities.[181] The interest of the Court is not to come into conflict with these legal obligations as long as the interest of the whistleblower, under Article 10, is ensured.

Analysis of case law indicates that whistleblowers can choose between internal reports and authorities, depending on national rules. However, CoE texts, such as Recommendation CM/Rec(2014)7, favour internal reporting, highlighting its benefits, though not all channels are considered equal for whistleblowers.[182]

By blowing the whistle internally, the whistleblower does not violate any obligations of secrecy or confidentiality. The states have the responsibility to incentivise employers to understand the value of internal reporting. This can be achieved by 'implementing a clear and strong legal framework that makes an employer liable for any detriment caused to anyone working for them for having exercised their right to report a concern or disclose information about wrongdoing according to law'.[183] Although there is no clear priority between internal reporting and reporting to the authorities, the Recommendation promotes internal whistleblowing as a sign of good corporate governance.

Finally, the Court appreciates the existence of internal channels for whistleblowing and recognises that employees should utilise them when they are not used.[184] For instance, in the *Soares* case, the Court noted that the applicant had internal channels for whistleblowing at his disposal. Still, he did not use them and also failed to disclose his information to a superior.[185] The Court confirmed he did not meet the criterion by not using internal channels or by not allowing his superiors to investigate rumours, indicating a preference for internal reporting.

Nevertheless, internal whistleblowing has drawbacks for the reporting person. The whistleblower may not be heard, as there is a possibility that the implicated persons are their superiors. Also, the whistleblower cannot assume that their superior/employer is ready and willing to solve the problems brought to their attention.[186] The whistleblower is faced with this dilemma, as they fear that their grievance will not be heard internally and making a public disclosure may have better results. Thus, a possible solution would be to reconsider the creation of a specialised body, where the whistleblower would have the opportunity to provide information without fearing internal retaliation and without having to address the media, a promising way of mitigating the damage for everyone involved.[187]

[181] Colneric (n 176) 236.

[182] Council of Europe Committee of Ministers, Recommendation CM/Rec(2014)7, Protection of whistle-blowers, (adopted by the Committee of Ministers at the 1198th meeting on 30 April 2014) Definitions, point c, p 7.

[183] ibid para 64.

[184] *Gawlik v Liechtenstein* (n 126) para 82.

[185] *Soares v Portugal* (n 126) para 47.

[186] G Sinzdak, 'An Analysis of Current Whistle-blower Laws: Defending a More Flexible Approach to Reporting Requirements' (2008) 96(6) *California Law Review* 1655.

[187] P Stephenson and M Levi, 'The Protection of Whistle-blowers - A Study on the Feasibility of a Legal Instrument on the Protection of Employees who Make Disclosures in the Public Interest', Council of Europe, CDCJ(2012)9FIN, 30.

Another important question concerns the amount of time a whistleblower should wait after reporting the incident internally before deciding to use an external channel. In the *Guja* case, the applicant has been waiting for six months, and the Prosecutor has not responded. The Court, in its analysis, was not explicit on this question, which will be posed in many new cases.[188] As a result, the understanding is that there is no 'magic number', but that the whistleblower has to wait for a reasonable amount of time before concluding that no action was being taken on their internal complaint.

O. To Punish or Not to Punish?

The Court recognised that the termination of the whistleblower's work contract is a severe sanction, which cannot be justified. In *Guja*, it noted that 'the heaviest sanction possible was imposed on the applicant'.[189] The Court, in its case law, argues that the termination of the work contract is a heavy sanction that cannot be justified. Certainly, terminating the work contract is a severe sanction that has numerous implications for the whistleblower.[190] Looking at it from a more social perspective, the whistleblower risks their professional career in order to blow the whistle. Consequently, they need better protection under labour law. It is positive that the Court considers dismissal as a heavy sanction, which cannot be justified. The Court recognised the fact that a severe sanction not only has negative repercussions for the employee but also for other employees who may, in the future, decide to report irregularities.[191]

The Court has not only faced dismissal as a sanction but also criminal sanctions against whistleblowers. In the *Bucur and Toma* case, the Court did not characterise the criminal sanction as 'the heaviest sanction'. Still, it focused more on the negative repercussions that a criminal sanction has on the applicant's career, as well as on other employees of the same public institution and public servants in general.[192] Based on these negative repercussions, the Court, without stating it clearly in its decision, implied that such a sanction cannot be acceptable for the whistleblower.[193] Someone would have expected the Court to immediately label a criminal law sanction as 'the heaviest sanction' because of its criminal nature. Since the Court recognised dismissal as a heavy sanction, it would be expected to do the same for criminal law sanctions. This does not mean that the Court saw the criminal law sanction as less critical or damaging, but it was not as severe as in the case of dismissal.

Finally, the Court recently answered a question that had not yet been addressed by the Strasbourg Court concerning whether 'lighter' sanctions, such as the refusal

[188] ibid 234.
[189] *Guja v Moldova* (n 85) para 95.
[190] ibid. See also *Heinisch v Germany* (n 119) para 91.
[191] *Guja v Moldova* (n 85) para 95.
[192] *Bucur and Toma v Romania* (n 89) para 119.
[193] ibid.

of promotion, can constitute a severe sanction in the Court's assessment. The recent case of *Halet v Luxembourg* offers new perspectives on 'lighter sanctions', and it is one of the first times the Court has confirmed that a sanction is reasonable for the whistleblower and does not create a chilling effect on future whistleblowers.[194] For this decision, the Court considered that the Luxembourg Courts had accepted, as a mitigating factor, the disinterested nature of the applicant's actions, and that the fine of €1,000 was modest.[195] The Court decided that the fine imposed was a relatively mild penalty, which will not have a chilling effect on the applicant's or other employees' right to freedom of expression. As a result, the Strasbourg Court, for the first time, recognised that a sanction can be reasonable and mild and does not have a chilling effect on whistleblowers' right to freedom of expression.[196] The Grand Chamber overturned this, emphasising that undue restrictions on whistleblowers chill free speech. It found Halet's criminal conviction and the requested sum disproportionate to their aims. The decision maintained the coherence of case law on sanctions for whistleblowers.

IV. Concluding Remarks

The Strasbourg Court, in its *Guja* judgment, was among the first to protect whistleblowers when their right to freedom of expression is violated. The Court, when it finds a violation of Article 10, awards damages (eg, €10,000 to Mr Guja, who lost his job and salary), but questions arise as to whether financial protection is sufficient, especially since whistleblowers are often stigmatised. It emphasises that the Court cannot force reintegration; this is the duty of national courts, which face challenges in enforcing such orders. A potential solution might be to improve financial compensation and require the employer to re-integrate them.

Furthermore, the Court granted protection under the aegis of Article 10. The Court has recognised the importance of the right to freedom of expression and its essential role in a democratic society. Several decades ago, the limits of the right to freedom of expression were determined by states, and they were scrutinised only by domestic judicial authorities. The situation changed due to the ECHR and the enforcement mechanisms of the Strasbourg Court. Some legal scholars argue about whether whistleblowing is a right or a duty.[197] From the wording of the Court's decisions, it is understood that whistleblowing is regarded as a right and not a duty. The whistleblower has the liberty (right) to decide whether to report or not, and they are not obliged to report, with no legal consequences in case of failure (duty).

[194] *Halet v Luxembourg* (n 139) para 111.

[195] ibid.

[196] Kafteranis (n 163) 2.

[197] MC Sordino, 'Lanceur d'alerte et droit pénal: entre méfiance et protection?' [2017] *Revue des sociétés*, Dalloz 206. See also I Hoedt-Rasmussen and D Voorhoof, 'Whistleblowing for Sustainable Democracy' (2018) 36 (1) *Netherlands Quarterly of Human Rights* 3, 4–5.

A key question is whether whistleblowing should be considered a human right. When individuals blow the whistle, they exercise their freedom of expression. Reporting is an aspect of this right, leading to the idea of a potential new right: the right to blow the whistle. The CoE and ECtHR confirm that whistleblowing falls under Article 10 of the ECHR. The Court has the authority under this article to define new rights based on existing ones, which the CoE could use to recognise whistleblowing as a human right.

The Court's rulings have enhanced human rights protections, but they lack enforcement power because it cannot compel Contracting Parties to fully respect rights. Political commitment is essential; for instance, the absence of political backing blocked a CoE Convention on whistleblowers, which could have strengthened the Court's authority. Although the Court has developed substantial case law, beginning with *Guja* and extending protections for whistleblowers under Article 10, it still cannot effectively enforce its decisions.

The advent of the Directive, along with the binding nature of EU law, might bring about changes in the near future. It may be beneficial for the Strasbourg Court to reconsider its case law in light of the Directive's provisions. The aim should be to provide uniform legal protection for whistleblowers across the CoE and the EU. The provisions of the Directive are seen as more lenient than the Court's strict standards for protecting whistleblowers. It is recommended to avoid tricky situations in which a whistleblower might not be protected by Strasbourg case law but could be under the EU Directive, or vice versa, as such ambiguities could cause uncertainty and confusion. There is no need for such a dichotomy, but the intention should be to harmonise the two approaches.

The recent case of *Halet v Luxembourg* is the first case decided by the ECtHR since the Directive on the protection of whistleblowers entered into force. It is interesting to comment on the ECtHR approach in relation to the Directive and the verdicts in *Halet v Luxembourg*. In its first decision, the Court took into consideration, when providing the legal framework, the Directive.[198] Nevertheless, the decision of the Court does not reflect the requirements as established by the Directive. The two dissenting judges highlighted this point.[199] The dissenting judges argued that the decision in *Halet v Luxembourg* failed to adequately take into account the legal developments regarding the protection of whistleblowers under the Directive. Notably, the Directive does not impose any balancing of damage caused to the employer by the employee.[200] The whistleblower is protected under the Directive if they fulfil the conditions of Article 6 and if they reasonably believe that wrongdoing occurred. The Strasbourg Court decided to follow its established reasoning and not consider the new developments in the Directive, thereby drawing a clear line between the two European levels of protection for whistleblowers. In the second decision by the Grand Chamber of the Court, the *Guja* criteria remained unchanged, and the Directive had no influence.

[198] *Halet v Luxembourg* (n 139) paras 50–51.
[199] ibid Annex para 10.
[200] ibid.

2

The US Legal Answers as a Blueprint for Europe

I. Understanding Whistleblowing in the US

The US legal approach to whistleblowing offers points worth analysing, especially in the banking and financial sectors. Europe's changes, notably the Directive, show US influence, particularly through the Sarbanes-Oxley Act (SOX)'s extraterritorial reach and European adoption of US whistleblower protections. SOX mandated European companies trading on US markets to establish internal whistleblowing mechanisms and structures.[1] For instance, French companies adopted internal whistleblowing systems after long debates due to the extraterritorial character of SOX.[2] European companies were directly influenced by SOX, and governments started considering the adoption of legislation on the protection of whistleblowers.[3] The influence of US legislation extends not only to the national level but also to the EU level.

The Market Abuse Regulation (MAR) shares similarities with the Dodd-Frank Act, as both respond to financial crises, emphasising scepticism of self-regulation while avoiding a return to the command-and-control model. They combine methods, notably valuing whistleblowers, who under MAR are depersonalised, anonymous, and whose personal motives do not matter anymore. The European Parliament's Resolution 2016/2224 (INI) advocates for protecting whistleblower anonymity and removing the good-faith requirement, drawing influence from US practices. US whistleblower protections shape EU policies, showing a tendency to prioritise efficiency rather than aligning with Member States' legal cultures.

Whistleblowing is a procedural way to free economies from reliance on personal bribes and relationships and reinstate transparency in the capital markets.[4] Individuals are a necessary component of combatting illegal activities and recovering funds that would otherwise be used for other social purposes. In

[1] Conseil d'État, *Le droit d'alerte: signaler, traiter, protéger* (2016) 23.

[2] ibid 24.

[3] For instance, in France the Law n° 2003-706 of 1 August 2003 related to the financial security is adopted (Loi n° 2003-706 de 1er Août 2003 relative à la sécurité financière).

[4] TM Dworkin, 'Whistleblowing, MNCs, and Peace' (2002) 35 *Vanderbilt Journal of Transnational Law* 457, 458–59.

the US, whistleblowing is a well-established concept dating back to 1863, when the first legislation related to whistleblowing was enacted.[5] At that time, Congress had built on a legal concept coming from the English legal tradition to pass a whistleblowing law to combat fraud during the Civil War. Despite this prominence of whistleblowing, the modern emphasis on it began with Ralph Nader, who, in 1971, emphasised its importance as a means to reduce organisational wrongdoing.[6] Different scandals during the first decades of the twenty-first century revealed a flaw in the legislation, which, inter alia, is intended to protect whistleblowers.[7] Corporate fraud and public health and safety disasters demonstrated the lack of whistleblower protection and prompted the US Congress to enact numerous Acts.

Until the 1990s, the legal protection of whistleblowers primarily consisted of protection from retaliation, with the possibility of recovering benefits and wages and retaining their jobs if they were lost due to reporting.[8] Legislators adopted that protection, believing fear of retaliation prevents whistleblowers from coming forward. However, legal protections against retaliation were ineffective. Most private-sector employees were at will, so, besides suing for wrongful termination and potential punitive damages (rare then), the protection was insufficient.[9] Whistleblower protection in the US varies between the public and private sectors. Public sector protections are standard for all public servants. Private-sector protections are industry-specific, as no overarching law covers all whistleblowers; instead, protections depend on the industry.

In the public sector, US public servants were initially protected by the Civil Service Reform Act (CSRA) adopted in 1978.[10] The CSRA banned retaliation against whistleblowers and established reporting channels, including the Office of Special Counsel (OSC), to handle reports on government wrongdoing. In 1989, the Whistleblower Protection Act (WPA) strengthened protections for employees in the public sector.[11] Despite the passage and subsequent revisions of the WPA, the public-sector anti-retaliation model was ineffective.[12] Nonetheless, some efforts, such as the enactment of the Whistleblower Protection Enhancement Act of 2012 and a more supportive OSC, may bring better results in the future.[13]

[5] Act of Mar. 2, 1863, ch. 67, § 6, 12 Stat. 696; False Claims Act, 31 U.S.C. §§ 3729–33 (1988) (formerly the False Claims Act of March 2, 1863, 31 U.S.C. §§ 3729–33 (1988). The objective of the Act was to punish government contractors who were, among other things, selling sawdust for gunpowder. See E Sangrey Callahan and T Morehead Dworkin, 'Do Good and Get Rich: Financial Incentives for Whistleblowing and the False Claims Act' (1992) 37 *Villanova Law Review* 273, 302.

[6] R Nader, 'Editorial: A Code for Professional Integrity', *New York Times*, 15 January 1971, 43.

[7] R Vaughn, *The Successes and Failures of Whistle-blower Laws* (Edward Elgar, 2012) 149.

[8] TM Dworkin and AJ Brown, 'The Money or the Media? Lessons from Contrasting Developments in US and Australian Whistleblowing Laws' (2013) 11(2) *Seattle Journal for Social Justice* 653, 656–57.

[9] TM Dworkin and JP Near, 'Whistleblowing Statutes: Are They Working?' (1987) 25 *American Business Law Journal* 241.

[10] Civil Service Reform Act, Pub. L. No. 95-454, 92 Stat. 1111 (1978).

[11] 5 U.S.C. § 1201 (1989).

[12] Dworkin and Brown (n 8) 657.

[13] Whistleblower Protection Enhancement Act of 2012, Pub. L. No. 112-199, 126 Stat. 1465 (2012).

Protection of private-sector whistleblowers is fragmented, unlike in the public sector. Various Acts protect them under different conditions. The SOX Act of 2002, enacted in response to scandals like Enron and WorldCom, is key legislation that safeguards whistleblowers worldwide from retaliation.[14] The 2008 crisis led to the enactment of the Dodd-Frank Wall Street Reform and Consumer Protection Act (Dodd-Frank), which significantly enhanced whistleblower protection by introducing financial rewards.[15] These rewards were designed on the basis of other successful reward systems, such as the Internal Revenue Service (IRS) rewards for reporting tax fraud and the False Claims Act (FCA) reward scheme for *qui tam* whistleblowers who report fraud involving government funds.[16] These Acts will be the primary focus of this part.

The US legislation on the protection of whistleblowers is notable for having transitioned from anti-retaliation protection to a rewards system.[17] Reward mechanisms succeed by encouraging compensation for whistleblowers who meet specific conditions. The failure of anti-retaliation provisions has led US lawmakers to adopt financial protections in their place.[18] The use of financial rewards along with the detailed whistleblowing legislation has particular roots in common-law-based legal systems, such as the US.[19]

While snitching is not accepted, using citizens to enforce laws privately is longstanding in common law countries. In the US, society and law value individualism, unlike in countries like France, Luxembourg, and Greece, where whistleblowing is viewed as a trait of totalitarian or Communist regimes.[20] This conceptual difference of whistleblowing has created an open culture for whistleblowers in the US, with the cornerstone of this openness being the use of financial rewards.

Whistleblowing legislation success in the US varies by sector. To access Dodd-Frank protections, such as anonymity and rewards, reports must involve securities law or SEC-related issues. SOX covers corporate governance. Tax matters and potential tax fraud should be reported to the IRS. Banking whistleblowing was ineffective until recent reforms, such as the Financial Institutions Reform, Recovery, and Enforcement Act, which enabled the DOJ to sue banks and officials for fraud involving US banking institutions.[21] Also, the enactment of the Anti-Money Laundering Act (AMLA) of 2020 and its subsequent amendments

[14] R Moberly, 'Sarbanes-Oxley's Whistleblower Provisions: Ten Years Later' (2012) 64 *South Carolina Law Review* 1, 11–21, 45–53.

[15] Dodd-Frank Wall Street Reform and Consumer Protection Act, 12 U.S.C. § 5301 (2010).

[16] Dworkin and Brown (n 8) 665.

[17] ibid 655.

[18] Dworkin and Near (n 9).

[19] Dworkin (n 4) 470.

[20] ibid 470–71.

[21] FDIC, 'Financial Institutions Reform, Recovery, and Enforcement Act (FIRREA)' (FDIC.gov, 12 June 2023) www.fdic.gov/publications/financial-institutions-reform-recovery-and-enforcement-act-firrea accessed 15 May 2025.

by the Anti-Money Laundering (AML) Whistleblower Improvement Act are steps towards rewards in the AML and sanctions areas.[22]

A. The First US Law on Whistleblowers: The False Claims Act

The US Congress enacted the False Claims Act (FCA), also known as Lincoln's law, in 1863 to combat fraudulent government contracts during the American Civil War.[23] The importance of the Act is that it is the first one to deal with 'whistleblowing', and it proves that the US legislator was far beyond their European counterparts. The Act was enacted at the end of the eighteenth century, a period when Europe lacked relevant legislation. Additionally, it has been considered the most successful whistleblower law.[24] The Act served as a basis for later US laws, enabling private citizens to sue contractors defrauding the government. If successful, they could claim a portion of the proceeds.

The FCA is based on an old common law principle called *qui tam*, which allows private citizens to bring a claim in court if governmental interests are defrauded. This idea goes back to the old common law doctrine of *qui tam pro domino rege quam pro se ipso*, which means that an individual sues in this issue for the King as well as for himself.[25] An individual who had information about a criminal or civil wrongdoing could sue on behalf of the Crown and be compensated if their claim was successful.[26] In the fourteenth century, British law enforcement relied on informers rather than the Crown. *Qui tam* actions were abolished in the UK in 1951 due to interpretation issues and misuse. However, the *qui tam* doctrine persists in US law, notably in the False Claims Act and other statutes.[27]

The FCA was initially effective but became less used over the course of a century, with few claims filed annually. Despite its disuse, federal contract fraud remained a significant concern for the US government, leading Congress to revise

[22] SM Kohn, 'The AML Whistleblower Program: A New Era for Money-Laundering Enforcement' (*International Banker*, 7 March 2024) internationalbanker.com/banking/the-aml-whistleblower-program-a-new-era-for-money-laundering-enforcement/ accessed 15 May 2025.

[23] False Claims Act 1863 31 U.S.C. §§ 3729-3733.The objective of the Act was to punish government contractors who were, among other things, selling sawdust for gunpowder. The FCA is considered the most important effort to protect whistleblowers since the Declaration of Independence. It should be noted, though, that, long before the FCA, other laws protected whistleblowers. For instance, the Continental Congress, in 1777, protected 10 American sailors, who sought protection as they had reported improper behaviour by the Continental Navy's most powerful man. See A Stanger, *Whistleblowers* (Yale University Press, 2019) 11.

[24] SM Kohn, *The New Whistleblower's Handbook – A Step by Step Guide to Doing What's Right and Protecting Yourself* (Lyons Press, 2017) 59.

[25] J Austin, 'To Reward or Not to Reward: A Cross-Jurisdictional Comparison of the Reasons Why Securities Regulators Have Adopted or Rejected Policies to Pay Whistleblowers' in S Lombard, V Brand and J Austin (eds), *Corporate Whistleblowing Regulation* (Springer, 2020) 68.

[26] T Faunce, K Crow and T Nikolic et al., 'Because They Have Evidence: Globalizing Financial Incentives for Corporate Fraud Whistleblowers' in AJ Brown, D Lewis and R Moberly et al. (eds), *International Handbook of Whistleblowing Research* (Edward Elgar, 2014) 382.

[27] Patent Act of 1842, ch 263 5, 5 Stat. 543, 544 (1842).

the FCA in 1986.[28] The Congress adopted different reward provisions during the late 1980s and early 1990s regarding certain kinds of governmental wrongdoing, in which rewards were discretionary and the amounts were small in many cases.[29] The revised FCA is characterised by the significant awards that are now available to whistleblowers. Consequently, after the revision of the FCA, its use increased significantly due to several positive changes, including the amount of the rewards, legal certainty, and the extension of the statute of limitations.[30]

After the FCA revision, claims rose, with successful ones potentially earning up to 30 per cent of recovery plus fines. Since these funds support defence and healthcare industries using billions of taxpayers' dollars, whistleblowers may often receive over a million dollars.[31] The government benefits from whistleblowers and taxpayers, as recovered funds help citizens. Employees in FCA-covered industries are more likely to claim financial rewards than those in other sectors.[32]

Despite the success of the FCA, it is limited to reporting misconduct that is detrimental to the US government, and it does not apply to revelations where misconduct is harmful to other parties.[33] A final issue with FCA rewards concerns their propriety and ethics, as financial incentives may lead to meritless claims. However, this is less problematic since a whistleblower cannot get a reward if the information is not new or does not lead to a recovery for the government.[34] If information is insufficient and unlikely to lead to recovery, the whistleblower may struggle to find a lawyer. The motive driven by financial reward is not a primary ethical concern. The government recoveries and correction of wrongdoing seem to outweigh the moral issues.[35]

B. Combatting Tax Wrongdoings: The Internal Revenue Service Whistleblowing Programme

The FCA was the founding stone of whistleblowing legislation in the US and was key in creating rewards for whistleblowers. Before discussing US banking and financial whistleblowing laws, some details on the IRS tax whistleblowing programme are needed. While not directly related to banking and finance, tax whistleblowing connects to financial institutions through scandals such as

[28] 1 U.S.C. §§ 3729–3733 (1988).

[29] Dworkin and Brown (n 8) 666.

[30] F Strasser, 'When the Big Whistle Blows' [1989] *National Law Journal* 43.

[31] P Loftus, 'Johnson & Johnson Ordered to Pay $327 Million', *Wall Street Journal*, 4 June 2011, online. wsj.com/article/S B10001424052702303745304576364621661093868.html accessed 15 May 2025. See also A Pasztor, 'Northrop Agrees to Pay $325 Million to Settle Suit', *Wall Street Journal*, 3 April 2009, at B1.

[32] A Dyck, et al., 'Who Blows the Whistle on Corporate Fraud?' (2010) 65 *Journal of Finance* 2213, 2215.

[33] N Stolowy, L Paugam and A Londero, 'The Whistleblower: An Important Person in Corporate Life? An Answer from Comparative Law' (2019) 3 *Journal of Business Law* 167, 178.

[34] 31 U.S.C. § 3730(e)(4)(A) (2012).

[35] Dworkin and Brown (n 8) 668.

Luxleaks and Swissleaks, which involve banks or their clients' tax regimes. These scandals also highlight banks' behaviour toward tax authorities, including leaks related to UBS in Switzerland and its misconduct in the US.[36] Bradley Birkenfeld, a UBS banker, was the person who provided information to the US authorities. Among the information he shared were tax-related wrongdoings, which led the US Senate to publish a report on tax havens and offshore banks.[37]

The facts above lead us to consider that tax whistleblowing is related to banks and financial institutions. In the US, the IRS is the government agency responsible for receiving and investigating tax whistleblowers' reports. The IRC's whistleblowing programme dates back to 1867.[38] The Secretary of the Treasury had the discretion to decide whether to give a reward if necessary for detecting a violation of revenue laws.[39] Earliest versions of the statute authorised the IRS to grant a reward if the information led to criminal tax violations.[40] That was the situation until 1996, when Congress added a clause which authorised an award to be given for information leading to civil violations, especially underpayments of tax obligations.[41] Different changes were adopted in the following years. In 1997, the award ceiling was raised from $100,000 to $2 million, and in 2004, the ceiling was increased to $10 million. Below these sums, the IRS had discretion to award an amount ranging from 1 to 15 per cent of the amount recovered.[42] The award could exceed 15 per cent only if a special agreement were made between the IRS and the whistleblower.

Despite the changes, the IRS whistleblower programme was not utilised. This is mainly due to the IRS's unchangeable discretion over the reward and the reward ceilings. In 2006, a new amendment provided new direction for tax whistleblowing.[43] Under the 2006 amendment, the whistleblower can challenge the IRS's reward in a tax court. It also authorised the IRS to create a Whistleblower Office to handle concerns and determine rewards, shifting this discretion from the Service District

[36] More about the scandal: RC Birkenfeld, *Lucifer's Banker: The Untold Story of how I Destroyed Swiss Bank Secrecy* (Greenleaf Book Group Press, 2016).

[37] US Senate Permanent Subcommittee on Investigations, Tax Haven Banks and US Tax Compliance (17 July 2008). It should be noted that Bradley Birkenfeld, who provided the information, was imprisoned before receiving his financial reward from the IRS.

[38] MM Kwon, 'Whistling Dixie About the IRS Whistleblower Program Thanks to the IRC Confidentiality Restriction' (2010) 29 *Virginia Tax Review* 447, 451.

[39] 26 U.S.C. § 7623(a); Treas. Reg. § 301.7623-l(a), (c) (as amended 1998). The US Court had constant case law on the fact that the IRS had broad discretion to decide whether to pay a reward or not and to determine the monetary amount of the reward.

[40] CP Rettig, 'The IRS Whistleblower Program: Making Money the Old Fashioned Way!' [2012] *Journal of Tax Practice & Procedure* 21.

[41] SW Matt Hu, 'Fine-Tuning the Tax Whistleblower Statute: Why Qui-tam is not a solution' (2014) 99 *Minnesota Law Review* 783, 787.

[42] Judicial review of the tax whistleblower claim was nonexistent. There was one way to challenge an IRS decision (raise a breach of an implied-in-fact contract claim) but it was not that effective. In addition, the absolute discretion of the IRS's District Director was a major obstacle as they had to decide if a reward should be given or not.

[43] D Ventry, Jr., 'Whistleblowers and Qui Tam for Tax' (2008) 61 *TAXLAW* 357, 361.

Directors.[44] Furthermore, the 2006 amendment created an additional provision where it is authorised for a tax whistleblower to receive a 15 to 30 per cent reward if the whistleblower alleges tax delinquencies of two million dollars or more.[45] Congress removed the $10 million award limit to attract high-dollar tax-abuse cases and reward whistleblowers accordingly.[46] Congress redesigned the tax whistleblowing programme to ensure maximum revenues with minimal programme expenses.

In 2018, Congress added section 7623(c) to the IRC, clarifying that 'proceeds' include taxes, penalties, interest, civil forfeitures, criminal fines, and non-tax penalties from reporting violations requirements.[47] The 'proceeds' are necessary for calculating rewards, and the new provision extends the term, potentially increasing the size of rewards. The 2006 and 2018 provisions have significantly improved the IRS whistleblowing programme by offering a clear entitlement to substantial compensation. However, in practice, the programme remains complex.

A primary issue arising is the time required for report processing. Following the implementation of the new provisions, more reports have been received, and the IRS is struggling to process them.[48] The IRS often takes a long time to process tips, with no clear deadline, risking programme survival if whistleblowers are discouraged from reporting. Also, the statute does not mandate awards. It states that

> if the Secretary proceeds with any administrative or judicial action … based on information brought to the Secretary's attention by an individual, such individual shall… receive as an award at least 15 per cent but not more than 30 per cent of the proceeds collected as a result of the action.[49]

The award lies within the discretion of the Whistleblower Office, and the sole criterion is the amount of the reward, as the Whistleblower Office should examine how substantially the whistleblower contributed to the action.[50] As a result, the whistleblower would give their tip to the IRS, but they are not certain of the reward, if any. If the IRS decides not to reward the whistleblower, they will leave empty-handed.[51]

Other reasons also lead to the complexity of the IRS whistleblower programme.[52] Despite criticism, the programme has led to significant cases, such as whistleblowers uncovering tax fraud and being rewarded. It shows that US law is shifting from anti-retaliation to rewarding tips with financial rewards. Employees of banks can use it to report tax wrongdoings, as demonstrated by UBS's Bradley C Birkenfeld,

[44] Matt Hu (n 41) 788.
[45] I.R.C. § 7623(b)(1).
[46] SJ Webber and K Davis-Nozemack, 'Lost Opportunities: The Underuse of Tax Whistleblowers' (2015) Accounting Faculty Publications, Paper 53, 11.
[47] J Nanavati, 'The IRS Whistleblower Regulations' [2018] *CPA Journal* 67.
[48] Webber and Davis-Nozemack (n 46) 13.
[49] IRC s 7623(b)(1).
[50] Nanavati (n 47) 67.
[51] Matt Hu (n 41) 791.
[52] Nanavati (n 47) 67.

who showed that banks can be involved in tax crimes and that the IRS can intervene. In the same vein, the EU Directive addresses tax whistleblowing and allows reporting of corporate tax wrongdoing.[53] It is possible that inspiration was partially drawn from the IRS whistleblowing programme, but this is not certain.

C. Responding to Corporate Failures: The Protection of Whistleblowers under the Sarbanes-Oxley Act

Capitalism and a 'laissez-faire' approach have limited the government's role in regulating corporations and financial markets.[54] As Ronald Reagan said in his first inaugural speech: 'Government is not the solution to a problem. Government is the problem.'[55] The government's role was to avoid intervention; the market could self-regulate and solve problems. The belief in the free market's transformative power has been a core American political idea since the country's founding. Following the collapse of the Soviet Union, reliance on the private sector increased. Business and government often had a contradictory relationship, sometimes as adversaries, sometimes as allies. Despite successes, the 2002 financial crisis exposed this approach's flaws, driven by corporate greed.[56]

Regulatory failures in the US contributed to significant economic losses. Certain whistleblower laws were enacted not only in response to the 2002 crisis but also to restore the public's confidence in the private sector.[57] Such a law is the SOX.[58] SOX was the answer of the US government to a series of corporate scandals and mismanagement that occurred in 2001.[59] Some of these corporate scandals are Enron, WorldCom, Global Crossing and Tyco.[60] These companies gained fame for accounting fraud and business abuses. When their wrongdoings became public, successful companies often went bankrupt quickly. These scandals cost employees and shareholders billions, leading the public to lose confidence in big companies, securities markets, and corporate governance in general.[61]

The abuses by these companies went beyond accounting fraud. Enron manipulated California's energy market, stole millions from ratepayers, and caused a crisis.

[53] Directive (EU) 2019/1937 of the European Parliament and of the Council of 23 October 2019 on the protection of persons who report breaches of Union law, [2019] OJ L395/17, Art 1(a)(x)(c).

[54] D Windsor, 'Capitalism' in LM Salinger (ed), *Encyclopaedia of White-Collar and Corporate Crime*, 2nd edn (Sage, 2013) 141.

[55] Stanger (n 23) 162.

[56] D Windsor, 'Enron Corp' in LM Salinger (ed), *Encyclopaedia of White-Collar and Corporate Crime*, 2nd edn (Sage, 2013) 303.

[57] Vaughn (n 7) 150.

[58] 18 U.S.C. § 1514A.

[59] K Rubinstein, 'Internal Whistleblowing and Sarbanes-Oxley Section 806: Balancing the Interests of Employee and Employer' (2007) 52 *New York Law School Law Review* 637, 638.

[60] RG. Vaughn, 'America's First Comprehensive Statute Protecting Corporate Whistleblowers' (2005) 57 *Administrative Law Review* 1, 2.

[61] Vaughn (n 7) 150.

Enron officials also bribed foreign officials from India and Guatemala.[62] Other companies faced human rights violations and environmental disasters. Employees reported concerns but were ignored. Notable whistleblowers include Sherron Watkins of Enron and Cynthia Cooper of WorldCom, both named 'Persons of the Year' in 2002 by *Time magazine*.[63]

Those events led President George W Bush to enact SOX, a response to public outcry and corporate scandals. Congress designed it to regulate corporate conduct better and reform the corporate sector.[64] Whistleblowing provisions in SOX are not tailored legislation but aim to promote transparency. The Senate Report noted that these provisions seek to break corporate silence and encourage employees to report misconduct and malfeasance.[65] SOX whistleblowing provisions were the most comprehensive private sector whistleblower law in the US and served as a model for later Acts.

Two provisions of the SOX aim to protect whistleblowers against workplace retaliation. The first one is section 1107, which applies to whistleblowers who report on any federal offence.[66] This provision was described as having the *potential to become the most important of all the SOX provisions because it could develop into a general whistleblower statute*.[67] Nevertheless, section 1107 does not provide for a civil remedy but imposes criminal liability on the employer who retaliates against the whistleblower.[68] The other section is section 806, which provides a civil cause of action for employees who were retaliated against.[69] Section 806 entails two broad categories of protected whistleblower conduct. First, the whistleblower who provides information and assists in the investigation; and second, the whistleblower who files or participates in a proceeding regarding an alleged violation as listed.[70] The Act covers employees of publicly traded companies.[71]

Before analysing sections 806 and 1107 of SOX, we should note the importance of SOX's protections against retaliation, which provide concrete labour law protections in the country, especially regarding the employment-at-will doctrine. This doctrine allows employers to 'dismiss their employees at will, be they many or few, for good cause, for no cause or even for cause morally wrong, without being

[62] ibid.

[63] J Morse and A Bower, 'The Party Crasher' (2002-2003) *TIME Magazine*, 53.

[64] SM Boyne, 'Financial Incentives and Truth-Telling: The Growth of Whistle-blowing Legislation in the United States' in G Thüsing and G Forst (eds), *Whistleblowing – A Comparative Study* (Springer, 2016) 290.

[65] Senate Report (2002) n° 107-46 5, 10.

[66] 18 U.S.C. §1513(e).

[67] TM Dworkin, 'SOX and Whistleblowing' (2007) 105 *Michigan Law Review* 1757, 1764.

[68] S Lombard, 'Regulatory Policies and Practices to Optimize Corporate Whistleblowing: A Comparative Analysis' in S Lombard, V Brand and J Austin (eds), *Corporate Whistleblowing Regulation* (Springer, 2020) 13.

[69] 18 U.S.C. §1514A(a) (2012).

[70] C Henkel, 'Whistleblower Rights and Protection Under U.S. Law in the Private Sector' in M Disant and D Pollet-Panousis (eds), *Les lanceurs d'alerte* (LGDJ éd., 2017) 339.

[71] 18 U.S.C. § 1514A(b)(1) (2012). The Supreme Court later determined that SOX also protected employees of the contractors of publicly traded companies.

thereby guilty of legal wrong'.[72] The doctrine, used in the late nineteenth century to support industrial expansion during the Industrial Revolution, justified greater employer freedom in hiring and firing to prevent business failure. The fact that SOX mandated the immediate reinstatement of employees demoted or terminated and added protections marked a victory for US employee rights.

Employees under SOX can report violations of federal criminal laws on mail, wire, or bank fraud, SEC rules, and federal provisions related to shareholder fraud.[73] Different remedies differ depending on the situation. Section 1107 targets whistleblowers reporting federal offences, imposing criminal liability on employers for retaliation, but offers no civil remedies. Conversely, section 806 allows civil remedies but only for securities violations or shareholder fraud. Once a whistleblower detects wrongdoing, they should classify it to identify available remedies, which can be challenging and may lead them to seek legal advice or report without legal protection. This could be avoided if a comprehensive corporate whistleblowing legal framework replaced sectoral legislation.

Under SOX, the whistleblower does not have to provide affirmative proof that an actual violation has occurred.[74] The whistleblower only needs to reasonably believe that the employer was involved in misconduct that violated securities laws.[75] The reasonable belief requirement allows any employee to blow the whistle, even without specific knowledge of federal securities laws. SOX does not define what constitutes a reasonable belief. There are two main theories: subjective, where the employee genuinely believes the conduct is illegal, and objective, where a reasonable person in their position would believe it is unlawful.[76]

As SOX does not define the concept of reasonable belief, US courts have analysed it. Regarding the subjective reasonable belief, the US courts have long held that subjective reasonableness requires only an actual or strong belief that an investigation is needed.[77] The objective reasonableness standard is hotly debated, with courts applying it since 2011 based on a reasonable person test. Objectiveness is judged by what a reasonable person with the same knowledge and training would know under the same circumstances as the whistleblower.[78] The whistleblower does not need to prove economic loss, materiality, reliance, or scienter to qualify for SOX protection. They only need to believe in good faith that their employer violated a listed provision of SOX.[79]

Under SOX, the disclosure must be made to a federal regulatory or law enforcement agency, a member of Congress, or a person with supervisory

[72] *Payne v W. & At. R.R. Co.*, 81 Tenn. 507, 519-20 (1884), *overruled on other grounds by* Hutton v. Watters, 132 Tenn. 527 (1915).

[73] 18 U.S.C. §1514A (2002).

[74] Henkel (n 70) 339.

[75] 18 U.S.C. § 1514A(a)(1).

[76] *Welch v Chao*, 536 F.3d 269, 277 (4th Cir. 2008).

[77] *Van Asdale v International Game Technology*, 577 F.3d 989 (9th Cir. 2009) and *Gale v US Dep't of Labor*, n° 08-14232 (11th Cir. June 25, 2010).

[78] *Sylvester v Parexel International LLC*, ARB Case n° 07-123, 13-14 (Dep't of Labor, May 25, 2011).

[79] *Wiest v Lynch*, 710 F.3d 121, 132 (3rd Cir. 2013).

authority over the employee to be granted protection.[80] Any disclosure to the media does not provide access to protection under SOX.[81] Reporting to Congress members or committees may lead to media disclosure, potentially harming the company if allegations are false. Initially, internal reporting was not favoured, but now SOX encourages it. Public company boards must set internal mechanisms for confidential, anonymous reports on questionable accounting or auditing issues.[82] This requirement does not extend to the reporting of other questionable matters.

What SOX utilised in relation to reporting was characterised by Professor Richard Moberly as a 'structural model'.[83] The fact that SOX required internal reporting to be addressed to the Board of Directors served a specific purpose: to bypass the blocking and filtering of reports that often occur at lower levels.[84] Similarly, the federal organisational sentencing guidelines promoted structural disclosure channels, and, as a motive, they drastically reduced possible criminal penalties for corporations that can prove they had adopted an effective programme to prevent and detect violations of law.[85] The guidelines were demanding of companies to exercise due diligence, requiring 'having in place and publicising a reporting system whereby employees and other agents could report criminal conduct by others within the organisation without fear of retribution'.[86] Even though the version mentioned above was repealed in 2016, the new version contains similar language: 'The organisation shall take reasonable steps … to have and publicise a system, which may include mechanisms that allow for anonymity or confidentiality, whereby the organisation's employees and agents may report or seek guidance regarding potential or actual criminal conduct without fear of retaliation.'[87]

Retaliation is conceived broadly.[88] The employer cannot discriminate against an employee who engaged in any protected activity, as mentioned in SOX.[89] More precisely, the employer may not commit the following: 'discharge, demote, suspend, threaten, harass, or in any other manner discriminate against in the terms and conditions of employment'.[90] Apart from the aforementioned types of retaliatory behaviour, other examples need to be mentioned, such as negative performance

[80] Sarbanes-Oxley Act, s 806(a)(1).
[81] 18 U.S.C. § 1514A.
[82] Sarbanes-Oxley Act, s 301.
[83] R Moberly, 'Sarbanes-Oxley's Structural Model to Encourage Corporate Whistleblowers' [2006] *BYU Law Review* 1107, 1127.
[84] R Moberly, 'Confidentiality and Whistleblowing' (2018) 96 *North Carolina Law Review* 751, 759.
[85] ibid. See also US Sentencing Guidelines Manual § 8A1.2 cmt. 3(k) (US Sentencing Comm'N 2003).
[86] ibid § 8A1.2 cmt. 3(k)(5).
[87] U.S. Sentencing Guidelines Manual § 8B2.1(b)(5)(C) (U.S. Sentencing Comm'N 2016).
[88] *Allen v Administrative Review Board*, 514 F.3d 468 (5th Cir. 2008).
[89] *Burlington Northern & Santa Fe Railway v White*, 548 U.S. 53, 98 FEP cases 385 (2006) where the type of actions that may constitute retaliation is extended under title VII of the Civil Rights Act of 1964.
[90] 18 U.S.C. § 1514A(a).

reviews,[91] hostile work environments,[92] the breach of an employee's right to confidentiality,[93] or constructive discharge claims.[94]

The civil liability, under section 806 of SOX, not only concerns the employer but also all officers, employees, contractors, subcontractors, or agents of a covered company. Those above may be named as respondents in a lawsuit and may be held liable with or without the employer.[95] In a SOX retaliation case, the whistleblower should prove that they engaged in a protected disclosure and were retaliated against.[96] If the whistleblower succeeds in proving the aforementioned, the respondent may avoid liability if they can provide sufficient proof that shows they had legitimate reasons for any adverse personnel actions.[97]

The Occupational Safety and Health Administration (OSHA) is responsible, under section 806, for handling complaints of retaliatory discharge. The retaliated employee has to file a complaint with the Secretary of Labour within 90 days of the alleged retaliation.[98] The secretary can investigate the complaint if the complainant 'has made a *prima facie* showing that the alleged protected activity was a contributing factor' in the retaliation the complainant suffered.[99] To establish a prima facie showing of retaliation, the employee should prove the following: they engaged in a protected activity, the employer knew about that activity, the employee suffered unfavourable personnel action, and the protected activity was a contributing factor in the unfavourable action.[100] The employer (as a defendant) has the chance to show, by 'clear and convincing evidence, that it would have taken the same unfavourable personnel action in the absence of the protected activity'.[101] Suppose the defendant fails to do so and the secretary has reasonable cause to believe that discriminatory behaviour has occurred. In that case, the secretary should issue a preliminary order to provide appropriate relief.[102]

After the preliminary order, both parties have 30 days to raise objections and request a hearing before an administrative law court; otherwise, it becomes final. If a hearing occurs, the secretary has 120 days to deny the complaint or give appropriate relief.[103] Once the final order is issued, every interested party has the right

[91] *Halloum v Intel Corp*, 2003-SOX-7 (ALJ Mar 4, 2004).

[92] *Avlon v American Express Co.*, 2008-SOX-51 (ALJ Sept 8, 2008).

[93] *Menendez v Halliburton Inc.*, ARB case nos 09-002, 09-003 (Dep't of Labor Sept 13, 2011).

[94] *Brown v Lockheed Martin Corp.*, ARB case n° 10-050, 9 (Dep't of Labor Feb 28, 2011).

[95] *Leznik v Nektar Therapeutics*, 2006-SOX-93 (ALJ Nov 16, 2007). See also JF Schulman, N Modesitt and DP Westman, *Whistleblowing: The Law of Retaliatory Discharge*, 3rd edn (Bloomburg BNA, 2016) 4–15.

[96] 18 U.S.C. §1514A(b)(2)(C).

[97] *Welch v Cardinal Bankshares Corp.*, 2003-SOX-15, 36 (ALJ Jan 28, 2004).

[98] 29 C.F.R. § 1980.103. When the employee becomes aware or should be reasonably aware of the employer's decision, the limitation period begins.

[99] 29 C.F.R. pt. 1980.

[100] 29 C.F.R. § 1980.104(b)(1).

[101] 29 C.F.R. §1980.104(c) (2006).

[102] 29 C.F.R. §1980.107(b). If the employer demonstrates that the employee is a security risk, OSHA may decide not to order reinstatement.

[103] 29 C.F.R. § 1980.110(c).

to lodge an appeal before the US Court of Appeals for the circuit in which they resided on the date of the violation or where the violation has taken place.[104] Then, the secretary has 180 days to issue a final decision. If there is no final decision from the secretary, the complainant has the right to request a *de novo* hearing in a Federal District Court.[105] Despite the fact that the aforementioned procedure was often described as a 'unique procedural innovation' for the combination of 'the efficiency of an administrative investigation with the safeguards of a federal court trial',[106] the whole process has received criticism for different reasons.

According to Moberly, during the first three years after the Act's enactment, only 3.6 per cent of SOX whistleblowers received relief through the Act's procedures, and only 6.5 per cent prevailed on appeal.[107] First, the 90 days were criticised as being too short, given the fact that 'most potential claimants don't realise what their rights are and how to pursue them in such a short period'. Additionally, the administrative law judges, who participated in the majority of the cases, interpreted the SOX requirements in a rather strict manner.[108] As a result of this narrow interpretation, numerous claims failed as a matter of law. Many of these claims failed because the claimant was unable to adequately demonstrate that the employer took action against them due to whistleblowing activity. The success of the causation element depends on the employee's ability to prove that the employer was aware of the whistleblowing activity and that, as a result, they were retaliated against.[109]

Another obstacle to the effective enforcement of SOX lies in the fact that it delegates enforcement to the Department of Labour and, more specifically, to OSHA.[110] OSHA, when SOX was enacted, handled 14 whistleblower laws but faced criticism for lacking expertise and a specialised bar for SOX claims, mainly due to the lack of a punitive damages remedy. Its administrative litigation was also criticised for judges who were rigid and refused relief from strict filing requirements and deadlines.[111] Finally, both administrative and federal law judges have dismissed claims, which appear to fall within the ambit of SOX's whistleblowing provisions but are not explicitly stated in SOX.

The imposition of criminal penalties under section 1107 of SOX was a significant improvement for whistleblower protection. Section 1107 reads: '[w]hoever knowingly, with the intent to retaliate, takes any action harmful to any person, including interference with lawful employment or livelihood of any person, for providing to a law enforcement officer any truthful information relating to the

[104] 29 C.F.R. § 1980.112(a).
[105] 29 C.F.R. § 1980.114(a).
[106] Moberly (n 14) 9.
[107] R Moberly, 'Unfulfilled Expectations: An Empirical Analysis of Why Sarbanes-Oxley Whistleblowers Rarely Win' (2007) 49 *William & Mary Law Review* 65, 67.
[108] Boyne (n 64) 293.
[109] Moberly (n 107) 100.
[110] Boyne (n 64) 293.
[111] ibid.

commission or possible commission of any federal offense' may be indicted.[112] The penalty ranges from a fine to up to ten years' imprisonment. Section 1107 applies to anyone engaging in prohibited behaviour in relation to any federal offence, unlike section 806 of SOX, which restricts whistleblowing to corporate fraud or accounting abuses. Enforcement of section 1107 is handled by the Department of Justice, not the Department of Labour, and it has extraterritorial jurisdiction, unlike section 806.

To sum up, the passage of SOX was an important piece of legislation for whistleblowers with concrete labour and criminal law protections. Nonetheless, SOX failed to adequately and effectively protect corporate whistleblowers. As Moberly noticed, in a phrase that summarises the problem of SOX: 'we ought to spend as much effort determining who is involved in whistleblower protection as deciding what those protections should formally entail'.[113] Regulatory failures and the problematic nature of SOX contributed to the financial crisis of 2008, from which new legislation was enacted as a response. The most significant was Dodd-Frank.

D. Enhancing Capital Markets Transparency and the Protection of Whistleblowers under the Dodd-Frank Act

The financial crisis of 2008, due in part to regulatory failures, nearly destroyed the US financial system, and it was compared to the Great Depression of 1929. Trillions of dollars of public money were disbursed, and that crisis became the worst recession since 1929.[114] However, a different development set the stage for this crisis: credit default swaps, an unregulated insurance that expanded from 2000 to 2008, undervaluing mortgage risk. Rating agencies failed to assess this risk, creating an environment in which lenders secured loans with minimal verification. This situation lowered house prices, causing more defaults. Major banks like Lehman Brothers invested in debt that lost value as defaults rose, found liabilities exceeding assets, and collapsed. This led to economic collapse in the US and a global recession.

Warnings coming from some regulators were not loud enough, and nobody hit the alarm button. Sophisticated financial professionals failed to consider the problematic aspects of these risks, along with the US government's 'too big to fail' policy, which contributed to this financial crisis and affected households worldwide. The crisis shed light on another failure of the financial system: the

[112] 18 U.S.C. § 1513(e).
[113] Moberly (n 14) 54.
[114] OJ Blanchard, 'The Crisis: Basic Mechanisms, and Appropriate Policies' (2008) MIT Department of Economics, Working Paper n° 09-01, papers.ssrn.com/sol3/papers.cfm?abstract_id=1324280 accessed 15 May 2025, where it is stated that $250 billion in subprime losses in the United States led to $4.7 trillion of losses in GDP and $26.4 trillion in losses in stock market values.

collapse of the largest Ponzi scheme in US history.[115] Harry Markopoulos tried for the first time in 2000 to expose the Ponzi scheme at stake.[116] Markopoulos investigated the securities firm held by Bernie Madoff to understand its success.[117] Markopoulos was not Madoff's employee, but was hired by Rampakt Investment Management to investigate Madoff's successful securities firm.[118] He first reported in 2000 but received no response from the SEC. Despite reporting again in 2001, 2005, 2007, and 2008, no action was taken. Madoff's fraud was uncovered only when he confessed to his sons, who reported him to the police, ending his scheme in 2008.[119] Markopoulos would later condemn the SEC before Congress for its failure to act earlier and prevent the expansion of the fraudulent scheme.[120]

These scandals and failures led to the adoption of the Dodd-Frank Act on 21 July 2010.[121] The purpose of the Act was to 'promote the financial stability of the United States by improving accountability and transparency in the financial system … [and] to protect consumers from abusive financial services practice'.[122] One significant legal innovation of the Act was the encouragement of corporate insiders to report on fraud in the securities industry by providing protection and financial rewards.[123] To this end, section 922 of the Act established the Securities and Exchange Commission's Whistleblower Program by the addition of section 21F to the Securities Exchange Act.

The whistleblower can report anonymously to the SEC. The Chairman of the SEC, in 2016, described the SEC's whistleblower programme as having had a

[115] F Shu-Acquaye, 'Dodd-Frank Wall Street Reform and Consumer Protection Act: The Evolution of Whistleblower Protections, Employment Contracts and Mandatory Arbitration Agreements' (2017) 15 *DePaul Business and Commercial Law Journal* 127, 130–131.

[116] Markopoulos was a securities fund manager working for a separate securities firm than Madoff's. See C Reinicke, 'Who is Harry Markopoulos? The Famed Madoff Whistleblower Could Make Millions After Publishing a Report Accusing GE of Fraud' (2019) *Business Insider*, markets.businessinsider.com/news/stocks/harry-markopolos-madoff-whistleblower-accounting-expert-who-is-he-2019-8-1028453215 accessed 15 May 2025.

[117] Madoff was the founder of a US securities firm with high profits. He orchestrated a fraudulent securities scheme and, at the end, billions of dollars were lost from investors. See Bernie Madoff Biography, hwww.biography.com/crime-figure/bernard-madoff accessed 15 May 2025.

[118] Markopoulos cannot be considered as a whistleblower under the common definition of whistleblower, who should have a 'working' relation with the reported person or company. He can be considered a whistleblower in a broader sense, as he alerted the authorities to a large fraud.

[119] MC Nunziato, 'Aiding and Abetting, a Madoff Family Affair: Why Secondary Actors Should be Held Accountable for Securities Fraud Through the Restoration of the Private Right of Action for Aiding and Abetting Liability Under the Federal Securities Laws' (2010) 73 *Albany Law Review* 603, 608.

[120] ME King, 'Blowing the Whistle on the Dodd-Frank Amendments: The Case Against the New Amendments to Whistleblower Protection in Section 806 of Sarbanes-Oxley' (2011) 48 *American Criminal Law Review* 1457, 1462–63.

[121] M Neal, 'Securities Whistleblowing under Dodd-Frank: Neglecting the Power of "Enterprising Privateers" in Favor of the "Slow-Going Public Vessel"' (2012) 15 *Lewis & Clark Law Review* 1107, 1117–18.

[122] Dodd-Frank Wall Street Reform and Consumer Protection Act, Pub. L. No. 111-203, 124 Stat. 1376 (2010) (codified as amended in scattered sections of 5, 7, 12, 15, 26, 28, 31, 42 U.S.C. (2012)).

[123] M Reeder, 'Proceeding Legally: Clarifying the SEC/Dodd-Frank Whistleblower Incentives' (2017) 7 *Harvard Business Law Review* 269, 271.

'transformative impact on enforcement' and said that whistleblowers have 'become key sources of very significant cases'.[124] In fiscal year 2023, the SEC received over 18,000 whistleblower tips, almost 50 per cent more than the previous record in 2022.[125] During 2023, the SEC awarded $600 million in whistleblower awards to 68 individuals. The numbers reveal the programme's success.

The SEC had a financial award programme in place since 1988, but it focused solely on insider trading-related information.[126] This award programme was enacted following the 1987 stock market crash, when the US Congress voted on various amendments to the Securities Exchange Act, aimed at preventing and sanctioning insider dealing.[127] The programme was not known, and this resulted in the fact that only five awards were made during its 20-year existence. Another problematic aspect of that programme was that the award could not exceed ten per cent of the amount recovered, and it was within the SEC's discretion to determine the amount.[128] The passage of SOX did not include awards and was less effective. In 2009, new incentives for whistleblowers were proposed after the SEC's failure to act on tips about Madoff and the financial crisis. The Dodd-Frank Act granted the SEC new powers, including the authority to award incentives to whistleblowers.

Following the passage of Dodd-Frank, the SEC presented its proposal for the rules related to the whistleblower's award system. The SEC gave the public one month to comment on its proposed rules. In the cost-benefit analysis accompanying the proposal, the following was stated: 'overall, enhanced whistleblower incentives should likely result in more frequent reporting of misconduct, which will result in greater deterrence of securities law violations and more effective and efficient enforcement on the part of the Commission'.[129] When the public consultation was concluded,[130] the SEC adopted its final rules on 25 May 2011, and they came into force on 12 August 2011.[131] Three Democratic SEC Commissioners voted in favour of the rules, while two Republican Commissioners voted against.

[124] MJ White, 'SEC Chair White Offers A New Model for Enforcement' (2016) www.sec.gov/news/speech/chair-white-speech-new-york-university-111816.html accessed 15 May 2025.

[125] US Securities and Exchange Commission, 2023 Annual Report to Congress – Whistleblower Program – (2023) www.sec.gov/files/fy23-annual-report.pdf accessed 15 September 2025.

[126] J Austin, 'To Reward or Not to Reward: A Cross-Jurisdictional Comparison of the Reasons Why Securities Regulators Have Adopted or Rejected Policies to Pay Whistleblowers' in S Lombard, V Brand and J Austin (eds), *Corporate Whistleblowing Regulation* (Springer, 2020) 69.

[127] Section 21A(e) of the Securities Exchange Act 1934 (Pub. L. 73–291, 48 Stat. 881, enacted June 6, 1934, codified at 15 U.S.C. § 78a et seq.) which was added by the Insider Trading and Securities Fraud Enforcement Act of 1988 (ITSEA), Pub. L. No. 100-704.

[128] Assessment of the SEC's Bounty Program, Report No. 474 (2010) 1 www.sec.gov/files/474.pdf accessed 15 May 2025.

[129] ibid.

[130] SEC received almost 500 comment letters in response to the proposed rules. Most commentators from the business industry raised concerns about internal reporting if the rules were to be voted on.

[131] Securities and Exchange Commission 'Whistleblowers Incentive and Protections Final Rules' (2011) 229 [Release No. 34-64545; File No. S7-33-10] www.sec.gov/rules/final/2011/34-64545.pdf accessed 15 May 2025.

They raised concerns over the negative impact that the new rules would have on internal compliance systems.[132]

The SEC's whistleblower programme was modelled after the IRS programme.[133] Under Dodd-Frank, the SEC has the power to award rewards to individuals who provide original information that leads to effective enforcement, and the monetary sanction imposed exceeds $1 million.[134] The whistleblower's reward should be at least 10 per cent, and up to 30 per cent.[135] The SEC has the discretion to decide the exact amount of the reward, taking into account the importance of the information and how this information resulted in the successful enforcement action, the degree of assistance the whistleblower provided, and the SEC's interest in deterring those violations.[136] A separate fund was established in order to administer the payments of the rewards.[137] The fund's name is 'Investor Protection Fund'.[138]

The question of whether the whistleblower could be protected under the anti-retaliation provision of Dodd-Frank if they did not report a securities law violation to the SEC, but internally arose in 2013, when two Courts of Appeal reached different conclusions. The Court of Appeals for the Fifth Circuit had ruled that employees must report to the SEC to be eligible for anti-retaliation protection under Dodd-Frank.[139] On the contrary, the Court of Appeals for the Second Circuit had a different approach. It granted protection to internal whistleblowers.[140] The Second Circuit decided that the definition of the whistleblower under Dodd-Frank was ambiguous and accorded *Chevron* deference to a 2011 SEC rule, which provided an explanatory definition of the term by referring to whistleblowers who report internally.[141]

[132] KL Casey 'Statement by SEC Commissioner: Adoption of Rules for Implementing the Whistleblower Provisions of Section 21F of the Securities Exchange Act of 1934' (2011), www.sec.gov/news/speech/2011/spch052511klc-item2.htm accessed 15 May 2025. TA Paredes 'Statement at Open Meeting to Adopt Final Rules for Implementing the Whistle-blower Provisions of Section 21F of the Securities Exchange Act of 1934' (2011), www.sec.gov/news/speech/2011/spch052511tap-item2.htm accessed 15 May 2025.

[133] S. REP. NO. 111-176, at 111 (2010).

[134] 15 U.S.C. § 78u-6(a)(1).

[135] 15 U.S.C. § 78u-6(b).

[136] 15 U.S.C. § 78u-6(c)(1)(B).

[137] Y Givati, 'Of Snitches and Riches: Optimal IRS and SEC Whistleblower Rewards' (2018) 55 *Harvard Journal on Legislation* 106, 117.

[138] 15 U.S.C. § 78u-6(g).

[139] *Asadi v G.E. Energy (USA),* LLC 720 F.3d 620 (5th Cir. 2013).

[140] *Berman v Neo@Ogilvy* 801 F.3d 145 (2d Cir. 2015).

[141] *Chevron U.S.A. Inc. v Natural Res. Def. Council, Inc.*, 467 U.S. 837, 843 (1984) ('If the statute is silent or ambiguous with respect to the specific issue, the question for the court is whether the agency's answer is based on a permissible construction of the statute.'). Chevron set up a two-part test: If Congress has spoken directly on an issue, the 'court, as well as the agency, must give effect to the unambiguously expressed intent of Congress'. *Chevron*, 467 U.S., 842-43. By contrast, if a statute is silent or ambiguous in respect to an issue, the court's review is limited to whether or not the agency's interpretation is a permissible construction of the statute. See S Leifer, 'Protecting Whistleblower Protections in the Dodd-Frank Act' (2014) *Michigan Law Review* 113:121, 131–40.

This circuit split was resolved by the Supreme Court in *Digital Realty Trust v Somers*.[142] The Supreme Court rejected the SEC's authority to define the 'whistleblower' for the purposes of anti-retaliation provisions.[143] The Court stated: 'when a statute includes an explicit definition, we must follow that definition'.[144] The definition of a whistleblower should be read in conjunction with §78u-6(h) of the Dodd-Frank anti-retaliation provisions. The whistleblower should provide information relating to a violation of the securities laws *to the Commission*.[145] This ruling creates a harsh time for whistleblowers, who relied upon internal reporting schemes and did not prefer to report to the SEC. In addition, it creates a negative atmosphere for internal compliance programmes, as promoted by SOX, where whistleblowers are encouraged to report to the SEC for protection under Dodd-Frank.[146]

In 2011, before the *Digital Realty* ruling, the SEC had issued its Final Rules, which encouraged whistleblowers to profit from internal compliance reporting mechanisms by offering a higher reward if the whistleblower used internal reporting systems.[147] Apart from higher rewards, the SEC had in place other types of compensation for having reported internally. The ruling in *Digital Realty* undermined all these SEC efforts. The Supreme Court based its ruling on the legislative history of Dodd-Frank and found that the purpose of Dodd-Frank's whistleblower provisions is to provide information to the SEC.[148] It seems evident that, under the current circumstances, the whistleblower should report to the SEC, rather than internally, if they want to be protected under Dodd-Frank, which offers more favourable protections than SOX.[149] In addition, whilst the SEC tried to ensure that internal reporting mechanisms would be respected (by allowing higher rewards and other advantages if the whistleblower reported internally), the Supreme Court's ruling resulted in something feared by whistleblowers: employers will be 'rewarded' if they react quicker and before the wrongdoing reaches the SEC.[150]

[142] *Digital Realty Trust, Inc v Somers*, n° 16-1276, 583 U.S. (2018).

[143] MK Ramirez, 'Whistling Past the Graveyard: Dodd-Frank Whistleblower Programs Dodge Bullets Fighting Financial Crime' (2019) 50 *Loyola University Chicago Law Journal* 617, 634.

[144] In *Digital Realty Trust v Somers*, Justice Ginsburg noted in the introduction part of the decision that 'Dodd-Frank delineates a more circumscribed class; it defines whistleblower to means a person who provides information relating to a violation of the securities laws to the Commission.'

[145] 15 U.S.C. §78u-6(a)(6).

[146] SR Sipe, CT Metrejean and Pearson, 'The SEC, The Courts and Whistleblowers: An Examination Into The Strength of The Anti-Retaliation Provisions Of The Dodd-Frank Act As Defined By Recent Federal Court Decisions' (2014–15) 19 *Journal of Legal Studies in Business* 8 (concerns have been raised long before the US Supreme Court decision).

[147] 17 C.F.R. § 240.21F-6 (2018).

[148] *Dig. Realty Tr., Inc. v Somers*, 138 S. Ct. 767, 777 (2018). See also Senate Report No. 111-76, 110 (2010) www.congress.gov/congressional-report/111th-congress/senate-report/76 accessed 15 May 2025: Congress's purpose was 'to motivate with inside knowledge to come forward and assist the Government to identify and prosecute persons who have violated securities laws and recover money for victims of financial fraud'.

[149] RH Filler and JW Markham, 'Whistleblowers—A Case Study in The Regulatory Cycle for Financial Services' (2018) 12 *Brooklyn Journal of Corporate, Financial & Commercial Law* 337–39.

[150] The SEC provides rewards to compliance officers who act as whistleblowers (under certain criteria). See US Securities and Exchange Commission, 'SEC awards 450,000 dollars to whistle-blower' (2020) www.sec.gov/news/press-release/2020-75 accessed 15 May 2025.

The Dodd-Frank Act has provisions protecting whistleblowers. While it works alongside SOX, it differs significantly. Section 21F extends the period for filing retaliation claims under SOX from 180 days to six years.[151] The employee must file their claim within three years of becoming aware, or reasonably should have been aware, of the facts relevant to their right of action. Additionally, the claim cannot be filed more than ten years after the violation occurred. While SOX requires filing via an administrative agency, Dodd-Frank allows direct action in a federal district court. The Dodd-Frank Act broadly protects more whistleblowers than SOX, including employees of private subsidiaries of public companies, contractors, and agents working for public companies. It covers past, present, and future employers under Dodd-Frank.

The Dodd-Frank Act prohibits the enforcement of arbitration agreements between whistleblowers and employers. Even if such an agreement exists, the SEC is not bound by it. Any action against individuals cooperating with the SEC on securities law issues is a prohibited violation.[152] The SEC respects this provision by bringing actions against employers who, by including arbitration or confidentiality agreements, tried to prevent employees from blowing the whistle.[153] A certain criticism has been spurred against this policy, as arbitration is faster and cheaper than going to the courts.[154] Arbitration keeps confidentiality and limits blacklisting, protecting whistleblowers. Despite criticism, the SEC's efforts to prevent gag orders have influenced agencies like the CFTC, which have adopted similar measures.[155]

An important aspect of the Dodd-Frank Act is the anonymity for whistleblowers. The whistleblower can contact the SEC and remain anonymous, which can prevent any possible retaliation from their employer. To better administer whistleblower protections, the Dodd-Frank Act created the 'Office of the Whistleblower'.[156] Additionally, it created an 'Office of Market Intelligence' to develop systems for reports and complaints. These offices have helped the Dodd-Frank Act succeed by enhancing protections and rewards for whistleblowers. Republicans opposed establishing the Office of the Whistleblower during negotiations, citing SEC cost issues. However, the Office proved crucial for better implementation and coordination of whistleblowing under Dodd-Frank, which offers more incentives and protections than other laws, making it a successful statute for whistleblower protection.

[151] 15 U.S.C. § 78u-6(h)(1)(B)(iii) (2010).

[152] 17 C.F.R. § 240.21F-17(a) (2018).

[153] Order Instituting Cease-and-Desist Proceedings, In re BlackRock, Inc., Exchange Act Release No. 79,804, 115 SEC Docket 5758 and Order Instituting Cease-and-Desist Proceedings, In re NeuStar, Inc., Exchange Act Release No. 79,593, 115 SEC Docket 4704.

[154] Sipe, Metrejean and Pearson (n 146) 6.

[155] 17 C.F.R. § 165.19 (2018); 17 C.F.R. app. § 165.20 (2018).

[156] GC Rapp, 'Four Signal Moments in Whistleblower Law: 1983–2013' (2013) *Hofstra Labour & Employment Law Journal* 30(2), 389, 400.

E. Whistleblowers in the Fight against Money Laundering

In the fight against money laundering and sanctions evasion, the US updated its anti-money laundering and sanctions whistleblower law. The new mechanisms were part of the Anti-Money Laundering Act of 2020 (AMLA) and the National Defence Authorisation Act (NDAA).[157] The Department of the Treasury administers the newly created whistleblower programme and provides for monetary awards to whistleblowers who report violations of the Bank Secrecy Act (BSA).

The 2022 amendments allow whistleblowers worldwide to report violations of US anti-money laundering and sanctions rules and receive rewards if successful. Reports can come from anyone with relevant information, not just US employees, as long as US regulators have jurisdiction. This encourages all with independent knowledge or evaluation of public information to come forward, even if the government is not aware of these details.

[157] FinCEN, 'The Anti-Money Laundering Act of 2020' (FinCEN.gov) www.fincen.gov/anti-money-laundering-act-2020 accessed 15 May 2025.

3

Sectoral Provisions on the Protection of Whistleblowers in the EU Banking and Financial Sector

I. The Adoption of Whistleblowing Provisions in the EU Banking and Financial Area

In the aftermath of the 2008 financial crisis, the EU has expanded the powers of several EU supervisors and regulators in the banking and financial services sector.[1] Several changes occurred, including the completion of the Banking Union and the creation of the Single Supervisory Mechanism (SSM), a key pillar providing EU banking supervisors with significant powers. These supervisors need information from ongoing supervision, other authorities, or internal personnel to identify possible wrongdoings. One specific mechanism through which supervisors can acquire information is whistleblowing.[2]

In addition, the financial crisis has sparked a discussion on how to prevent them. Several stories of whistleblowers who reported breaches of banking and financial rules came to the fore, demonstrating that whistleblowing is a helpful tool in detecting wrongdoing.[3] Whistleblowing provisions began in the US, and the banking and financial sectors in Europe followed. Several EU laws in banking and finance include whistleblowing requirements. These are sector-specific, focusing on whistleblowing within the framework of these industries.[4] These provisions vary across legal acts but share common traits. This chapter focuses on sectoral whistleblowing rules in EU banking and financial laws. We will review them chronologically to identify similarities, differences, and the European Commission's pattern in their adoption.

[1] S Loosveld, 'EU Financial Supervisory Powers, Whistleblowing and Self-Reporting' (2019) 34(9) *Journal of International Banking Law and Regulation* 317.

[2] ibid 322.

[3] J Coffee Jr., *Corporate Crime and Punishment – The Crisis of Underenforcement* (Berrett-Koehler Publishers, 2020) 97.

[4] D Kafteranis, 'Sectoral Provisions and the Directive on the Protection of Whistle-blowers: No to a Complex Relationship' (Oxford Business Law Blog, 4 June 2020) www.law.ox.ac.uk/business-law-blog/blog/2020/06/sectoral-provisions-and-directive-protection-whistle-blowers-no accessed 15 May 2025.

The central rationale for enacting whistleblowing rules under EU law is that whistleblowers are seen as a means of strengthening the enforcement of EU law.[5] In the ex-post EU intervention in the banking and financial sector, the EU legislator acknowledged the added value of whistleblowing as a helpful tool to encourage reporting and to promote the need for information by the enforcement bodies that need to detect violations of EU rules.[6] In addition, the introduction of whistleblowing rules follows incidents that harmed the public interest, which would have been avoided had whistleblowers been heard.

The European Commission, in its Communication of 8 December 2010 entitled 'Reinforcing sanctioning regimes in the financial services sector', had highlighted that financial market rules are often not respected and applied correctly.[7] During the recent economic crisis, the European Commission explored ways to strengthen sanctions and ensure the enforcement of EU rules. One approach was to add standard protections for whistleblowers in the banking and finance sectors, addressing the lack of consistency among Member States in encouraging disclosures. After public consultation, the Commission planned to include whistleblowing provisions in the new financial legislation sector.

A. Sectoral Provisions in the EU Banking Sector

i. The Single Supervisory Mechanism (SSM)

Despite the evolution of the EU financial sector over the last 30 years, a truly European integration of supervisors had remained absent.[8] The 2008 crisis ended the paradox of an integrated EU credit market with free movement but fragmented supervision. The collapse of financial institutions highlighted the need for a common supervisory authority.

This led to the creation of the Single Supervisory Mechanism (SSM).[9] Under the new regulatory framework, the European Central Bank (ECB) is responsible for the prudential supervision of significant banks along with the national

[5] The only instrument where the rationale for introducing whistleblowing rules was different is Directive 2016/943 (Trade Secrets Directive) where the whistleblower is granted protection by means of a derogation with a view to safeguarding freedom of expression.

[6] European Commission's Analysis of the Member States' Legislative Framework, Annex 6 (2017) 90–91 ec.europa.eu/info/sites/info/files/1-11_annexes.pdf accessed 15 May 2025.

[7] European Commission, Reinforcing Sanctioning Regimes in the Financial Services Sector [2010] SEC(2010) 1946 final, 2, eur-lex.europa.eu/LexUriServ/LexUriServ.do?uri=COM:2010:0716:FIN:EN:PDF accessed 15 May 2025.

[8] M Haentjens and P Gioia-Carabellese, *European Banking and Financial Law* (Routledge, 2015) 73.

[9] European Central Bank Regulation (EU) 468/2014 of 16 April 2014 establishing the framework for cooperation within the Single Supervisory Mechanism between the European Central Bank and national competent authorities and with national designated authorities (SSM Framework Regulation) [2014] OJ L141/1.

supervisory authorities.[10] To carry out the supervisory duties, the ECB needs information about possible breaches of the relevant legislation. One of these sources is the SSM whistleblowing programme, which allows potentially pertinent information to reach the ECB from third parties, such as employees of credit institutions.[11]

Under Article 23 of the SSM Regulation, the ECB has specific obligations regarding whistleblowing.[12] The ECB shall ensure that adequate mechanisms and procedures exist for the reporting of breaches of EU prudential rules by credit institutions, financial holding companies, mixed financial holding companies or competent authorities in the eurozone.[13] More details on these whistleblowing obligations are available in Articles 36–38 of the SSM Framework Regulation.[14] Any person can report directly to the ECB, in good faith, if they have reasonable grounds to believe that their reporting shows breaches of relevant EU law by the supervised institution or by the supervisors themselves.[15]

The report should not address areas outside the ECB's competence, such as money laundering or consumer protection. Whistleblowers should contact the relevant national authorities for such issues. If the report concerns a significant institution (supervised by the ECB), the ECB will investigate. If it concerns a less substantial institution, the ECB will assess whether there are breaches of ECB regulations and forward the report to national authorities. The ECB must ensure the whistleblower's identity remains confidential.

While anyone can report to the ECB, it is more common for employees of credit institutions to do so. Reports concern breaches of EU banking rules, with the ECB as recipient. The key missing element is protection for whistleblowers, as the ECB leaves this to Member States. Without safety guarantees, whistleblowers will not feel secure, undermining the programme's success. The interaction between the ECB's programme and the Directive is notable, as transposition is now complete and whistleblowing laws across Member States are operational.

It is not only the ECB that has to adopt whistleblowing programmes, but also the credit institutions. Under EU law, whistleblowing platforms are needed for credit institutions. These requirements are set out in Article 71 of the Capital

[10] CV Gortsos, 'European Banking Union Within the System of European Banking and Monetary Law' in MP Chiti and V Santoro (eds), *The Palgrave Handbook of European Banking Union Law* (Palgrave Macmillan, 2019) 24.

[11] G Lasagni, *Banking Supervision and Criminal Investigation – Comparing the EU and US Experiences* (Springer, 2019) 137–38.

[12] European Parliament and European Council Regulation (EU) 1024/2013 of 15 October 2013 conferring specific tasks on the European Central Bank concerning policies relating to the prudential supervision of credit institutions [2013] OJ L287/63 (SSM Regulation), Art 23.

[13] The prudential rules can be found in Art 4(3) of the SSM Regulation.

[14] Regulation No 468/2014 (n 9).

[15] European Central Bank, Information on the use of the breach reporting mechanism (BRM), www.bankingsupervision.europa.eu/framework/breach/html/index.en.html accessed 15 May 2025.

Requirements Directive IV (CRD IV).[16] Member States should ensure that the national competent supervisory authorities will 'establish effective and reliable mechanisms to encourage reporting of potential or actual breaches' of both the Capital Requirements Regulation (CRR) and the national provisions transposing the CRD IV.[17]

These whistleblowing structures should meet minimum standards, including procedures for receiving breach reports and being able to provide a follow-up.[18] They should provide three protections: first, shielding whistleblowers from retaliation, discrimination, or unfair treatment; second, safeguarding the personal data of both the whistleblower and the accused under EU data protection rules.[19] Finally, confidentiality should be provided to the whistleblower to the extent that disclosure of their identity is necessary under national law or in the context of further judicial proceedings or investigations.[20] Internally, credit institutions should establish procedures that facilitate internal alerts and whistleblowing under Article 71(3) of the CRD IV.[21] Credit institutions should establish a 'specific, independent and autonomous channel' for internal disclosure, with protection requirements that match those set by the supervisory authorities.[22]

The EU's diverse provisions create confusion for whistleblowers. They vary across legal instruments, and the Directive may make things worse. For example, reporting to the ECB requires good faith, but the Directive only requires reasonable grounds. Suppose the employee cannot be protected under the aforementioned sectoral rules. In that case, whistleblowers can seek protection under the Directive because the ECB is an external authority to which they can report directly. The Directive will likely become the preferred option due to its lower

[16] European Parliament and European Council Directive 2013/36/EU of 26 June 2013 on access to the activity of credit institutions and the prudential supervision of credit institutions and investment firms, amending Directive 2002/87/EC and repealing Directives 2006/48 and 2006/49/EC [2013] OJ L176/338. The recently adopted European Parliament and European Council Directive 2019/36/EU of 20 May 2019 amending Directive 2013/36/EU as regards exempted entities, financial holding companies, mixed financial holding companies, remuneration, supervisory measures and powers and capital conservation measures (CRD V) [2019] OJ L150/253 does not add anything to the existing provisions of CRD IV. CRD V and CRD VI did not bring any changes. CRR II and CRR III did not bring any changes as well.

[17] European Parliament and European Council Regulation (EU) 575/2013 of 26 June 2013 on prudential requirements for credit institutions and investment firms and amending Regulation (EU) 648/2012 [2013] OJ L176/1. See also Directive 2013/36 ibid.

[18] Directive 2013/36 (n 16) Art. 71(2).

[19] Although the CRD IV refers to European Parliament and European Council Directive 95/46/EC of 24 October 1995 on the protection of individuals with regard to the processing of personal data and on the free movement of such data and on the free movement of such data [1995] OJ L281/31, it is now replaced by the General Data Protection Regulation 2016/679 on the protection of natural persons with regard to the processing of personal data and on the free movement of such data (known as GDPR).

[20] Investigations, in this point, are meant either by the supervisory authorities or by the criminal authorities and they are not related to internal investigations.

[21] P Mulbert and A Wilheml, 'CRD IV Framework for Banks' Corporate Governance' in D Busch and G Ferrarini (eds), *European Banking Union* (OUP, 2020) 241.

[22] Directive 2013/36 (n 16) Art 71(3).

requirements for protection.[23] As the sectoral provisions are more demanding in protecting whistleblowers, they may render them inoperative compared to the Directive, as employees will seek protection under the Directive's provisions. As the Directive is more detailed and precise, it may become the preferred option for whistleblowers shortly.

ii. Directive 2019/20234 on the prudential supervision of investment firms

Another key whistleblowing provision in banking is supervision of investment firms. Directive 2019/2034 supplements rules like Regulation (EU) 575/2013 and Directive 2013/36.[24] These rules are based on Basel Committee standards for large banking groups and aim to harmonise supervisory practices in the EU and with the European Banking Authority and ESMA.

Under Article 22, 'Reporting of breaches', Member States must ensure effective reporting mechanisms for employees to report breaches of national laws implementing the Directive and Regulation 2019/2033. These mechanisms should have specific procedures for receiving, treating, and following up reports, with secure communication channels. Employees reporting breaches by investment firms are protected against discrimination, retaliation, and unfair treatment. Personal data must be protected under GDPR, maintaining confidentiality unless disclosure is legally required. Investment firms should also establish internal reporting systems, with social partners able to set these up if they follow the outlined procedures for authorities.

B. Ariadne's Thread: Sectoral Provisions in the EU Financial Sector

i. UCITS Directive 2009/65

Whistleblowing provisions are found in the Undertakings for Collective Investment in Transferable Securities (UCITS) Directive, adopted in 2009.[25] The UCITS Directive is the fruit of a long evolution of EU fund law since 1985.[26] The latest reforms, stemming from the 2009 UCITS Directive, relate to the financial crisis and Madoff's failure. The sector features detailed harmonisation, reinforced by

[23] Kafteranis (n 4).

[24] Directive (EU) 2019/2034 of the European Parliament and of the Council of 27 November 2019 on the prudential supervision of investment firms, [2019] OJ L314/64–114.

[25] European Parliament and European Council Directive 2009/65/EC of 13 July 2009 on the coordination of laws, regulations and administrative provisions relating to undertakings for collective investment in transferable securities (UCITS) [2009] OJ L302/32.

[26] N Moloney, *EU Securities and Financial Markets Regulation*, 3rd edn (OUP, 2014) 212.

administrative and legislative measures, and various supervisory measures have been adopted.

The UCITS Directive's whistleblowing regime is based on the 2014 UCITS V reforms, aiming to align sanctions with post-crisis securities and market reforms regulation.[27] Articles 99 and 99(a-e) were adopted to enhance the sanctioning regime, where practical, proportionate, and dissuasive administrative sanctions must be available.[28] The need to sanction brought the need to report information, which will enable investigations.[29] This task is addressed by whistleblowing.

Article 99d of the UCITS Directive sets out rules on whistleblowing. Member States are required to set up systems allowing whistleblowers to report (potential) violations of national laws implementing the Directive to the appropriate authorities.[30] These mechanisms should have procedures for the receipt and follow-up of reports, protect personal data, ensure confidentiality unless lifted for investigations or judicial proceedings, and protect against discrimination, retaliation, and unfair treatment.[31] The personal scope is limited to employees of investment companies, management companies and depositaries.[32] Nonetheless, the European Securities and Markets Authority (ESMA) has noticed that former employees or any other person can report their concerns directly to the ESMA's reporting channel, provided that the reporting is done in a personal capacity and in good faith.[33]

Apart from the reporting channels that the national authorities should establish, ESMA also has an obligation. ESMA should provide reporting channels, and whistleblowers can choose to report either to national authorities or directly to ESMA, as provided for in the UCITS Directive.[34] Furthermore, the whistleblower should not incur any liability for having disclosed the information to the relevant authorities. This means that no restriction on the whistleblower's ability to provide information can be imposed, either by contract or by law.[35] Finally, Member States should require management companies, investment companies, and depositaries to establish internal reporting procedures, enabling employees to report through a specific, independent, and autonomous disclosure channel.[36]

[27] ibid 259.

[28] Criminal sanctions might be used as well, but the Commission must be notified about it, and certain measures should be put in place that will facilitate the cooperation between national competent authorities and the ESMA.

[29] D Zetzsche and D Nast, 'Funds' in M Lehmann and C Kumpan (eds), *European Financial Services Law* (Beck – Hart – Nomos, 2019) 1446.

[30] Directive 2009/65/EC (n 25) Art 99(d)(1).

[31] ibid Art 99(d)(2)(a-d).

[32] ibid Art 99(d)(2)(b).

[33] Loosveld (n 1) 323.

[34] Directive 2009/65/EC (n 25) Art 99(d)(3).

[35] ibid Art 99(d)(4).

[36] ibid Art 99(d)(5).

ii. Directive 2014/56 on Statutory Audits of Annual Accounts and Consolidated Accounts

In Recital 17 of Directive 2014/56 on statutory audits of annual accounts, the importance of whistleblowing is highlighted due to the ability of whistleblowers to bring new information to the attention of competent authorities.[37] Whistleblowers face obstacles due to limited protection and incentives. Member States should implement measures to shield them from retaliation and harm, including safeguarding personal data, ensuring fair trial rights, and allowing them to be heard before decisions affecting them. The Directive mentions no financial incentives, but Article 30e covers reporting breaches of the Directive.

Article 30e has provisions similar to those discussed earlier. Most EU banking and financial sector whistleblowing rules follow a similar pattern. Member States should ensure that their competent authorities adopt effective mechanisms to encourage reporting breaches of the Directive or Regulation No 537/2014.[38] The minimum conditions for whistleblowing mechanisms are establishing procedures for receiving and following up reports, protecting personal data, and safeguarding the rights of the accused party.[39] These rights include the right to a defence, the right to be heard before a decision is made concerning them, and the right to seek an effective remedy before a court against any decision taken on their behalf.[40] These rights for the accused are rare in other sectoral provisions. Member States should also ensure that audit firms establish effective internal reporting mechanisms for employees to report breaches of the Directive and the Regulation.

iii. MiFID II – Directive 2014/65

Directive 2004/39/EC, commonly known as MiFID I, was adopted to regulate investment firms and regulated markets.[41] Since November 2007, MiFID I, along with the MiFID I Implementing Directive and the MiFID I Implementing Regulation, has served as the reference text for financial instruments.[42] MiFID I aimed to

[37] European Parliament and European Council Directive 2014/56/EU of 16 April 2014 amending Directive 2006/43/EC on statutory audits of annual accounts and consolidated accounts Text with EEA relevance [2014] OJ L158/196, Recital 17.

[38] European Parliament and European Council Regulation (EU) 537/2014 of 16 April 2014 on specific requirements regarding statutory audit of public-interest entities and repealing Commission Decision 2005/909/EC [2014] OJ L158/77.

[39] Directive 2014/56 (n 37) Art 30e(2).

[40] ibid Art 30e(2)(c).

[41] European Parliament and European Council Directive 2004/39/EC of 21 April 2014 on markets in financial instruments amending Council Directives 85/611/EEC and 93/6/EEC and Directive 2000/12/EC and repealing Council Directive 93/22/EEC [2004] OJ L145/1–47.

[42] European Parliament and European Council Directive 2006/73/EC of 10 August 2006 implementing Directive 2004/39/EC as regards organisational requirements and operating conditions for investment firms and defined terms for the purposes of the Directive [2006] OJ L241/26–58 (MiFID I Implementing Directive).

provide a high level of financial market transparency, investor protection, and better competition among trading venues.[43] The financial crisis has unveiled gaps and problematic aspects of MiFID I, leading to the adoption, in 2014, of the Directive 2014/65/EU (Markets in Financial Instruments Directive – known as MiFID II) along with the adoption of the Markets in Financial Instruments Regulation (MiFIR), and a significant number of implementing measures known as Level 2 legislation.[44] While MiFID I was considered strict, MiFID II and MiFIR are even more stringent, aiming to regulate financial markets better and increase transparency, significantly impacting the EU financial sector.

To ensure effective enforcement of MiFID II, Article 73 sets rules on internal and external whistleblowing, similar to MAR provisions on whistleblowing.[45] The need for whistleblowing is justified by the secrecy surrounding the financial markets industry, which necessitates information from the inside to initiate proceedings or investigations.[46] Encouraging whistleblowing is vital for reporting breaches of EU financial law, especially in capital markets. Article 73, together with Articles 67 and 69, requires Member States to ensure that their national authorities enact laws safeguarding whistleblowers.

External whistleblowing is the first option available to the whistleblower under Article 73(1).[47] By external whistleblowing, it is meant that the whistleblower should report outside their financial institution to a competent authority. The authority varies from one country to another.[48] The provision requires Member States to ensure that the national competent authorities establish effective whistleblowing mechanisms for reporting actual or possible infringements of MiFID II.

Specific minimum standards should be established by the competent authorities to facilitate whistleblowing.[49] Procedures should be established to receive reports and ensure secure communication. Whistleblowers need protection for reporting infringements, and personal data protection must comply with

European Commission Regulation 1287/2006 of 10 August 2006 implementing Directive 2004/39/EC as regards record-keeping obligations for investment firms, transaction reporting, market transparency, admission of financial instruments to trading, and defined terms for the purpose of that Directive [2006] OJ L241/1 (MiFID I Implementing Regulation).

[43] D Busch and G Ferrarini, 'Who's afraid of MiFID II?' in D Busch and G Ferrarini (eds), *Regulation of the EU Financial Markets* (OUP, 2016) para 1.01.

[44] European Parliament and European Council Directive 2014/65/EU of 15 May 2014 on markets in financial instruments and amending Directive 2002/92/EC and Directive 2011/61/EU Text with EEA relevance [2014] OJ L173/349. European Parliament and European Council Regulation (EU) 600/2014 of 15 May 2014 on markets in financial instruments and amending Regulation (EU) 648/2012 [2014] OJ L173/84.

[45] Directive 2014/65 (n 44) Art 73.

[46] JA Kammerer, 'Title VI Competent Authorities' in M Lehmann and C Kumpan (eds), *European Financial Services Law* (Beck – Hart – Nomos, 2019) 373.

[47] Directive 2014/65 (n 44) Art 73(1).

[48] P Yeoh, 'Whistleblowing: Motivations, Corporate Self-Regulation, and the Law' [2014] *International Journal of Law & Management* 459, 465 et seq.

[49] CV Gortsos, 'Public Enforcement of MiFID II?' in D Busch and G Ferrarini (eds), *Regulation of the EU Financial Markets* (OUP, 2016) para 19.76.

EU rules. Although general, it is surprising that Article 73 lacks the authority to specify technical or detailed requirements.

MiFID II includes provisions for internal whistleblowing within financial institutions, allowing whistleblowers to report if the entity is an investment firm, market operator, or similar, including breaches by third-country firms. Member States must require these entities to develop 'appropriate procedures' for reporting infringements, though no specific guidelines are provided. These procedures should be tailored to each entity's size, type, and structure, taking into account factors such as the severity of the breach and the employee's role. Protecting whistleblowers from retaliation is crucial, with anonymity being an important safeguard.

There is no priority between internal and external whistleblowing. Whistleblowers can report either internally or to authorities without choosing one. Internal reporting helps employers, but authorities need information for investigations. Unlike Article 32 of MAR, MiFID II is silent on financial rewards; while not prohibited, they are not permitted under current law. Implementing rewards likely conflicts with MiFID II.

iv. Market Abuse Regulation No 596/2014

Under EU law, market abuse encompasses market manipulation, insider dealing, and unlawful disclosure of inside information.[50] Certain legal instruments, at the EU level, regulate these behaviours. First and foremost, the Market Abuse Regulation (MAR), and second, a Directive on criminal sanctions for market abuse (MAD II).[51] In addition, the European Commission has adopted a variety of measures, under MAR, that introduce regulatory technical standards and implementing technical standards.[52]

[50] European Parliament and European Council Regulation (EU) 596/2014 of 16 April 2014 on market abuse (market abuse regulation) and repealing Directive 2003/6/EC and Commission Directives 2003/124/EC, 2003/125/EC and 2004/72/EC [2014] OJ L173/1, Art 1.

[51] ibid. See also European Parliament and European Council Directive 2014/57/EU of 16 April 2014 on criminal sanctions for market abuse (market abuse directive) [2014] OJ L173/179.

[52] Amongst these acts are the following: European Commission Implementing Regulation (EU) 2016/378 of 11 March 2016 laying down implementing technical standards with regard to the timing, format and template of the submission of notifications to competent authorities in accordance with Regulation (EU) No 596/2014 [2016] OJ L72/1. European Commission Delegated Regulation (EU) 2016/522 of 17 December 2015 supplementing Regulation (EU) No 596/2014 as regards an exemption for certain third countries public bodies and central banks, the indicators of market manipulation, the disclosure thresholds, the competent authority for notifications of delays, the permission for trading during closed periods and types of notifiable managers' transactions [2016] OJ L88/1. European Commission Implementing Regulation (EU) 2016/523 of 10 March 2016 laying down implementing technical standards with regard to the format and template for notification and public disclosure of managers' transactions in accordance with Regulation (EU) No 596/2014 [2016] OJ L88/19. European Commission Delegated Regulation (EU) 2016/908 supplementing Regulation (EU) No 596/2014 of the European Parliament and of the Council laying down regulatory technical standards on the criteria, the procedure and the requirements for establishing an accepted market practice and the requirements for maintaining it, terminating it or modifying the conditions for its acceptance [2016] OJ L153/3.

The EU legislator adopted these rules on market abuse to 'ensure the integrity of financial markets in the Union and to enhance investor protection and confidence in those markets'.[53] The European Commission highlights whistleblowing as a key purpose of MAR, noting that whistleblower reports can provide important firsthand information on potential breaches. However, the Commission warns that informants may hesitate to come forward due to fear of reprisals or lack of incentives.[54] For this reason, the European Commission proposed to include whistleblowing provisions in the MAR.

The inclusion of whistleblowing provisions in the MAR reflects international trends, as similar provisions have been adopted in other post-crisis financial and securities legislation at the EU level.[55] MAR establishes whistleblowing procedures and protections, acknowledging the value of whistleblowing.[56] The importance of whistleblowing lies in the ability to intensify enforcement capability through enhanced discovery. Certain paragraphs of the whistleblowing provisions in MAR were the subject of controversy during negotiations on the Regulation.[57] The European Commission had initially opted for a provision that would oblige Member States to provide for specific whistleblowing mechanisms where information would be shared between the reporting person and the relevant competent authorities, and to provide for the possibility of financial rewards.[58] The European Council, then, proposed that whistleblowers should report internally at first before reporting to the relevant national authorities.[59] The proposal of the Council was not retained, but MAR requires employers to put in place internal reporting structures.

Article 32 of the MAR, titled 'Reporting of Infringements', organises whistleblowing. It details rules for creating internal mechanisms or reporting to competent authorities. Developed alongside Articles 22 and 23, it covers obligations of national authorities. It also links to data protection and professional secrecy under Article 28. The first two paragraphs concern competent authorities, while the third and fourth focus on employers (financial institutions).[60]

[53] Explanatory Memorandum of the Proposal for a Regulation on Market Abuse (2011), 2, eur-lex.europa.eu/legal-content/EN/TXT/HTML/?uri=CELEX:52011PC0651&from=EN accessed 15 May 2025.

[54] European Commission Proposal for a Regulation on insider dealing manipulation (market abuse) [2011] COM(2011) 651 final, Recital 36.

[55] F Holger and SK Ulrich, 'Financial Incentives for Whistleblowers in European Capital Markets Law? Legal Policy Considerations on the Reform of the Market Abuse Regime' (2012) ECGI Law WP No 189/2012, ssrn.com/abstract=2124678 accessed 15 May 2025.

[56] Regulation (EU) 596/2014 (n 52) Recital 74. See also S Wilson, 'The New Market Abuse Regulation and Directive on Criminal Sanctions for Market Abuse: European Capital Markets Law and New Global Trends in Financial Crime Enforcement' (2015) 16 *ERA Forum* 427, 437.

[57] JA Kammerer, 'Market Behaviour' in M Lehmann and C Kumpan (eds), *European Financial Services Law* (Beck – Hart – Nomos, 2019) 866.

[58] Proposal for a Regulation (n 54) Art 29 (1) and (2).

[59] European Parliament and European Council, Proposal for a Regulation o on insider dealing and market manipulation (market abuse) – Presidency compromise [2012] 10198/12, Art 29 (1, 1a).

[60] Kammerer (n 57) 866.

The European Commission, in respect of Article 32(5), adopted the Implementing Directive 2015/2392 on MAR, which lays down more detailed rules on the relationship between national competent authorities and whistleblowers.[61] ESMA is the responsible authority that prepared the Implementing Directive.[62]

Article 32(1) requires Member States to ensure their authorities establish effective reporting systems for potential or actual infringements, with secure channels, data protection, and safeguards outlined in the Implementing Directive. These channels must differ from regular ones, ensure information completeness, integrity, confidentiality, restrict access, and be stored securely. Reports can be made in person, by phone, electronically, or on paper.

Article 32(3) covers internal whistleblowing, involving reports to the workplace. It aims to create internal channels for employees to report MAR infringements. While clear, it remains vague on some issues. The Member State acts more as a guarantor than a responsible party for establishing proper structures. The scope is broad, requiring all financial sector employers to set up reporting mechanisms. Design factors include the institution's size, structure, employee position, and breach severity. Failure occurs if the reporting structure faces sanctions or does not exist, risking ineffective internal reporting. A key to success is anonymity.[63]

Reporting possible MAR infringements to the authorities is seen as a private enforcement tool.[64] The employee should feel safe to report to the authorities, and they should be protected against unfair reprisals, such as any retaliation or discrimination. This protection applies not only when the whistleblower reports to the competent authority but also when they report internally. Furthermore, Article 23(4) should be considered as a further protection for whistleblowers, as it reads that a

> person making information available to the competent authority in accordance with this Regulation shall not be considered to be infringing any restriction on disclosure of information imposed by contract or by any legislative, regulatory or administrative provision, and shall not involve the person notifying in liability of any kind related to such notification.

Since the whistleblower provides information to the competent authority, Article 23(4) should apply. Also, Article 32(4) covers financial rewards, but due to issues, no Member State has yet used them.

[61] European Commission Implementing Directive (EU) 2015/2392 of 17 December 2015 on Regulation (EU) No 596/2014 of the European Parliament and of the Council as regards reporting to competent authorities of actual or potential infringements of that Regulation [2015] OJ L332/126.

[62] European Securities and Markets Authority, Final Report ESMA's technical advice on possible delegated acts concerning the Market Abuse Regulation [2015] ESMA/2015/224, paras 164 et seq.

[63] M Wundenberg, 'Compliance in Wertpa-pierfirmen' in R Veil (ed), *Europäisches Kapitalmarktrecht* (Mohr Siebeck, 2014).

[64] R Veil, 'Enforcement of Capital Markets Law in Europe – Observations from a Civil Law Country' (2010) 11 *European Business Organization Law Review* 409, 417. See also D Kafteranis, 'A New Enforcement Tool: A Directive to Protect Whistle-blowers' (2020) 41 *Business Law Review* 50.

v. Regulation No 909/2014 on Improving Securities Settlement in the EU and on Central Securities Depositories (CSDR)

Another reporting scheme has been adopted by Regulation No 909/2014 on improving securities settlement in the EU and on central securities depositories (CSDR).[65] Article 65's wording and structure mirror previous examples. Member States must ensure that competent authorities adopt effective mechanisms to encourage reporting of potential or actual infringements under the CSDR.

There are specific (minimum) requirements for these reporting structures. First, there should be special procedures for receiving and following up on these reports, including the establishment of safe reporting channels.[66] Second, protection should be offered to employees who report breaches of the CSDR. The protection should include protection against retaliation, discrimination, and other forms of unfair treatment.[67] Finally, the personal data should be protected in accordance with the EU and national legal frameworks, and the identities of both persons should not be revealed unless necessary under national law for subsequent investigations or judicial proceedings.

The reporting scheme involves whistleblowing to an external authority and regulates internal reporting in Article 65. Member States should require institutions to have autonomous, independent procedures for employees to report breaches of the CSDR. This internal channel can also be delegated to social entity partners.

Furthermore, the same standards of protection required for external whistleblowing structures should also be applied to internal reporting schemes. As noted earlier, Article 65 is similar to the other sectoral provisions on whistleblowing in the EU banking and financial sector, demonstrating a paternalistic approach by the EU legislature on the issue, where the exact requirements are adopted in several EU acts without any specific analysis of the reasons that led to the adoption of these requirements.[68]

vi. RPIIPs – Regulation No 1286/2014

Another provision on whistleblowing is found in Regulation No 1286/2014 on key information documents for packaged retail and insurance-based investment products (known as RPIIPs).[69] This Regulation details the format and content of the key

[65] European Parliament and European Council Regulation (EU) 909/2014 of 23 July 2014 on improving securities settlement in the EU and on central securities depositories and amending Directives 98/26/EC and 2014/65/EU and Regulation (EU) 236/2012 (CSDR) [2014] OJ L257/66, Art 65.

[66] Regulation No 909/2014 (n 65) Art 65(2)(a).

[67] ibid Art 65(2)(b).

[68] It should be mentioned that the European Commission made no impact assessment for the CSDR (consequently, whistleblowing was not discussed).

[69] European Parliament and European Council Regulation (EU) 1286/2014 of 26 November 2014 on key information documents for packaged retail and insurance-based investment products (PRIIPs) [2014] OJ L352/1.

information document prepared by RPIIP manufacturers and their provision to retail investors, enabling retail investors to understand and compare the key features and risks of RPIIPs.[70] Under Article 28 of the RPIIPs, whistleblowing obligations are imposed on both the employer and the national competent authorities. Similar to MAR and MiFID II, the EU legislator has retained the same model of internal reporting and whistleblowing to the relevant competent authorities in PRIIPR.

National authorities should establish effective whistleblower reporting systems for reporting RPIIP infringements. Article 28 sets minimum standards, including procedures for receiving breach reports and ensuring follow-up.[71] Second, protection should be available to the whistleblower. This protection should extend to protection against discrimination, retaliation, and other forms of unfair treatment.[72] Finally, the identity of the whistleblower should be protected at every stage of the procedure, unless disclosure is required by national law in the context of further investigation or judicial proceedings.[73] This confidentiality clause is common in whistleblowing policies but offers no real benefit to whistleblowers. A major concern is that their names could be disclosed, and this type of confidentiality does not ensure anonymity. While true anonymity would be ideal, no EU legal provision on whistleblowing provides for this, not even the Directive.

Article 28 allows Member States discretion to adopt extra mechanisms under their laws. It requires them to ensure that financial services employers establish internal reporting procedures for PRIIPs infringements, which should be specific, independent, and autonomous. RPIIPs do not mandate these mechanisms, leaving their necessity to Member States, and they conflict with other EU whistleblowing laws that require internal reporting. RPIIPs also lack provisions on monetary rewards.

vii. Regulation 2015/2365 on Transparency of Securities Financing Transactions and of Reuse (SFTR)

Similar to the CSDR, Regulation 2015/2365 on transparency of securities financing and reuse (SFTR) includes whistleblowing provisions; however, no impact assessment was conducted before their adoption.[74] Under Article 24, competent authorities should establish reporting mechanisms to allow the reporting of actual or potential breaches of Articles 4 and 15 to other competent authorities. There are certain (minimum) requirements that these reporting mechanisms should respect.[75]

[70] S Gerhards and K Rothenhofer, 'Packaged Retail and Insurance-based Investment Products Regulation (PRIIP)' in M Lehmann and C Kumpan (eds), *European Financial Services Law* (Beck – Hart – Nomos, 2019) 1033.

[71] Regulation 1286/2014 (n 69) Art 28(2)(a).

[72] ibid Art 28(2)(b).

[73] ibid Art 28(2)(c).

[74] European Parliament and European Council Regulation (EU) 2015/2365 of 25 November 2015 on transparency of securities financing transactions and of reuse and amending Regulation (EU) 648/2012 (SFTR) [2015] OJ L337/26.

[75] ibid Art 24(2).

First, there should be in place specific procedures for the receipt and follow-up of the reports made, and, for that purpose, a secure communication reporting channel should be established.[76] Second, employees who report infringements should have protection against retaliation, discrimination, and unfair treatment. Additionally, personal data and informant identity should be protected in accordance with EU rules, unless disclosure is necessary for investigations or judicial proceedings.[77]

In addition to reporting to authorities, Article 24 mandates internal reporting. Financial institutions must establish whistleblowing mechanisms for employees. Unlike external reporting, internal reporting does not have the same level of protection safeguards. This suggests that each provision stems from similar principles but was adopted inconsistently. Overall, the lack of uniformity complicates the EU banking and financial laws on whistleblowing.

viii. Directive 2016/97 on Insurance Distribution (IDD)

Another instrument in the financial sector that includes whistleblowing provisions is the Insurance Distribution Directive (IDD) 2016/97.[78] The current provision on whistleblowing (Article 35 of the IDD) was already included in the Commission Proposal, even though the matter was not explicitly mentioned in the Impact Assessment.[79] The Impact Assessment focused on broad issues such as inadequate sanctions and enforcement and considered various regulatory options favouring harmonisation. Aside from a summary of Article 35 in the Explanatory Memorandum, it lacked a detailed analysis of whistleblowing, effectiveness, or the role in the Impact Assessment.

Whistleblowing in the IDD is regulated under Article 35, in a manner similar to other provisions analysed. Member States should ensure competent authorities establish effective reporting mechanisms to encourage and facilitate reporting of national legal provisions on IDD.[80] The IDD's scope covers employees of insurance or reinsurance distributors and, when possible, others reporting breaches within these institutions. Whistleblower protections include protection against retaliation, discrimination, and unfair treatment, as well as safeguarding the identities of both the whistleblower and the 'accused', unless national law purposes require disclosure.[81] Finally, the national competent authorities should have appropriate procedures for receiving and following up on the reports made.[82]

[76] ibid Art 24(2)(a).
[77] ibid Art 24(2)(c).
[78] European Parliament and European Council Directive 2016/97/EU on insurance distribution (recast) (2016) OJ L26/19.
[79] European Commission Proposal for a Directive on insurance mediation (recast) [2012] COM(2012) 360 final, Art 30.
[80] Directive 2016/97 (n 78) Art 35(1).
[81] ibid Art 35(2)(b) and (c).
[82] ibid Art 35(2)(a).

ix. IORP – Directive 2016/2341

In 2016, the EU adopted a recast version of the Institutions for Occupational Retirement Provision (IORP II) Directive to encourage long-term investment through occupational pension funds.[83] The IORP II Directive came into force to complete Directive 2003/41/EC.[84] The new rules, under IORP II, aimed to enhance specific areas of interest.[85] Among the four categories of interest for the EU, there was a need to ensure good governance and risk management.[86] Under these new good governance and risk management rules, certain reporting obligations, akin to whistleblowing, have been imposed.

Article 24 outlines the modalities of whistleblowing within the framework of the IORP II Directive.[87] The holders of a key function should inform the competent authority of the IORP if the administrative, supervisory or management body (internally) does not take action in specific scenarios.[88] First, the holder of a key function is a person who does either the risk management, the internal audit, or, if applicable, an actuarial function.[89] The holder of a key function may be a person or an organisational unit. The holder of a key function should inform the competent authorities when a substantial risk exists that the IORP will not comply with specific essential statutory requirements, provided that this has been reported internally. It should pose a threat to the interests of members and beneficiaries.[90]

The other scenario is when the holder of the key function has observed a significant breach of the laws or regulations related to the IORP and has reported it internally.[91] The wording of the provisions is unclear as to whether the key function holder should first inform internal stakeholders and, if no action is taken, then report to authorities, or report to both simultaneously. It is likely the first, as good governance suggests informing internal stakeholders first, then reporting to

[83] European Commission, Occupational pension funds – rules governing the activities and supervision of institutions for occupational retirement provision ec.europa.eu/info/business-economy-euro/banking-and-finance/insurance-and-pensions/occupational-pension-funds_en#documents accessed 15 May 2025.

[84] P Borsjé and H van Meerten, 'A European Pensions Union: Towards a Strengthening of the European Pension Systems' in F Pennings and G Vonk (eds), *Research Handbook on European Social Security Law* (Edward Elgar, 2015) 394–403.

[85] K Van Hulle, 'Risk Disclosure in the European Insurance Industry: Implications for Occupational Pension Funds' in OS Mitchell, R Maurer and JM Orszag (eds), *Retirement System Risk Management – Implications of the New Regulatory Order* (OUP, 2016) 80–82.

[86] The other categories are: clarifying cross-border activities of IORPs, providing clear and relevant information to members and beneficiaries, and ensuring that supervisors have the necessary tools to effectively supervise IORPs. See also N Searle, 'EU Directive on Institutions for Occupational Retirement Provisions (IORP II)' (2016) *The National Law Review* www.natlawreview.com/article/eu-directive-institutions-occupational-retirement-provision-iorp-ii?amp accessed 15 May 2025.

[87] European Parliament and European Council Directive 2016/2341/EU of 14 December 2016 on the activities and supervision of institutions for occupational retirement provision (IORPs) [2016] OJ L354/37, Art 24.

[88] ibid Art 24(5).

[89] ibid Art 24(1).

[90] ibid Art 24(5)(a).

[91] ibid Art 24(5)(b).

authorities if needed. The Directive also mandates that Member States ensure legal protection for those who report to relevant authorities.[92]

x. Prospectus Regulation 2017/1129

Whistleblowing provisions exist in Regulation 2017/1129 (known as the Prospectus Regulation).[93] In Recital 77, the importance of whistleblowing is recognised as an essential source of information for the competent authorities to enable them to detect and to impose sanctions for breaches of the Prospectus Regulation.[94] Therefore, the whistleblower should be protected from retaliation to be able to report.[95]

Under Article 41, whistleblowing provisions outline that authorities should establish effective reporting mechanisms to encourage reporting of actual or potential issues or infringements.[96] This time, responsibility falls to the relevant authorities, not the Member State. The state has no role; the authority should adopt whistleblowing clauses. This raises questions about oversight and regulation and whether the state will regulate or the authority will oversee the system.

Reporting mechanisms for authorities must meet minimum requirements, including procedures for the receipt and follow-up of reports, as well as secure channels for receipt.[97] Second, the whistleblower should enjoy appropriate protection against discrimination, retaliation, and other types of unfair treatment either by their employer or by a third relevant party.[98] Finally, the protection of personal data should be ensured by complying with EU rules on this matter, and the identities of both the whistleblower and the other party should also be protected.[99] The protection of the identity can be levied if there is a need for disclosure under national laws for further judicial proceedings or investigations.

Besides reporting to authorities, the Prospectus Regulation mandate relevant employers in financial services to establish internal reporting mechanisms for employees to report breaches of the Regulations.[100] This internal reporting channel should be specific, autonomous, and independent, with Member States responsible for ensuring private parties establish such schemes.

Finally, the Prospectus Regulation is the second legal instrument, following the MAR, which allows the adoption of financial rewards for whistleblowers.[101]

[92] ibid Art 24(6).

[93] European Parliament and European Council Regulation (EU) 2017/1129 of 14 June 2017 on the prospectus to be published when securities are offered to the public or admitted to trading on a regulated market, and repealing Directive 2003/71/EC [2017] OJ L168/12.

[94] ibid Recital 77.

[95] ibid.

[96] ibid Art 41(1).

[97] Regulation No 2017/1129 (n 93) Art 41(2)(a).

[98] ibid Art 41(2)(b).

[99] ibid Art 41(2)(c).

[100] ibid Art 41(4).

[101] ibid Art 41(3).

The provision is more detailed than in the MAR but still vague. Member States can grant rewards to whistleblowers for breaches of the Prospectus Regulation under certain conditions: the information must be new, not legally required to be reported, and lead to sanctions. Similar to MAR, the Regulation establishes certain conditions but grants Member States discretion. So far, no state has adopted such financial incentives.

xi. Whistleblowing in the EU financial sector post the Directive

Following the adoption of the Whistleblowing Directive, EU financial sector rules refer to it. Regulation 2020/1503 on European crowdfunding highlights the importance of whistleblowing in bringing new information to authorities.[102] Article 47 amends the Whistleblowing Directive so it can be applicable for reporting breaches of Regulation 2020/1503. Another example is the Directive 2022/2464 on corporate sustainability reporting.[103] As the European Commission enacts delegated acts under the Directive, it needs to take into account the Whistleblowing Directive when establishing sustainability reporting standards in Article 29b. Another example is Regulation 2023/1114 on Markets in Crypto Assets (MiCAR).[104] Recital 115 emphasises the importance of whistleblowing for providing new information to authorities. Under MiCAR, whistleblowing should follow the provisions of the Whistleblowing Directive.

The new approach to whistleblowing in EU financial legislation emphasises the need for uniformity. Since the adoption of the Whistleblowing Directive, most provisions now refer to it, indicating its growing significance. However, earlier legislation predates the Directive and has different regulations, which can cause confusion. A unified, clear reporting process is necessary to facilitate whistleblowing, but the coexistence of sectoral rules and the Directive may make whistleblowing more challenging. In addition to causing confusion, Member States might face challenges when transposing these new EU legal acts – which mandate that whistleblowing complies with the Whistleblowing Directive. They may need to amend their national whistleblowing laws or include references to these laws in their transposition laws of the relevant EU legal framework. The annexe of the Whistleblowing Directive contains all the previous whistleblowing provisions enacted within the EU. Should this annexe be updated accordingly? Should national laws be amended as well? These questions will be addressed in the coming years, as the interaction between the Whistleblowing Directive and other EU legal acts will become clearer.

[102] Regulation (EU) 2020/1503 of the European Parliament and of the Council of 7 October 2020 on European crowdfunding service providers for business, [2020] OJ L347/1–49.

[103] Directive (EU) 2022/2464 of the European Parliament and of the Council of 14 December 2022 as regards corporate sustainability reporting, [2022] OJ L322/15–80.

[104] Regulation (EU) 2023/1114 of the European Parliament and of the Council of 31 May 2023 on markets in crypto-assets, [2023] OJ L150/40–205.

C. Confusion of Whistleblowers in the Anti-Money Laundering Area

i. EU AML Framework

Another example of whistleblowing provisions is in the EU legislation on preventing and countering money laundering and terrorist financing.[105] Directive 2015/849, known as the 4th AML Directive, sets out how whistleblowing can occur regarding money laundering and terrorist financing.[106] Regulation 2015/847 completes the whistleblowing provisions by establishing rules on information accompanying the transfer of funds and on how an employee can blow the whistle about breaches of this Regulation.[107] The legislative field of money laundering and terrorist financing is evolving in response to changing needs.[108] The recent AML reform at the EU level has brought significant changes, notably with the creation of the Anti-Money Laundering Authority (AMLA) and the adoption of an AML single rulebook.[109]

The AML reporting framework, based on Article 61 of the 4th and 5th AML Directives and reinforced by the 2024 AML Regulation, requires Member States to ensure competent authorities or self-regulatory bodies establish effective reporting mechanisms for employees to report breaches of the EU AML transposition framework.[110] The Regulation mandates minimum requirements for effective reporting and the protection of whistleblowers. Secure communication channels, specific procedures for receiving and following up reports, protection for whistleblowers and accused persons, adherence to EU data protection rules, and confidentiality of whistleblowers are essential, unless disclosure of the identity is required by law.[111]

[105] Loosveld (n 1) 324.

[106] European Parliament and European Council Directive 2015/849/EU of 20 May 2015 on the prevention of the use of the financial system for the purposes of money laundering or terrorist financing, amending Regulation No 648/2012/EU, and repealing Directive 2005/60/EC and Commission Directive 2006/70/EC (Text with EEA relevance) [2015] OJ L141/73.

[107] European Parliament and European Council Regulation (EU) 2015/847 of 20 May 2015 on information accompanying transfers of funds and repealing Regulation (EC) 1781/2006 [2015] OJ L141/1.

[108] CFS Del Mundo, 'How Countries Seek to Strengthen Anti-Money Laundering Laws in Response to the Panama Papers, and the Ethical Implications of Incentivizing Whistleblowers' (2019) 40 *Northwestern Journal of International Law & Business* 87, 103.

[109] The EU has adopted the AML package in May 2024: www.consilium.europa.eu/en/press/press-releases/2024/05/30/anti-money-laundering-council-adopts-package-of-rules/#gsc-main-content accessed 15 May 2025.

[110] Directive 2015/849 (n. 106) Art 61(1). See also European Parliament and European Council Directive 2018/843 of 30 May 2018 amending Directive 2015/849/EU on the prevention of the use of the financial system for the purposes of money laundering or terrorist financing, and amending Directives 2009/138/EC and 2013/36/EU [2018] OJ L156/43. European Parliament and European Council Directive 2018/1673 of 23 October 2018 on combatting money laundering by criminal law [2018] OJ L284/22, Art 1(39). Regulation (EU) 2024/1624 of the European Parliament and of the Council of 31 May 2024 on the prevention of the use of the financial system for the purposes of money laundering or terrorist financing ('2024 AML Regulation').

[111] Directive 2015/849 (n 106) Art 61(2)(a)-(e). Directive 2018/843 (n 110) Art 1(39)(b). Regulation 2024/1624 (n 110) Art 14.

Internal reporting procedures should also be established, with a clear, anonymous, independent, and specific reporting channel.[112] Employees and representatives reporting suspicions of money laundering or terrorist financing should be protected from threats, retaliation, or adverse employment actions. They have the right to complain to their employer without fear of reprisal.

Under the Regulation, Member States must establish effective reporting mechanisms for employees to report breaches to competent authorities, meeting the minimum requirements set out in Article 69. Payment service providers, with authorities' input, should create internal reporting systems for employees or people in suitable positions to report breaches via an independent, anonymous channel, scaled to their size and nature. On 18 December 2019, the European Banking Authority (EBA) was tasked with establishing a permanent Standing Committee on AML and Countering Terrorism Financing (AMLSC). [113] The Committee has powers in the areas of money laundering and terrorist financing but has not produced any results so far on whistleblowing.

With the adoption of AMLA, the EU would gain new powers to receive reports on breaches of AML legislation.[114] Under Article 90 of Regulation 2024/1620, AMLA should create dedicated reporting channels for breaches of Regulations 2024/1624 and 2023/1113, and Directive 2024/1640. The Whistleblowing Directive should also apply to protecting these persons. AMLA can request additional information from reporting entities and supervisory authorities without risking the reporting person's identity. These new powers increase reassurance but also add complexity to the AML reporting scheme.

There is confusion about whistleblowing on money laundering and terrorist financing as a broader right and the duties to report suspicious activities under the EU AML framework. Under Regulation 2024/1624, employees in the banking and financial sector must report suspicious transactions to the Financial Intelligence Units (FIUs). Whistleblowing, regulated under Article 14 of the 2024 Regulation, aligns with the voluntary nature of whistleblowing as enriched in Directive 2019/1937. Whistleblowing is a right – employees are not obligated to report and face no legal consequences for not doing so. However, they must report suspicious transactions or face penalties in the context of money laundering.

The coexistence of these regimes causes confusion. Having two reporting regimes might seem helpful, but different legal consequences and protections can discourage reporting. This weakens efforts to improve enforcement, transparency, and compliance in the financial sector. Therefore, a distinction should be made

[112] Regulation 2024/1624 (n 110) Art 60.

[113] European Banking Authority, Mandate of the Standing Committee on anti-money laundering and countering terrorist financing (AMLSC) [2020] EBA/DC/2020/309, www.eba.europa.eu/sites/default/documents/files/document_library/About%20Us/Legal%20Framework/Updated%20Files%2026022019/854476/2020%2001%2022%20BoS%20ESAs%20Review%20-%20AMLSC%20mandate.pdf accessed 15 May 2025.

[114] European Parliament and European Council Regulation of 31 May 2024 establishing the Authority for Anti-Money Laundering and Countering the Financing of Terrorism and amending Regulations No 1093/2010, No 1094/2010 and No 1095/2010, [2024] OJ 19.6.2024.

between the duty to report and the right to report.[115] A single law should clearly define whistleblowing and its legal scope, separating it from mandatory reporting. Duties to report must be explicit and distinct from whistleblowing. Institutions should educate staff on these differences. Whistleblowing policies should promote transparency, not just exist in compliance.

D. Puzzled and Confused Whistleblower

The aforementioned legal provisions on sectoral whistleblowing in the EU banking and financial sector are set out in point A of the annexes to the Whistleblowers Directive.[116] These sectoral provisions are *lex specialis*, overriding the Whistleblowers Directive. The detailed analysis was intentional. Despite similarities, minor differences can significantly impact whistleblower protections. These provisions cause confusion and legal complexity. Whistleblowers must consult relevant rules for each report, which may discourage them from coming forward.

From the overview of these sectoral provisions, it becomes clear that the scope of whistleblower protection at the EU level is limited, aiming to ensure the enforcement of specific EU acts in specific EU areas.[117] It does not cover one sector but specific sectors with precise instruments. In addition, certain areas are not covered at all. An example of this is the transport safety area, where specific whistleblowing rules exist for air and maritime transport safety. At the same time, there are no provisions concerning road and rail transport safety. The content and level of whistleblowing provisions differ across instruments, and they are limited in most cases.[118]

Specific instruments offer reporting channels but mostly lack protections for whistleblowers. When protection exists, it only shields against retaliation, with no mention of criminal, civil, or administrative safeguards. Member States can decide to extend the scope of protection, but this is not always certain. These factors create legal gaps and uncertainty.[119] The whistleblower is confused by this piecemeal, sectoral approach, which impedes whistleblowing. This fragmentation thus has a negative impact on the effectiveness of existing EU rules protecting whistleblowers.

An optimal solution is to render sectoral provisions inoperable and replace them with the Whistleblowers Directive. This ensures legal clarity, as whistleblowers would consult only one law, clarifying rules and protections. Having both causes unnecessary confusion for authorities and whistleblowers.[120]

[115] I Hoedt-Ramussen and D Voorhoof, 'Whistleblowing for Sustainable Democracy' (2018) 36(1) *Netherlands Quarterly of Human Rights* 3, 4–5.

[116] European Parliament and European Council Directive 2019/1937/EU of 23 October 2019 on the protection of persons who report breaches of Union law [2019] OJ L305/17, 55–56.

[117] Commission's Analysis of the Member States' Legislative Framework (n 6) 92–93.

[118] ibid.

[119] ibid 93.

[120] D Kafteranis et al., 'The Citizens' Role in combatting Economic Crimes: Insights from Tax Offences, Money Laundering, and Sanctions Evasion' [2025] *European Law Journal* 1–24.

4

A Controversial Legal Basis to Address an Urgent Need for an EU Protection of Whistleblowers

I. The Rocky Way towards the EU Directive on the Protection of Whistleblowers

A. The European Parliament's Pressure with its Resolutions

The EU lacked a comprehensive legal framework to protect whistleblowers.[1] The European Parliament has worked to protect whistleblowers, especially since the Lisbon Treaty.[2] It has approved several Resolutions focusing on whistleblowing. While not legally binding, these resolutions invite the European Commission to propose legislation on the issue.[3] Article 225 of the Treaty on the Functioning of the EU (TFEU) and Article 133 of the European Parliament's rules of procedure are the legal bases of this soft law instrument.

The European Parliament's Resolutions call on the Commission to propose legislation on whistleblowing, but not solely on it.[4] For instance, in a Resolution of 23 October 2013 on organised crime, corruption and money laundering, in paragraph 14, the Parliament asked the Commission to present a whistleblower protection programme which will enhance the fight against corruption.

This example demonstrates that whistleblowing was complementary to the fight against corruption, seen as a tool to combat corruption and related wrong-doings. It was a sectoral provision. Several scandals, including Luxleaks and the Panama Papers, influenced the demands of the European Parliament. The need for transparency at the EU level had been reflected in several Resolutions

[1] G Georgiadou, 'The European Commission's Proposal for Strengthening Whistleblower Protection' (2018) 3 *EU Criminal Law Review* 166.

[2] S White, 'A Matter of Life or Death – Whistleblowing Legislation in the EU' (2018) 3 *EU Criminal Law Review* 171.

[3] D Chalmers, 'The Democratic Ambiguity of EU Law Making and its Enemies' in A Arnull and D Chalmers (eds), *The Oxford Handbook of European Union Law* (OUP, 2015) 312.

[4] D Kafteranis, 'The Role of the European Parliament in the Adoption of the Directive on the Protection of Whistle-blowers' (2020) 4 *Revue des affaires européennes* 903.

of the European Parliament calling for the introduction of whistleblowers' protection.[5]

For instance, the Resolution of 25 November 2015 on tax rulings and other measures of a similar nature or effect mirrors the step towards the introduction of a European legal framework for the protection of whistleblowers.[6] It invited the European Commission *to propose, by June 2016, an EU legislative framework for the effective protection of whistleblowers.* The European Parliament began to abandon the sectoral approach to protecting whistleblowers and moved towards the need for a horizontal legal framework.

Despite the Resolution, the European Commission remained unresponsive. For that entire period, the European Commission did not propose a horizontal legal framework on the protection of whistleblowers.[7] The matter evolved, and the European Commission faced greater pressure following the adoption by the European Parliament of the Resolution of 24 October 2017 on legitimate measures to protect whistleblowers acting in the public interest when disclosing the confidential information of companies and public bodies.[8] This Resolution was an essential step towards the adoption of an EU Act on the protection of whistleblowers.[9]

The Resolution emphasised the need for a legal framework that covers whistleblowing across all relevant fields. It highlighted the importance of whistleblowers in uncovering illegalities and their significance to various sectors of EU interest, such as consumer protection and financial markets. The European Parliament urged the European Commission to propose a common EU legal framework by the end of 2017. The Commission responded nearly a year later.

B. Finally, the Proposal for a Directive by the Commission

The European Commission proposed a Directive in April 2018 to protect whistleblowers reporting breaches of Union law, aiming to enhance enforcement where

[5] European Parliament, Resolution of 16 December 2015 on bringing transparency, coordination and convergence to corporate tax policies in the Union [2015] P8_TA(2015)0457, recommendation A7 and European Parliament, Resolution of 6 July 2016 on tax rulings and other measures similar in nature of effect [2016] P8_TA(2016)0310, paras 44–46.

[6] European Parliament, Resolution of 25 November 2015 on tax rulings and other measures similar in nature or effect [2015] P8_TA(2015)0408, paras 144–145.

[7] T Racho, 'La possibilité d'un encadrement juridique des lanceurs d'alerte par l'Union Européenne' (2016) 10 *Revue des Droits de l'Homme* 1, 3.

[8] European Parliament, Resolution of 24 October 2017 on legitimate measures to protect whistle-blowers acting in the public interest when disclosing the confidential information of companies and public bodies [2016] (2016/2224(INI)).

[9] D Kafteranis, 'Protection of Whistleblowers in the European Union: The Promising Parliament Resolution and the Challenge for the European Commission' (Oxford Business Law Blog, 14 December 2017) www.law.ox.ac.uk/business-law-blog/blog/2017/12/protection-whistleblowers-european-union-promising-parliament accessed 15 May 2025.

underreporting delayed progress.[10] These specific areas of under-enforcement are: financial services; prevention of money laundering and terrorist financing; product safety; transport safety; public procurement; protection of the environment; nuclear safety; food safety; protection of privacy and personal data; consumer protection; and breaches of competition law. The proposal's text was inspiring and innovative, in line with international standards, including those of the Council of Europe.[11]

The proposal broadly defined a whistleblower, protecting them in both public and private sectors. It adopted the 'three-tier' model of disclosure, requiring the whistleblower to report internally first, then to the relevant competent authorities, and, as a last resort, to the public. Internal reporting was prioritised, but this was not reflected in the final text of the Directive, which allows the whistleblower to choose freely between internal reporting and reporting to the competent authorities. The proposal adopted the reasonable belief test, omitting the problematic good-faith requirement. Protection was ensured through sanctions against retaliation, reversing the burden of proof in court for whistleblowers, and providing legal aid. The proposal targeted breaches of EU law and was unrelated to national laws on classified information.

The proposal saw the whistleblower as key to a fair single market, ensuring a level playing field in which they can report breaches of EU rules, especially in the financial sector. Whistleblowing focuses on enforcement issues, serving as a useful enforcement tool to ensure a safe internal market. Therefore, Article 114 TFEU was preferred as the legal basis over Article 153. Article 153 TFEU was discarded because it offered limited protection to employees and was considered a costly regulatory intervention, as it would have applied even in cases where there was no connection to EU law.

The Commission stated, 'by boosting corporate transparency, social responsibility and financial and non-financial performance, whistleblower protection can complement measures to increase business transparency on social and environmental matters'.[12] The proposal followed the regulatory idea of responsive regulation, whereby self-regulation through internal whistleblowing is the base of the regulatory pyramid, which then escalates to external reporting, either to the authorities or to the media, where the reputational damage of the corporation is more severe.[13] The need to protect the market was the principal motive for proposing legislation, and protecting whistleblowers was an accessory.

[10] European Commission Proposal for a Directive of the European Parliament and of the Council on the protections of persons reporting on breaches of Union law: 2018/0106 (COD) [2018] 6.

[11] Council of Europe Committee of Ministers, Recommendation CM/Rec(2014)7, Protection of whistle-blowers, (adopted by the Committee of Ministers at the 1198th meeting on 30 April 2014).

[12] European Commission Communication COM(2018) 214 on strengthening whistleblower protection at EU level [2018] 5.

[13] O Lobel, 'New Governance as Regulatory Governance' in D Levi-Faur (ed), *The Oxford Handbook of Governance* (OUP, 2012) 76–77.

II. Defining the Directive: The Puzzle of Legal Bases

The European Commission has struggled to find a legal basis to propose legislation since the European Parliament first called for whistleblower protection.[14] The Directive was adopted by combining 12 legal bases.[15] Whistleblowing could not fall within a single field of exclusive or shared competence, as there was no stand-alone legal basis that would have allowed its adoption on a single legal basis. As a result, the correct legal basis was not a single one but a combination of multiple legal bases, enabling the adoption of the Directive. The discussion of the legal bases is essential, as it may be one of the Directive's weaknesses should a case reach the Court of Justice of the European Union (CJEU).

Since the start of the legal basis debate, two key issues have emerged: what the legal basis should be and whether it should be horizontal or sectoral intervention.[16] Recalling the rich discussion among the different EU institutions will help us clarify the rationale for not adopting a Directive with a single legal basis, the final choice of legal bases, and the reasons for not including specific articles in the Directive. The debate over the legal basis was complex and formalistic. The EU decided to exclude legal bases based on procedural issues rather than taking the time to reorganise the Directive's adoption by dividing it into several legal instruments, each specific to the competences attributed under the legal basis used for its adoption.[17]

The discussion on the legal basis of the Directive started on 24 October 2017 with the European Parliament's Resolution on 'Legitimate measures to protect whistleblowers acting in the public interest.' The European Parliament called on the Commission to determine the appropriate legal basis to enable the EU to take action on whistleblowing and insisted that there should be a horizontal legislative proposal. It insisted that several legal foundations can encourage the adoption of an EU legal act, without, though, mentioning which those bases are.[18] The Resolution did not make any suggestions regarding the choice of legal bases, except for the Committee on Constitutional Affairs of the European Parliament's

[14] V Abazi, 'The European Union Whistleblower Directive: A Game Changer for Whistleblowing Protection?' [2020] *Industrial Law Journal* 1.

[15] European Parliament and European Council Directive 2019/1937/EU of 23 October 2019 on the protection of persons who report breaches of Union law [2019] OJ L305/17, first page where the different legal bases are given.

[16] The European Commission had already done a first analysis on the legal basis in the Impact Assessment where it stressed the need for multiple legal foundations as a single legal basis was not possible to be found.

[17] The proposal to divide the Directive into several EU legal instruments based on the legal basis, scope and competence was expressed by the Legal Service of the European Council in its Opinion. European Council, Opinion of the legal service on the legal basis for the proposal for a directive on the protection of persons reporting on breaches of Union law (2018) JUR_14620/18, 23.

[18] E Andreis, 'Towards Common Minimum Standards for Whistleblower Protection across the EU' (2019) 4(2) European Papers 575, 577–78, www.europeanpapers.eu/en/europeanforum/towards-common-minimum-standards-for-whistleblower-protection-across-eu accessed on 15 May 2025.

opinion on the Resolution.[19] The Committee proposed as legal bases Article 114 TFEU on the approximation of national legislation regarding the functioning of the internal market and Article 153(2)(b) on working conditions.

A. The Proposal for a Directive: The Multiplicity of Legal Bases

Following the European Parliament's resolution on whistleblower protection, the European Commission proposed a Directive on reporting breaches of Union law on 23 April 2018. The European Commission did not present a horizontal legislative proposal, as the European Parliament had wished, but instead adopted a sectoral EU legislative act. The European Commission's rationale for this choice was the absence of a legal basis in the Treaties that specifically allows the EU to regulate whistleblowing. The Commission added that no initiative could have been taken based on the EU Charter of Fundamental Rights, as it cannot serve as a standalone legal basis.[20] Furthermore, although fraud and corruption are common violations of EU law that hamper the proper functioning of the internal market, they do not provide a self-standing legal basis in the Treaties that would have allowed the adoption of a horizontal EU legal act.

The Commission stated that a pan-sectoral EU legal act can be adopted on several legal bases set out in the Treaties. This pan-sectoral approach means the Directive covers certain areas of EU interest but not all. This pan-sectoral approach is justified by the limited competences the EU has, and, thus, a horizontal approach cannot be envisaged. The European Commission justified this statement as follows: these legal bases aim to strengthen whistleblowing as a means of enhancing the enforcement of EU law in specific fields, and they should be combined with other Treaty Articles that address other policy domains. Consequently, instead of a horizontal proposal that would cover every sector, it chose to propose an EU legal act that covers specific EU policy areas, primarily to protect the internal market and the EU's financial interests.

The European Commission's choice was rational and logical, as it could not exceed its competencies. The lack of a self-standing legal basis in the Treaties for an EU legal instrument on the protection of whistleblowers was an obstacle that could not be overlooked. In addition, whistleblowing involves sensitive sectors, such as political corruption or national security, which touch on issues of Member States' sovereignty, where the EU cannot intervene.

Finally, the proposal was based on the following Articles: 16, 33, 43, 50, 53(1), 62, 91, 100, 103, 109, 114, 168, 169, 192, 207, and 325 of the TFEU, as well as

[19] European Parliament Committee on Constitutional Affairs, Opinion on legitimate measures to protect whistle-blowers acting in the public interest when disclosing the confidential information of companies and public bodies [2017], para 6.

[20] The European Commission highlighted, though, that any legislative act on the protection of whistleblowers would have a positive impact on the right to freedom of expression.

Article 31 of the Euratom Treaty. The purpose of all these Articles is to ensure the proper functioning of the internal market and to implement Union policies effectively.[21] This is achieved by introducing new provisions on whistleblowers' protection, ensuring common minimum standards across Europe, and strengthening the existing EU sectoral provisions on whistleblowing.

Amendments were proposed during the legislative process to modify the Directive's scope of application. Articles 19 para 2, 77 para 2, 78, 79, 83 para 1, 153, 154, 157 and 352 TFEU were proposed for addition by the European Parliament.[22] Articles 77 para 2, 78, and 79 TFEU relate to the common immigration and asylum policy; Article 83 para 1 TFEU deals with criminal law policy; and Articles 153, 154, and 157 TFEU relate to social policy. Article 352 TFEU relates to the 'flexibility clause', which empowers the EU to adopt measures necessary to attain its objectives where the Treaty does not provide a specific legal basis.[23] The European Parliament extended the areas of EU interest to include areas beyond those proposed by the Commission.

It is interesting to note the debate surrounding Article 153 TFEU, as workers' rights are closely linked to whistleblowing. The European Economic and Social Committee requested that the Commission include the protection of workers' rights under Article 153 TFEU. This Article concerns employees' rights and is thus relevant to whistleblowers' protection. Despite proposals from the European Parliament and the European Economic and Social Committee to include it, the Commission had already discarded this option in its impact assessment for several reasons.[24]

First, the Article's personal scope would have been limited to employees, excluding all other categories of unprotected whistleblowers, such as self-employed persons or contractors, who are now protected under the Directive.[25] Nevertheless, it should be noted that the definition of 'worker' under Article 45 TFEU and the

[21] The policy areas that were basically covered by the Proposal are the following: the proper functioning of the single market, product safety, transport safety, environmental protection, nuclear safety, food and feed safety, animal health and welfare, public health, consumer protection, protection of privacy and personal data, security of network and information systems, competition, and the financial interests of the EU.

[22] European Parliament Committee on Legal Affairs, Report on the proposal for a Directive on the protection of persons reporting on breaches of Union law [2018] A8-0398/2018.

[23] M Kellerbauer and M Klamert, 'Article 352' in M Kellerbauer, M Klamert and J Tomkin (eds), *Commentary on the EU Treaties and the Charter of Fundamental Rights* (OUP, 2019) 2073.

[24] The European Commission had already discarded Article 50(2)(g) TFEU which aimed at enhancing the integrity of the private sector because of, inter alia, its limited scope of application (only the private sector).

[25] N Kountouris, 'The Concept of 'Worker' in European Labour Law: Fragmentation, Autonomy and Scope' [2017] *Industrial Law Journal* 1, 30, where Kountouris analyses the meaning of worker under EU law and case law stating: 'It is also increasingly apparent that the EU law making institutions and, withing their prerogatives, the European social partners, may have to interject in order to consolidate the acquis and, possibly, to redirect its development on the basis of more solid constitutional and policy foundations.' Although the European Commission insisted that the definition of worker, under Article 153 TFEU, would be limited, the case law of the CJEU demonstrates the extensive interpretation of worker. There is a pressing need to find a common definition of the term aligning EU law and case law.

case law of the CJEU is broad.[26] The concept of worker under Article 45 TFEU is autonomous, built upon the need to ensure the freedom of movement within the EU and to serve the internal market. The CJEU has interpreted the term 'worker' broadly, encompassing various types of work.[27] As a result, the Commission may have erred on this point, as the definition of worker under Article 45 TFEU is rather broad.

Second, the protection offered under Article 153 TFEU would have been limited. The protection would focus solely on the worker's safety and health, leaving aside other important forms of protection, such as financial market protection or transportation security. Moreover, requiring Member States to investigate a report properly exceeds the scope of safety and health at work. Ultimately, this Article would lead to more reports of work-related grievances than to the detection of Union law breaches, which is a key purpose of the Directive.[28]

While Article 153 TFEU was excluded as a legal basis, the Directive requires the European Commission to review expanding its scope to social rights (workers' rights) during the 2023 revision, with any amendments proposed by 2025.[29] Article 153 TFEU concerns social rights, ie, labour law, which remains largely a national competence, and the EU has somewhat restricted access to this area.[30] The use of this Article would not have been compatible with the legislative procedure, as well as its limited personal scope.

The European Commission was correct in excluding it, as whistleblowing is often confused with work-related grievances. Work-related problems do not constitute a breach of Union law and are not always indicative of wrongdoing; instead, they reflect behaviours that disturb the worker. Given the importance of reporting those behaviours, the Directive would not have been the right place to include them, due to the confusion they could have caused; however, a separate legal instrument may have been adopted to address Article 153 TFEU requirements.[31] The Directive

[26] M Kellerbauer and D Martin, 'Article 45' in M Kekkerbauer, M Klamert and J Tomkin (eds), *The EU Treaties and the Charter of Fundamental Rights – A Commentary* (OUP, 2019) 607–34.

[27] ACL Davies, A Bogg and C Costello, 'The Role of the Court of Justice in Labour Law' in A Bogg, C Castello and ACL Davies, *Research Handbook on EU Labour Law* (Edward Elgar, 2016) 114–21.

[28] It should be noted that reports of personal grievances might not be whistleblowing. See D Lewis, 'Is a Public Interest Test for Workplace Whistleblowing in Society's Interest?' (2014) 57(2) *International Journal of Law and Management* 141, 144.

[29] Such intention has not been communicated by the Commission yet and the reexamination of the Directive has been postponed for 2026. For more information ec.europa.eu/info/law/better-regulation/have-your-say/initiatives/14468-Whistleblower-Protection-Directive-evaluation_en accessed on 15 May 2025.

[30] P Syrpis, 'The EU and National Systems of Labour Law' in A Arnull and D Chalmers, *The Oxford Handbook of European Union Law* (OUP, 2015) 955.

[31] F Hendrickx, 'Completing Economic and Social Integration: Towards Labour Law for the United States of Europe' in N Countouris and M Freedland (eds), *Resocialising Europe in a Time of Crisis* (CUP, 2013) 75. In general, Hendrickx argues that 'A firm legal basis for fundamental (social) rights may remove some of the objections that have been raised in the fear that labour law is viewed as overly instrumental in a European context. Such a basis might impact on the discussion (and therefore also the Court's case law) surrounding the balance between social rights and market freedoms.'

would have inspired this legal instrument, focusing on workers' rights in the workplace and on how to report related grievances.[32]

B. Wisdom from the Legal Committees

After the proposal for a Directive was published, the European Parliament's Legal Committee and the Council's Legal Service provided their opinions on the legal bases.[33] The opinions of the European Parliament's Legal Committee are superficial, focusing only on procedural issues and offering no alternatives. On the contrary, the Legal Service of the Council provided a thoughtful analysis of alternative legal options but refused to publicly share its opinion, which was obtained only through official document requests. However, some parts of the opinion were missing, deemed as confidential.

Both Committees confirmed that the European Commission can use various legal bases under specific conditions. The proposal should pursue multiple interconnected objectives or components, with none being secondary or unrelated. In such cases, several legal bases can be employed. The second condition is that these several legal bases can be used *if they are indissociably linked, without one being secondary and indirect in relation to the others, but only if they entail incompatible decision-making procedures.* The CJEU has extensive case law on the legal bases. Several legal bases can be used, but it should be examined to what extent there are differences in terms of legislative procedures, the nature of the competence or the legal instruments. The issue of procedural differences is one that the Court has extensively scrutinised, and the Committees have also scrutinised in the proposal.

Procedural incompatibilities led to the exclusion of specific Articles. The European Parliament's Legal Committee, in its initial opinion, excluded several bases. For instance, Article 83(1) TFEU, related to criminal offences and sanctions, was rejected as a legal basis because its third paragraph contains an 'emergency brake' allowing one Member State to refer the file to the European Council and suspend the ordinary legislative process. In addition, Article 83, with Articles 77–79, can apply to Ireland if it opts in per Protocol No 21, and no measure applies to Denmark under Protocol No 22.[34] Though the aforementioned does not affect

[32] Syrpis (n 30) 957. The situation is rather pessimistic for Syrpis about the desire of the EU to protect social rights by legislating in the field due to the major focus being the internal market which actually contributes towards the dismantling of protective labour law.

[33] European Parliament, Committee on Legal Affairs, Opinion on the legal basis for the proposal for a directive on the protection of persons reporting on breaches of Union law (2018) JURI_AL (2018) 629554; European Parliament, Committee on Legal Affairs, Opinion on the legal basis for the proposal for a directive on the protection of persons reporting on breaches of Union law (2019) JURI_AL (2019) 637335.

[34] When the opinion was published, the United Kingdom (UK) was still an EU member but then left the EU. As a result, Protocol n° 21 only applies to Ireland.

the legislative process, it may cause the proposal to split in the Council. Therefore, these Articles could not be used as legal bases.[35]

The Council's Legal Service examined several proposed legal bases and presented its opinion. It followed the Legal Committee's reasoning, excluding legal bases for procedural reasons, but suggested splitting the proposal into separate legal acts. It identified four categories. The first category includes public procurement, financial services, anti-money laundering measures, product and transport safety, environmental protection, nuclear safety, food safety, animal health and welfare, public health, consumer protection, privacy and data security, and network security systems. The second category concerns provisions of primary law in the areas of competition law and state aid. The third category concerns the financial interests of the Union, as defined in Article 325 TFEU. The fourth and final category concerns breaches affecting the internal market, with a special focus on tax policy and law. The Council's Legal Service proposed a different solution: rather than keeping the proposal as it was, it suggested splitting it into separate legal acts.

First, the legal act resulting from the aforementioned first category should adopt measures to enhance the enforcement of Union law.[36] This act should target key areas like financial services and consumer protection, combining Article 114 TFEU with other legal bases to form a first Directive. Moving to competition law and state aid, the Legal Service said neither Article 114 TFEU nor other legal bases can be used. The reason is that Articles 103 and 109 TFEU are the correct legal bases for measures in that area, but they provide non-legislative procedures that cannot be combined with the ordinary legislative process. Concerning the EU's financial interests, it was argued that its basis, Article 325(4) TFEU, can be added to the other legal bases.

The Legal Service expressed the view that Article 114 TFEU cannot be used to pursue the enforcement of Union law related to the fight against corporate tax avoidance/evasion. It believed Articles 113 and/or 115 TFEU are the correct legal bases but require unanimity and European Parliament consultation, making them incompatible with the ordinary legislative process. As a result, the Legal Service proposed not to include this policy field. In summary, the Legal Service proposed maintaining the proposal on correct legal foundations and adopting various legal acts in nuclear safety, competition law, state aid, and corporate tax law.

The UK Parliament's Committee on European Scrutiny raised significant concerns about the use of numerous legal bases.[37] The Committee stated that it

[35] Articles 352, 154 and 19(2) TFEU were also excluded for similar reasons. For a detailed discussion on the issue of the legal basis on criminal law see D Kafteranis, 'From Obscurity to Limelight: The Whistle-blowers' Protection under EU Law' in V Mitsilegas and SJ Wortman (eds), *Whistleblowing, Transparency and Criminal Law: A Comparative Perspective* (Brill, 2021).

[36] The Legal Service proposed some minor changes mostly related to nuclear safety and the use of Art 31 of the Euroatom Treaty.

[37] Parliament of the United Kingdom, European Scrutiny Committee, Whistleblowing and Breaches of EU law (2019), point 1.9, publications.parliament.uk/pa/cm201719/cmselect/cmeuleg/301-lxx/30104.htm accessed 15 May 2025.

is unusual to see a Directive with so many legal bases spanning such a breadth of legal areas. The Committee on European Scrutiny emphasised that acts breaching corporate tax rules cannot be included in the Directive, as this should be under Article 115 TFEU, which needs unanimity and allows Member States to veto proposals to safeguard national sovereignty over tax policy. A minority of states agreed on this point but failed to amend the provision.[38]

C. The Final Decision on the Legal Bases

Reaching the final agreement, decisions had to be made. The co-legislative bodies decided to delete Articles 33 TFEU (linked to the strengthening of customs cooperation within the EU), 62 TFEU (that sets the procedure to adopt measures about services), 103 TFEU (related to competition matters) and 109 TFEU (related to the procedures for state aid) from the text of the Directive as well as Article 207 TFEU. The European Parliament's Committee on Legal Affairs confirmed the legal foundations of the Directive in a second opinion on the final legal bases.

These legal bases are: Articles 16 TFEU (protection of data), 43(2) TFEU (common agricultural and fisheries policy), 50 TFEU (freedom of establishment), 53(1) TFEU (self-employed persons and mutual recognition of academic and professional qualifications), 91 TFEU (transport safety), 100 TFEU (means of transport), 114 TFEU (internal market), 168(4) TFEU (health safety), 169 TFEU (consumer protection), 192(1) TFEU (energy), and 325(4) TFEU (protection of the EU's financial interests) and Article 31 of the Euroatom Treaty.

The focus of the Directive is on protecting the internal market and EU financial interests. Despite this, the final text completes the section on legal bases by adding the necessary articles for the specific areas of EU interest. Nevertheless, the European Parliament left open the possibility, during the 2023 review of the Directive, of extending its scope to other areas of interest, especially to improve the working environment and protect employees' health and safety. This means that Articles 153 and 157 TFEU may be added as legal bases; however, this has not yet occurred. The Directive stands on multiple thin ropes, which may prove to be a weakness.

D. Is the Whistleblower Stable? Remarks on the Choice of Legal Bases

Each Article used as a legal basis for the Directive represents a specific area of EU interest for which the EU has the power to legislate. A unique legal basis was not possible for this Directive. It ultimately had 12 Articles as legal bases, compared to

[38] The Opinion was prior to Brexit.

the 16 in the proposal. Already from the proposal, the fact that there were so many legal bases was a source of criticism from institutional actors. Worth mentioning is the reaction of the UK Parliament (before Brexit), which stated: 'it is very unusual to see a Directive which cites legal bases in so many numbers, and across such a breadth of EU legal areas'.[39] The Luxembourg Chamber of Employees (Chambre des salariés) highlighted that the Proposal refers to an unprecedented number of legal bases (*fait référence à un nombre sans précédent de bases juridiques*).[40] When, usually, the debate about the legal bases is about the use of a single or a dual legal basis, the use of 12 Articles is rather strange.

An EU legal act can be adopted on a dual legal basis. The analysis shows that the CJEU has case law on the matter, focusing on legislative procedure and the nature of the competence or legal instrument to determine if a dual legal basis can be used. At present, it is not the dual legal basis that poses questions, but the twelve legal bases used. As Tridimas observes, 'increasing the quantity of legal bases cannot improve their quality'.[41] The Directive could not have been based on Article 114 TFEU. It is worth recalling that Article 114 TFEU cannot be used to strengthen EU law enforcement because it cannot be directly linked to the internal market and is not applicable where more specific legal bases exist. It is peculiar that many see strengthening Union law enforcement and Article 114 TFEU as the cornerstone of this Directive. This fact implies that the other Articles are merely supplementary to strengthening Union law enforcement and, thus, protecting the internal market.

Article 114 TFEU aims to harmonise laws in a specific area and to improve the functioning of the internal market.[42] As a result, there is no specific area of law where it applies. When a measure may affect the internal market, Article 114 TFEU may apply. The use of this Article has been challenged numerous times before the CJEU, even when another, more specific legal basis was available. The relevance of all these to the Directive is that, for certain areas of EU interest, more specific Articles would have been used. For instance, as the Legal Service of the Council noted, rules on corporate tax covered by the Directive should have been adopted under Article 115, which is based on the special legislative procedure. Using both Articles 114 and 115 would not have been compatible, as they have different legislative procedures.

The CJEU has, to a certain extent, provided answers to these questions by developing the 'centre of gravity' theory or the *lex specialis derogate legi generali* principle. Given the absence of any case law, at least for the time being, on the Directive, we cannot speculate on the answers the Court might provide should

[39] Parliament of the United Kingdom (n 37) point 1.9.

[40] Chambre des Salariés, 'Protection des lanceurs d'alerte' (2018) www.csl.lu/bibliotheque/publications/268723fee5.pdf accessed 15 May 2025.

[41] T Tridimas, 'Terrorism and the ECJ: Empowerment and Democracy in the EC Legal Order' (2009) 34(1) *European Law Review* 103, 110.

[42] Case C-376/98, *Federal Republic of Germany v European Parliament and Council of the European Union* (Tobacco Advertising), ECLI:EU:C:2000:544.

such questions arise before it. Nevertheless, the discussion can focus on the democratic concerns these choices raise at the EU and national levels. The quest for the Articles that are under the same legislative procedure leaves aside other Articles with a different and, maybe, 'tougher' legislative procedure. In the example of tax-related whistleblowing, by not utilising Article 115 TFEU, Member States have less power, as they lose the special legislative procedure and the associated rights. Concurrently, this means the European Parliament will have greater powers and serve as a co-legislator on the issue. This situation mirrors the general trend toward a qualified majority over unanimity. The same applies to Article 83 TFEU, which was not selected as a legal basis because of its emergency break procedure and the particular status of Ireland and Denmark.[43]

The problem posed in this scenario is which legislative procedure should have priority and to what extent national or European legislators will be better equipped to resolve the issue. For instance, if Article 115 TFEU were to be used, a different legislative procedure (requiring unanimity) would have been required, and this situation would have been more time-consuming. Politics in the internal market concern how quickly the legislative procedure can be carried out.[44] This whole process and the final choices reveal the technocratic character of the EU, raising democratic issues. The emphasis is on economic interests, leaving aside the societal or democratic issues that arise. The issue of whistleblowing is not only a legal concern, but it also relates to society and culture. Regulating it at the EU level under these circumstances may give the impression to citizens and states that their views were not taken into account in the process. The EU's focus is on protecting the internal market rather than protecting whistleblowers, taking into account national ideas, opinions, and specificities on this delicate issue.

The refusal to rely on Article 153 TFEU as a legal basis also mirrors the Directive's focus on market protection. The protection of whistleblowers is a secondary issue, as the primary concern is ensuring the market's well-functioning. One may argue that, although the focus is on protecting the market, the whistleblower is adequately protected under the Directive. This statement is correct, but we object that, symbolically,[45] the concern should have been about whistleblowers and their rights, not the market. In addition, and apart from the symbolism, there may be repercussions shortly regarding the rationale of the Directive if a case comes

[43] JW Ouwerkerk, 'Criminalization Powers of the European Union and the Risks of Cherry-Picking between Various Legal Bases: The Case for a Single Legal Framework for EU-Level Criminalization' (2017) 23 *Columbia Journal of European Law* 503, 542–43. Ireland has a flexible opt-out from legislation adopted in the AFSJ whereas Denmark has a stricter opt-out from AFSJ.

[44] G Davies, 'Democracy and Legitimacy in the Shadow of Purposive Competence' (2015) 21(1) *European Law Journal* 2, 14.

[45] The preference for Art 114 TFEU over Art 153 demonstrates an emphasis to the economic implications of whistleblowing rather than the acceptance of EU legislation and institutions by the citizens. For this reason, it would be an important symbolism to adopt legislation under Art 153 TFEU for the EU to demonstrate a more social approach.

before the CJEU. Under a teleological interpretation, a possible dispute between an employer and a whistleblower before the CJEU may end in the employer's favour.

As Weatherill notices, 'Any argument that the Court is not locked into a congenital tendency to prioritise economic rights over social and political rights must reckon with the abominable December 2017 rulings of the Grand Chamber of the Court of Justice in *Viking Line* and *Laval*.'[46] It remains to be seen whether a case arises, what the CJEU would highlight, and, of course, the amendments that the European Commission will propose in 2026 and whether these amendments will rely on Article 153 TFEU as a legal basis.

E. When It All Goes Wrong: Criminal Law

When the proposal for the Directive was presented, the European Commission did not include any criminal law-related legal basis. Although the Commission's impact assessment mentioned combatting criminal offences such as corruption and fraud through whistleblowing, it did not refer to the Treaties' criminal law bases. The use of criminal law bases would have been expected, as the Directive aims to detect crimes through whistleblowing and to protect whistleblowers from criminal liability. The first (and only) consideration of Article 83 TFEU was made by the European Parliament's Committee on Legal Affairs in its opinion on the legal basis for the proposal. The Committee on Legal Affairs mentioned that five amendments were tabled, which, among *other things*, suggested the use of Article 83 TFEU as a possible legal basis.[47]

Following the adoption of the Lisbon Treaty, the EU's criminal law competence was consolidated by the withdrawal of the third pillar.[48] Article 83 TFEU became the legal basis for the approximation of substantive criminal law. Nonetheless, the exact limits of this competence are still a matter of debate.[49] Under Article 83, paragraph 1, minimum rules can be adopted by means of a Directive in accordance with the ordinary legislative procedure, concerning the definition of criminal offences and sanctions in the areas of particularly serious crimes with a cross-border dimension resulting from the nature or impact of such offences or from a special need to combat them on an everyday basis.[50] This approximation, under Article 83(1), may take place to enable the effective implementation

[46] S Weatherill, *The Internal Market as a Legal Concept* (OUP, 2017) 125.

[47] The amendments mentioned by the Committee were not found until now. It may be the case that there were internal documents for which there is no public access.

[48] V Mitsilegas, *EU Criminal Law* (Hart Publishing, 2009) 107.

[49] V Mitsilegas, *EU Criminal Law After Lisbon. Rights, Trust and the Transformation of Justice in Europe* (Hart Publishing, 2016) 4–5, 19–21, 53–68.

[50] These offences are listed as such: terrorism, trafficking in human beings and sexual exploitation of women and children, illicit drug trafficking, illicit arms trafficking, money laundering, corruption, counterfeiting of means of payment, computer crime and organised crime. There is the possibility to add others in the list by unanimous decision of the Council and the consent of the European Parliament.

of certain Union policies.[51] The other component, Article 83 paragraph 2, aims to approximate criminal law when it '(…) proves essential to ensure the effective implementation of a Union policy in an area which has been subject to harmonisation measures'.

The lack of effective enforcement and implementation of Union rules at the national level has led to the adoption of the Directive, which aims to enhance the proper application of Union law in specific areas. [52] The whistleblower must report wrongdoing of a criminal, civil, or administrative nature. Therefore, the whistleblower is a crime-fighting measure adopted to combat crime, among *other purposes*. Apart from its crime-fighting purpose, the Directive aims to protect whistleblowers from criminal liability, and Member States should adopt criminal sanctions for anyone who retaliates against them. All these could justify the use of Article 83 TFEU as a legal basis.

Nevertheless, the Directive could not rely on Article 83(1) for the following reasons. First, Article 83(1) defines particularly serious crimes with a cross-border dimension and their associated sanctions. Although the Directive refers to desirable criminal sanctions for persons who retaliate against whistleblowers, it does not establish minimum rules for defining sanctions in areas of severe crimes with a cross-border dimension. Furthermore, the Directive does not define any criminal offence with a cross-border dimension. It only defines whistleblowing as a tool for detecting cross-border crimes. Therefore, the use of Article 83(1) TFEU would not have been possible for this Directive.

On the contrary, Article 83(2) could have served as a legal basis for the Directive, given its wording and purpose. The adoption of the Directive clearly aims to harmonise this specific area under EU law. The purpose of Article 83(2) is to approximate criminal law when it '(…) proves essential to ensure the effective implementation of a Union policy in an area which has been subject to harmonisation measures'. The Directive aims to harmonise criminal law across Member States to protect whistleblowers as an effective enforcement tool. This enforcement tool will not only report civil or administrative wrongdoings but also criminal offences. They will be a valuable asset for the investigation, detection, and prosecution of serious crimes. To achieve this, the Directive was based on the premise that whistleblowers would not be criminally liable for charges arising from their reporting.

The criminal immunity of the whistleblower under the Directive is seen as a means to approximate criminal law in areas where harmonised measures have been adopted. However, for several reasons, the use of Article 83(2) TFEU is problematic. The case law of the CJEU has demonstrated a certain reluctance on the Court's part to rely on Article 83(2) as a legal basis for criminal law issues.[53]

[51] K Ambros, *European Criminal Law* (CUP, 2018) 319.

[52] D Kafteranis, 'A New Enforcement tool: A Directive to Protect Whistle-blowers' (2020) 41 *Business Law Review* 50.

[53] J Oberg, 'The Legal Basis for EU Criminal Law Harmonisation: A Question of Federalism?' (2018) 43(3) *European Law Review* 366, 367.

The Court has decided that other legal bases, rather than Article 83(2), should be considered as more relevant. A notable case to consider is *Ireland v Parliament and Council*, a pre-Lisbon judgment, in which Ireland challenged the legal basis of the Data Retention Directive.[54] Ireland argued that the Directive should have been adopted under the pre-Lisbon legal basis on criminal law, as it is a crime-fighting measure, not under what is now Article 114 TFEU. The Court rejected Ireland's argument, finding that the Directive was predominantly related to the functioning of the internal market rather than the prosecution and investigation of crime.[55]

The Court followed the same path in other pre-Lisbon cases, such as *Ship Pollution* and *Environmental Crimes*.[56] In these judgments, the Court stated that the legal bases of Articles 100(2) TFEU (transport policy) and 192 TFEU (environmental policy) had priority over the criminal law provisions of the third pillar. In its reasoning, the Court carefully considered the main purpose of the legal instrument. For instance, in *Commission v Council*, the Court stated that, by analysing the aim and the content of the framework decision, the main purpose is the protection of the environment; thus, the legal basis of Article 175 EC. This approach should be considered in light of the strong preference for the Community pillar over the three-pillar structure.[57] Nonetheless, the Court did not change its approach even after the Lisbon Treaty and the 'communitarisation' of criminal law. In conflicts between legal bases inside and outside the Area of Freedom, Security and Justice (AFSJ), the Court uses its 'main aim' doctrine. If a measure primarily benefits a non-AFJS legal basis, that basis takes priority over an AFJS basis. The Court insisted that this should apply even though complementary elements to criminal law might exist.[58]

Among the legal bases of the Directive, the 'central' legal basis is Article 114 TFEU, because the protection of whistleblowers aims to enhance the integrity of the internal market. In addition, Article 325(4) TFEU plays a central role in the adoption of the Directive, as whistleblowers will assist the EU in its fight against fraud affecting its financial interests. Both these legal bases are considered as

[54] Case C-301/06 *Ireland v Parliament and Council* [2009] ECR I-00593. The Directive 2006/24/EC of the European Parliament and of the Council of 15 March 2006 on the retention of data generated or processed in connection with the provision of publicly available electronic communications services or of public communications networks and amending Directive 2002/58/EC [2006] OJ L105/54.

[55] Oberg (n 53) 374. It should be noted, though, that in the *Digital Rights* judgment, the Court underlined that the main objective of the Data Retention Directive was to ensure that data is available for the purpose of the investigation, detection and prosecution of serious crime and that ultimately it is a measure aimed at enhancing public security. See Case C-293/12 *Digital Rights Ireland and Seitlinger and Others* [2014] ECLI:EU:C:2014:238, paras 41–43.

[56] Case C-176/03 *Commission v Council (environmental sanctions)* [2005] ECR I-07879, paras 38–53 and Case C-440/05 *Commission v Council (Ship-Source Pollution)* ECLI:EU:C:2007:625, paras 52–74.

[57] E Herlin-Karnell, 'Annotation, Case Comment Case C-301/06, Ireland v. Parliament and Council' (2009) 46 *Common Market Law Review* 1667.

[58] Case C-137/12 *Commission v Council* ECLI:EU:C:2013:675, paras 70–72.

alternatives to the use of Article 83(2) TFEU.[59] Article 114 TFEU is regarded as a legitimate legal basis for EU criminalisation measures.[60]

First, the application of Article 114 TFEU ensures the uniform implementation of specific EU policies. It avoids any 'Delaware effects', where a state seeks to create favourable conditions for corporations and offers low regulatory standards.[61] The EU needs common minimum standards that are uniform across Member States, and this can be ensured through Article 114 TFEU. Although its main purpose is the protection of the internal market, it has been widely used as a key tool to promote EU integration, particularly in sensitive areas of national policy. It is not limited to the internal market; it also has broader regulatory powers granted by the EU institutions.[62]

The use of Article 83(2) TFEU might be problematic, as it has a limited scope, and some countries have a particular status when adopting measures under it.[63] Moreover, the other legal basis favoured as a core basis for the Directive was Article 325(4) TFEU. The use of Article 325(4) TFEU, rather than Article 83(2) TFEU, seems a more convenient option due to its benefits. First, Article 325(4) TFEU is not bound by the strict conditions of Article 83(2) TFEU to serve as a legal basis. The use of Article 83(2) TFEU is possible when criminal law is essential, and there are previous harmonisation measures in place.[64] This is not the case for Article 325(4) TFEU, where the Union has a broad competence to enact any criminal or non-criminal measures against illegal activities affecting the EU's financial interests. The Whistleblower Directive, besides its role to protect the integrity of the internal market, also aims to protect the EU's financial interests. As a result, the use of Article 325(4) TFEU seemed a more convenient choice.

The need to protect the internal market and the EU's financial interests justifies the adoption of the Directive, primarily under Articles 114 and 325(4) of the TFEU. The other legal foundations used complement the main goals and cover the sectors in which whistleblowing is promoted. It would also have been desirable

[59] P Whelan, 'Contemplating the Future: Personal Criminal Sanctions for Infringement of EC Competition Law' (2008) 19 *King's Law Journal* 364, 369. M Zuleeg, 'Criminal Sanctions to be Imposed on Individuals as Enforcement Instruments in European Competition Law' in CD Ehlermann and I Atanasiu (eds), *European Competition Law Annual 2001: Effective Private Enforcement of EC Antitrust Law* (Hart Publishing, 2003) 456–57.

[60] European Commission, 'Amended proposal for a Directive of the European Parliament and of the Council on criminal measures aimed at ensuring the enforcement of intellectual property rights', COM (2006) 168 final.

[61] WL Cary, 'Federalism and Corporate Law: Reflections upon Delaware' (1974) 83 *Yale Law Journal* 663, 663–68.

[62] D Wyatt, 'Community Competence to Regulate the Internal Market' in Michael Dougan and Samantha Currie (eds), *50 Year of the European Treaties: Looking Back and Thinking Forward* (Hart Publishing, 2009) 135–36.

[63] E Herlin-Karnell, 'The Fight against White-Collar Crime as European Financial Crisis Rescuer: Regulatory Challenges and the Tough on Crime Approach' in L Hinojosa and JM Beneyto (eds), *European Banking Union: The New Regime* (Kluwer Law International, 2015) 37.

[64] J Öberg, 'Union Regulatory Criminal Law Competence after Lisbon Treaty' (2011) 19 *European Journal of Crime, Criminal Law and Criminal Justice* 289, 313–17.

to utilise Article 83(2) TFEU to emphasise the criminal law character.[65] Criminal law should have been considered an effective instrument for implementing Union policies, a means to an end. It would have protected legal and Union interests by avoiding adverse effects on the internal market. In addition, the Directive is not only designed to combat crimes through whistleblowing, but also to protect whistleblowers by granting them immunity from criminal prosecution. This protection is not related to the special part of criminal law, but to the general part.

The EU criminal law legal bases do not explicitly confer competence to set out norms affecting the general part of criminal law at the national level.[66] The competence of the EU is to criminalise, ie, to define criminal offences and to adopt criminal sanctions.[67] This need to criminalise can be justified on the grounds of addressing security threats (securitised criminalisation) and the necessity of using criminal law to ensure the effectiveness of EU law (functional criminalisation). Under Article 83 TFEU, the EU has a specific competence: to establish, by means of Directives, minimum rules concerning the definition of criminal offences and sanctions in the areas of particularly serious crimes with a cross-border dimension. The list of criminal offences is set out in Article 83(1) TFEU. Article 83(2) TFEU attributes to the EU the competence to approximate national criminal laws and regulations when such approximation is essential for ensuring the effective implementation of an EU policy in an area where harmonisation has already occurred. Article 83 TFEU addresses the specific aspect of criminal law, excluding the general part. Although the EU has the competence to approximate minimum rules, this does not encompass the structures and definitions of the general part.

The CJEU has already defined certain concepts of the general part of criminal law and has elaborated new concepts for which the Treaties do not provide specific legislative competence.[68] In the *Intertanko* judgment, the Court interpreted the concept of 'serious negligence',[69] taking into consideration the different legal systems to define the concept. Nonetheless, it is not certain that such competence exists for the EU legislator. Criminal law touches upon the constitutional and criminal law traditions of Member States, which means that the general part of criminal law cannot be created indirectly by the Court when such explicit competence does not exist for the Union legislator.[70] As there is a lack of Union

[65] E Herlin-Karnell, *The Constitutional Dimension of European Criminal Law* (Bloomsbury Publishing, 2012) 52; JAE Vervaele, 'European Criminal Justice in the European and Global Context' (2019) 10(1) *New Journal of European Criminal Law* 7, 15. Both authors elaborate on the criminal enforcement debate under EU law.

[66] A Klip, *European Criminal Law. An Integrative Approach*, 3rd edn (CUP, 2016) 196.

[67] V Mitsilegas, 'EU Criminal Law Competence after Lisbon: From Securitised to Functional Criminalisation' in DA Arcarazo and CC Murphy (eds), *EU Security and Justice Law* (Hart Publishing, 2014) 110.

[68] U lõhmus, 'European Criminal Law: Can a General Part be Developed through Case Law?' in A Klip (ed), *Substantive Criminal Law of the European Union* (Maklu, 2011) 199.

[69] Case C-308/06 *Intertanko and Others* [2008] ECR I-04057.

[70] P Faraguna, 'Taking Constitutional Identities Away from the Courts' (2016) 41 *Brooklyn Journal of International Law* 492.

competence for the harmonisation of the general part of criminal law, it is peculiar that in the Whistleblower Directive, criminal immunity rules are adopted without any reference to the EU criminal law basis.

An alternative to using a criminal law basis for measures under the general part of criminal law would be Article 67 TFEU. It paints a picture of crime prevention at the Union level, as it provides for a more general Union competence in this area. This Article could have been used, as its design seems closer to the general part of criminal law. Unfortunately, Article 67 TFEU was never considered by the EU legislator for the Directive, and the analysis above is merely a thought on how the problem of a criminal-law basis might have been resolved. In summary, the Directive lacks a criminal law basis, and the Committee on Legal Affairs of the European Parliament's refusal to invoke Article 83(2) TFEU was based solely on procedural grounds.

In its first opinion, the Committee argued that the use of Article 83(2) TFEU is not possible because it is not procedurally compatible with the other legal bases. Measures under other legal bases, such as Article 114 TFEU, can be adopted by the ordinary legislative procedure. Although paragraphs two and three of Article 83 TFEU provide for the ordinary legislative procedure, it is paragraph three that creates the procedural incompatibility. The reason is the 'emergency brake', under which Member States may suspend the procedure and refer the file to the European Council.

Consequently, this provision creates a procedural obstacle because of its uniqueness, as no other provision has an 'emergency break'. Additionally, a problematic aspect of Article 83(2) TFEU is the opt-out arrangements enjoyed by certain Member States. Measures adopted under the criminal law basis do not apply to Denmark (Protocol No 22), and they will apply to Ireland only if it opts in (Protocol No 21).[71] This event is not problematic in relation to the legislative procedure, but rather due to the possible split within the Council. Member States will be divided into groups, which may complicate negotiations.

The procedural incompatibility was the only reason why Article 83(2) TFEU was not used as a legal basis for the Directive. In light of CJEU case law, the use of Article 83(2) TFEU in conjunction with other legal bases would have been refused as procedurally incompatible. On the contrary, it would have been optimal to design a separate EU legal act for the criminal law elements of whistleblower protection. Indeed, such an act would have divided the Member States and compromised the protection of whistleblowers. Still, it would have allowed Member States to negotiate the criminal law aspects of a measure that affects the fundamental elements of their criminal justice systems correctly. In addition, this choice would have favoured Member States' sovereignty, as it would have adopted a more restrictive approach, which is necessary when the EU interferes with criminal law.[72]

[71] The same would have been the case for the UK prior to Brexit.

[72] Judgment of German Federal Constitutional Court of 30 June 2009, *Lisbon Judgment*, Case 2 BvE 2/08, 5/08, 2 BvR 1010/08, 1022/08, 1259/08, 182/09 (2009) paras 226, 231, 237–42.

The procedural incompatibility with the other legal bases of the Directive has excluded the criminal law legal basis. Although this is a reasonable decision, it leaves unanswered the questions addressed above. The procedural obstacles serve as a shield to a deeper theoretical discussion of the EU's competences. The Luxembourg Court has a Union-friendly policy in criminal law, which remains national-centred. The question is whether we can continue with the negative integration as the Court has done, or should the EU change its policy and structure? It is not an easy task to provide an answer to that question. However, these 'competence cocktails', where different types of competences fall within one policy area, may have dramatic consequences for legal basis litigation.

5

Shaping The Concept of Blowing the Whistle: Definition

I. Unveiling: Who is the Person Behind the Whistleblower?

Legal protection for whistleblowers requires a clear understanding of their identities and traits. This is challenging, with varied legal definitions and no consensus in academic literature on the best one.[1] A consensus was reached on defining a whistleblower, as given by Miceli and Near (1985). It reads as follows: whistleblowing is 'the disclosure by organisation members (former or current) of the illegal, immoral or illegitimate practices under the control of their employers to persons or organisations that may be able to effect action'.[2] The definition emphasises whistleblowing but omits motives or other aspects.[3]

Researchers in the field of whistleblowing widely accept the definition above.[4] However, this definition has been criticised as narrow, leading some academics to prefer broader ones.[5] Others define a whistleblower narrowly, stating it is not just

[1] R Haigh and P Bowal, 'Whistleblowing and Freedom of Conscience: Towards a New Legal Analysis' (2012) *Comparative Research in Law & Political Economy*, Research Paper No. 1974982, 6–12.

[2] JP Miceli and MP Near, 'Organizational Dissidence: The Case of Whistle-Blowing' (1985) 4 *Journal of Business Ethics* 1, 4. Reasons for adopting this definition are discussed by R Smith, 'The Role of Whistle-Blowing in Governing Well: Evidence from the Australian Public Sector' (2010) 50(6) *American Review of Public Administration* 704, 708, and include maintaining consistency with how whistleblowing has been defined by governments (including its definition within legislation), maintaining consistency with other academic work, and using a definition 'that allows for a wide range of propositions about whistle-blowing to be tested'.

[3] G Ferguson, *Global Corruption – Law, Theory and Practice*, 3rd edn, vol 1 (UVIC Press, 2008) 1009.

[4] ibid.

[5] D Banisar, 'Whistleblowing: International Standards and Developments' in IE Sandoval (ed), *Contemporary Debates on Corruption and Transparency: Rethinking State, Market, and Society* (World Bank, Institute for Social Research, UNAM, 2011) 4, where the following definition is given: 'whistleblowing as a means to promote accountability by allowing for the disclosure by any person of information about misconduct while at the same time protecting the person against sanctions of all forms'. See M Skivenes and SC Trygstad, 'When Whistle-Blowing Works: The Norwegian Case' (2010) 63(7) *Human Relations* 1071, 1077, where the definition of Miceli and Near is criticised. See also B Fasterling, 'Whistleblower Protection: A Comparative Law Perspective' in AJ Brown et al (eds), *International Handbook on Whistleblowing Research* (Edward Elgar, 2014) 334.

about informing but also involves a person or organisation accused and challenged by the process.[6] These definitions are debated in academia, which helps researchers identify whistleblowers. A key point is the distinction between whistleblowers and others who are often considered whistleblowers.[7]

Whistleblowers are employees or members of an organisation who disclose illegal or unethical wrongdoing, expecting a solution. They differ from others in literature based on these characteristics.[8] The others, not whistleblowers or 'bell-ringers', are individuals unaffiliated with organisations who report issues, hoping for solutions.[9] Journalists cannot be considered whistleblowers because their role is to disseminate information from whistleblowers.[10] They have not discovered the wrongdoing themselves, but the whistleblower provides the information. This shows that the whistleblower should have a work-related relationship and encounter the wrongdoing during that relationship.[11]

Legal science approaches the definition differently, with no consensus on what constitutes a whistleblower. Characteristics vary based on a country's legal, political, social, and economic context.[12] This divergence in legal literature is expected to be remedied in the EU with the Directive on reporting breaches of Union law. This chapter analyses the whistleblower definition and its innovative aspects. The Directive's broad definition aligns with international best practices on whistleblower protection.[13] However, some aspects of the definition, such as the concepts

[6] PB Jubb, 'Whistleblowing: A Restrictive Definition and Interpretation' (1999) 21 *Journal of Business Ethics* 77, 79. S Bok, 'Whistle-Blowing and Professional Responsibilities' in JC Callahan (ed), *Ethical Issues in Professional Life* (OUP, 1998) 321.

[7] MP Miceli, S Dreyfus and JP Near, 'Outsiders 'Whistle-blowers': Conceptualising and Distinguishing 'Bell-Ringing' Behaviour' in AJ Brown et al (eds), *International Handbook on Whistleblowing Research* (Edward Elgar, 2014) 71. See also European Commission Staff Working Document, Impact Assessment accompanying the document of the proposal for a Directive of the European Parliament and of the Council on the protection of persons reporting on breaches of Union law [2018] COM(2018) 218 final, 7–8.

[8] Miceli, Dreyfus and Near (n 7) 71.

[9] ibid 72–73.

[10] ibid 74. Recital 46 of the Directive states that whistleblowers are important sources for investigative journalists. By protecting the whistleblower, we are also safeguarding the role of investigative journalists as 'watchdogs'. In that sense, the journalist is not a whistleblower, but they are considered an important source of information.

[11] In Recital 30 of the Directive, it is highlighted that the Directive is not applied to persons who, having given their informed consent, have been identified as informants or registered as such. The Directive is clear on the need for a work-based relationship.

[12] Ferguson (n 3) 1010.

[13] The international best practices have various sources and try to extract the good elements for a whistleblower law. Amongst others, see United Nations Office on Drugs and Crime, 'The United Nations Convention against Corruption: Resource Guide on Good Practices in the Protection of Reporting Persons' (August 2015), www.unodc.org/documents/corruption/Publications/2015/15-04741_Person_Guide_eBook.pdf accessed 15 May 2025; See also Transparency International, 'Recommended Draft Principles for Whistleblowing Legislation' (2009), www.transparency.org/files/content/activity/2009_PrinciplesForWhistleblowingLegislation_EN.pdf accessed 15 May 2025; T Devine and S Walden, 'International Best Practices for Whistleblower Policies' (2013) *Whistleblower*, www.whistleblower.org/sites/default/files/pictures/Best_Practices_Document_for_website_March_13_2013.pdf accessed 15 May 2025; *CleanGovBiz*, 'Whistleblower Protection: Encouraging Reporting' (July 2012), www.oecd.org/cleangovbiz/toolkit/50042935.pdf accessed 15 May 2025.

of a self-standing criminal offence and reasonable grounds, may pose problems for future whistleblowers due to their ambiguity.

A. The Definition of the Whistleblower

Before the Directive, Member States lacked a standard definition of whistleblowing, and there was no international consensus on what constitutes a whistleblower.[14] The European Commission highlighted this fact when presenting the proposal for a Directive.[15] Depending on the country, definitions of a whistleblower vary. Examples will illustrate these differences, showing that the Directive now establishes common minimum standards, promoting uniformity in who qualifies as a whistleblower.[16] Despite minimum standards, defining whistleblowers remains challenging after transposition. Several Member States have not correctly transposed the Directive, and specific definitional issues persist.[17]

An example of a legal whistleblower definition is France's Law Sapin II, recently amended by Law No 2022-401 of 21 March 2022, which transposes the Directive.[18] Article 6 defines a whistleblower as a person who, in good faith and without financial interest, reports a crime, a misdemeanour, a treaty violation, a legal breach, or a public-interest threat.[19] Despite the transposition of the Directive, France's legal definition of whistleblowers still requires good faith, which will be analysed below.[20] The definition excludes legal entities.[21]

Irish legislation on whistleblower protection aligns more closely with the Directive.[22] The term 'worker' is broad and encompasses employees, contractors, trainees, and agency workers. Irish legislation removes the good-faith requirement,

[14] European Commission, Impact Assessment (n 7) 6.

[15] ibid 6.

[16] G Georgiadou, 'The European Commission's Proposal for Strengthening Whistleblower Protection' (2018) 3 *European Criminal Law Forum* 167.

[17] European Commission, 'Report from the Commission to the European Parliament and the Council on the implementation and application of Directive (EU) 2019/1937 on the protection of persons who report breaches of Union law' COM(2024) 269 final, 3 July 2024.

[18] Law n° 2016-1691 of 6 December 2016 related to transparency, the fight against corruption and the modernisation of economic life, JORF n°0287, Art 6. Law n° 2022-401 of 21 March 2022 aiming to improve the protection of whistleblowers, JORF n° 0068.

[19] The translation was made by the author. The original text in French is the following: '*Un lanceur d'alerte est une personne physique qui signale ou divulgue, sans contrepartie financière directe et de bonne foi, des informations portant sur un crime, un délit, une menace ou un préjudice pour l'intérêt général, une violation ou une tentative de dissimulation d'une violation d'un engagement international régulièrement ratifié ou approuvé par la France, d'un acte unilatéral d'une organisation internationale pris sur le fondement d'un tel engagement, du droit de l'Union européenne, de la loi ou du règlement*'.

[20] V Magner and Y Paclot, 'Un nouveau champ de protection pour les lanceurs d'alerte' (2019) 4 *RAE-LAE* 699, 701.

[21] E Daoud and S Sfoggia, 'Lanceurs d'alerte et enterprises: les enjeux de la loi Sapin II' (2017) *AJ Pénal Dalloz* 71, 72; See also F Chaltiel Terral, *Les lanceurs d'alerte* (Dalloz éd., 2018) 70–71.

[22] Protected Disclosures Act 2014, No 14 of 2014, ss 1–3; See also J Hyde, 'The Protected Disclosures Act 2014: An Overview' (2014) 11 *Irish Employment Law Journal* 2. For a profound analysis: A Kerr and L Kierans, *Protected Disclosures Act 2014*, 2nd edn (Round Hall Press, 2024).

requiring only that the worker reasonably believe the information is correct. It emphasises the substance over the motives of the whistleblower.[23] Despite the abolition of the good faith requirement, a 'bad faith' whistleblower lacks the same protection as a 'good faith' one. The Protected Disclosures Act of 2014 offers less protection to informants acting in 'bad faith,' where their motivation was beyond investigating the wrongdoing.[24]

From the French and Irish examples, it is clear that the whistleblower definition varies across countries despite the Directive. In France, whistleblowers must report in good faith, while in Ireland, they only need reasonable grounds to believe the information is accurate. This inconsistency causes confusion, especially in cross-border cases, due to the lack of a uniform definition.[25] If a whistleblower can choose where to report – such as Ireland or France – they may opt for Ireland, where protections are less strict. This example shows that French law may not effectively use whistleblowers as an enforcement tool, potentially leading to forum shopping cases.

The adoption of the Directive and its definition of a whistleblower should have brought the much-needed homogeneity about the features of whistleblowers.[26] Having common minimum standards for defining a whistleblower would reduce insecurity and complexity, as was the case before.[27] The EU drew inspiration from the Council of Europe and the European Court of Human Rights case law on whistleblower protection to draft its definition, which will be analysed in the following sections.[28]

B. Natural Person

Starting with the definition from Article 4 of the Directive, the reporting individual must be employed in the public or private sector and should have obtained relevant information through their work environment.[29] This person reports and prevents breaches of the law, safeguarding society.[30] First, the term 'reporting person' under the Directive refers to a natural person who reports or makes a public disclosure of breaches acquired in a work-related context.[31]

[23] Protected Disclosures Act 2014, No 14 of 2014, s 5(7).

[24] ibid s 11(1)(e).

[25] European Commission, Impact Assessment (n 7) 28.

[26] V Abazi, 'The European Union Whistleblower Directive: A Game Changer for Whistleblowing Protection?' [2020] *Industrial Law Journal* 1, 17.

[27] European Parliament and European Council Directive 2019/1937/EU of 23 October 2019 on the protection of persons who report breaches of Union law [2019] OJ L305/17, Recital 5.

[28] European Commission, Impact Assessment (n 7) 6.

[29] Directive 2019/1937 (n 27) Art 4(1) and Recital 1.

[30] ibid Recital 1.

[31] ibid Art 5(7).

The reporting person is a natural one, so legal persons are excluded from whistleblowing.[32] Under French Law Sapin II, as amended by Law No 2022-401, whistleblowing is limited to individuals, excluding legal entities such as associations or organisations in the public interest.[33] The French Senate has, since 2016, preferred to protect only natural persons, not legal persons. Their Rapporteur had stated that 'the whistleblower is, above all, an important stimulus, a responsible citizen and consequently a physical person'.[34]

Allowing legal persons to blow the whistle would have been ideal for organisations in this field, but the problem would be that they are not in a work-based relation *stricto sensu*.[35] Additionally, it is essential to permit one institution to report a breach by another during cooperation; however, more detailed procedures are necessary.[36] Currently, the Directive excludes legal persons, but Member States can extend the personal scope to include them.[37]

C. Public, Private Sector and EU Officials

The reporting person should work in either the public or private sector.[38] The Directive ends the debate on protecting whistleblowers in public and private sectors in

[32] Under the European Commission's leniency programme, legal persons (undertakings) can report competition breaches, even though they may be involved in the offence, unlike whistleblowers. Notably, while legal persons can report cartels, they are excluded from whistleblower protections. The Commission also allows anonymous reporting in competition law, despite the Whistleblowers Directive lacking such provisions. See European Commission Notice on Immunity from fines and reduction of fines in the cartel cases (2006/C 298/11). See also O Odudu and D Bailey, 'The Single Economic Entity Doctrine in EU Competition Law' (2014) 51 *Common Market Law Review* 1721 and European Commission, Anonymous Whistleblower Tool, ec.europa.eu/competition/cartels/whistleblower/index.html accessed 15 May 2025.

[33] Daoud and Sfoggia (n 21) 72.

[34] F Pillet, 'Rapport rélatif à la transparence, à la lutte contre la corruption et à la modernisation de la vie économique pour le Sénat', 22 June 2016, 47, www.senat.fr/rap/l15-712-1/l15-712-11.pdf accessed 15 May 2025.

[35] In these cases, the legal person can seek protection as a 'watchdog' as long as it exercises a fundamental freedom, freedom of expression, under the case law of the European Court of Human Rights. See *Animal Defenders International v UK* App no 48876/08 (ECtHR, 27 May 2004) para 103; and *Vides Aizsardzības Klubs c Lettonie* App no 57829/00 (ECtHR, 27 May 2004) para 42.

[36] Inspiration could be drawn from the Leniency Program already in place for the detection of secret cartels, where an involved corporation can report to the European Commission about the other participating corporations to the secret cartel. See J Malinauskaite, *Harmonisation of EU Competition Law Enforcement* (Springer, 2020) 124–25.

[37] Council of Europe, Parliamentary Assembly, Committee on Legal Affairs and Human Rights, 'Improving the Protection of Whistleblowers all over Europe' (2019) 2, website-pace.net/documents/19838/5636250/20190624-WhistleblowerProtection-EN.pdf/69a1e5b5-5bb5-4c50-bbf8-16423d020aff accessed 15 May 2025 where it is proposed to allow legal persons to blow the whistle on illegal practices (but this begs the question: where is the work-based relation?) or to enjoy protection as 'whistleblowing facilitators' like the journalists who use the whistleblowers as sources.

[38] Directive 2019/1937 (n 27) Art 4(1).

academic literature by requiring protection for both worker groups.[39] It is interesting, though, to notice that the Directive does not include the EU staff members in its definition.[40] As protection should be granted to public sector employees, it is reasonable to consider that EU staff members should fall under this category.

To the contrary, the Directive does not cover EU officials and other employees, who are required to abide by the internal reporting procedures as outlined in Articles 22a, 22b, and 22c of the Staff Regulations of the European Union.[41] There is only one possibility for EU officials and servants to report and be covered by the Directive: they may *report breaches that occur in a work-related context outside their employment relation with the Union institutions, bodies, offices or agencies*.[42] EU employees may report breaches when dealing with unrelated public or private entities.

Excluding EU officials and servants from the Directive is a significant gap that needs to be addressed.[43] Since each EU institution creates its own rules, whistleblower protection is fragmented, which the Directive aims to address at the Member State level. To enforce EU law effectively, EU workers should be able to report and be protected.[44] The European Parliament and the Committee on Constitutional Affairs expressed the desire to include EU officials in their proposed amendments to the Directive.[45] The European Commission did not mention including EU officials, likely because there was no legal basis and no relevant precedent.

D. Work-Related Context

The reporting person should acquire the information on breaches within a 'work-related context'.[46] This 'work-related context' includes past or current

[39] T Devine, 'International Best Practices for Whistleblower Statutes' in D Lewis and W Vandekerckhove (eds), *Developments in Whistleblowing Research* (International Whistleblowing Research Network, 2015) 9, www.track.unodc.org/Academia/Documents/151110 IWRN ebook 2015.pdf accessed on 15 May 2025, wherein he notes that whistleblower protection should protect all citizens who have relevant disclosures regardless of their formal employment status.

[40] D Lewis, 'The EU Directive on the Protection of Whistleblowers: A Missed Opportunity to Establish International Best Practices?' (2020) 9(1) *E-Journal of International and Comparative Labour Studies* 1, 8.

[41] Directive 2019/1937 (n 27) Recital 23. See also European Parliament and European Council Regulation No 31 (EEC), 11 (EAEC) laying down the Staff Regulations of Officials and the Conditions of Employment of Other Servants of the European Economic Community and the European Atomic Energy Community [1962] OJ L1385/62.

[42] Directive 2019/1937 (n 27) Recital 23.

[43] European Parliament Committee on Constitutional Affairs, Opinion for the Committee on Legal Affairs on the proposal for a Directive on the protection of persons reporting on breaches of Union law [2018] C8-0159/2018, 3.

[44] Transparency International, 'Whistleblower Protection in the EU: Analysis of and Recommendations on the Proposed EU Directive' (2018) 8 www.transparency.org/whatwedo/publication/whistleblower_protection_in_the_eu_analysis_of_and_recommendations accessed 15 May 2021.

[45] European Parliament, Explanatory Statement on the Draft European Parliament Legislative Resolution on the proposal for a directive on the protection of persons reporting on breaches of Union law (COM(2018)0218-C8-0159/2018-2018/0106(COD).

[46] Directive 2019/1937 (n 27) Art 5(9).

work activities through which the whistleblower encountered breach-related information, and the whistleblower risks retaliation if they report it.[47] The term 'work-related context' is viewed as a barrier because it might leave out important details about wrongdoings.

In Recital 36, the restriction to 'work-related' is justified because there exists an 'economic vulnerability vis-à-vis the person on whom de facto they depend for work. Where there is no such work-related power imbalance, [...] there is no need for protection against retaliation'. Recital 36 contradicts the European Parliament's October 2017 Resolution, which defined a whistleblower as anyone who reports or discloses information in the public interest, including unlawful acts or threats that endanger the public, often related to their work.[48]

The Directive limits whistleblowing to work-related issues in the public or private sector, as aforementioned, and excludes other persons, such as citizens, from reporting. This aligns with the Irish PDA 2014 or the case law of the European Court of Human Rights.[49] Extending the scope to persons without a work-based relationship was not discussed during negotiations, but it is worth considering the French approach and arguing that the Directive's approach is correct given the EU's competences.

E. The French Approach to the Question of Work-Related Context

Under French law, a whistleblower must be a physical person, which includes all citizens, not just employees. The law's definition is broad and unique.[50] However, this definitional innovation in Article 6 of the French law contrasts with Article 8, which describes the channels whistleblowers can use to report to the employer.[51]

[47] ibid. The text is in line with Art 3(10) of the Proposal for a Directive and with Art 6(9) of the European Parliament Resolution.

[48] European Parliament, Resolution of 24 October 2017 on legitimate measures to protect whistle-blowers acting in the public interest when disclosing the confidential information of companies and public bodies [2016] (2016/2224(INI)), point 14. Principle 3 of the G20's High-Level Principles for the Effective Protection of Whistleblowers' (2019) www.bmjv.de/SharedDocs/Downloads/EN/G20/G20_2019_High-Level-Principles_Whistleblowers.pdf?__blob=publicationFile&v=1 accessed 15 May 2025 where it states, as well: 'G20 countries should seek to provide appropriate protection of persons reporting corruption to competent authorities outside of an employment situation including confidentiality' Osaka, 2019.

[49] Protected Disclosures Act 2014, No 14 of 2014, s 5 where it is stated that the worker should have noticed the relevant wrongdoings in the due course of their work. See *Guja v Moldova* App no 14277/04 (ECtHR, 12 February 2008) para 97. See also *Medžlis Islamske Zajednice Brčko and Others v Bosnia and Herzegovina* App no 17224/11 (ECtHR, 27 June 2017) para 80, where the Strasbourg Court states that, in order to invoke the relevant case-law on the protection of the whistle-blowers, a work-based relation should have been established at first.

[50] P Pailler, 'Le nouveau statut de lanceur d'alerte' [2017] *Revue du droit bancaire et financier* 1, 2.

[51] Law n° 2016-1691 of 6 December 2016 related to transparency, the fight against corruption and the modernisation of economic life, JORF n°0287, Art 8.

This obligation restricts the whistleblower definition to employee-employer relationships. French senators raised this contradiction to the French Constitutional Court (Conseil Constitutionnel).[52]

The applicants argued that confusion between Articles 6 and 8 regarding the distinction between a physical person and an employee contradicts the constitutional goals of law accessibility and clarity.[53] These constitutional objectives stem from Articles 4, 5, 6, and 16 of the 1789 Declaration of the Rights of the Person and of the Citizen, requiring the legislator to adopt precise provisions.[54] In addition, the applicants raised the point that Article 6 defines the term whistleblower imprecisely. They argued that this imprecision is contrary to the principle of legality for misdemeanours and crimes, as expressed in Article 34 of the French Constitution,[55] contrary to the principles of equality and proportionality of sanctions, because the definition in Article 6 is determinant and related to the criminal irresponsibility of the whistleblower under Article 7 of the French law.[56]

The French Constitutional Court initially ruled that the criteria defining a whistleblower are clear, countering claims of vagueness.[57] The Constitutional Court ruled that differentiating between Article 6's use of 'physical' person and Article 8's employee-employer interaction in reporting procedures does not violate the Constitution or its objectives.[58] The Constitutional Court noted that Article 6 defines a whistleblower as any person, but Article 8 limits Law Sapin II's protection to employees or collaborators reporting workplace illegalities.[59] The fact that the definition in Article 6 not only includes employees or collaborators of an organisation but also extends to every physical person does not render the provision unintelligible.[60] The purpose of French law is to ensure that this broad definition applies not only to cases under Article 8 but also to other whistleblowing procedures outside the professional framework.[61]

Many laws limit whistleblowers to workers, portraying them as inspectors rather than activists. Extending the term 'whistleblower' to citizens without a work relationship would create a civic duty, which is outside the Directive's purpose.[62]

[52] Conseil Constitutionnel, Décision n° 2016-741 DC du 8 Décembre 2016 www.conseil-constitutionnel.fr/decision/2016/2016741DC.htm accessed 15 May 2025.

[53] ibid points 3–5.

[54] République Française, Déclaration des Droits de l'Homme et du Citoyen de 1789, arts 4, 5, 6 and 16 www.legifrance.gouv.fr/Droit-francais/Constitution/Declaration-des-Droits-de-l-Homme-et-du-Citoyen-de-1789 accessed 15 May 2025.

[55] République Française, Constitution du 4 octobre 1958, Art 34 www.legifrance.gouv.fr/affichTexte.do?cidTexte=LEGITEXT000006071194 accessed 15 May 2025.

[56] Décision n° 2016-741 (n 52) points 3–5.

[57] ibid point 6.

[58] ibid point 7.

[59] ibid.

[60] ibid points 8–9.

[61] ibid.

[62] Miceli, Dreyfus and Near (n 7) 76. The authors refer to the concept of bystander intervention.

Normal citizens can still report crimes with proof by going to the Prosecutor's office or police station, fulfilling their civic duties.[63]

The whistleblower needs to be a worker because workplaces are often secretive or complicated to access from the outside. Citizens cannot do this unless they work there. The Directive aims to gather information on breaches of Union law from within, so workers, not outsiders, are the right people. Member States can expand whistleblowing beyond employment, as under UK law, where disclosures under section 43B of ERA 1996 qualify for protection regardless of how the worker obtained the information.

F. The Meaning of Worker

The Directive succeeded in providing a broad category of what constitutes a work-related context.[64] The proposal for a Directive, as presented by the European Commission, had a more restrictive approach to the persons who can be considered as whistleblowers.[65] This restrictive approach was criticised by the European Parliament, its committees, and whistleblower protection groups like Transparency International. They also called for broadening the scope of the Directive.[66] Transparency International and others demanded a broader scope.[67] These voices and their proposals were heard, leading to a broader scope in the Directive. This is because more reporting persons will be protected, and these actors' expertise in whistleblowing legislation contributed to the decision.

The reporting person may be a worker within the meaning of Article 45(1) TFEU, including civil servants or self-employed, as enriched in Article 49 TFEU.[68] Member States should consult their national laws to determine the definition of 'worker', since the Directive does not specify it, likely assuming it is understood. This would avoid confusion with Article 45(1) of the TFEU. They may expand or exclude categories as relevant to Article 45(1) TFEU.

The definition given to the worker under Article 45 TFEU is broad.[69] The concept of worker is autonomous under EU law, as it defines the field of

[63] C Delmas, 'The Civic Duty to Report Crime and Corruption' (2014) 9(1) *Les ateliers de l'éthique* 50, 51.

[64] ibid 8.

[65] European Commission Proposal for a Directive of the European Parliament and of the Council on the protections of persons reporting on breaches of Union law: 2018/0106 (COD) [2018], Art 2.9.

[66] European Parliament, Draft European Parliament Legislative Resolution (n 45) Art 2; European Parliament Committee on Economic and Monetary Affairs, Opinion for the Committee on Legal Affairs on the Proposal for a Directive on the protection of persons reporting on breaches of Union law [2018] C8-0159/2018, 3.

[67] Transparency International (n 44) 8.

[68] Directive 2019/1937 (n 27) Art 4(1)(a) and 4(1)(b).

[69] M Kellerbauer and D Martin, 'Article 45' in M Kekkerbauer, M Klamert and J Tomkin (eds), *The EU Treaties and the Charter of Fundamental Rights – A Commentary* (OUP, 2019) 607–34.

application of one of the fundamental freedoms guaranteed by the Treaties.[70] This fundamental freedom is the freedom of movement, essential to the functioning of the internal market. Article 45(2) TFEU connects elements such as monetary compensation and employment to the concept of a worker, illustrating the EU's interpretation of it.[71] The autonomous concept of 'worker' applies across the EU, but EU law shows that national laws define what constitutes a worker.[72] Despite the importance of these elements at the EU and national levels, the Treaties lack a clear definition of 'worker'.

The Luxembourg Court interprets 'worker' broadly, including those performing services under direction for a limited time for pay.[73] The CJEU's decision in *Lawrie-Blum* has served as the basis for defining a worker and has developed its case law to date.[74] The CJEU has defined the term 'worker' under EU law, clarifying the concept and introducing new categories and characteristics.[75] The CJEU broadly interprets Article 45 TFEU, emphasising freedom of movement and the internal market, rather than the employment relationship alone. It focuses on the genuine economic nature of services, offering a flexible worker definition that benefits workers like whistleblowers.

Despite the Luxembourg Court's broad interpretation of Articles 45 and 49 TFEU, issues arise with the CJEU's approach, as its case law evolves and different concepts are at stake. The problem with the test (of who is a worker) is the ongoing addition of requirements.[76] The aim is not to analyse these ongoing changes in depth but to show they may be discriminatory and exclude some persons from the definition of workers under Articles 45 and 49 TFEU. They could also violate the principle of effectiveness (*effet utile*). Although the Court has recently adhered to this principle, its protection is still vulnerable because of inconsistent approaches by the EU judges. A more consistent interpretation is needed to uphold the principle of effectiveness.

For example, a person with a disability should meet the same genuine activity threshold as an able-bodied person, and someone offering informal, essential care might not be considered a worker as a paid employees work.[77] The CJEU's approach overlooks elements like physical or mental work adaptations or unavailability, applying a uniform test for genuine work that can cause discrimination, especially for disabled persons. The analysis suggests that the Directive should define 'worker' in accordance with national and EU law, while respecting equality before the law. Also, case law under Article 45 TFEU supports whistleblowers,

[70] S Giubboni, 'Being a worker in EU law' (2018) 9(3) *European Labour Law Journal* 223, 224.

[71] Kellerbauer and Martin (n 69) 611.

[72] ibid.

[73] See also Case C-456/02 *Trojani v Centre public d'aide sociale* [2004] ECR 1-7573.

[74] Case C-66/85 *Deborah Lawrie-Blum v Land Baden-Württemberg* [1986] EU:C:1986:284.

[75] ACL Davies, A Bogg and C Costello, 'The Role of the Court of Justice in Labour Law' in A Bogg, C Castello and ACL Davies (eds), *Research Handbook on EU Labour Law* (Edward Elgar, 2016) 114–21.

[76] C O'Brien, 'Social Blind Spots and Monocular Policy Making: the ECJ's Migrant Worker Problem' (2009) 46 *Common Market Law Review* 1107, 1117.

[77] D Chalmers, G Davies and G Monti, *European Union Law* (OUP, 2010) 854.

emphasising that 'worker' should be understood in the context of the Directive and Article 45 TFEU, with reference to relevant case law.

Civil servants, public employees, or anyone in the public sector are considered 'workers' under this Directive. This includes employees reporting or disclosing issues, even after their contracts end, as well as those in recruitment or pre-contractual stages who have information about breaches. Volunteers and trainees, paid or unpaid, are also covered. The term 'worker' includes part-time, fixed-term, contract and agency workers and those in employment relationships.

Shareholders and members of an undertaking's management, including non-executive members, can report under the Directive. Persons working for contractors, subcontractors, and suppliers are also covered. The Directive's protections extend to facilitators and third parties, like colleagues, relatives, or entities with an ownership interest, who may face retaliation. These whistleblowers are not necessarily employees but are 'work' connected to the source of information about potential misconduct.

For example, in aeroplane safety, a supplier is closer to the source of information about potential misconduct in manufacturing or maintenance. These individuals can face retaliation, such as boycotts, contract losses, blacklisting, or other measures. Since they may not always seek damages under labour law, they should be protected by the Directive. The Directive must protect them due to their vulnerability to those involved in the wrongdoing.

In summary, the 'worker' definition under the Directive is a small victory for whistleblowers. It is broad, covering various work-related relationships, and extends beyond traditional definitions. This wide scope, as interpreted under Article 45 TFEU and reinforced by case law, is crucial for whistleblower protection, as many workers can now benefit from the Directive's protections.

G. The Innovative Definition of the Whistleblower under the Directive

Despite the limitations in the material scope of the Directive, given the competences of the EU, the scope and therefore the definition of the whistleblower is broad and not limited.[78] Advocates of whistleblowers' protection welcomed the new definition as a positive step toward international best practices. This issue occurs because these definitional elements are frequently absent in advanced EU sectoral provisions and previous national laws.[79]

[78] S White, 'A Matter of Life or Death – Whistleblowing Legislation in the EU' (2018) 3 *European Criminal Law Forum* 172. The characterisation of the definition as innovative had already been done when the European Commission proposed the Directive.

[79] ibid.

The Directive adopts a broad definition of a 'reporting person'.[80] Initially, it appears there is no difference between the public and private sectors, as everyone is protected regardless of employment status.[81] The Directive extends protection beyond work-related contexts to include current and former workers, dependants like contractors and subcontractors, trainees, volunteers, job applicants, shareholders, and management members.[82] All these elements may characterise the definition of a whistleblower under the Directive as innovative.

H. Framing the Reasonable Grounds Concept

The worker's definition is the primary aspect of a whistleblower under the Directive, with other requirements to follow.[83] These two requirements in Article 6 are cumulative, so the whistleblower must meet both. The first one is that the whistleblower has *reasonable grounds to believe that the information on breaches reported was accurate at the time of reporting and that information fell within the scope* of the Directive. The second requirement is that the whistleblower must adhere to the reporting channels as outlined in Articles 7, 10, and 15 of the Directive. This second requirement is analysed in the following chapter.

The first requirement consists of two parts: analysing 'reasonable grounds' and reviewing 'information on breaches' to comprehend the Directive and its potential implications. First, the whistleblower should believe the reported information is accurate, considering the circumstances and the available information at that time.[84] Additionally, they should have reasonable grounds to believe that the information is covered by this Directive.[85] This requirement might deter future whistleblowers. Requiring disclosure of reasonable grounds before protection is granted leaves reporters uncertain whether they must prove their grounds, making them vulnerable to unfounded attacks.

The reasonable grounds requirement protects against malicious reports, ensuring that whistleblowers acting in good faith are safeguarded, while those providing false or misleading reports are not protected.[86] An exception applies if the whistleblower provided inaccurate information in good faith due to an honest mistake.[87] The challenge is to distinguish honest errors from malicious reports. While the Directive does not consider whistleblower motives, in this case, motives matter.

[80] Magner and Paclot (n 20) 700.

[81] Many actors were proposing that. See Transparency International, 'Whistleblower Protection and the UN Convention Against Corruption' (2013) 13, www.transparency.org/whatwedo/publication/whistleblower_protection_and_the_un_convention_against_corruption accessed 15 May 2025.

[82] European Commission, Impact Assessment (n 7) 9.

[83] Directive 2019/1937 (n 27) Art 6.

[84] ibid Recital 32.

[85] ibid.

[86] ibid Recitals 32 and 91. See also European Commission, Impact Assessment (n 7) 33–34.

[87] ibid Recital 32. See also E Andreis, 'Towards Common Minimum Standards for Whistleblower Protection across the EU' (2019) 4(2) *European Papers* 575, 580.

Honest mistakes imply good faith, while malicious reports relate to bad faith. The new requirement of reasonable grounds without ulterior motives creates challenges for future whistleblowers and may impede the process.

Some actors welcomed the concept of reasonable grounds, as it moves away from the motives test and offers a more lenient way to verify information.[88] Transparency International and the Council of Europe welcomed this step, noting it complies with international best practices on whistleblower protections.[89] Under these circumstances, 'reasonable grounds' means a reasonable belief that others with similar knowledge, training, and experience should also agree that a wrongdoing may occur.[90] However, their interpretation does not match the Directive, which focuses on the reasonable grounds of the whistleblower rather than the nature of their motives. The European Commission's recent report on the transposition of the Directive notes that some member states have wrongly transposed this requirement by considering motives for protection.[91]

I. Information About a Breach

Additionally, the whistleblower is required to disclose details about a breach, which are separated into two components: the information itself and the breach itself. The Directive briefly explains 'information' in Article 5(2), defining it as including reasonable suspicions. Recital 43 mentions 'positive evidence' when considering whether the reporting person can provide evidence or raise suspicions, but it is unclear whether this refers to documental, oral, or taped evidence. Recital 94 discusses the whistleblower's liability with specific references to documents, emails, and files, but these are only in the preamble, not the main text.

The preamble offers the only explanations, though its legal value is ambiguous. The Court of Justice of the European Union (CJEU) has decided in case C-134/08 that 'the preamble to a Community act has no binding legal force and cannot be validly relied on either as a ground for derogating from the actual provisions of the act in question or for interpreting those provisions in a manner clearly contrary to their wording'.[92] In whistleblower cases, the ambiguity might lead parties or the CJEU to interpret the Directive's legal provisions using the preamble as a guide, but this is not certain. They may also choose not to refer to it. Future case law will clarify what 'information' means in this context.

[88] Lewis (n 40) 18.

[89] Transparency International (n 44) 3; Council of Europe (n 36) 14–15; Tom Devine, 'Assessment of European Union Whistleblower Directive', (2019) GAP Blog, www.whistleblower.org/blog/assessment-of-european-union-whistleblower-directive/ accessed 15 May 2025.

[90] Transparency International (n 44) 3.

[91] European Commission Report 2024 (n 17) 5.

[92] Case C-134/08 *Hauptzollamt Bremen v J. E. Tyson Parketthandel GmbH hanse j.* [2009] ECR I-02875, paras 16 and 32.

The information on breaches or suspicions may relate to actual or potential violations at the institution where the reporting person works or worked, or at another institution with which they have been in contact, including attempts to conceal such breaches.[93] The Directive allows whistleblowers to report current breaches, suspicions of future violations, or attempts to conceal them.[94] A whistle-blower should have reasonable grounds for suspicion. But what does 'reasonable suspicion' mean? Does it mean a worker in the same position would think so, or that the whistleblower, analysing the facts, suspects a problem? Reporting an actual breach is easier than reporting a potential one. Standards should clarify what constitutes reasonable suspicion and what actions are expected of the whistleblower.

The whistleblower should report a breach of the law.[95] Under the Directive, a breach refers to an unlawful act or omission concerning Union acts within the scope of Article 2, or that undermines the purpose of the EU rules.[96] The breach report must relate to the sections outlined in Article 2 of the Directive.[97] The Directive leaves the possibility for Member States to extend protection under national law to areas not covered by EU legislation.[98] Despite the broad areas of EU interest for which a report can be made, the Directive was characterised as providing sectoral protection,[99] and it was also criticised for creating different national

[93] Directive 2019/1937 (n 27) Art 5(2).

[94] ibid.

[95] ibid Art 5(1).

[96] ibid.

[97] (a) breaches falling within the scope of the Union acts set out in the Annex (Parts I and Part II) ***to this Directive*** as regards the following areas:
(i) public procurement;
(ii) financial services, ***products and markets and*** prevention of money laundering and terrorist financing
(iii) product safety;
(iv) transport safety;
(v) protection of the environment;
(vi) ***radiation protection and*** nuclear safety;
(vii) food and feed safety, animal health and welfare;
(viii) public health;
(ix) consumer protection;
(x) protection of privacy and personal data, and security of network and information systems.
breaches affecting the financial interests of the Union as defined by Article 325 TFEU and as further specified in ***relevant Union measures***;
(c) breaches relating to the internal market, as referred to in Article 26(2) TFEU, ***including breaches of the competition and State aid rules, and*** as regards acts which breach the rules of corporate tax or arrangements whose purpose is to obtain a tax advantage that defeats the object or purpose of the applicable corporate tax law.

[98] Directive 2019/1937 (n 27) Art 1(2).

[99] N Veronika and C Naomi, 'Whistleblowing in the European Union: A New Directive to Protect Citizens, Democracy and Rule of Law' (2019) Blueprint for Free Speech, 2, static1.squarespace.com/static/5e249291de6f0056c7b1099b/t/5ed119f3deae375165af97b4/1616776389329/EU_NEW_DIRECTIVE_ANALYSIS_V5_ONLINE.pdf accessed 15 May 2025.

legislations: one transposing the Directive and one related to what falls outside the material scope of the Directive, thus addressing issues related to national law.[100]

Initially, the Directive is seen as an EU sectoral approach, not a horizontal legal framework.[101] The European Union adopted a legal framework that took into account its limited powers.[102] The EU legal framework is sectoral and cannot cover areas beyond its competence.[103] The Directive is a horizontal legal act on whistleblower protection within the EU's competences. Member States must decide whether to extend their scope to cover issues addressed only by national law.[104] The 2024 European Commission report on transposition found that some Member States opted for a restricted transposition, focusing only on the areas covered by the Directive.

Furthermore, it is valuable to examine the sectoral approach to whistleblower legislation, as it leads to protection provisions being distributed across different legal frameworks.[105] This means whistleblowers are protected when reporting something specific covered by the legislation. For example, EU law includes a provision under the EU Regulation on Market Abuse that allows reporting insider dealing and market manipulation to authorities.[106] Other sectoral clauses pertain to banking supervision or anti-money laundering.[107] On the contrary, horizontal

[100] R Brockhaus and D Kafteranis, 'No More Piecemeal Tactics: Call for a Comprehensive Implementation of EU's Whistleblowing Directive' (2020) VerBlog, dx.doi.org/10.17176/20200710-235503-0 accessed 15 May 2025.

[101] White (n 78) 171–72.

[102] The impact assessment had found that the Treaties cannot provide for a specific legal basis to regulate the legal position of whistleblowers, at the EU level, in general. The right to freedom of expression, as enshrined in the Charter of Fundamental Rights, would have been a legal basis for a horizontal approach but it cannot serve as a standalone legal basis. See European Commission, Impact Assessment (n 7) 30–31.

[103] The EU is bound to the principle of conferral. In addition, reportable wrongdoing can only apply in areas where Member States have previously agreed on sharing competences. See P Craig and G de Burca, *EU law -Text, Cases and Materials*, 6th edn (OUP, 2015) 75 and V Nad and C Naomi, 'Whistleblowing in the European Union: a New Directive to Protect Citizens, Democracy and Rule of law' (2019) Blueprint for Free Speech static1.squarespace.com/static/5e249291de6f0056c7b1099b/t/5ed119f3de-ae375165af97b4/1616776389329/EU_NEW_DIRECTIVE_ANALYSIS_V5_ONLINE.pdf accessed 15 May 2025, 2.

[104] The French Senate has issued its concerns on this issue in its opinion on the Proposal for a Directive. The French Senate stated that, even though the Directive has a limited scope of application (only to wrongdoings related to EU law), its transposition will result in a problem of harmonisation as France will be 'obliged' to amend its existing legislation in order to avoid the co-existence of two different legal frameworks. See Sénat, Rapport fait sur la proposition de directive sur la protection des personnes dénoncent les infractions au droit de l'Union N° 638 (2018), 8.

[105] Government Reform Unit, Department of Public Expenditure and Reform, Protected Disclosures Bill 2013 – Regulatory Impact Analysis, 10 July 2013.

[106] European Parliament and European Council Regulation (EU) 596/2014 of 16 April 2014 on market abuse (market abuse regulation) and repealing Directive 2003/6/EC and Commission Directives 2003/124/EC, 2003/125/EC and 2004/72/EC [2014] OJ L173/1.

[107] European Parliament and European Council Directive 2015/849/EU of 20 May 2015 on the prevention of the use of the financial system for the purposes of money laundering or terrorist financing, amending Regulation No 648/2012/EU, and repealing Directive 2005/60/EC and Commission Directive 2006/70/EC (Text with EEA relevance) [2015] OJ L141/73, 73–117 and European Central Bank Regulation (EU) 468/2014 of 16 April 2014 establishing the framework for cooperation within the Single Supervisory Mechanism between the European Central Bank and national competent authorities and with national designated authorities (SSM Framework Regulation) [2014] OJ L141/1.

legislation has as its core element the protection of whistleblowers in every possible area of interest, which may also be referred to as pan-sectoral legislation.[108] The purpose of horizontal legislation is to provide a legal framework for protecting whistleblowers across all fields of interest. This is what the EU did, limited to the EU's areas of interest. For the EU, it concerns a matter of competence rather than a decision to limit its areas of interest.[109]

Furthermore, the reported breach should be related to an unlawful act or omission or an act or omission that may defeat the purpose of the law.[110] The act or omission should fall within the Directive's scope, regardless of legality or the law's intent. While unlawful acts are clear, doubts exist about acts that defeat the object or purpose of the law. According to Recital 42, there are abusive practices, as defined by the case law of the CJEU,[111] that are not unlawful in formal terms but defeat the purpose of the law. For instance, this is the case of corporate law taxation.[112]

The Directive aims to combat breaches that 'can give rise to unfair tax competition and extensive tax evasion, distorting the level playing field for businesses and resulting in a loss of tax revenues for Member States and the Union budget as a whole'.[113] The Directive covers tax breaches related to the internal market, including violations of corporate tax rules such as tax evasion, arrangements aimed at obtaining tax advantages that undermine tax law, and breaches of competition and state aid rules.[114] The Directive omits protection for whistleblowers reporting tax avoidance.[115] Furthermore, tax whistleblowing confusion stems from the overlap between the Directive and sector-specific rules, such as violations involving special tax provisions schemes.[116]

Scrutinising the Directive's tax whistleblowing regime, obtaining a tax advantage by evading legal rules may not be illegal, but it defeats the purpose of the law and causes unfair tax evasion and competition. This undermines fair business

[108] The Final Report of the Tribunal of Inquiry into Certain Planning Matters and Payments (2012) 2644, www.planningtribunal.ie/images/finalReport.pdf accessed 15 May 2025.

[109] Directive 2019/1937 (n 27) Recital 106. The European Union has chosen these specific EU areas of interest as it identified a problem of enforcement of its policies. The material scope may be extended in the future if new elements come to the fore but still limited to the EU areas of interest (competence).

[110] ibid Art 5(1).

[111] Case C-33/74 *Van Binsbergen v Bestuur van de Bedrijfsvereniging voor de Metaalnijverheid* [1974] ECR 1299, para 13; Case C-255/02 *Halifax plc, Leeds Permanent Development Services Ltd, County Wide Property Investments Ltd v Commissioners of Customs & Excise* [2006] ECR I-1609; Case C-251/16 *Edward Cussens and Others v T.G. Brosman* [2017] ECLI:EU:C:2017:881.

[112] Directive 2019/1937 (n 27) Recital 18.

[113] ibid.

[114] A Lachapelle, 'And thus Tax Whistleblowing was Born! Comment on the Directive on Whistleblowers in Tax Matters' (2020) 588 *Tijdschrift voor Fiscaal Recht* 798, 804.

[115] ibid 807.

[116] For an extensive analysis of tax whistleblowing under the Directive and its coexistence with sectoral provisions on tax reporting, see K Pantazatou, 'The New Directive on Whistleblowers' Protection: Any Impact on Taxation?' (2019) Kluwer International Tax Blog, 22 May 2019, kluwertaxblog.com/2019/05/22/the-new-directive-on-whistleblowers-protection-any-impact-on-taxation/ accessed 15 May 2025.

practices and reduces tax revenues for Member States.[117] What comes to mind is the Luxleaks case, where two whistleblowers revealed specific tax rulings between companies and the Luxembourg tax authorities. The interest in the Luxleaks case lies in the fact that the two employees exposed an obscure tax practice, but not one that is illegal.[118] The practice of 'tax rulings' is not unlawful and is common in many EU countries.[119] This book's purpose is not to analyse the nature of 'tax rulings' but to highlight that whistleblowers have exposed an obscure practice, not a wrongdoing. Since the scandal was revealed before the Directive's adoption, it is likely to have inspired this requirement.[120]

The meaning of 'abusive practices' under CJEU case law is not well-defined, and legal scholarship on the issue is limited. It is a judge-made law concept.[121] The CJEU has continually evolved its approach to abusive practices under EU law.[122] The concept is developed across EU areas, including free movement of persons and services, social security, company law, and, recently, tax law.[123] In February 2006, the Court, in the *Halifax* case, referred to the abusive practices as the 'principle of prohibiting abusive practices'.[124]

The Court has stated in recent cases that EU law has a general principle prohibiting abusive practices, which does not require national law implementation before it applies to a private party.[125] To that extent, it also covers abuses of national law which cannot be justified on constitutional grounds.[126] Although rich, the case law of the Court of Justice on abusive practices appears confusing. Legal scholarship has only recently focused on this issue due to its implications in tax law.[127]

[117] Directive 2019/1937 (n 27) Recital 18.

[118] CA Luxembourg, 15 Mars 2017, n° 117/17 X, point 3 les causes justificatives, b) le fait justificatif du lanceur d'alerte, where the Luxembourg Court of Appeal has noticed: '*Il se dégage encore de cette jurisprudence que l'illicéité du comportement divulgué n'est pas un critère de l'application du statut protecteur du lanceur d'alerte ; peut le cas échéant invoquer la protection de la Convention, l'agent qui dénonce un dysfonctionnement grave*.'

[119] Lachapelle (n 114) 805.

[120] ibid 818.

[121] JP Maublanc, 'Réévaluation de l'abus de droit à la lumière de la jurisprudence communautaire sur les pratiques abusives' [2007] *Revue du Marché commun et de l'Union européenne* 267, 269 ('*construction prétorienne communautaire*').

[122] The concept has been developed in the case law of the Court of Justice since 1974. See *Van Binsbergen v Bestuur van de Bedrijfsvereniging voor de Metaalnijverheid* (n 111) para 13.

[123] R de la Feria, 'Prohibition of Abuse of (Community) Law: The Creation of a New General Principle of EC Law through tax' (2008) 45 *Common Market Law Review* 395.

[124] Case C-255/02 *Halifax plc, Leeds Permanent Development Services Ltd, County Wide Property Investments Ltd v Commissioners of Customs & Excise* [2006] ECR I-1609, where the case concerned the interpretation of EU secondary legislation on Value Added Tax (VAT).

[125] *Edward Cussens v Brosman*, (n 111).

[126] D Leczykiewicz, 'Prohibition of Abusive Practices as a General Principle of EU Law' (2019) 56 *Common Market Law Review* 703.

[127] S Vogenauer, 'The Prohibition of Abuse of Law: An Emerging General Principle of EU law' in R de la Feria and S Vogenauer (eds), *Prohibition of Abuse of Law: A New General Principle of EU Law?* (Hart Publishing, 2011) 522.

This book focuses on the banking and financial sector, where abusive practices have had no direct impact.[128] The strong EU market abuse and securities laws make the concept of abusive practices in financial law unnecessary. Although abusive practices are not evident in financial services, their presence in corporate and tax laws can influence financial institutions, as these areas are interconnected. Corporate taxation is notable because, under the Directive, whistleblowers can report related misconduct. This book does not extensively analyse abusive practices but emphasises that whistleblowers can report them, which is problematic given the uncertainty and complexity in the interpretation of case law.

The whistleblower may be unsure if a practice is abusive, as the Luxembourg Court assesses cases individually. The reporting person often lacks legal expertise, and professionals outside the legal field can blow the whistle. For example, in the Luxleaks case, Antoine Deltour, the first whistleblower, could not understand the nature of the tax rulings, so a former tax advisor helped clarify that they were abusive but not illegal.

Additionally, the concept of abusive practices contradicts the principle of legal certainty.[129] Taking tax law as an example, it requires that 'rules imposing charges on the taxpayer must be clear and precise so that he may know without ambiguity what his rights and obligations are'.[130] The creation of the principle of prohibiting abusive practices is hindered by a lack of awareness, which harms legal certainty more than the principle of abuse of law itself.[131] Apart from the repercussions of the prohibition of abusive practices for legal certainty, it is worth noting that it creates ambiguity for whistleblowers, as they cannot be certain whether a particular practice is abusive.[132]

Whilst the need to report abusive practices under the Directive aims to encompass all the specific sectors covered by the Directive, it targets the field of corporate taxation or corporate arrangements in particular.[133] The Directive encourages whistleblowers to report breaches and arrangements that may cause unfair tax competition and tax evasion in order to protect the internal market.[134] The aim is to create a safer place within the internal market where businesses do not distort

[128] T Tridimas, 'Abuse of Rights in EU Law: Some Reflections with Particular Reference to Financial Law' in de la Feria and Vogenauer (n 127) 181–83.

[129] This belief results from the need that rules of law should be known, clear, precise, predictable and certain. In that case, the term is neither clear nor precise and, as a result, against the principle of legal certainty. See J van Meerbeeck, 'The Principle of Legal Certainty in the Case-Law of the European Court of Justice: From Certainty to Trust' (2016) 41(2) *European Law Review* 275.

[130] Case C-169/80 *Administration des douanes v Société anonyme Gondrand Frères and Société anonyme Garancini* [1981] ECR 1931.

[131] de la Feria (n 123) 411.

[132] A problem of legal coherence is observed as the interpretation of abusive practices threatens the protection of whistleblowers. Consequently, the whistleblower will not be able to foresee the applicable law to his or her actions (if the Directive is applied or not). See A Portuese, O Gough and J Tanega, 'The Principle of Legal Certainty as a Principle of Economic Efficiency' (2014) 44 *European Journal of Law and Economics* 131, 133–36.

[133] Directive 2019/1937 (n 27) Art 2(1)(c).

[134] ibid Recital 18.

the level playing field, and Member States do not lose their tax revenues.[135] Various opinions have been expressed regarding the above.

First, the EU's competence in corporate taxation is unclear, as there is no clear competence under the Treaties.[136] Naturally, and without any specific competence, the EU attempts to extend its powers indirectly to protect the internal market and enhance transparency and the exchange of information in the field of taxation.[137] Despite these noble arguments, it cannot justify requiring a whistleblower to report abusive corporate tax practices, nor explain why this is part of the Directive.

Second, by accepting the EU's indirect competence in corporate taxation, the whistleblower will be uncertain about what constitutes an abusive practice.[138] As mentioned earlier, the Court of Justice's case law is often confusing rather than enlightening, which does not facilitate effective reporting. To a certain extent, this fact is contrary to the principle of legal certainty, as the whistleblower should be sure what to report. Reporting on abusive practices, a concept that is complex and poorly defined, contradicts the principle of legal certainty and places the whistleblower in a delicate position if they decide to report such matters.

Finally, the concept of abusive practices is rooted in EU law, not national law. The Court has expanded it into national law despite constitutional issues. The whistleblower must report an abusive practice internally or to authorities. The problem is that, whether internally or with the authorities,[139] they will not know whether there is an abusive practice. This will be up to the EU or national judges.[140] Even if you go directly to the authorities, nothing will likely be done, because the authorities may have authorised themselves to engage in the abusive practice (except in cases involving cross-border issues). Additionally, this abusive practice often stems from national, rather than EU, law, which limits the whistleblower's scope under

[135] ibid.

[136] Indirect taxes have been harmonised at EU level. Direct taxation (such as corporate taxation) is not harmonised where it is observed a rapid and large expanding body of case-by-case and therefore uncoordinated case law of the Court, often fatal for the national direct tax measures. See PJ Wattel, 'Introduction' in PJ Wattel, O Marres and H Vermeulen (eds), *European Tax Law* (Wolters Kluwer, 2018) 5–7.

[137] Directive 2019/1937 (n 27) Recital 18.

[138] de la Feria (n 123) 411.

[139] Under the existing secondary EU legislation, such as DAC6, an undertaking should report to the tax authorities any 'aggressive tax planning'. This means that the whistleblower may report something that may have already been reported by their corporation. As Pantazatou highlights, 'In such a scenario, the risk of over-reporting, over-disclosure and an overflow of information to the tax authorities would arise. This problem would become even more evident in lack of an intermediary overseeing EU institution that could/would clarify questions as to the objective scope of the Directive.' See Pantazatou (n 116).

[140] In the 'Luxleaks' case, the Court of Appeal examined this criterion and noticed that the two defendants could report neither internally nor to the authorities. The Court of Appeal noticed that they could not report internally or externally, as the reprehensible facts were not illegal. The Court of Appeal justified their choice to inform the public about these obscure tax practices to incite public debate. See CA Luxembourg, 15 Mars 2017, n° 117/17 X., point 3 les causes justificatives, b) le fait justificatif du lanceur d'alerte.

the Directive.[141] The only solution for the whistleblower will be to make a public disclosure if they fulfil the strict conditions.[142]

The question arises whether reporting corporate taxation is void since the process lacks a solid basis and is uncertain. Reporting such issues is problematic, especially given the potential for abuse. The process is unclear, and reporting legally uncertain matters undermines the whistleblower's legitimacy. Whistleblowers may remain silent due to doubts about the definition of an abusive practice.[143] Therefore, the Directive should be revised for clarity to support whistleblowing, or else the obligation to report corporate tax abuses becomes pointless, providing only a Pyrrhic victory.

Besides the issues defining abusive practices, whistleblowers face another obstacle: the Directive's scope and the need to report breaches of Union law. This might discourage reporting national law violations. The Directive encourages Member States to expand its scope to include the provision of national laws.[144]

The French Senate criticised this point during negotiations, noting that Member States must include both national and EU law in the transposition of the Directive to avoid two separate legislative frameworks: one for transposing the Directive and another for reporting outside its scope (national law issues).[145] The European Commission's recent report welcomed some Member States extending the material scope beyond the Directive, while implying others have not followed this recommendation. [146]

The whistleblower may not be able to distinguish between Union and national law.[147] If some Member States adopt two laws, the whistleblower must differentiate between national and Union law, which is challenging.[148] Practically, the whistleblower is not always a lawyer or legally knowledgeable.[149] In the banking and financial sector, for example, many employees are economists, financial analysts,

[141] Leczykiewicz (n 126) 725.

[142] Directive 2019/1937 (n 27) Art 15.

[143] As Pantazatou notes, 'While good faith and certain objective knowledge are not prerequisites in the attribution of the whistleblower status and the protection that comes with it, one may wonder whether in this scenario the whistleblower would be protected if he mistakenly reported something that he perceived as a breach of EU tax law and/or an abusive practice. The lack of a commonly accepted definition of what constitutes (tax) abuse as a general principle of EU law would only exacerbate the problem.' See Pantazatou (n 116).

[144] Directive 2019/1937 (n 27) Art 2(2).

[145] Sénat (n 104), 8.

[146] Commission Report (n 17) p 3.

[147] Andreis (n 87), 585.

[148] White (n 78) 174. This point was already criticised when the proposal for a Directive had been presented. See: European Court of Auditors, Opinion No 4/2018 of 9 November 2018 concerning the Proposal for a Directive of the European Parliament and of the Council on the protection of persons reporting on breaches of Union law.

[149] E Feldman, 'Whistleblower Protection' in R Byrne and W Binchy (eds), *Annual Review of Irish Law* (Round Hall, 2011) 616–23, where she criticised that the whistleblowing provisions of the 2011 Criminal Justice Act (Ireland) were not clear and precise. As a result, it would be difficult for whistleblowers, without a legal background, to understand the meaning and purpose of these provisions. In a similar way, an employee without a legal background will not be able to discern between Union and national laws.

IT experts, or other professionals with no direct relation to the law. How can these employees distinguish between Union and national laws?

The national legislator should clarify the distinction between national and Union law to help whistleblowers, who still need to navigate complexities. It would be better for the transposing laws of the Directive to allow employees to report suspected breaches of Union law and national law for simplicity.[150] In that way, the whistleblower will feel more secure, and protection will be granted easily.

J. Uncovering the Concept of the Self-Standing Criminal Offence

Under the Directive, the whistleblower must not have committed a self-standing criminal offence when they acquired the information.[151] The whistleblower should report only information related to the breach, not any superfluous details. This could be problematic, as recent European cases show that whistleblowers often face charges such as theft or breach of secrecy.[152] This requirement acts as a Sword of Damocles over whistleblowers, as they must handle documents that could be seen as theft or a breach of secrecy obligations, without knowing whether they will ultimately be protected under the Directive. The Directive addresses the idea of a self-standing criminal offence in the recitals rather than in the main body of the text. Recital 91 states that a whistleblower should report only with reasonable grounds necessary to reveal a breach. Reporting unnecessary information without such grounds risks dismissal of whistleblower protections.

Recital 92 clarifies the issue of a self-standing criminal offence. In addition to the reasonable grounds test and report-related information, the whistleblower must have lawfully accessed the reported information or documents. For instance, they can copy or remove these documents from the organisation. The Directive mentions two criminal offences: trespassing and hacking. It offers immunity in civil, administrative, and labour law when information is obtained indirectly, such as via emails or non-work-related files, or by taking photos or entering restricted areas. However, it does not grant criminal immunity in these cases, making it a self-standing criminal offence. Even if the whistleblower avoids civil, administrative, or labour liability, they can still face criminal charges, leaving a protection gap.

[150] Directive 2019/1937 (n 27) Recital 32 where it is proposed that the whistleblower should be protected if they had reasonable grounds to believe that the reported breach falls within the Directive's scope. The recital is only soft law, and such a provision does not exist in the Directive. The proposal made is to entail it in the Directive without the need of reasonable grounds but only believing it.

[151] ibid Art 21(3).

[152] See to that end the Luxleaks case, where the two whistleblowers were accused of theft and breach of professional secrecy. See TA Lux, 29 Juin 2016, n° 1981/2016, CA Luxembourg, 15 Mars 2017, n° 117/17 X, CSJ, cass., 11 Janvier 2018, n° 3911 and CSJ, cass., 11 Janvier 2018, n° 3912.

In addition, with the advent of digitalisation, the workplace has changed, now featuring digital information.[153] Consequently, the whistleblower may easily be criminally charged for accessing digital information without permission.[154] This should be clarified to limit criminalisation to computer hacking for personal gain. More attention should be given to acts or omissions unrelated to reporting or unnecessary to it. Does the Directive aim for a proportional safety net that allows whistleblowers to report only what is needed? If there is a reason to include the concept of a standalone criminal offence, it should be clearer. The current wording causes confusion and may discourage future whistleblowers.

K. Do We Really Care About the Motive of the Whistleblower?

The debate about what defines a whistleblower centres on their motives and the public interest nature of their disclosures.[155] The whistleblower's motives are translated into the requirement that the reporting be done in good or bad faith. In contrast, the public-interest requirement concerns the information's impact on the public. For both requirements, different concepts are being developed around their meaning and value, influenced by national and European legislation. In the first part, the analysis will focus on the good-faith requirement, outlining the two interpretations and presenting the approach adopted by the Directive. In the second part, the public interest requirement will be analysed to understand the concept and examine how it is embodied in the Directive.

The 'in good faith' provision is a contentious concept in international, European, and national whistleblowing laws.[156] Despite its dominance some years ago, many countries have abandoned the 'in good faith' requirement in favour of a 'public interest' concept.[157] The good faith requirement can be found in several international instruments.[158] It can also be found in laws like the UK's Public Interest Disclosure Act (PIDA) and France's Law Sapin II.[159] The British legislation on the

[153] R Bosua, S Milton, S Dreyfus and R Lederman, 'Going Public: Researching External Whistleblowing in a New Media Age' in AJ Brown, D Lewis, R Moberly and W Vandekerckhove (eds), *International Research Handbook on Whistle-blowing* (Routledge, 2014) 250.

[154] S Waserman, 'Improving the Protection of Whistleblowers all over Europe' (2019) Council of Europe, Committee on Legal Affairs and Human Rights 15.

[155] S Oelrich, 'Making Regulation Fit by Taking Irrationality into Account: The Case of the Whistleblower' (2019) 12 *Business Research* 175, 181.

[156] ibid.

[157] ibid. See also J Alibert and JP Foegle, 'Première victoire d'un lanceur d'alerte en référé sous l'empire de la loi "Sapin II"' [2019] *La Revue des droits de l'homme*, 5–6, journals.openedition.org/revdh/6313 accessed 15 May 2025.

[158] For example, the OECD Anti-Bribery Convention, the United Nations Convention against Corruption (UNCAC) and the Civil Law Convention of the Council of Europe on Corruption.

[159] UK Public Interest Disclosure Act 1998 and Law N° 2016-1691 of 6 December 2016 related to transparency, the fight against corruption and the modernization of economic life, JORF n°0287.

protection of whistleblowers was the first adopted in Europe, and it required good faith for protection.[160] The good-faith requirement had been criticised, leading the British legislator to remove it in 2013.[161] The French legislation followed a similar path under Law Sapin II, but it abolished the good-faith requirement when the Directive was transposed.

Under Article 6 of French law on whistleblower protection, individuals must report in good faith without financial gain. Good faith means acting without personal benefit and in the public interest, in line with the European Court of Human Rights' case law, especially in the landmark case of *Guja v Moldova*. The Court's six criteria include good faith in recognising and protecting whistleblowers' right to freedom of expression.[162] Personal grievances should not drive whistleblowing. The good faith requirement under French law was expected, as French courts had already interpreted it.[163]

The European Court of Human Rights states that a bona fide whistleblower must have acted in good faith and believed the information was accurate, disclosing it in the public interest.[164] The Strasbourg Court excludes whistleblowers acting in bad faith, motivated by personal gain, financial expectations, or antagonism, from protection. It stresses that those driven by personal gain or antagonism do not warrant the same protection as good-faith whistleblowers.

In the *Soares* case, the Strasbourg Court doubted the applicant's good faith after the national courts' decision. It noted that the applicant accused another employee of misusing public money but lacked evidence, relying on rumours.[165] The Strasbourg Court reaffirmed the national courts' findings that the applicant did not act in good faith. In the *Langner* case, it based its analysis on the facts and concluded that the applicant's unfounded allegation of a serious crime was a defamatory accusation rather than public criticism.[166]

The Strasbourg Court, having adopted a case-by-case analysis, scrutinises the whistleblower's motives to determine whether they acted in good faith. This fact conflicts with the proposed practices of the Council of Europe. In Resolution 1729 in 2010, the Council of Europe stated that: 'any whistleblower shall be considered as having acted in good faith provided he or she had reasonable grounds to believe that the information disclosed was true [...]'.[167] In 2014, the Council of Europe's Recommendation CM/Rec(2014)7 confirmed the approach adopted in

[160] J Ashton, '15 Years of Whistleblowing Protection under the Public Interest Disclosure Act 1998: Are We Still Shooting the Messenger?' (2015) 44(1) *Industrial Law Journal* 29, 35.

[161] For criticism, see Secretary of State for Health, *Shipman Inquiry 5th Report* (Cm 6394, 2004) and Ashton (n 160) 51–52.

[162] *Guja v Moldova* (n 49) paras 92–94.

[163] Code du travail, Art L.1132-3 and L.1161-1, Cass. soc., 5 juillet 2011, n° 10-23.319, Cass. soc., 6 juin 2012, n° 10-28.345 and Cass, soc., 29 octobre 2013, n° 12-22.447.

[164] *Guja v Moldova* (n 49) para 77.

[165] *Soares v Portugal*, App no 79972/12, §46 ECHR 2016.

[166] *Langner v Germany*, App no 14464/11, §§47–49, ECHR 2015.

[167] Council of Europe Parliamentary Assembly, 'Resolution 1729 (2010), Protection of Whistleblower's (adopted by the Parliamentary Assembly at the 17th sitting on 29 April 2010), para 6.2.4.

the 2010 Resolution.[168] Under its principle 22, the intention is to grant protection to the whistleblower, independent of their motives. In a recent report of the Parliamentary Assembly, the same point was made.[169] To that extent, the texts of the Council of Europe differ from the case law of the Strasbourg Court, demonstrating that the good-faith requirement can easily become dangerous and unpredictable in the Court's application.

Before analysing the Directive's perspective on good faith, it is essential to review the objective and subjective analysis of the requirement. In its objective analysis, good faith ignores the whistleblower's motives, like antagonism, and focuses on whether the reported facts were accurate at the time.[170] The whistleblower should reasonably believe in the report's authenticity and the truthfulness of the facts.[171] From an objective analysis of the good-faith requirement, the focus is on the merits of the information provided to avoid false reporting.[172]

In its subjective analysis, the good-faith requirement concerns the motives of the whistleblower, such as personal interests, animosity, or revenge, that may cause harm.[173] The whistleblower blows the whistle because they expect something in return and have personal interests to satisfy, rather than protecting the public with the report.[174] For the subjective analysis, our focus is on the messenger, not the information transmitted.[175] The whistleblower's intentions are in the spotlight and will be assessed to determine whether the employee is a whistleblower. The subjective aspect of good faith also eliminates any pecuniary advantage for the whistleblower, such as financial rewards. Being financially compensated is considered bad-faith whistleblowing because the ultimate motive is the money received, rather than the importance of reporting wrongdoing to prevent subsequent harm.[176]

From the aforementioned analysis of the good-faith requirement, it is clear that it is a complex and nuanced concept that can easily shift in meaning and interpretation before the courts. The Directive has opted for an objective analysis of the good-faith requirement. First, the Directive states, in a clear way, that: 'the motives

[168] Council of Europe Committee of Ministers, 'Recommendation CM/Rec(2014)7, Protection of Whistle-blowers' (adopted by the Committee of Ministers at the 1198th meeting on 30 April 2014).

[169] Council of Europe (n 36) 15.

[170] Conseil d'Etat, 'Le droit d'alerte: signaler, traiter, protéger' (2016) 73. See also JP Foegle, 'Un renforcement en demi-teinte du statut du lanceur d'alerte dans - l'Europe des droits de l'homme' [2015] *La Revue des droits de l'homme*, Actualités Droits-Libertés, 9–10, revdh.revues.org/1073 accessed 15 May 2025 and Transparency International. 'A Best Practice Guide for Whistleblowing Legislation' (2018) 15, www.transparency.org/whatwedo/publication/best_practice_guide_for_whistleblowing_legislation accessed 15 May 2025.

171Conseil d'Etat (n 170) 73.

[172] Transparency International (n 170) 15.

[173] Conseil d'Etat (n 170) 73.

[174] ibid.

[175] Transparency International (n 170) 15.

[176] F Barrière, 'Les lanceurs d'alerte' [2017] *Revue des sociétés* 191, 194; Conseil d'Etat (n 170) 76. The whistleblowers should not have reporting as a regular activity (like a job), but they should act in the public interest avoiding any pecuniary advantage for their act.

of the reporting persons in reporting should be irrelevant in deciding whether they should receive protection'.[177] Before the final text of the Directive, there was no discussion on the subjective perception of good faith. While it does not require a personal motive test for whistleblowers, it also does not offer financial rewards or compensation.[178] It clearly differentiates whistleblowers from informants who report breaches for monetary reward.[179] If motives do not matter, why exclude financial rewards?[180]

Although the issue of financial rewards is analysed elsewhere, some preliminary comments can be made here about the whistleblower's motives and rewards. Exclusion of rewards may be justified under the objective analysis of the good-faith requirement, as the Directive requires that the whistleblower reasonably believe, based on the circumstances and available information, that the reported matters are factual, in accordance with the good-faith principle discussed above.[181]

The interest is in the truthfulness or honest belief that the information was accurate, not in the whistleblower's motivation.[182] In that way, abusive or malicious reporting of wrong or misleading information will not be protected under the Directive.[183] It is clear, thus, that the Directive focuses on the information rather than the whistleblower's personal motivation. What is unclear is whether the breach constitutes a threat or harm to the public interest, where the interest in excluding financial rewards also lies.

L. Public Interest or Not: The Dilemma

The Directive is confusing on the point of public interest. The Directive's recitals specify that the breach must threaten or harm the public interest.[184] Although the public interest requirement is clear in the Directive's preamble, it is not mentioned in the related articles, which state only that the information must be accurate at the time of reporting.[185] There is a discrepancy between the recitals and the

[177] Directive 2019/1937 (n 27) Recital 32.

[178] S Andreadakis, 'Enhancing Whistleblower Protection: It's All About the Culture' (2019) 30(6) *European Business Law Review* 859, 868 (many whistleblowers have argued that their choice was driven by strong moral preferences and not any financial incentives, a concept that the Directive seems to adhere to).

[179] Directive 2019/1937 (n 27) Recital 30. See D Kafteranis, 'The Question of One Million Dollars: Financial Rewards or Not for the Whistle-blowers' (2021) 36 (4) *International Journal of Banking Law and Regulation* 160. See also ch 7, financial rewards, p 366.

[180] European Commission, Impact Assessment (n 7) 36. The European Commission considers that introducing financial rewards will shift the purpose of reporting away from the public interest to the personal gain of whistleblowers, thus making reporting appear as a commercial transaction which may discredit the whistleblowing process.

[181] Directive 2019/1937 (n 27) Recital 32 and Art 6(1).

[182] ibid Recital 32.

[183] ibid.

[184] ibid Recitals 1, 5, 31 and 37.

[185] ibid Art 6(1)(a).

articles of the Directive regarding the public interest requirement. It may be that the Directive intends to exclude interpersonal grievances from its scope, referring instead to harm or a threat to the public interest. However, this causes confusion for future whistleblowers about the meaning of 'public interest'. When harm or a threat poses a risk to the public interest, whistleblowers face a new, ambiguous obstacle to reporting.[186]

The distinction regarding the public-interest requirement is between public and private interests.[187] The whistleblower should report harm or threats in the public interest, not private interest. While public interest will be analysed, private interest offers interesting considerations. As mentioned earlier, the Directive aims to exclude reports related to personal grievances or breaches of individual working conditions.[188] These types of personal grievances or violations of individual working conditions fall within the private interest sphere and are therefore not protected under the Directive. The whistleblower should be a responsible citizen who distances themselves from their interests and considers the public interest.[189] This report type may be interpersonal and conflictual, but it also justifies public interest. If an employer harms employees, causing psychiatric issues or suicides, is that not in the public interest? When a whistleblower reports, are they reporting harm or a threat to public interest (human lives)? Judges at the national or European level will determine it if this question comes up. The judges will determine the meaning of public interest, which is not easily defined and varies from case to case. The European Commission provided examples such as law violations, human rights, public health, and environmental risks, but the list is not exhaustive.[190] This situation presents two different conflicting aspects for the whistleblower.

The first aspect, which can be characterised as an advantage for the whistleblower, is that judges determine the concept of public interest in the context of legal rights in different factual situations.[191] Depending on the facts of the case and the timing of the whistleblowing, judges have the power to recognise a particular event as of public interest and, thus, allow for whistleblowers' protection. On the other hand, the second aspect, which is a disadvantage for the whistleblower, is that the whistleblower may not know in advance with sufficient certainty how the public interest will be applied.[192] Previous court decisions have indicated when a particular event falls within the concept of public interest, but this is not sufficient to reassure the whistleblower about their claim.[193] This may discourage the whistleblower from reporting certain events when they are unsure whether the public interest requirement is met.

[186] E Boot, *The Ethics of Whistleblowing* (Routledge, 2019) 24–25.
[187] European Commission, Impact Assessment (n 7) 8.
[188] ibid.
[189] Conseil d'État, rapport public, *L'intérêt général*, ED n° 50 (1999) 357.
[190] European Commission, Impact Assessment (n 7) 7.
[191] Lewis (n 40) 141.
[192] ibid.
[193] ibid.

Furthermore, the European Parliament, in its October 2017 Resolution, defines the whistleblower as someone who reports in the public interest and in the European public interest.[194] The European public interest is as vague as the broader concept of public interest. European law lacks a clear definition of public interest, even though terms like 'general' or 'common interest' are used.[195] Under European law, the concept of public interest can refer to the interests of public institutions or private interests. It is not strictly defined and varies depending on the context.

In conclusion, the Directive has not dismissed the good-faith requirement but has adopted an objective approach in which the interest lies in the truthfulness of the facts rather than the personal motives of the whistleblower. The interest lies in the transposition of this point from Member States, who may seek to extend the good-faith requirement to a subjective analysis.[196] France has maintained the good-faith requirement, defended by the Cour de Cassation, Conseil d'état, and Défenseur des droits.[197] French courts and the Défenseur des droits say good faith means the honesty of the whistleblower to avoid malicious intent, but it is a case-by-case approach in which the concept varies. France overlooks the Directive's emphasis on reported information rather than the whistleblower's intent.

The concept of the public interest requirement is problematic, as explained. First, it is not clear from the Directive whether this is a requirement for whistleblowers under the new EU legal framework. This is a focal point that the European Commission should clarify after the transposition period. If the public interest requirement is to be introduced, it would be important to clarify the concept of public interest or, at least, provide concrete guidelines on it at the EU level.

[194] Resolution (n 51) para 14.

[195] C Hossfeld, Y Muller-Lagarde, D Alexandre, M Poschke and L Zevounou, 'L'intérêt public européen/European public interest: Rapport de recherche final' (2018) ANC – Rapport de recherche – Autorité des normes comptables 1, 15.

[196] S Gerdemann, 'Position paper on the national implementation of the Directive for the protection of persons reporting on breaches of Union law' (2019) point 7, www.whistleblower-net.de/wp-content/uploads/2020/05/Paper-National-Implementation-WBD.pdf accessed 15 May 2025.

[197] Defenseur des droits (2024) Biennial Report on the protection of whistleblowers in France 2022-2023. Court of Cassation, Soc., 16 September 2020, No 18-26.696, published in the bulletin. Court of Cassation, Soc., 13 January 2021, No 19-21.138, published in the bulletin. Conseil d'État, 8 December 2023, No 435266, in Tables.

6

The Dilemma for the Whistleblower

Report Internally or Externally?

I. The Proceduralisation of Blowing the Whistle

Historically, whistleblowing was regarded as disobedience, involving the public disclosure of wrongdoing without prior internal or official channels reporting. Now, protection demands compliance with legal and procedural requirements. The whistleblower must first meet legal definitions and then adhere to reporting channels.

Consequently, defining whistleblowing procedures is essential in legislation and guarantees the protection of whistleblowers' legal rights.[1] At the European level, there seems to be a specific approach, known as the 'three-tier model'.[2] In a nutshell, this means the whistleblower should report internally first – within their workplace. Second, if they cannot report internally for different reasons,[3] the whistleblower should report to the relevant competent authorities. Third, if reporting to the relevant competent authorities is not possible, the whistleblower can then disclose the information to the public.[4]

This chapter analyses the channels of 'blowing the whistle' as outlined in the Directive, demonstrating how EU rules seek to make whistleblowing a more effective tool for compliance.[5] One reason the EU adopted the Directive was to enforce rules more effectively in key areas within its scope.[6] The whistleblower is an essential tool for better enforcement of EU rules and for assisting competent authorities in detecting wrongdoing.[7] This relationship between whistleblowers and competent

[1] J Lewis, J Bowers QC, M Fodder and J Mirchell, *Whistleblowing – Law and Practice*, 3rd edn (OUP, 2017) 101.

[2] W Vandekerckhove, 'European Whistleblower Protection: Tiers or Tears?' in D Lewis (ed), *A Global Approach to Public Interest Disclosure*: (Edward Elgar, 2010) 15–35.

[3] For instance, it may be the case that there are no internal reporting structures, or the recipients of internal reports are also involved in the wrongdoing.

[4] R Bosua, S Milton, S Dreyfus and R Lederman, 'Going Public: Researching External Whistleblowing in a New Media Age' in AJ Brown, D Lewis, R Moberly and W Vandekerckhove (eds), *International Research Handbook on Whistleblowing* (Routledge, 2014) 251.

[5] European Parliament and European Council Directive 2019/1937/EU of 23 October 2019 on the protection of persons who report breaches of Union law [2019] OJ L305/17.

[6] European Commission, Proposal for a Directive of the European Parliament and of the European Council on the protection of persons reporting breaches of Union law COM(2018) 218 final, 6, ec.europa.eu/info/sites/info/files/placeholder_8.pdf accessed 15 May 2025.

[7] D Kafteranis, 'A New Enforcement Tool: A Directive to Protect Whistle-blowers' (2020) 41 *Business Law Review* 50.

authorities will be at the centre of the analysis. The role of whistleblowers as enforcement tools will be examined to assess their potential to achieve positive outcomes.

The first part examines the 'three-tier model' and the laws of some states to better introduce the concept of 'reporting' channels. Then, it focuses on the EU Directive, showing how negotiations led to a lenient reporting approach.[8] Additionally, various aspects will be examined to outline the advantages and disadvantages of reporting channels as described in the Directive.

II. To Whom to Trust my Reporting: National Legislations and the ECtHR Case Law

'Blowing the whistle' is a complex process in which an employee reports to their employer or a designated person.[9] The literature distinguishes between internal and external whistleblowing.[10] Internal reporting involves reporting wrongdoings at work or to a third party designated by the employer. External whistleblowing refers to reporting outside the workplace, with two main forms of external whistleblowing. Employees should either report to an external authority or disclose information publicly, such as through the media.[11]

Another distinction between internal and external whistleblowing concerns the hierarchy of signalling pathways.[12] The common model in Europe is the 'three-tier' approach, where whistleblowers first report internally to designated persons. If that fails or proves ineffective, they can report to authorities and, as a last resort, go public.[13] Various countries have adopted this model in different variations and formats, including those with existing legislation protecting whistleblowers, such as the Irish and French whistleblowing laws, as well as the case law of the European Court of Human Rights (ECtHR or Strasbourg Court).[14] The French and ECtHR approaches were similar, while the Irish approach had specific minor differences.

[8] By 'lenient', the whistleblower is free to report either internally or to the authorities. This freedom comes in contrast with the strict approach of obligatory internal reporting as proposed by the European Commission in the proposal for the Directive.

[9] W Vanderkerckhove, AJ Brown and E Tsahuridu, 'Managerial Responsiveness to Whistleblowing: Expanding the Research Horizon' in AJ Brown, D Lewis, R Moberly and W Vandekerckhove (eds), *International Research Handbook on Whistleblowing* (Routledge, 2014) 299–300.

[10] ibid.

[11] ibid.

[12] D Kafteranis, 'Reporting to the Boss or the Authorities: The Ongoing Dilemma of the Whistleblower' [2018] *Cambridge Law Review* 10.

[13] UK Public Interest Disclosure Act 1998, the Irish Public Disclosures Act 2014 and the French Law Sapin II.

[14] Protected Disclosures Act 2014, No 14 of 2014, ss 5–10; Law No 2016-1691 of 6 December 2016 related to transparency, the fight against corruption and the modernisation of economic life, JORF n°0287, Art 8; *Guja v Moldova* App no 14277/04 (ECtHR 12 February 2008); V Junod, 'Lancer l'alerte: quoi de neuf depuis 'Guja'?: (Cour eur. dr. h., 'Bucur et Toma c. Roumanie', 8 janvier 2013)' (2014) 98 *Revue trimestrielle des droits de l'homme* 459–82.

The Strasbourg Court, in *Guja v Moldova* and subsequent whistleblowing cases, held that whistleblowers must follow the specified procedural path.[15] One of the six criteria under Article 10 of the ECHR for whistleblower protection concerns how information is disclosed: it should first be shared internally with a superior, then with a competent authority or body.[16] If this is impossible, the information can be disclosed to the public as an *ultima ratio*.[17] Only if those conditions are met should the whistleblower be considered for protection. Its case law has served as a blueprint for various national legislations, including the French and Irish laws on whistleblowers' protection.

Under French Law Sapin II (named after the minister who enacted it), the whistleblower had to report internally, then to authorities if the internal system failed, and finally, to disclose to the public.[18] The Law Sapin II established procedural steps for whistleblowers to obtain protection.[19] Reporting, driven by freedom of expression, must align with discretion and loyalty and be proportional. Law Sapin II specified the steps employees should follow.[20] The Law Sapin II approach changed with the Waserman Law amendments, which transposed the Directive.[21] The new law allows whistleblowers to report

[15] *Guja v Moldova* (n 14). See also *Heinisch v Germany*, App no 28274/08, ECHR 2011 and *Bucur et Toma v Roumania*, App no 40238/02, ECHR, 2013.

[16] N Colneric, 'Does the Case Law of the European Court of Human Rights Show that the Convention States of the European Convention on Human Rights Must Prescribe Priority of Internal Whistleblowing as a Rule?' (2018) 6 *Soziales Recht* 232.

[17] *Guja v Moldova* (n 14).

[18] See Law No 2016-1691 Art 8, which reads: 'I. Reporting of information should be brought to the attention of a direct or indirect line manager of the employer or to a person appointed by the employer. In the absence of any by the aforementioned person to verify, in a reasonable amount of time, the admissibility of the report, the report is addressed to the judicial authorities, the administrative authorities or to the professional orders. As a last resort, in case that the aforementioned authorities and orders did not treat the report within three months, the employee can report to the public.
II. In case of an imminent and important danger or in the presence of a risk with irreversible damages, reporting can be done directly to the authorities or orders mentioned above. It can be made public too.
III. Appropriate procedures for collecting reports from staff members or external or occasional collaborators should be established by the public or private corporations that have at least fifty employees, the administrative state entities, the municipalities of at least 10000 citizens, as well as by the public inter-municipality cooperation establishments (EPICs) to which they are members, the departments and the regions under specific conditions as they will be decreed by the Council of State (Conseil d'Etat).
IV. Every person can address his/her report to the Advocate of Human Rights in order to orient this person to the appropriate organisation which will receive the report.'

[19] Tribunal Administratif de Châlons-en-Champagne, n° 1701162 du 13 Février 2018. See also S Dyens, 'Le bénéfice de la protection due au lanceur d'alerte est conditionné au respect de la procédure d'alerte' [2018] *AJ Collectivités Territoriales* 404.

[20] P Pailler, 'Le nouveau statut de lanceur d'alerte'[2017] *Revue du droit bancaire et financier* 1, 3.

[21] R Gauvain and O Marleix, Rapport d'information (…) sur l'évaluation de l'impact de la loi n° 2016-1691 du 9 décembre 2016 relative à la transparence, à la lutte contre la corruption et à la modernisation de la vie économique, dite 'loi Sapin 2' (2021) www.vie-publique.fr/rapport/281075-evaluation-de-limpact-de-la-loi-sapin-2_accessed 15 May 2025.

internally or to authorities, removing the previous requirement to report internally at first.[22]

The Irish approach initially aligns with the same reasoning as the abovementioned procedural requirements for whistleblowing. The Protected Disclosures Act 2014 (PDA) adopted a stepped disclosure regime, but unlike others, it does not require whistleblowers to report internally at first. Instead, it incentivises internal reporting before reaching authorities or the public. Protection conditions are tied to these incentives. Reporting to their employer is the most straightforward approach, with no additional criteria required for protection.[23] The whistleblower could report directly to authorities, but should believe the information is accurate and that the recipient is the right person to inform.[24] Finally, the whistleblower could disclose the information publicly, but stricter conditions would then be required to protect them.[25] Although it is not expressly required, the Act requires the worker to report to their employer or to another person who has the legal responsibility to accept their concerns.[26]

III. The Innovative Approach of the EU Directive

A. The Proposal for a Directive: The Commission's Insistence on Compulsory Internal Reporting

The European Commission proposed the Directive to protect whistleblowers and suggested a 'three-tier model' for the reporting process.[27] Under Article 13 of the Proposal, protection depended on compliance with the disclosure channels.[28] Under the proposal, the whistleblower was obliged to report internally at first and could only report to authorities if conditions in Article 13(2) were met. Public disclosure was a last resort if certain conditions applied.[29] The proposal promoted a strict conditional model requiring internal reporting, allowing whistleblowers to report externally only under certain conditions.[30] The Commission's stance demonstrated its strong preference for internal reporting, viewing whistleblowers as an internal resource for employers.

[22] S Andreadakis and D Kafteranis, 'Internal Whistleblowing in the US after Digital Realty Trust v Somers: Any Lessons to be Learnt from Europe?' (2025) 54(2) *Industrial Law Journal* 357.

[23] Protected Disclosures Act 2014, number 14 of 2014, s 6.

[24] ibid s 7.

[25] ibid s 8.

[26] ibid s 5.

[27] European Commission, Proposal for a directive (n 6).

[28] ibid.

[29] ibid Art 13(4).

[30] G Georgiadou, 'The European Commission's proposal for Strengthening Whistleblower Protection' (2018) 3 *European Criminal Law Forum* 167.

B. Heated Debate in the EU Parliament

Following the European Commission's proposal, one of the points of debate among different institutional actors was the three-tier reporting model.[31] There was disagreement among committees and stakeholders; some argued for changing the Proposal to allow internal reporting and reporting to authorities under the same protection threshold. Others supported the Commission's approach, requiring internal reporting first. The former was defended by the European Economic and Social Committee, the Committee on the Environment, Public Health and Food Safety, and the Economic and Monetary Affairs Committee, who called for equal access to both channels without prior use of internal channels.[32]

Other voices supported maintaining the current reporting scheme or argued that providing detailed reporting rules would violate the principle of proportionality in the system.[33] This point was heavily debated during negotiations between the European Parliament and the Council. The Council favoured keeping the Proposal's model, but Parliament pressed for change. The Parliament's proposed change was ultimately adopted in the Directive.[34]

C. The Influence from the Other Side of the Atlantic

US whistleblower laws have also influenced this new approach to reporting channels. As shown in previous chapters, the 2008 financial crisis and early 2000s scandals prompted the US to pass laws addressing financial misconduct. One step was promoting whistleblowing to rebuild trust and reform corporate governance. The Sarbanes-Oxley Act (2002) included internal whistleblowing

[31] European Parliament and European Council, 'Proposal for a Directive of the European Parliament and of the Council on the Protection of Persons Reporting Breaches of Union Law: Progress Report', February 2019, 4.

[32] EESC, 'Opinion of the European Economic and Social Committee on Communication from the Commission to the European Parliament, the Council and the European Economic and Social Committee Strengthening Whistleblower Protection at EU Level' (COM (2018) 214 final). See also European Commission, 'Proposal for a Directive of the European Parliament and of the Council on the Protection of Persons Reporting Beaches of Union Law' (COM (2018) 218 final), C 62/155, February 2019, 4; CEPHFS, 'Opinion of the Committee on the Environment, Public Health and Food Safety for the Committee on Legal Affairs on the Proposal for a Directive of the European Parliament and of the Council on the Protection of Persons Reporting on Breaches of Union Law' (September 2018) 3–4. See also CEMA, 'Opinion of the Committee on Economic and Monetary Affairs for the Committee on Legal Affairs on the Proposal for a Directive of the European Parliament and of the Council on the Protection of Persons Reporting on Breaches of Union Law' (September 2018) 3.

[33] European Court of Auditors, 'Opinion n° 4/2018 concerning the Proposal for a Directive of the European Parliament and of the Council on the Protection of Persons Reporting Breaches of Union Law' (2018) 5. The Swedish Parliament, Opinion on the Application of the Principles of Subsidiarity and Proportionality (Proposal for a Directive of the European Parliament and of the Council on the Protection of Persons Reporting on Breaches of Union Law) (June 2018) 4.

[34] European Parliament and European Council, Proposal for a Directive (n 31) 4.

rules to encourage compliance but faced criticism for inadequate whistleblower protection.[35]

Meanwhile, a banking crisis prompted the enactment of the Dodd-Frank Act in 2010.[36] New provisions for whistleblowers were adopted, offering benefits and giving the SEC new powers. The SEC can now provide financial rewards to whistleblowers under specific conditions.[37] This drew potential whistleblowers, who seemed protected whether reporting internally or to the SEC. The SEC confirmed this, but the US Supreme Court disagreed in *Digital Realty Trust Inc. v Somers.*[38]

The Court ruled that a whistleblower can seek protection under the Dodd-Frank Act only if they report to the SEC.[39] The US relies more on external whistleblowing and trust in authorities. SOX's internal systems failed, leading Congress to grant the SEC greater power under Dodd-Frank.[40] Congress decided whistleblowers should report to the SEC for protection under Dodd-Frank, confirmed in *Digital Realty Trust Inc. v Somers*, emphasising external reporting to authorities over internal reporting.[41]

The National Whistleblower Center (NWC), a US non-profit supporting whistleblowers worldwide, expressed its stance during the Directive negotiations. Stephen M Kohn, NWC's board chairman, emphasised the need for a lenient reporting approach.[42] He argued that a strict hierarchy between internal and external whistleblowing would impede companies from trading stocks in the US due to different regulations.[43] He highlighted the risk of a self-defeating Directive, in which EU employees might notify US authorities rather than national authorities for better protection.[44] This evidence is backed by the fact that, between 2011 and 2018, over 1,000 European employees notified the SEC.[45] Although US influence

[35] BH Earle and GA Madek, 'The Mirage of Whistleblower Protection Under Sarbanes-Oxley: A Proposal for Change' (2007) 44 *American Business Law Journal* 1, 19–24.

[36] 15 U.S.C. § 78n (2012).

[37] Dodd-Frank Wall Street Reform and Consumer Protection Act (Dodd-Frank Act), Pub. L. No. 111-203, §§748, 922, 124 Stat. 1380, 1381 (2010) (codified in 15 U.S.C. § 78n (2012)).

[38] *Digital Realty Trust Inc. v Somers*, 138 US 767 (2018).

[39] BJ McAllister, 'The Impact of the Dodd-Frank Whistle-blower Provisions on FCPA Enforcement and Modern Corporate Compliance Programs' (2017) 14 *Berkley Business Law Journal* 45, 51–52. The conflict was between the definition of whistleblower in s 21F(a)(6) and the requirements to qualify as a whistleblower when an employee makes an internal disclosure under s 21F(h)(1)(A)(iii). The US courts were divided on this issue before the decision of the Supreme Court.

[40] R Vaughn, *The Successes and Failures of Whistle-blower Laws* (EE Publications, 2012) 153.

[41] *Somers* (n 38) 777. See also Senate Report No. 111-76, 110 (2010). The Congress's purpose was 'to motivate with inside knowledge to come forward and assist the Government to identify and prosecute persons who have violated securities laws and recover money for victims of financial fraud'.

[42] SM Kohn, 'Letter to the President of the European Parliament in relation to the Proposal for a Directive of the European Parliament and of the Council on the Protection of Persons Reporting Breaches of Union Law' (2019) 7 www.whistleblowers.org/wp-content/uploads/2019/02/EU-WB-Directive-Letter-2.7.19.pdf accessed 15 May 2025.

[43] ibid 7.

[44] ibid 7.

[45] US Securities and Exchange Commission, 'Annual Reports of the Office of the Whistleblower', www.sec.gov/reports?aId=edit-tid&year=All&field_article_sub_type_secart_value=Reports+and+Publications-AnnualReports&tid=59 accessed 15 May 2025.

was indirect, these statistics reveal a key aspect that should have been considered during the Directive negotiations.

D. Victory for the Whistleblowers: The Final Text of the Directive

Despite the three-tier model in laws, Strasbourg Court case law, and some institutions opposing flexibility, the Directive aligns with the European Parliament, allowing whistleblowers to report internally or to authorities without first reporting internally.[46] The Directive adopts a relaxed approach, easing procedural aspects.[47] The European Commission's strict categorisation of whistleblowing has drawn criticism from various actors and scholars.[48] This new approach, under the Directive, introduces an innovation that appears to ease the whistleblower's life.

IV. Internal and External Reporting to the Authorities

The Directive details internal and external reporting channels and their proper use.[49] For example, whistleblowers should get clear information about how their report will be handled, including whether an investigation will occur soon. Proper use of the reporting channel is essential for protection. They can choose internal or external channels without repercussions. Though the Directive favours internal and authority reporting, it restricts public disclosure as a last resort. Usually, whistleblowers must report internally or to authorities before informing the public.

The Directive guides the organisation of internal channels and sets out authorities' obligations as whistleblower recipients.[50] The analysis of these features will be provided in the following sections. The reporting employee can choose where to address themselves, without strict procedural obligations.[51]

[46] Directive 2019/1937, Art 10.

[47] P Portier, 'Les canaux de signalement interne et externe selon le droit européen, une avancée par rapport à la loi Sapin 2?' (2019) 4 *RAE-LAE* 705, 707.

[48] ES Callahan and TM Dworkin, 'Who Blows the Whistle to the Media, and Why: Organisational Characteristics of Media Whistle-blowers' (1994) 96 *American Business Law Journal* 151, 168.

[49] Portier (n 47) 707.

[50] Directive 2019/1937, Arts 7–15.

[51] S White, 'A Matter of Life or Death – Whistleblowing Legislation in the EU' (2018) 3 *European Criminal Law Forum* 172.

A. Why the New Approach adopted by the Directive is Innovative?

The issue of internal or external whistleblowing has long been a topic of interest to legal scholars in the field.[52] Scholars in the US and Europe have discussed the problematic nature of the strict separation between internal and external whistleblowing.[53] The various legal regimes in countries such as France, Ireland, and the US caused confusion for employees.[54] The technical legal requirements, like where to report, were often unclear, making it hard for the whistleblower to understand and follow them.[55] The whistleblower felt uncertain about which path to follow, leaving them dissatisfied and discouraged from reporting.

The negotiators of the Directive considered the criticisms above and decided to adopt a more lenient approach on where and to whom to blow the whistle.[56] This new approach is innovative, offering whistleblowers a choice of reporting channels. It replaces the previous, complex, and uncertain process with a flexible system that grants protection regardless of whether they report internally or to authorities.[57] The whistleblower can choose their reporting channel, a key step in protecting them. However, the Directive still encourages, but does not require, internal reporting before external reporting.[58] Disclosure to the public is considered a last resort, and it becomes the first option only under strict conditions, in accordance with relevant legislation and Strasbourg Court rulings.[59] The chapter analyses whistleblowing paths, how they operate, and the issues they raise.

V. Encouraging, not Obliging, Internal Whistleblowing: A Tool for Internal Compliance

A. The General and Vague Meaning of Information

Article 5(4) of the Directive defines internal reporting as the communication of breaches within a legal entity. Employees must report violations of Union law

[52] J Mendelsohn, 'Calling the Boss or Calling the Press: A Comparison of British and American Responses to Internal and External Whistleblowing' (2009) 8 *Global Studies Law Review* 723, 723–24.

[53] Vanderkerckhove, Brown and Tsahuridu (n 9) 299–300.

[54] Kafteranis (n 12) 10.

[55] E Feldman, 'Whistleblower Protection' in R Byrne and W Binchy (eds), *Annual Review of Irish Law 2011* (Roundhall, 2011) 616–23.

[56] J Vallet-Pamart, 'Genèse de la directive protégeant les lanceurs d'alerte' (2019) 4 *RAE-LAE* 681, 687.

[57] Transparency International, 'Building on the EU Directive for Whistleblower Protection – Analysis and Recommendations' (2019) Position Paper, 2 www.transparency.org/whatwedo/publications accessed 15 May 2025.

[58] Directive 2019/1937, Recitals 33 and 47.

[59] ibid Art 15.

at work. Notably, the whistleblower reports breaches, which are documented in accordance with the Directive.[60] These documents should be related to the violation, and the whistleblower should take only what is necessary to avoid superfluous information.[61] A new burden is placed on the whistleblower, who must carefully gather and submit all the required documents to prove the alleged breach. The Directive does not specify the types or scope of 'document'. The whistleblower may use emails, faxes, taped calls, and other evidence to prove the breach. These could be admissible in court, depending on national law and case law. The whistleblower can report internally, but it is unclear from the Directive what type of information is required.

The Directive sets out obligations for internal reporting and the design of whistleblowing channels.[62] The Directive invites Member States to encourage the use of internal reporting before external reporting (to the authorities) when a breach can be addressed internally, and the whistleblower believes they will not face retaliation.[63] According to Article 10, the Directive does not require whistleblowers to report internally before reporting to the authorities, but Article 7 suggests internal reporting should be encouraged.[64] The interesting point is to observe how Member States will encourage internal reporting and to what extent they may render it quasi-obligatory.[65]

In the preamble to the Directive (Recital 33), explanations are provided on encouraging internal reporting. The whistleblower may feel more at ease reporting internally, a view supported by empirical studies showing that most whistleblowers report internally.[66] Reporting internally allows those closest to the problem to be informed and find solutions. Recital 33 emphasises the need to balance the whistleblower's right to freedom of expression with the employer's right to conduct business, advising whistleblowers to choose the most appropriate channel that

[60] ibid Recital 92.

[61] E Andreis, 'Towards Common Minimum Standards for Whistleblower Protection across the EU' (2019) 4(2) *European Papers* 575, 580 www.europeanpapers.eu/en/europeanforum/towards-common-minimum-standards-for-whistleblower-protection-across-eu accessed 15 May 2025.

[62] Directive 2019/1937, ch II.

[63] ibid Art 7.

[64] A Handley, 'New EU Whistleblowing Directive – What UK Financial Services Firms need to know' (2019) Hogan Lovells Publications, www.hoganlovells.com/en/publications/new-eu-whistleblowing-directive-what-uk-financial-services-firms-need-to-know accessed 15 May 2025.

[65] See, for instance, the Irish legislation where internal whistleblowing is not obligatory, but it is implied to be the first path the whistleblower should take. The Act incentivises internal reporting. Although it is not expressly required, the wording of the Act requires the worker to report to his employer or to another person that has legal responsibility for reporting. Public bodies have the obligation to establish internal procedures for the disclosure of information from the public servants. As for the private sector, the employer has the responsibility to enact and incentivise internal reporting. The Workplace Relations Commission has prepared a draft code of practice in order to give guidelines to the employers related to the new law and the internal whistleblowing structures that should be designed and put in place. This Code is not of an obligatory nature, but it is considered as guidance for the employers.

[66] R Moberly, 'To Persons or Organisations that may be Able to Effect Action: Whistle-blowing Recipients' in AJ Brown, D Lewis, R Moberly and W Vandekerckhove (eds), *International Research Handbook on Whistleblowing* (Routledge, 2014) 277.

balances these conflicting rights.[67] The whistleblower may prefer to report internally first out of loyalty to their employer.

B. What Should Employers Do? Step One: Establish Internal Reporting Channels

Under Article 8 of the Directive, legal entities in both the public and private sectors must establish internal reporting mechanisms and procedures for reporting.[68] A private-sector legal entity is one with 50+ employees, while a public-sector legal entity is a public legal entity or is controlled by such an entity.[69] In practice, private-sector legal entities with more than 50 employees must establish internal reporting channels.[70]

Special provisions are being applied to legal entities in the banking and financial sector. According to the Directive, the 50-employee threshold does not apply in this case.[71] Legal entities in banking and finance should adopt internal reporting mechanisms regardless of size due to their unique risks. Following the 2008 crisis, the EU established provisions on whistleblowing in this sector.[72] For example, the SSM Regulation in the EU banking sector and the MAR in the EU financial sector.[73] These instruments required establishing reporting channels and protecting employees.[74] In the Annexes of the Directive, these areas are specified, and for these areas, internal reporting schemes should be independently established regardless of the number of employees.[75]

Public sector legal entities should establish internal reporting schemes, except municipalities with fewer than 10,000 inhabitants or fewer than 50 employees, and other entities with fewer than 50 employees which Member States may exempt.[76] The Directive allows Member States to allow municipalities to share or jointly

[67] Directive 2019/1937, Recital 33.

[68] ibid Art 8. In ch 5, adequate analysis is done about to whom the Directive is addressed. It is significant that the Directive applies to workers at the national level but not to EU officials.

[69] ibid Arts 8(3) and 6(9)

[70] A Keenan, 'The EU's Whistleblowing Directive' (2019) blogs.orrick.com/financial/ accessed 15 May 2025.

[71] Directive 2019/1937, Art 8(4).

[72] ibid Recital 7.

[73] Regulation 1024/2013 conferring specific tasks on the European Central Bank concerning policies relating to the prudential supervision of credit institutions (2013) OJ L287/63 (SSM Regulation) and Regulation 596/2014 on market abuse (2014) OJ L173. For an extensive analysis of the pre-existing rules on whistleblowing in the EU banking and financial sector, see ch 3.

[74] For more details on the coexistence of these sectoral provisions and the Directive, see D Kafteranis, 'Sectoral Provisions and the Directive on the Protection of Whistle-blowers: No to a Complex Relationship?' (2020) *Oxford Business Law Blog* (OBLB) www.law.ox.ac.uk/business-law-blog/blog/2020/06/sectoral-provisions-and-directive-protection-whistle-blowers-no accessed 15 May 2025.

See also M Lehmann and C Kumpan (eds), *European Financial Services Law* (Beck – Hart – Nomos, 2019).

[75] Directive 2019/1937, Annex Parts I.B and II. See also ch 3.

[76] Directive 2019/1937, Art 8(9).

operate internal reporting schemes, provided these channels are autonomous and separate from external reporting mechanisms.[77]

Member States should monitor the fulfilment of these duties.[78] The design of internal reporting mechanisms should involve social partners, as mandated by national law.[79] These internal reporting mechanisms should enable employees and other interested parties engaged in work-related activities to report issues. Reporting channels can be managed internally by a responsible person or department, or assigned to a third party, provided that the safeguards and requirements of the Directive are followed, notably the independence and impartiality of the assigned persons and/or department.[80] Member States can request private-sector legal entities to establish internal reporting mechanisms, despite being exempted, if they believe the activities pose significant risks, provided they notify the European Commission.[81] Private sector entities can share resources to receive and investigate reports, ensure confidentiality, provide feedback, and address breaches.[82]

C. Step Two: Designing the Reporting Channels

In addition to the obligation to establish internal reporting channels, the Directive provides specific guidance on their design.[83] First, channels should be designed and operated securely to protect the confidentiality of the whistleblower and any other parties mentioned.[84] Access to non-authorised members of staff should be prohibited.[85] The reporting person should get acknowledgement of their report within seven days or less.[86] Confidentiality concerns arise when, for example, a department with three employees (one male, two female) includes a male report that could reveal his identity. This highlights the need to prioritise safeguarding whistleblowers' confidentiality.

Once the above requirements are met, the legal entities must appoint an independent and impartial person or department to follow up on whistleblower reports, communicate with them, request additional information if needed, and provide feedback.[87] The Directive allows this person or department to be the same as or different from the one receiving reports.[88] This provision may cause confusion by implicating multiple internal actors, thereby increasing the whistleblower's

[77] ibid Art 8(8).
[78] Handley (n 64).
[79] Directive 2019/1937, Art 8(1).
[80] ibid Art 8(5).
[81] ibid Art 8(9).
[82] ibid Art 8(6).
[83] Handley (n 64).
[84] Directive 2019/1937, Art 9(1)(a).
[85] ibid.
[86] ibid Art 9(1)(b).
[87] ibid Art 9(1)(c).
[88] ibid.

exposure. This issue and other problems of internal whistleblowing will be discussed further below.

The designated person or department must diligently follow up on the report.[89] The Directive's text is ambiguous regarding anonymous reporting.[90] The report must be kept confidential, but national laws should specify how designated persons or departments follow up on anonymous reports.[91] Consequently, internal reporting can be anonymous if permitted by national legislation.[92] The Directive does not require Member States to protect anonymous whistleblowers, but it extends protection to those who are identified and suffer retaliation.[93] If the person meets the Directive's criteria, they can seek protection by referencing the Directive.[94] The paradox is that the Directive cannot include provisions on anonymous reporting but only protects these persons if their identity is revealed. But could an anonymous person facing retaliation be protected under the Directive?

These internal reporting structures should operate within the time limits specified by the Directive.[95] The responsible person or department must update the whistleblower on the progress of the report within three months of acknowledgement, or, if no acknowledgement is sent, after the seven-day period. Usually, they should acknowledge receipt within seven days.[96] When informing the reporting person about follow-up, the three-month period can start after seven days, even without acknowledgement of receipt. Does this mean the responsible person or department is not required to inform the report recipient of receipt?

The Directive details methods for reporting to the responsible person or department.[97] The whistleblower can communicate their concerns orally or in writing via telephone or voice messaging systems or request a meeting with the responsible person or department within a reasonable timeframe. Such meetings should occur outside the workplace to avoid stigmatisation. The timeframe can range from seven days to three months, depending on the Directive. Employers should determine this timeframe and provide clear, accessible information on reporting options, both internally and externally, including the relevant authorities at national and European levels.[98]

[89] ibid Art 9(1)(d).

[90] Transparency International, 'Building on the EU Directive for Whistleblower Protection – Analysis and Recommendations' (2019) Position Paper, 2 www.transparency.org/whatwedo/publications accessed 15 May 2025.

[91] D Lewis, 'The EU Directive on the Protection of Whistleblowers: A Missed Opportunity to Establish International Best Practices?' (2020) 9(1) *E-Journal of International and Comparative Labour Studies* 1, 21.

[92] Directive 2019/1937, Art 9(1)(e).

[93] Transparency International (n 90) 9.

[94] Directive 2019/1937, Recital (35) and Art 5(2).

[95] ibid Art 9(1)(f).

[96] ibid Art 9(1)(b).

[97] Directive 2019/1937, Art 9(2).

[98] ibid Art 9(1)(g).

VI. Internal Helpful and Compliance Tool: Blowing the Whistle in your Workplace

The EU Directive promotes internal reporting and urges Member States to encourage it.[99] The whistleblower may be more motivated to report internally than externally.[100] Recital 33 of the Directive notes that whistleblowers usually prefer internal reporting and need specific reasons to go to authorities. Internal reporting benefits both employees and employers, as explained below.

A. The First Choice: Report to your Boss

Favouring internal channels offers advantages; the reporting person might feel more comfortable reporting internally than to authorities or the public.[101] The whistleblower reports internally to respect their loyalty to their employer and believes the problem will be resolved more efficiently within the organisation.[102] This belief is justified because the employer is closer to the problem, and receiving early information enables quicker action. Internal reporting is seen as a new form of loyalty, termed 'rational loyalty' by scholars.[103]

Internal reporting helps the company to address issues early before they become scandals or attract publicity.[104] From the organisation's perspective, internal disclosures are preferred and encouraged to prevent public attention, negative publicity, or scandals.[105] Reporting to authorities instead of internally can cause severe financial or reputational damage to the organisation and expose the whistleblower to legal liability, as confidential information will be shared externally.

Reporting internally does not breach professional secrecy.[106] Confidentiality is crucial in banking and finance, and it must be protected.[107] This protection is reflected legally in the duty of professional secrecy.[108] Among the EU Member

[99] Handley (n 64).
[100] V Abazi, 'The European Union Whistleblower Directive: A Game Changer for Whistleblowing Protection?' [2020] *Industrial Law Journal* 1, 10–11.
[101] Commission, Commission Staff Working Document, Impact Assessment accompanying the document of the proposal for a Directive of the European Parliament and of the Council on the protection of persons reporting on breaches of Union law COM(2018) 218 final, 9 eur-lex.europa.eu/legal-content/EN/TXT/PDF/?uri=CELEX:52018SC0116&from=EN accessed 15 May 2025.
[102] Directive 2019/1937, Recital 33.
[103] W Vandekerckhove, *Whistleblowing and Organizational Social Responsibility: A Global Assessment* (Ashgate, 2006) 124–34.
[104] T Barnett, 'A Preliminary Investigation of the Relationship between Selected Organizational Characteristics and External Whistleblowing by Employees' (1992) 11 *Journal of Business Ethics* 949, 950.
[105] ibid. See also Vaughn (n 40) 323.
[106] A Bather and M Kelly, 'Whistleblowing: The Advantages of Self-Regulation' (2005) University of Waikato Working Paper Series 82, 6.
[107] B Sissela, *Secrets: On the Ethics of Concealment and Revelation* (Vintage Publishing, 1989) 136.
[108] Moberly (n 66) 751.

States, secrecy is protected under criminal law, as in France and Luxembourg, or under tort law, as in Ireland.[109] Reporting internally keeps the protected information within the workplace, avoiding potential breaches of secrecy. Reporting to authorities risks violating professional confidentiality, which could be a criminal offence under the Directive.[110] The employer may accuse the whistleblower of violating professional secrecy, a criminal offence under national law. Granting immunity to the whistleblower is complex and unclear under the Directive.[111] Consequently, reporting internally would prevent breaching the whistleblower's duty of professional secrecy and entail fewer legal risks.

Ultimately, a clear internal whistleblowing policy fosters good corporate governance, vital for the corporation's growth.[112] Corporate governance regulates how institutions are run to ensure legality and sustainability.[113] The purpose of corporate governance is to establish an ethical climate for business activities.[114] A well-functioning internal reporting scheme demonstrates strong corporate governance by signalling a commitment to listening to employees and correcting wrongdoing. It benefits the company's image and often resolves issues faster than involving authorities. While advantageous, internal reporting also has drawbacks, which will be discussed next.

Culture is crucial for success in corporate governance and whistleblowing.[115] Laws mandate corporations to set up internal reporting schemes, but whistleblower stories often show these are ineffective. Laws exist, but practice often fails. Better efforts are needed to improve corporate culture, shifting from secrecy to honesty, integrity, and transparency.[116] This change should come from within; corporations must foster strong values and an open culture to encourage and safely retain whistleblowers.

Regulators cannot change culture but can influence corporations to foster trust, integrity, and transparency. Each company must create an open, ethical environment that promotes whistleblowing. Change starts with leadership setting a good example. Though culture is deeply rooted and socially complex, reasonable efforts

[109] Art 226-13 of the French Criminal Law Code and Art 458 of the Luxembourg Criminal Law Code. The duty of confidentiality is a judge-made principle; see *Tournier v National Provincial and Union Bank of England* [1924] 1 KB 461 (CA). The Supreme Court of Ireland recognised the duty of confidentiality in the Irish legal order by affirming the decision in *National Irish Bank Limited v Radio Telefis Eireann* [1998] 2 IR 465, 494.

[110] Directive 2019/1937, Art 21(3). As discussed above, this requirement seems problematic and not clear and comes in contrast with recital 36 where it is stated that the whistleblower should be protected, inter alia, from the breach of the duty of confidentiality or loyalty.

[111] ibid Recital 92 and Art 21(2).

[112] Kafteranis (n 12) 21.

[113] RV Aguilera, M Goyer and LR Kabbach de Castro, 'Regulation and Comparative Corporate Governance' in M Wright, D Siegel, K Keasey and I Filatotchev (eds), *The Oxford Handbook of Corporate Governance* (OUP, 2013) 31.

[114] A Knell, *Corporate Governance: A Practical Implementation Guide for Unlisted Companies* (CIMA Publishing, 2006) 6.

[115] S Andreadakis 'Enhancing Whistleblower protection: It's All About the Culture' (2019) 30(6) *European Business Law Review* 859.

[116] ibid 870.

can build a safe environment for whistleblowers. As Dr Andreadakis notices: 'Apparently, culture has become a buzzword, and this is positive, because this is what all the attempts and initiatives should focus on: how to shape a company's culture and how to combine law and culture in a sustainable way.'[117]

B. When It Goes Wrong: The Problematic Aspects of Internal Whistleblowing

A key issue in internal reporting in the banking and financial sector is its connection to compliance.[118] Banks and financial institutions in Europe must have an independent Compliance Department to oversee activities and ensure compliance with the law.[119] Each Member State has its own compliance rules for companies and financial institutions, inspired by the EU's AML and CTF laws.[120] The compliance officer and team ensure the institution follows laws and regulations independently, unaffected by other departments or executives. The question is: What is the relationship between compliance and internal whistleblowing?

First, the Directive does not specify how compliance, companies, states, and whistleblowing relate. For banking and financial institutions, internal whistleblowing could fall under this Department, seen as the most competent. The whistleblower can support the Compliance Department by reporting illegal acts. Conversely, the Directive allows Member States to determine how internal reporting is conducted in companies and financial institutions. This allows each to manage it differently, with some assigning it to the Compliance Department, others leaving it to the institution, or designating other Departments. This variability may weaken the compliance function, especially when other Departments handle whistleblowing.

There is a risk that the whistleblower may undermine the Compliance Department's work or identify the wrongdoings, creating tension and possibly being seen as replacing compliance officers.[121] In the scenario where a whistleblower addresses their concerns to another Department, the Compliance Department

[117] ibid 874.

[118] M Filoromo and Z Arbitman, 'Can Compliance Officers be Whistleblowers' (2019) Corporate Compliance Insights, www.corporatecomplianceinsights.com/can-compliance-officers-be-whistleblowers/ accessed 15 May 2021.

[119] Basel Committee on Banking Supervision, 'Compliance and the Compliance Function in Banks' (2005) www.bis.org/publ/bcbs113.pdf accessed 15 May 2025. See also European Securities and Markets Authority (ESMA), 'Final Report – Guidelines on Certain Aspects of the MiFID Compliance Function Requirements' (2012) www.esma.europa.eu/sites/default/files/library/2015/11/2012-388.pdf accessed 15 May 2025.

[120] For an overview of the AML and CTF EU legislation, see finance.ec.europa.eu/financial-crime/anti-money-laundering-and-countering-financing-terrorism-overview_en accessed 15 May 2025. For a national example, see Luxembourg www.cssf.lu/fileadmin/files/Lois_reglements/Circulaires/Hors_blanchiment_terrorisme/cssf04_155.pdf accessed 15 May 2025.

[121] G Parsons Miller, 'The Compliance Function: An Overview' in JN Gordon and WG Ringe (eds), *The Oxford Handbook of Corporate Law and Governance* (OUP, 2018) 15.

could be exposed and unable to react.[122] Compliance and whistleblowing may overlap if reports concern a lack of compliance, especially if the Compliance Department fails. Employees should report issues anonymously to senior officials, such as the CEO, with protections against retaliation. In banking and finance, internal whistleblowing should be directed to Compliance, but anonymous channels are vital.[123] Banking and financial institutions may see whistleblowing as a duty, not just a right, encouraging internal reporting.[124]

Another scenario the Directive should regulate is the compliance officer's ability to report to authorities. Under the Dodd-Frank Act, the SEC receives employee reports, investigates them, and may financially compensate whistleblowers.[125] The SEC generally does not accept reports from Compliance or Internal Audit employees.[126] Nevertheless, the compliance officer may report to the SEC under certain conditions.[127] In 2015, the SEC awarded $1 million to a compliance officer who revealed critical fraud information that could have hurt the company and investors.[128]

This financial award is the second given to a compliance officer.[129] This example shows the fragility of compliance, as the officer reporting directly to authorities can undermine the core purpose of the compliance doctrine.[130] The EU or Member States may prohibit compliance officers from becoming whistleblowers unless they first report internally. Their role, tied to legal compliance, requires reporting wrongdoing internally or to authorities under specific conditions. This clarity supports their sensitive role.

Summarising the relationship between compliance and whistleblowing, we can say it is complex. The Compliance Department enforces rules and detects non-compliance, while whistleblowers report wrongdoing during discovery and disclosure. Whistleblowers also enforce rules, roles typically for authorities and courts. Compliance controls rule application and intervene when needed.[131] Thus, a clear line is required in order to define where whistleblowers should intervene and where the Compliance Department lacks authority. Either the Compliance Department manages whistleblowing, or boundaries are to be set for harmonious cooperation.

Despite the benefits of internal channels, there are difficulties and risks in internal reporting. Employers need a positive attitude toward employees

[122] C Sylvia and E Stabile, 'Rethinking Compliance: The Role of Whistleblowers' (2016) 84 *University of Cincinnati Law Review* 451, 456.

[123] Parsons Miller (n 1) 15.

[124] ibid.

[125] 15 U.S.C. § 78n (2012).

[126] 17 C.F.R. § 240.21F-4(b)(4)(iii)(B).

[127] 17 C.F.R. § 240.21F-4(b)(4)(v).

[128] U.S. Securities and Exchange Commission, 'SEC announces million-dollar whistleblower award to compliance officer' (2015) www.sec.gov/news/pressrelease/2015-73.html accessed 15 May 2025.

[129] U.S. Securities and Exchange Commission, 'SEC announces $300,000 whistleblower award to audit and compliance professional who reported company's wrongdoing', www.sec.gov/news/press-release/2014-180 accessed 15 May 2025.

[130] Sylvia and Stabile (n 122) 456.

[131] C Parker and V Lehmann Nielsen, 'Compliance: 14 questions' in P Drahos (ed), *Regulation Theory – Foundations and Applications* (ANU, 2017) 218.

reporting wrongdoing that may harm the business.[132] There is an oxymoron in internal whistleblowing: the employee should report wrongdoing to the relevant person or department, but sometimes the person responsible for accepting whistleblowing concerns may be involved or have assisted in the wrongdoing. This paradox can create a hostile environment for the whistleblower.[133] Apart from those mentioned above, the employee may face other difficulties if they pursue internal options. The company may try to minimise the importance of the report or destroy evidence related to the wrongdoing it seeks to protect. When the internal environment is not conducive to whistleblowing, a whistleblower can report directly to authorities, thereby avoiding negative consequences within the organisation.[134]

VII. Enforcing the Law: The Whistleblower as a *Deus ex Machina* for the Competent Authorities

The whistleblower can report directly to authorities and receive protection under the Directive or choose to report internally if the issue is not suitable for external reporting to be investigated. The Directive allows reporting internally or externally without consequences. This part focuses on external reporting, as detailed in Chapter III of the Directive, which covers reports to authorities. 'External reporting' is defined as reporting to authorities, while 'public disclosure' refers to a public, not external, disclosure.

Under Article 10, whistleblowers can report breaches of Union law via internal channels or by directly contacting the competent authority, in accordance with Articles 11 and 12.[135] Under Article 5, external reporting means providing information on breaches to the competent authorities, which are any national authorities that receive reports under Chapter III and provide feedback, including follow-up on the report.[136]

Member States should designate authorities responsible for receiving reports and providing feedback or follow-up.[137] Competent authorities should have sufficient resources to perform their functions.[138] Member States should consider the relevant EU areas covered by the Directive and appoint responsible national authorities.[139]

[132] K Kenny, 'Censored: Whistleblowers and Impossible Speech' (2017) 71 *Human Relations* 16–27.
[133] Vaughn (n 38) 324.
[134] R Moberly, 'To Persons or Organisations that may be able to Effect Action: Whistle-blowing recipients' in AJ Brown, D Lewis, R Moberly and W Vandekerckhove (eds), *International Research Handbook on Whistle-blowing* (Routledge, 2014) 278.
[135] Directive 2019/1937, Art 10.
[136] ibid Arts 5 (5) and (12).
[137] Lewis (n 91) 10.
[138] Directive 2019/1937, Art 11(1).
[139] Cleary Gottlieb, 'New EU Directive Strengthens Protection of Whistleblowers' (2019) Alert Memorandum, www.clearygottlieb.com accessed 15 May 2025.

The EU areas of interest under the Directive include public procurement, safety, environment, nuclear, food, health, consumer and privacy protection, EU financial interests, the internal market, and the financial services sector (including banks).[140] Additionally, authorities are obligated to inform the whistleblower about their report.[141] Member States should provide financial resources to competent authorities to enable them to exercise their functions under the Directive effectively.

A. Obligation to Establish Independent External Reporting Channels

Member States should ensure that authorities establish independent channels to handle whistleblower information.[142] The Directive states two criteria for considering external reporting channels independent and autonomous.[143] Channels must be designed, set up, and operated to ensure information completeness, integrity and confidentiality, and restrict access to authorised staff.[144] The second criterion is that authorities must store data following specific rules for future investigations.[145]

B. Form of Reporting

The Directive details how whistleblowers can report to authorities.[146] External reporting can be done in writing, orally, via phone or voice message, and, if requested, through a physical meeting within a reasonable time.[147] This reasonable timeframe is not specified in the Directive, leaving it to the discretion of Member States.[148] Time is crucial when a whistleblower reports to authorities due to potential internal cover-ups, inefficiencies, or corruption.[149] If a whistleblower requests a meeting, it should be scheduled promptly within a set timeframe. If the report is received outside designated channels or by an uninvolved staff member, they must not disclose any whistleblower information and must immediately forward it to the responsible persons.[150]

[140] Directive 2019/1937, Art 2(1).
[141] Transparency International (n 90) 2.
[142] Directive 2019/1937, Art 11(2)(a). See also S Feinstein and T Devine, 'A Comparative Analysis of US v EU Whistleblower Law' (2019) *Whistleblower* whistleblower.org/blog/a-comparative-analysis-of-u-s-v-e-u-whistleblower-law/ accessed 15 May 2025.
[143] ibid Art 12.
[144] ibid Art 12(a).
[145] ibid Art 12(b).
[146] ibid Art 12.
[147] Directive, Art 12(2).
[148] Lewis (n 91) 11.
[149] Mendelsohn (n 52) 741.
[150] Directive 2019/1937, Art 12(3).

C. Training of Staff Members

Member States should ensure competent authorities nominate and train responsible staff.[151] These staff members should provide information on reporting procedures and stay in contact with whistleblowers for feedback or additional information.[152] Responsible staff should receive targeted training according to the Directive.[153] This training should include specific training on the data protection rules applicable to the Directive.[154] Staff contact details should be publicly accessible for whistleblowers.[155] Finally, staff and authorised individuals should access the report while strictly adhering to confidentiality, data protection and professional secrecy when sharing data within or outside the authority or during enforcement activities, such as investigations.[156]

D. Record-Keeping Rules

The Directive details the formalities and duties for recording.[157] The rules are thorough, offering little discretion to Member States.[158] The Directive outlines recording duties, helping whistleblowers understand and use this documentation in court. Detailed rules protect against abuse and are essential for future legal actions.[159]

The Directive details record-keeping rules for internal reports by private and public entities and external reports to authorities.[160] Responsible legal entities and authorities must record every report, in accordance with the confidentiality rules set out in Article 16 of the Directive.[161] Reports should be stored only as long as necessary and proportionate to legal and authority requirements under the Directive.[162]

The Directive lacks clear guidelines on what is necessary and proportionate, leaving that to Member States' discretion. It would be better if the drafters set limits, such as no more than three months or a range of three months to a year, to promote cohesion. The Directive highlights that EU data protection regulations must apply to data storage and processing.[163] In addition to setting time limits,

[151] ibid Art 12(4).
[152] ibid Art 12(4).
[153] ibid Art 12(5).
[154] ibid Recital 74.
[155] ibid Recital 75.
[156] ibid Recital 77.
[157] Handley (n 64).
[158] Lewis (n 91) 13.
[159] Andreis (n 66), 581.
[160] Directive 2019/1937, Art 18.
[161] ibid Arts 16 and 18(1).
[162] ibid.
[163] Directive 2019/1937, Art 17. See also General Data Protection Regulation 2016/679 on the protection of natural persons with regard to the processing of personal data and on the free movement of such

Member States must ensure compliance with EU data protection rules when transposing the Directive.[164]

Furthermore, the Directive specifies how to store information depending on the reporting method. If transmitted via a recorded phone call or voice system, authorities must follow specific storage rules regardless of the reporter's consent.[165] One way to store this oral report is to record the conversation in a durable, retrievable format.[166] The second way is to prepare a complete and accurate transcript by staff members responsible for handling the reports.[167] In this scenario, the reporting person should be able to review, ratify, and sign the transcript. This raises questions about the time limits for responsible persons to prepare the transcript – should it be done immediately or later? Also, how should the whistleblower give consent – orally or in writing? These questions are currently unanswered, but experience will guide future practice.

If the reporting person uses an unrecorded phone or voice messaging system, legal entities and authorities can document the oral report with accurate minutes prepared by responsible staff.[168] The reporting person should review, modify, and agree with the prepared document. The Directive requires the whistleblower to sign the document if they agree, showing their explicit approval.[169] Suppose the whistleblower meets staff from the legal entity or authority. In that case, staff must keep complete, accurate records of the meeting in a durable, retrievable form, and the whistleblower should give consent.[170] The documentation should be completed in one of the following ways: either by recording the discussion or by preparing a document with the meeting minutes, which staff members should prepare.[171] Staff should give the reporting person a chance to review, verify, and approve the minutes, which they demonstrate by signing the document.[172] Apart from the above timeframe concerns, a final question is: if the whistleblower disagrees with the document, what then? Should another staff member prepare a new one? Can they challenge the previous one in court to have it annulled and replaced?

data (known as GDPR) and Directive 2016/680 on the protection of natural persons with regard to the processing of personal data by competent authorities for the purposes of the prevention, investigation, detection or prosecution of criminal offences or the execution of criminal penalties, and on the free movement of such data OJ L119/89.

[164] T Douville, 'Directive (UE) 2019/1937 du 23 octobre 2019 sur la protection des personnes qui signalent des violations du droit de l'Union – Aspects relatifs à la protection des données à caractère personnel' (2019) *R.A.E-L.E.A.*, 709.

[165] Directive 2019/1937, Art 18(2).

[166] ibid Art 18(2)(a).

[167] ibid Art 18(2)(b).

[168] ibid Art 18(3).

[169] ibid Art 18(3).

[170] ibid Art 18(4).

[171] ibid Art 18(4).

[172] Handley (n 64) 9.

E. Rights of Whistleblowers

Authorities must acknowledge whistleblower reports within seven days after receipt.[173] If the reporting person requests or confirms that the report risks the whistleblower's identity, the authority can be exempted from confirming receipt within seven days.[174]

Furthermore, authorities should follow up on reports and give feedback.[175] This should be completed within a reasonable timeframe, not exceeding three months, and in exceptional cases, six months.[176] The whistleblower has the right to be informed of the investigation's outcomes in accordance with national law.[177] Furthermore, authorities should promptly share necessary information with other Union institutions, bodies, or agencies for investigation, when legally permitted. This is especially crucial for the banking sector, where the ECB has vital powers on whistleblowing.

F. Duties of Competent Authorities: Public Access to Whistleblowing via Competent Authorities

Member States shall ensure their authorities publish clear, accessible information on reporting procedures on their websites.[178] The Directive specifies the information whistleblowers should find on the authority's website, with options for more detail if the legislator chooses. It should include how whistleblowers qualify for protection and contact details for external reporting, such as addresses, phone numbers, and whether calls are recorded.[179] Secondly, the authority should specify to the reporting person how it may request clarifications or additional information, including the timeframe and content of the feedback.[180]

Furthermore, the website should include information on the confidentiality regime under the Directive and personal data protection under EU law.[181] The website information section should include details on follow-up for reports, remedies and procedures against retaliation, and options for confidential advice during report preparation.[182] An explanatory document should be available for whistleblowers detailing when they will not breach confidentiality when reporting

[173] Directive 2019/1937, Art 11(2)(b).
[174] ibid Art 11(2)(b).
[175] ibid Art 11(2)(c).
[176] ibid Art 11(2)(d).
[177] ibid Art 11(2)(d).
[178] Directive 2019/1937, Art 13.
[179] ibid Art 13(a) and (b).
[180] ibid Art 13(c).
[181] ibid Art 13(d).
[182] ibid Art 13(e) and (f).

to authorities.[183] The relationship between confidentiality and whistleblowing is interesting, as noted in other parts of this book. The Directive seeks to justify breaching professional secrecy based on the whistleblower's status, relying on national law. This depends on factors like criminal or civil law protections.[184]

Lastly, the website should include contact details for an independent administrative authority, if applicable, that can support the whistleblower, as provided in Article 20(2).[185] Article 20(2) does not leave the impression that this single independent administrative authority must be created, stating: 'Member States may provide for financial assistance and support, including psychological support, for reporting persons in the framework of legal proceedings.' The support in Article 20(2) applies only during legal proceedings, not reporting. Article 20(3) mentions an information centre or an administrative authority, referring to a single independent authority, but Member States are not obliged to create one.

The issue of a single, independent administrative authority for whistleblowers, at the national or EU level, is discussed in other parts of the book. Competent authorities should review the procedures for receiving reports and their follow-up at least once every three years.[186] Member States should review at least once every three years, or more often if appropriate, taking into account the experience of their own and other competent authorities, to adapt methods based on lessons learnt.[187]

G. Powers of the Competent Authorities vis-à-vis the Reports Made

Member States can allow authorities to ignore minor breaches after analysing their severity.[188] The power of competent authorities, if granted by Member States, should not affect other obligations or procedures for addressing the breach or the protection to be offered to the whistleblower.[189] If authorities decide not to follow up on the reported breach, the whistleblower should be informed of this decision and the grounds for it.[190] Authorities can choose not to follow up on repetitive reports that lack new, meaningful information compared to previous reports.[191]

[183] ibid Arts 13(g) and 21(4).

[184] D Kafteranis, 'From Obscurity to Limelight: The Whistle-blowers' Protection under EU Law' in V Mitsilegas and SJ Wortman (eds), *Whistleblowing, Transparency and Criminal Law: A Comparative Perspective* (Brill, 2021).

[185] Directive 2019/1937, Art 13(h).

[186] ibid Art 14.

[187] Directive 2019/1937, Art 14.

[188] ibid Art 11(3).

[189] ibid.

[190] ibid.

[191] ibid Art 11(4).

If new legal or factual information emerges, the authority may investigate further. The whistleblower should be informed of the reasons for the decision.[192]

Furthermore, in high-volume report cases, authorities can prioritise serious breaches or critical provisions under the Directive, postponing less severe or relevant reports.[193] If they delay addressing the report, authorities must still notify the whistleblower within seven days that the report has been received.[194] Member States must ensure that authorities receiving reports transfer them promptly and securely to the right authority if they lack the competence to act.[195]

The whistleblower should be promptly informed of this transmission between authorities.[196] The powers of authorities are broad, giving them discretion in handling reports. Key questions include the criteria for serious breaches, whether they should issue guidelines, and whether whistleblowers can challenge refusals in courts. Member States must clarify their authority and powers to prevent abuses against whistleblowers.

VIII. Who Will Enforce EU Law: God Save the Whistleblower

A. The Challenging Nature of Enforcing EU Law

A significant challenge in implementing Union law is its enforcement, as highlighted by the European Commission in a Communication entitled 'EU law: Better Results through Better Application'.[197] The European Commission noted that: '[O]ften, when issues come to the fore – car emission testing, water pollution, illegal landfills, transport safety and security – it is not the lack of EU legislation that is the problem, but rather the fact that the EU law is not applied effectively [...]'.[198] The European Commission recognised that enforcing EU law remains a challenge, and it decided to focus *more strongly on enforcement to serve the general interest*.[199] One of the reasons for proposing legislation to protect whistleblowers was to enhance the enforcement of Union law.[200]

The EU depends on Member States to correctly implement Union law.[201] It assumes Member States' compliance with EU rules and procedures to enhance

[192] ibid.
[193] ibid Art 11(5).
[194] ibid Art 11(2)(b).
[195] ibid Art 11(6).
[196] ibid Art 11(6).
[197] C/2016/8600, OJ C18/10.
[198] ibid.
[199] ibid.
[200] European Commission, Proposal for a Directive (n 6) 6.
[201] R Bieber and F Maiani, 'Enhancing Centralised Enforcement of EU Law: Pandora's Toolbox?' (2014) 51 *Common Market Law Review* 1057, 1058.

various EU sectors of interest, such as financial markets. Member States should have adequate mechanisms to detect and remedy breaches of Union law when necessary.[202] In addition to traditional enforcement, where authorities act on breaches, this EU Directive introduces a private enforcement tool, allowing citizens to enforce the law by referring issues to authorities or institutions. This model has a long history in common law and US legislation.

B. Private Enforcement in the US

Private enforcement centres on citizens, who are often better equipped to spot illegalities and irregularities. They can sue directly under the *qui tam* provisions or report the issues to the authorities.[203] The citizen becomes a new enforcement tool, replacing traditional mechanisms by which authorities usually identify and address wrongdoing. In this new enforcement, the whistleblower is key in uncovering misconduct. The idea of private enforcement relates to *qui tam* writs, which originate from common law principles.[204] The idea is that the *qui tam writ* lets citizens sue if the state's interests are ignored.[205] The *qui tam writ* influenced the 1863 False Claims Act, the first law in US history to protect whistleblowers.[206] Various state actors, such as the IRS and the SEC, use whistleblowers to enforce rules, offering protection and rewards.[207]

Effective regulation depends on both state enforcement and private intervention.[208] Regulatory authorities often lack the budget, resources, or information needed to investigate or prosecute violations of the law.[209] Thus, enforcement may originate from market actors through internal reporting or by reporting to authorities to assist their work.[210] Referring to US legislation and its tendency to enforce rules by using citizens is deliberate. In the corporate and financial sectors, US trends often influence Europe due to reliance on US trade and

[202] ibid.

[203] The *qui tam* writ, dating back to Lincoln's presidency, is the first example where the US government authorised citizens to sue individuals that committed fraud against federal economic interests. See D Freeman Engstrom, 'Harnessing the Private Attorney General: Evidence from Qui Tam Litigation' (2012) 112 *Columbia Law Review* 1244, 1246.

[204] Freeman Engstrom ibid 1246.

[205] ibid.

[206] False Claims Act (FCA), 31 U.S.C. §§ 3729–3733.

[207] Y Givati, 'Of Snitches and Riches: Optimal IRS and SEC Whistleblower rewards' (2018) 55 *Harvard Journal on Legislation* 112. For a European perspective on financial rewards and whistleblowing, see Dimitrios Kafteranis, 'Rethinking Financial Rewards for Whistle-blowers under the Proposal for a Directive on the Protection of Whistle-blowers Reporting Breaches of EU Law' (2019) Nordic Journal of European Law 38.

[208] J Fischer, E Harshman, W Gillespie and H Ordower, 'Privatizing Regulation: Whistleblowing and Bounty Hunting in the Financial Services Industries' (2000) 1 *Dickinson Journal of International law* 117, 118–19.

[209] ibid.

[210] ibid 119.

multinationals.[211] Following the economic crises, Sarbanes-Oxley and Dodd-Frank introduced key rules on corporate enforcement, where whistleblowers are part of the solution but not the main focus.[212] These Acts significantly impact the EU corporate and financial sectors.[213] This influence led to whistleblower protection and its use as an enforcement tool.

C. The EU's Perspective on the Whistleblower as an Enforcement Tool

The whistleblower aims to boost corporate responsibility through internal reporting, informing authorities, and occasionally involving the public. Enforcement of EU law, however, is not within the EU's powers, which are limited to ensuring the effectiveness of law in accordance with Article 19 TEU and Article 47 of the Charter of Fundamental Rights.[214] EU law enforcement is handled at the national level, as the EU cannot intervene.[215] Apart from EU competition law, enforcement is usually governed by national law. Recently, the EU has been introducing enforcement rules affecting both national systems and the EU.[216] One of these enforcement measures is the whistleblower.[217] The success of this enforcement tool is dubious given the EU's multi-level enforcement system.

First, the Directive sets minimum standards, allowing Member States discretion to adopt additional rules. Adopting a Regulation would be more efficient, but issues such as proportionality and consensus on the fragile legal basis argue against this option.[218] Moreover, the Directive's reporting scope in parts of the EU causes confusion about its relationship with national law and European policies.[219] This problem was difficult to solve because the EU has limited powers and cannot extend its application *ratione materiae*. Therefore, the Directive had to restrict reports of Union law rather than national law.

[211] C Bradley, 'Breaking Up is Hard to Do: The Interconnection Problem in Financial Markets and Financial Regulation: A European (Banking) Union Perspective' (2014) 49 *Texas International Law Journal* 271.

[212] Sarbanes–Oxley Act of 2002 (Pub.L. 107–204, 116 Stat. 745, enacted July 30, 2002) as amended by Dodd-Frank Wall Street Reform and Consumer Protection Act (Pub. L. No. 111-203, § 929-Z, 124 Stat. 1376, 1871, 2010).

[213] MC Cardilli, 'Regulation without Borders: The impact of Sarbanes-Oxley on European Companies' (2003) 27(2) *Fordham International Law Journal* 786; M Greenberger, 'The Extraterritorial Provisions of the Dodd-Frank Act Protects US Taxpayers from Worldwide Bailouts' (2012) 80(4) *UMKC Law Review* 1.

[214] M Klamert and B Schima, 'Article 19' in M Kekkerbauer, M Klamert and J Tomkin (eds), *The EU Treaties and the Charter of Fundamental Rights – A Commentary* (OUP, 2019) 183–84.

[215] S Andersen, *The Enforcement of EU Law* (OUP, 2012) 42.

[216] M Scholten, 'Mind the Trend! Enforcemet of EU law has been moving to 'Brussels' (2017) 24(9) *Journal of European Public Policy* 1348.

[217] Kafteranis (n 7) 50.

[218] European Commission, Proposal for a Directive (n 6) 6.

[219] Directive 2019/1937, Art 2 (material scope).

A first observation is that distinguishing between EU and national law is often difficult, and this will be a demanding task for the whistleblower.[220] The transposition of EU law at the national level is not always easy for employees to discern.[221] Determining whether a rule involves EU or national law may be easier for specialists like lawyers, but challenging for employees without legal expertise. While whistleblowers are expected to understand the misconduct and report it, determining whether it falls under national or EU law adds complexity. This distinction may discourage future whistleblowers. The best solution was for Member States to adopt a catch-all approach, where national laws implementing the Directive cover wrongdoings under both legal frameworks.[222] While some Member States, such as France and Luxembourg, chose the 'catch-all' approach, others, such as Greece, limited the material scope in line with the Directive.

Moreover, the Directive's limited material scope may lead to two laws at the national level: one transposing the Directive and another for whistleblowing on breaches of national law outside its scope.[223] Member States can choose to expand the law's scope when transposing the Directive to include breaches related to national law, not just those covered by the Directive. This was optional, giving Member States the freedom to follow or not. If they do not expand the scope and stick to the Directive's wording, two law types will arise, causing confusion and complexity for whistleblowers, which may impede reporting.[224] Hence, the transposition of the Directive and Member States' material scope choices could cause disputes and enforcement difficulties for whistleblowing.

A final comment is that the whistleblowing rules from the Directive do not apply to EU officials. This point should be discussed, despite it being common knowledge that a Directive cannot apply to EU officials.[225] The EU has created a new enforcement tool, the whistleblower, to strengthen law enforcement in some areas, but it gives less importance to whistleblowing within EU institutions. Rules for EU officials should be under the Staff Regulation of 2004 but are often not

[220] Kafteranis (n 7) 50.

[221] ibid.

[222] The view of enlarging wrongdoings of national law has been expressed by the Council of Europe. See Council of Europe, Parliamentary Assembly, Committee on Legal Affairs and Human Rights, 'Improving the protection of whistleblowers all over Europe', 2 (2019) website-pace.net/documents/19838/5636250/20190624-WhistleblowerProtection-EN.pdf/69a1e5b5-5bb5-4c50-bbf8-16423d020aff accessed 15 May 2025. See also R Brockhaus and D Kafteranis, 'No more Piecemeal Tactics: Call for a comprehensive implementation of EU's Whistleblowing Directive' (2020) Verfassungsblog on Constitutional matters verfassungsblog.de/no-69a1e5b5more-piecemeal-tactics/ accessed 15 May 2025.

[223] The French Senate has issued concerns in its opinion on the Proposal for a Directive. It stated that even though the Directive has a limited scope of application (only to wrongdoings related to EU law), its transposition will result in a problem of harmonisation as France will be 'obliged' to amend its existing legislation in order to avoid the co-existence of two different legal frameworks. See Sénat, Rapport fait sur la proposition de directive sur la protection des personnes dénoncent les infractions au droit de l'Union (2018) N° 638, 8.

[224] Kafteranis (n 7).

[225] Directive 2019/1937, Recital 2 and Art 4 (personal scope).

applied correctly.[226] The Directive may have led to new reporting rules for EU officials, inspired by those in the Directive.

EU officials hold key positions and are part of the enforcement system, providing access to information to detect and report wrongdoing. Including EU officials in the Directive or adopting new rules would have strengthened their protection and clarified whistleblowing guidelines.[227] Their inclusion in the Directive or in new regulations inspired by it could have improved law enforcement and the fight against misconduct within EU institutions. A negative aspect is the lack of an independent EU body to coordinate implementation and assist whistleblowers.

IX. The Competent Authorities

The whistleblower can report to external authorities responsible for facilitating the process.[228] The Directive does not specify which authorities should be qualified but outlines their characteristics. Member States are responsible for designating competent authorities, allowing each to have a different perspective.[229] In the banking and financial sector, these authorities should supervise the industry, including relevant EU institutions such as the ECB and ESMA.[230] This section focuses on national authorities; the next discusses the roles of the ECB and ESMA.

The Directive specifies desired characteristics of the competent authorities across all sectors, not just banking and finance. However, the attribution power remains national, with no mandatory requirements. Its preamble gives examples of these authorities, including judicial bodies, regulatory agencies, central authorities, law enforcement, anti-corruption agencies, and ombudspersons.[231] Member States have broad discretion in choosing the authorities to receive reports and in appointing a competent authority under the Directive. While investigating and remedying issues are desirable powers for these authorities, they are not mandatory.

[226] Regulation No 31 (EEC), 11 (EAEC) laying down the Staff Regulations of Officials and the Conditions of Employment of Other Servants of the European Economic Community and the European Atomic Energy Community (2004) OJ 45 1385, Art 22a; European Ombudsman, 'Only two EU institutions have adopted the required rules on whistle-blowing' (2014) www.ombudsman.europa.eu/en/summary/en/59134 accessed 15 May 2025; S White, 'The Whistleblower in the European Union's Institution: Is the Bird Tamed?' (2010) 540 *Revue du Marche Commun et de l'Union Europeenn*, 441–45. In the recent case T-793/22, the European Parliament was condemned for failing to protect an internal whistleblower (curia.europa.eu/juris/document/document.jsf?text=&docid=289971&pageIndex=0&doclang=FR&mode=req&dir=&occ=first&part=1&cid=6199228) accessed 15 May 2025.

[227] European Parliament Committee on Constitutional Affairs, Opinion for the Committee on Legal Affairs on the proposal for a Directive on the protection of persons reporting on breaches of Union law [2018] C8-0159/2018, 3.

[228] Directive 2019/1937, Art 10.

[229] Lewis (n 91) 10.

[230] In Recital 69 of the Directive, ESMA is mentioned as an EU body that should have in place external reporting channels. Interestingly, the ECB is not mentioned in the Directive as a competent authority, even though it can be the recipient of whistleblowers' reports.

[231] Directive 2019/1937, Recital 65.

Focusing on banking and finance will be challenging because EU countries have supervisory bodies such as Central Banks and Financial Supervisory Authorities.[232] These bodies have administrative powers to investigate and remedy issues within their legal scope. Criminal law issues must be referred to the Public Prosecutor for investigation and appropriate remedial action. For example, France and Ireland have whistleblower protections and specific authorities in the banking and financial sector.

Under France's 'Sapin II' law, an employee could report to a judicial, administrative, or professional legal body only if the internal report was not addressed in a reasonable time.[233] The authorities responsible for the banking and financial sector are defined by French law, Sapin II, Article 16 (as modified by the Waserman Law).[234] These two authorities are: the Financial Markets Authority (Autorité des Marches Financiers – AMF) and the Prudential Control and Resolution Authority (Autorité de Contrôle Prudentiel et de Résolution).[235] An employee at a bank or financial institution can report concerns to two authorities that have procedures for handling them. Legislation allows the employee to choose which authority to report to.[236] The employee can also report to a judicial authority or their professional body.

In Ireland, under the Protected Disclosures Act 2014 (PDA 2014), the reporting person can contact a prescribed person.[237] The Minister for Public Expenditure and Reform may proscribe persons who, by reason of their responsibilities or functions, are likely to be recipients of disclosures of relevant wrongdoing within their prescribed matters.[238] The minister issued a list of prescribed persons per sector.[239] The Central Bank of Ireland is the designated authority for the banking and financial sector.[240] When addressing a prescribed person, the worker should reasonably

[232] S Looseveld, 'EU Financial Supervisory Powers, Whistleblowing and Self-reporting' (2019) 34(9) *Journal of International Banking Law and Regulation* 317, 317–18. For Ireland, see Protected Disclosures Act 2014 (s 7(2)) Order 2014, SI No 339 of 2014, 3. For France, see Law No 2016-1691 of 6 December 2016 related to transparency, the fight against corruption and the modernization of economic life, JORF n°0287 Art 16.

[233] Law No 2016-1691, Art 8 sub. I.

[234] Loi n° 2022-401 du 21 mars 2022 visant à améliorer la protection des lanceurs d'alerte (1), JORF n°0068, 22 mars 2022.

[235] ibid Art 16.

[236] Paille (n 20) 3.

[237] Protected Disclosures Act 2014, number 14 of 2014, s 7. 'The Minister for Public Expenditure and Reform Michael McGrath TD signs order updating list of persons prescribed to receive protected disclosures under Section 7 of the Protected Disclosures Act 2014' (Government of Ireland, 25 September 2020) www.gov.ie/ga/an-roinn-caiteachais-phoibli-bonneagair-athchoriuchain-seirbhise-poibli-agus-digitiuchain/preaseisiuinti/the-minister-for-public-expenditure-and-reform-michael-mcgrath-td-signs-order-updating-list-of-persons-prescribed-to-receive-protected-disclosures-under-section-7-of-the-protected-disclosures-act-2014/ accessed 15 May 2025.

[238] ibid.

[239] Protected Disclosures (Whistleblowing): List of prescribed persons (Government of Ireland, 25 September 2020) www.gov.ie/en/department-of-public-expenditure-infrastructure-public-service-reform-and-digitalisation/collections/protected-disclosures-whistleblowing-list-of-prescribed-persons/ accessed 15 May 2025.

[240] ibid.

believe the wrongdoing is within their responsibility and that the information is substantially accurate to be protected under the Act.[241]

The examples show that authorities in banking and finance are involved in supervision. Ireland has a list of prescribed persons; France allows reporting to authorities or bodies under Law Sapin II. These authorities handle issues within their competencies and pass others to appropriate agencies. This process can be confusing, complex, and uncertain for whistleblowers, making it difficult to identify the right authority. The Directive seeks to simplify reporting and clarify the role of competent authorities.[242]

A fictional scenario illustrates these concerns. An employee at a large financial institution with a good salary has just bought a house and car. He notices something unusual in one of the accounts, suspects fraud by a superior, and investigates. He suspects the fraud relates to securities regulation and wonders where to report it: to the financial authorities or to the Prosecutor. The whistleblower must decide where to report, which involves understanding the wrongdoing and identifying the correct authority. This process may discourage them, leading to inaction if they lack confidence.

A. Reporting to European Authorities

In addition to the national competent authorities, the Directive also allows reporting directly to the European Anti-Fraud Office (OLAF) or the European Public Prosecutor's Office (EPPO).[243] Additionally, national competent authorities should refer cases to the aforementioned EU bodies. The whistleblower, who will choose to report directly to these two bodies, should report matters within their respective competencies.[244] Reporting to EU bodies might be preferable for whistleblowers but could lead to a more complex, confusing process.

The problem lies in the vagueness of the rules on whistleblowing and the EPPO. In the Directive, the provision on the EPPO's ability to receive whistleblowing concerns from national competent authorities or individual whistleblowers is located in a single recital rather than in the Articles.[245] In the Regulation on the EPPO, the only reference to whistleblowers appears in one recital.[246] Both recitals are highly problematic, as they lack clarity on which cases whistleblowers should

[241] ibid s 7 and (section 7(2)) Order 2014, SI No 339 of 2014.

[242] For the criticism raised in the US about the competent authorities, see C Berkebile, 'The Puzzle of Whistleblower Protection Legislation: Assembling the Piecemeal' (2018) 28 *Indiana International & Comparative Law Review* 1, 23.

[243] Directive 2019/1937, Recital 72.

[244] European Parliament, Directorate General for Internal Policies, 'The Future Cooperation between OLAF and the European Public Prosecutor's Office (EPPO) 10–16, www.europarl.europa.eu/RegData/etudes/IDAN/2017/603789/IPOL_IDA(2017)603789_EN.pdf accessed 15 May 2025.

[245] Directive 2019/1937, Recital 71.

[246] Regulation 2017/1939 of 12 October 2017 implementing enhanced cooperation on the establishment of the European Public Prosecutor's Office ('the EPPO') OJ L238/1, Recital 50.

report to the EPPO, and the recitals do not carry the same legal weight as the articles. Thus, it is optimal for the Member States and the European Union to establish a new body or institution to guide whistleblowers. Even if this institution operates only at the EU level, it should be able to guide whistleblowers on the country's national-level requirements.[247]

B. An EU Office for the Whistleblowers

The 2017 European Parliament Resolution proposed creating an EU body to collaborate with whistleblowers.[248] The proposal from the European Parliament favoured the European Ombudsman as the responsible organ for establishing and coordinating an EU Office for whistleblowers. Since the EU Ombudsman was willing and able to investigate internal complaints, the European Parliament asked the European Commission to consider taking on this role.[249]

During negotiations, several EU actors supported this idea. The European Parliament's Committee on the Environment, Public Health, and Food Safety proposed creating an EU Whistleblower body in its opinion on the Directive.[250] The Committee proposed establishing a European Whistleblower Protection Office with certain powers to coordinate whistleblowing.[251] The Office's purpose would be to receive and investigate whistleblowers' reports and notify authorities. It would be independent and impartial, advising and supporting whistleblowers under the European Ombudsman or an independent EU body. The EU Ombudsman has the credentials and a positive public image to serve as the main EU whistleblowing coordinator.[252] Attributing whistleblowing coordination and protection to the European Ombudsman reflects a changing public attitude.[253] The European Commission did not act on the issue despite the European Parliament's request.

The Directive does not clearly require Member States to create an Office for Whistleblowers, but it indirectly opens this possibility to them. Article 20 of the Directive sets out measures Member States may take to support whistleblowers, including access to independent information, legal aid in criminal and

[247] The concept of an Office that assists whistleblowers or investigates their concerns can be found in the US. For instance, the US Office of Special Counsel is an independent federal investigative and prosecutorial agency; see osc.gov/Pages/about.aspx accessed 15 May 2025. Similar offices can be found in Europe too such as the Dutch House of Whistleblowers (Huis voor Klokkenluiders) or the Federaal Ombudsmeam in Belgium which provide advice and support to the whistleblowers.

[248] European Parliament, Resolution of 24 October 2017 on legitimate measures to protect whistle-blowers acting in the public interest when disclosing the confidential information of companies and public bodies [2016] (2016/2224(INI)) para 55.

[249] ibid.

[250] CEPHFS, Opinion (n 32) 3.

[251] ibid.

[252] N Creutzfeldt, 'Trusting the Middle-Man: Impact and Legitimacy of Ombudsmen in Europe' (2016) Project report – University of Westminster, 4, www.law.ox.ac.uk/sites/files/oxlaw/ombuds_project_report_nc_2.pdf accessed 15 May 2025.

[253] Kafteranis (n 7).

cross-border civil cases, and financial assistance.[254] Article 20, paragraph 3 states that support measures can be provided by an information centre or an independent administrative authority. The Directive allows Member States to establish an information centre or an independent authority to support whistleblowers.[255]

A European Whistleblower Protection Office offers many benefits. The EU's complex governance involves multiple Member States, which can make reporting and protection difficult for whistleblowers. A dedicated Office would advise and coordinate among Member States, oversee the implementation of the Directive, and evaluate progress with the European Commission. It would serve as a secure intermediary in transnational cases, ensuring the Directive is properly applied and protecting whistleblowers.[256]

Despite the benefits of an EU whistleblowers body, legal challenges exist. Limited EU competences, especially legal bases, deter the establishment of a coordinating EU whistleblowing body. Finding legal bases for the Directive proved challenging, leading to a pan-sectoral Directive rather than a uniform EU approach to protecting whistleblowers. Under the principle of conferral, the EU *shall act only within the limits of the competences conferred upon it by the Member States in the Treaties to attain the objectives set out therein*.[257] The EU has historically expanded its competences through teleological interpretation.[258] In the case of whistleblowing, which is not an EU competence to legislate on, this expansion, by teleological interpretation, was necessary to protect the internal market and the economic interests of the EU.

The above raises the question of whether the EU has the competence to establish such a body. EU bodies or agencies are an institutionalised collaboration between the EU and Member States' administrations.[259] These EU agencies have both instrumental and final decision-making powers in individual decision-making.[260] Creating EU bodies requires a Treaty legal basis or an EU legislative act.[261] The European Commission can sub-delegate powers to an EU body when it has them. Since most EU bodies are established by Treaty articles or legislative acts based on these articles, a missing legal basis prevents the creation of an EU body. Without a Treaty basis, an EU body cannot adopt measures to harmonise or approximate national laws.[262]

[254] Directive 2019/1937, Art 20.

[255] ibid Art 20(3).

[256] K Loyens and W Vandekerckove, 'Whistleblowing from an International Perspective: A Comparative Analysis of Institutional Arrangements' (2018) 8 *Administrative Sciences* 30, 12 (discussing the tendency to install governmental whistleblowing agencies and its advantages).

[257] Art 5(2) TFEU.

[258] R Schutze, 'EU Competences – Existence and Exercise' in A Arnull and D Chalmers (eds), *The Oxford Handbook of European Union Law* (OUP, 2015) 76–78.

[259] J Mendes, 'The EU Administrative Institutions, Their Law, and Legal Scholarship' in P Cane et al (eds), *The Oxford Handbook of Comparative Administrative Law* (OUP, 2021) 533.

[260] ibid 534. Joined Cases 9/56 and 10/56 *Meroni v ECSC High Authority* [1957-8] ECR English Special Edition 13, paras 150–52.

[261] HC H Hoffman, 'General principles of EU law and EU administrative law' in C Barnard and S Peers (eds), *European Union Law* (OUP, 2020) 217.

[262] ibid 219.

The creation of an EU body on whistleblowing becomes problematic in light of the above. The EU's lack of clear authority to regulate whistleblowing, and the use of multiple legal bases to justify the Directive's legality, do not empower the Commission to establish an EU body. The Commission is limited by its competences on whistleblowing under the Treaties' articles. The positive aspects of an EU body on whistleblower protection are mainly coordinating or advisory, not regulatory powers. To that extent, we should reconsider the need for an EU body to protect whistleblowers since national authorities can do this and have regulatory or investigatory powers.

The recent EU framework invites Member States to designate competent authorities in line with their legal systems. The whistleblower will face a complicated situation, needing time to choose the right authority to address their concerns. Issues in the banking and financial sector tend to be inherently complex, and determining the competent authority is not easy. An optimal solution would be to establish a body at both the national and EU levels (an Office for whistleblowers) with the authority to receive concerns and provide guidance. The Commission can initiate an investigation into establishing an EU office for whistleblowers, taking into account its authority under Article 23 of the Directive and the potential reforms in 2026.[263]

X. The Particular Status of the ECB and the ESMA

In the EU banking and financial sector, the ECB and ESMA, alongside national authorities, handle whistleblowers' concerns. Concerning the banking sector, following the adoption of the Single Supervisory Mechanism (SSM), the ECB has the power to receive and address concerns raised by employees of supervised banks. In the same spirit, a whistleblower can report concerns to ESMA about specific issues related to capital markets. It is worth examining these institutions' powers to receive allegations and how this aids whistleblowing.

A. The Big Banker: What can the ECB do for the Whistleblowers?

After the 2009 financial crisis, the ECB gained significant supervisory powers over banks.[264] Among these powers, the ECB can receive whistleblowing concerns. Three EU acts attribute these powers to the ECB: Directive 2013/36/EU on access

[263] For this initiative: ec.europa.eu/info/law/better-regulation/have-your-say/initiatives/14468-Whistleblower-Protection-Directive-evaluation_en accessed 15 May 2025.

[264] European Central Bank, 'Guide to Banking Supervision' (November 2014) www.bankingsupervision.europa.eu/ecb/pub/pdf/ssmguidebankingsupervision201411.en.pdf accessed 15 May 2025.

to the activity of credit institutions and the prudential supervision of credit institutions and investment firms (CRD IV),[265] Regulation No 1024/2013 conferring specific tasks on the European Central Bank concerning policies relating to the prudential supervision of credit institutions (SSM Regulation)[266] and Regulation No 468/2014 establishing the framework for cooperation within the Single Supervisory Mechanism between the European Central Bank and national competent authorities (SSM Framework Regulation).[267]

The CRD IV and its Article 71 require national authorities to *establish effective and reliable mechanisms to encourage the reporting of potential or actual breaches of national provisions transposing* CRD IV and Regulation No 575/2013.[268] The mapping of national initiatives in this field is outside the scope of this book.[269] Nevertheless, the ECB can receive reports under the SSM Regulation and Framework Regulation.[270] Under Article 23 of the SSM Regulation, the ECB must establish a whistleblowing mechanism.[271] The SSM Framework Regulation, in Article 36, requires the ECB to establish a whistleblowing mechanism.[272] The two legal acts will be read and analysed together to understand the ECB's role as a 'competent authority'.

There are specific requirements for reporting to the ECB and for protection. The report should address banking regulations governing the supervision of a Significant Institution (SI). If the ECB finds that it concerns a Less Significant Institution (LSI), it should transfer it to the national authority. The reporting person should report in good faith and have reasonable grounds to believe that a breach has occurred. Data protection rules are applied, and the whistleblower's confidentiality is ensured. The ECB should establish procedures for receiving and following up on reports, ensure protection for the accused, and cooperate harmoniously with national authorities for the exchange of documents and information.

These provisions lack essential elements for whistleblowers, such as a clear definition. It is at the ECB's discretion to accept anyone as a whistleblower. Taking an actual bank employee makes sense, but what about ex-employees or contractors?

[265] Directive 2013/36/EU of the European Parliament and of the Council of 26 June 2013 on access to the activity of credit institutions and the prudential supervision of credit institutions and investment firms, amending Directive 2002/87/EC and repealing Directives 2006/48/EC and 2006/49/EC, OJ L176/338, Art 71.

[266] European Parliament and European Council Regulation (EU) No 1024/2013 of 15 October 2013 conferring specific tasks on the European Central Bank concerning policies relating to the prudential supervision of credit institutions, OJ L287/63, Art 23.

[267] European Parliament and European Council Regulation (EU) No 468/2014 of 16 April 2014 establishing the framework for cooperation within the Single Supervisory Mechanism between the European Central Bank and national competent authorities and with national designated authorities, OJ L141/1, Art 36.

[268] Directive 2013/36/EU, Art 71.

[269] For a detailed analysis of national initiatives, see S Allegrezza (ed), *The Enforcement Dimension of the Single Supervisory Mechanism* (Wolters Kluwer Italia, 2020).

[270] See www.bankingsupervision.europa.eu/about/ssmexplained/html/whistleblowers.en.html accessed 15 May 2025.

[271] European Parliament and European Council Regulation (EU) No 1024/2013, Art 23.

[272] European Parliament and European Council Regulation (EU) No 468/2014, Art 36.

These provisions do not specify the type or manner of protection. How can the ECB protect a whistleblower? If legal issues arise, they may involve national or EU law, but protection remains a national law issue. The concern is how the ECB will protect this whistleblower, as it cannot intervene in national legal proceedings. The Directive aims to protect whistleblowers reporting to the ECB as a competent authority, but this needs further clarification through transposition and case law. Currently, the protection is unclear, increasing insecurity for whistleblowers.

Furthermore, the ECB's reporting mechanism has significant limitations: it only allows reporting of wrongdoing about supervised entities, not potential breaches of the ECB or national banking supervisors. As a result, reports cannot be made to competent national authorities or the ECB regarding possible wrongdoing. In addition, reporting should strictly relate to the ECB's supervisory tasks and not cover other areas, such as money laundering or terrorist financing. The ECB cannot accept these issues and cannot forward them to other authorities.[273] This point contradicts the ECB staff's duty to report on fraud, corruption, or other illegal activities that harm EU financial interests. Misusing the reporting system could be a crime in some countries, and the ECB might pursue criminal action if the report was not made in good faith. This conflicts with the Directive, which does not require good faith.

The ECB is slowly progressing in establishing a robust internal reporting mechanism, which has been criticised for its slow pace.[274] An administrative circular issued by the Executive Board in 2006 is the first document related to internal whistleblowing.[275] This document requires managers and encourages staff to report breaches of professional obligations to their senior managers. Anonymity may be maintained, but the reporter's identity will always be disclosed to the manager receiving the report.[276] If an administrative inquiry begins, it clarifies the facts without always leading to disciplinary action.

Furthermore, the ECB must report to OLAF (the European Anti-Fraud Office) on fraud, corruption, or any other wrongdoing affecting the EU's

[273] European Central Bank, 'Information on the use of the breach reporting mechanism (BRM)', www.bankingsupervision.europa.eu/banking/breach/form/shared/pdf/BRM_important_legal_information.pdf accessed 15 May 2025. See also D Kafteranis, 'The Pilatus Bank Scandal: Time to Reconsider Banking Supervision, Anti-money Laundering and Whistle-blower's Protection in the EU' (European Law Blog, 5 December 2018) europeanlawblog.eu/2018/12/05/the-pilatus-bank-scandal-time-to-reconsider-banking-supervision-anti-money-laundering-and-whistle-blowers-protection-in-the-eu/ accessed 15 May 2025.

[274] Transparency International, 'Two sides of the same coin? Independence and accountability of the European Central Bank' (2017) 57 transparency.eu/resource/two-sides-of-the-same-coin-independence-and-accountability-of-the-european-central-bank/ accessed 10 April 2025. See also the recent letter from Mario Draghi to Sven Giegold, where it is mentioned that better internal reporting mechanisms are one of the priorities of the ECB, www.ecb.europa.eu/pub/pdf/other/ecb.mepletter190927_Giegold~bdb5d44333.en.pdf accessed 15 May 2025.

[275] European Central Bank, 'Administrative Circular 1/2006 on Internal Administrative Inquiries', www.ecb.europa.eu/ecb/access_to_documents/document/pa_document/shared/data/ecb.dr.par2017_0075_circular_administrative_enquiries.en.pdf?9a30fd53b47d52420f77f5e75e5ffcb2 accessed 15 May 2025.

[276] Transparency International (n 274) 57.

financial interests.[277] A 2016 ECB decision states that if an ECB employee comes across any information related to fraud, corruption, or any wrongdoing affecting the financial interests of the EU, they must report it to the Director of Internal Audit, their manager, or a relevant member of the Executive Board.[278] The whistleblower should suffer no negative consequences for having reported the information above.

Although these provisions supported internal whistleblowing, they were not entirely sufficient.[279] The internal whistleblowing practice was based on an administrative circular that lacked essential information, including follow-up timelines and expectations for inquiries.[280] Moreover, the 2006 administrative circular is outdated due to significant evolutions since then. The ECB announced plans to change and redesign its internal whistleblowing policies.[281] It has recently modified its internal whistleblowing mechanisms to encourage internal whistleblowing.[282]

On 20 October 2020, the ECB enhanced its staff rules, introducing a whistle-blowing tool and stronger protections.[283] The new regulations on the ECB's internal whistleblowing system are more precise and detailed. The good-faith requirement is abolished, as is the case under the Directive on the protection of whistleblowers, and the reporting employee must have reasonable grounds to believe that wrong-doing is occurring.[284] Additionally, the whistleblower can report information and reasonable suspicions of breaches or potential breaches.[285] A clear distinction is made between whistleblowers and witnesses,[286] anonymous whistleblowing is enabled,[287] and protection against retaliation is given.[288] The employee can still use the previous ECB whistleblowing rules, but the new rules offer an alternative reporting channel.[289] The new rules mark a step toward a more effective ECB internal reporting policy, but their effectiveness remains to be seen after adoption.

[277] OLAF Regulation (No 883/2013) and the respective ECB Decision ECB/2016/456.

[278] Art 3 Decision (EU) 2016/456 of the ECB of 4 March 2016 concerning the terms and conditions for European Anti-Fraud Office investigations of the ECB, in relation to the prevention of fraud, corruption and any other illegal activities affecting the financial interests of the Union (ECB/2016/3).

[279] Transparency International (n 274).

[280] ibid.

[281] European Central Bank, Letter from Danièle Nouy to Mr Sven Giegold regarding whistle-blower protection at the ECB (2017) www.bankingsupervision.europa.eu/ecb/pub/pdf/ssm.mepletter170630.en.pdf?f508ce662d57696b218f9f355ea2e5aa accessed 15 May 2025.

[282] See the letter from Mario Draghi to Sven Giegold where it is mentioned that better internal reporting mechanisms are one of the priorities of the ECB, www.ecb.europa.eu/pub/pdf/other/ecb.mepletter190927_Giegold~bdb5d44333.en.pdf accessed 15 May 2025.

[283] Decision of the European Central Bank of 20 October 2020 amending the European Central Bank Staff Rules as regards the introduction of a whistleblowing tool and enhancements to the whistleblower protection (ECB/2020/NP37).

[284] ibid Recital 3.

[285] ibid Art 1(1)(c).

[286] ibid Art 1(1)(g).

[287] ibid Art 1(0.4bis.5.2).

[288] ibid Art 1(0.4bis.6).

[289] ibid Art 1(0.4bis.2.2).

In 2024, the ECB received 421 whistleblower reports, about 19 per cent more than the previous year, 2023.[290] Of the 421 reports, 124 involved breaches of EU law and 117 fell within the ECB's supervisory remit. The remaining reports involved non-prudential violations, such as consumer protection issues, and were outside the ECB's whistleblowing scope. It is an improvement that the ECB is more transparent, now providing official statistics. Nevertheless, questions remain, such as follow-up on reports not relevant to the ECB's programme, especially if transferred to other authorities.

B. A Queen Without Powers: The Case of ESMA

Turning to the EU authority for the financial sector, ESMA lacks the ECB's essential powers. Its role is limited, but certain issues can be reported directly to it.[291] Under the UCITS (Undertakings for Collective Investment in Transferable Securities) Directive,[292] a market participant can submit a confidential report to the ESMA regarding an infringement of national provisions transposing the Directive.[293] The next reporting avenue for ESMA involves the Credit Rating Agencies (CRA) Regulation and the European Market Infrastructure Regulation (EMIR), enabling supervisory activities.[294] These are the EU legal acts for which ESMA can accept whistleblowing concerns.

Under the UCITS Directive, a natural person (employee or former employee) of an investment company, management company, or depositary must report, in good faith and personally, any infringements of national provisions transposing the Directive.[295] Reports can be made by any person in good faith about possible infringements of national laws implementing the Directive. Concerning the CRA Regulation and the EMIR Regulation,[296] reports can be made to ESMA by individuals or groups acting in good faith, employed or previously employed by a

[290] European Central Bank, 'ECB Annual Report on supervisory activities 2024' (2024) www.bankingsupervision.europa.eu/press/other-publications/annual-report/html/ssm.ar2024~700cba1314.en.html accessed 15 May 2025.

[291] ESMA, www.esma.europa.eu/whistleblowers-corner accessed 15 May 2025.

[292] M Lehmann and C Kumpan (eds), *European Financial Services Law* (Beck – Hart – Nomos, 2019) 1446.

[293] ESMA (n 291). See also Directive 2009/65/EC of 13 July 2009 on the coordination of laws, regulations and administrative provisions relating to undertakings for collective investment in transferable securities (UCITS), OJ L 302/32.

[294] ESMA (n 291). See also Regulation (EC) No 1060/2009 of 16 September 2009 on credit agencies (CRA), OJ L302/1 and Regulation (EU) No 648/2012 of 4 July 2012 on OTC derivatives, central counterparties and trade repositories (EMIR), OJ L201/1.

[295] ESMA (n 291).

[296] C Kumpan and R Grutze, 'Credit Rating Agency Regulation' in M Lehmann and C Kumpan (eds), *European Financial Services Law* (Beck – Hart – Nomos, 2019) 1289. See also P Lucantoni, 'Securities Clearing and Settlement – European Markets Infrastructure Regulation' in M Lehmann and C Kumpan (eds), *European Financial Services Law* (Beck – Hart – Nomos, 2019) 1670–72.

supervised entity, and acting in a personal capacity. The information helps ESMA detect potential breaches of the CRA and EMIR Regulations.[297]

The report can be submitted via specific forms on ESMA's website and sent by post or email. The ESMA guarantees anonymity unless the whistleblower consents to disclose their identity. Personal data is protected, and all report information will be processed in accordance with data protection rules.[298] Misusing the reporting mechanism may be a criminal offence in some Member States, as noted on the ESMA website.[299]

Although ESMA allows reporting breaches of EU laws to enhance supervision, certain issues may prevent future whistleblowers and undermine ESMA's role as a competent authority. Provisions show a lack of protection; whistleblowers can report to the ESMA, but there are no safeguards. The ESMA does not analyse, as the ECB does, how it will protect whistleblowers. The legal basis is problematic because the ESMA website requirements are not found in EU laws or official documents.

In addition, ESMA has been criticised for lacking a hotline for whistleblower calls.[300] ESMA's website has also been found to be dysfunctional and not easy to access.[301] Finally, the good faith requirement is questioned as the Directive is transposed, since a future whistleblower might choose the Directive's provisions over ESMA's whistleblowing process, which does not require good faith. It is essential to reconsider ESMA's role as the competent authority to adapt and enforce whistleblowing soon.

XI. Public Disclosure or What to Think at the End

In whistleblowing literature, there is a tendency to distinguish between internal and external cases of reporting.[302] Internal whistleblowing is when an employee reports wrongdoing to a superior or colleague. External whistleblowing involves reporting to an outside authority believed to have the power to correct the wrongdoing.[303] Although there is no clear consensus on the recipients of external whistleblowing, many scholars see it as reporting to union representatives, NGOs, the media, law enforcement, or advocacy groups.[304] For the Directive,

[297] ESMA (n 291).
[298] ibid.
[299] ibid.
[300] M Marriage, 'Esma and the Invisible Whistleblower Hotline' *Financial Times* (18 December 2016) www.ft.com/content/59162a1e-c3a6-11e6-9bca-2b93a6856354 accessed 15 May 2025.
[301] ibid.
[302] MP Miceli and JP Near, *Blowing the Whistle: The Organizational and Legal Implications for Companies and Employees* (Lexington Books, 1992).
[303] H Park, J Blenkisopp, M Kemal Oktem and U Omurgonulsen, 'Cultural Orientation and Attitudes toward Different Forms of Whistle-blowing: A Comparison of South Korea, Turkey, and the U.K.' (2008) 82(4) *Journal of Business Ethics* 929, 930.
[304] MP Miceli and JP Near, 'The Relationships among Beliefs, Organizational Position, and Whistle-blowing Status: A Discriminant Analysis' (1984) 27 *Academy of Management Journal* 687–705; M Miceli

external reporting has two parts: reporting to authorities and public disclosure of wrongdoing.[305]

The act of blowing the whistle, as Ralph Nader coined the term 'whistleblower' and developed this idea, has the meaning it has today: a public disclosure.[306] Public disclosure involves whistleblowers sharing information publicly, using available means. Information and technological revolutions are vital to effective public disclosure.[307] New technologies allow nearly everyone to collaborate and connect online across time and space.[308] Technological advances impact the whistleblower. Digitalisation allows easy collection and dissemination of information. Evidence can be quickly gathered, stored securely, and shared online.[309] The whistleblower can publicly report via technological advancements, but this is a last resort if other options fail. The whistleblower can initially exercise this option only under restrictive conditions.

A. The Last Resort: Disclosing to the Public

The whistleblower can disclose information publicly if specific conditions are met, and public disclosure should be the last resort option. The Directive's preamble emphasises timely follow-up and feedback on reports to prevent unnecessary *public disclosures*.[310] Consequently, the requirements for making a public disclosure are strict. The Directive encourages internal or authority reporting, making public disclosure harder.

Chapter IV of the Directive, entitled 'Public Disclosures', and Article 15 outline the rules applicable to it.[311] 'Public disclosure' refers to making information about breaches available to the public.[312] The Directive does not analyse 'public domain' but implies it involves informing many people about a breach and making information publicly available via media or the internet.[313] Recital 45 gives examples of how information might appear in the public domain: 'directly to the public

and JP Near, 'Retaliation against Whistle-blowers: Predictions and Effects' (1986) 71 *Journal of Applied Psychology* 137–45; JG Caillier, 'Public Service Motivation and Decisions to Report Wrongdoing in U.S. Federal Agencies : Is this Relationship Mediated by the Seriousness of the Wrongdoing' [2016] *The American Review of Public Administration* 1, 2.

[305] Directive 2019/1937, Art 15.

[306] Nader, Petkas, and Blackwell (n 1) vii.

[307] Bosua, Milton, Dreyfus and Lederman (n 4) 250.

[308] ibid.

[309] Panama Papers are considered the biggest leak in history (2.6 terabytes) and Paradise Papers are the second biggest (1.4 terabytes). See A Greenberg, 'How reporters pulled off the Panama Papers, the biggest leak in whistleblower history' (*Wired*, 4 April 2016) www.wired.com/2016/04/reporters-pulled-off-panama-papers-biggest-leak-whistleblower-history/ accessed 15 May 2021.

[310] Directive 2019/1937, Recitals 58 and 68; See also European Commission, Proposal for a directive (n 6) Recital 50.

[311] ibid Art 15.

[312] ibid Art 6(6).

[313] European Commission, Impact Assessment (n 101) 34.

through online platforms or social media, or to the media, elected officials, civil society organisations, trade unions or professional and business organisations'.[314] The whistleblower should disclose publicly information about a breach within the scope of the Directive and fulfil one of the conditions set out in Article 15.[315] The conditions are not cumulative, but if only one is met, the whistleblower can be protected.

The first condition the whistleblower must fulfil to be protected for making a public disclosure is that they reported internally and externally, or directly externally (to the authorities). Still, no action was taken in response to the report within the timeframes set out in the Directive.[316] The whistleblower can report either internally or to the authorities, without any priority given to either channel. As a result, if the whistleblower reported internally and then to the authorities, or has reported directly to the competent authorities, and no action has been taken, they can make a public disclosure. Interestingly, if the whistleblower had reported internally but not to the authorities, they could still make a public disclosure and remain protected. This requirement highlights the need to limit public disclosure by establishing different layers of 'protection' across the internal, external, and public tiers.

Apart from respecting reporting channels, whistleblowers must consider the Directive's timeframes. If reporting internally and then to authorities, they must wait up to three months for follow-up after internal reports, and another three (or up to six in justified cases) after reporting to authorities.[317] That means the whistleblower should wait from six to nine months, and if there is no follow-up, they can make a public disclosure. The Directive provides ample time, both internally and with the competent authorities, to follow up on the report. However, this waiting period may pose an obstacle to public disclosure.

First, the whistleblower must carefully calculate the timeframe before publicly revealing information. This adds to the already complicated whistleblowing process and becomes problematic if urgent action is needed. An example from banking and finance illustrates this. An employee at a Luxembourg financial institution discovers securities fraud and reports it internally but receives no response. Realising the fraud is escalating beyond the institution to other branches, he waits three months before reporting to the authorities. The fraud continues to grow, and he must wait another three or six months before public disclosure. This raises questions about the system's efficiency.

The example shows that the process can be slow and might not fix the wrongdoing. Allowing wrongdoing to become dangerous risks focusing on procedures over the goal of correcting and preventing harm. The time rules are appropriate, as they aim to frame the process and provide clarity to the whistleblower and the

[314] Directive 2019/1937, Recital 45.
[315] ibid Art 15(1).
[316] ibid Art 15(1)(a).
[317] Directive 2019/1937, Arts 9(1)(f) and 11(2)(d) respectively.

involved parties.[318] On the other hand, wrongdoing in the banking and financial sector may need to be addressed quickly, as it may escalate into something even more serious, given the fluidity of capital markets. To that end, it may be helpful to reconsider these strict timeframes and redesign public disclosures.

To sum up, the whistleblower has the opportunity to make a public disclosure if they have exhausted internal reporting and reporting to the authorities without success. In that case, the whistleblower can make a public disclosure and be protected under the Directive. The following condition is a bit more complicated. Article 15 specifies two conditions for whistleblowers to make protected public disclosures as the first choice. First, the reporter must have reasonable grounds to believe one of these conditions applies, with 'reasonable grounds' defined as in the Directive and discussed earlier.[319]

The two conditions are presented in Article 15, paragraph 1(b).[320] The first condition is when *the breach may constitute an imminent or manifest danger to the public interest, such as in an emergency or when there is a risk of irreversible damage.*[321] Analysing this sentence is complex. The use of 'may' suggests that a whistleblower can suspect, not necessarily be certain, that a breach poses an imminent or obvious danger to the public interest. They only need suspicion, not proof.

The other concept to be understood is the imminent and manifest danger to the public interest. The Directive provides two examples of what may constitute an imminent or manifest danger to the public interest. This can be either an emergency or a risk of irreversible damage. The list of examples is not exhaustive. All the aforementioned concepts are ambiguous, making it difficult for whistleblowers to understand them. Many questions arise: What defines an imminent danger? How do we interpret the public interest – national, European, or international? How should we understand emergencies or irreversible risks?

The concept of imminent or manifest danger is not deeply analysed in the Directive or accompanying documents. Member States have discretion when implementing the Directive to clarify it. The French Law Sapin II (amended by the Waserman Law) specifies the exact requirement for public disclosure.[322] Although this requirement has existed in French law since 2016, its precise nature remains unclear. Clarification is needed from European or national judges, which may lead to different interpretations.[323] Since the Directive is laconic, it is wise to note that the whistleblower must carefully analyse the situation and decide how to proceed.

The second condition of Article 15 para 1(b)(ii) is when, in the case of external reporting, the whistleblower has reasonable grounds to believe that *there is a risk of*

[318] Moberly (n 134) 292.
[319] Directive 2019/1937, Art 15(1)(b).
[320] ibid.
[321] ibid Art 15(1)(b)(i).
[322] Law No 2016-1691, Art 8 sub. II.
[323] Abazi (n 100) 10–11. Dr Abazi also believes that EU judges will interpret this provision and more clarifications will become available. In addition, she invites EU courts to be inspired by the case law of the European Court of Human Rights.

retaliation or there is low prospect of the breach being effectively addressed, due to the particular circumstances of the case, such as those where evidence may be concealed or destroyed, or where an authority may be in collusion with the perpetrator of the breach or involved in the violation.[324] If this condition is met, the whistleblower may choose to inform the public and be protected under the Directive.[325] These circumstances include concealed or destroyed evidence, collusion with the perpetrator, or involvement by authority in the violation.[326] The wording of this provision seems confusing.

First, the reference to external reporting in the first part of the provision requires that an internal report has been made. In that sense, the employee reported internally. Still, they are afraid to go to the competent authority, fearing retaliation or that the breach will not be effectively handled, which would prevent them from making a public disclosure. There is controversy surrounding this requirement. On the one hand, the whistleblower believes that reporting to the competent authority is futile due to potential retaliation or the incompetence of the competent authority. Thus, it is better to make a public disclosure likely to cause reprisals, as the authority may not handle the report.

In addition, the ineffectiveness of the competent authority is being conflated with problems in internal reporting. It is clear that the competent authority's involvement in the breach is an obstacle, but the possibility of concealing or destroying evidence is an internal issue. Does that mean the whistleblower could bypass internal reporting and go straight to the public? Additionally, if the whistleblower goes public, evidence is more likely to be destroyed or concealed as the company attempts to eliminate proof. The wording should clarify whether internal reporting is necessary and offer a better solution to these delicate situations.[327]

B. Achieve the Impossible: Defining the Public Interest

Defining and understanding 'public interest' is the next step for the whistleblower making a public disclosure under the first condition (Article 15 para 1(b)(i)). The concept of the 'public interest' is complex and difficult to define.[328] This concept has sparked significant debate about its meaning and content.[329] Black's Law Dictionary defines 'public interest' as: (1) the public's general welfare needing recognition and protection, and (2) something the public has a stake in, especially if it justifies regulation. What constitutes public interest cannot be determined by absolute rules.[330]

[324] Directive 2019/1937, Art 15(1)(b)(ii).
[325] Abazi (n 100) 12.
[326] Directive 2019/1937, Art 15(1)(b)(ii).
[327] See to that extent, Kafteranis (n 12) 24–25.
[328] N Dunne, 'Public Interest and EU Competition Law' (2020) 65(2) *The Antitrust Bulletin* 256, 257.
[329] G Anthony, 'Public Interest and the Three Dimensions of Judicial Review (2013) 64 *Northern Ireland Legal Quarterly* 125, 127.
[330] *Chesterton Global Ltd & anr v Nurmohamed & anr* (2017) EWCA Civ 979.

Another definition of public interest in Barron's Law Dictionary provides more insight. According to Barron's Law Dictionary, public interest is *that which is best for society as a whole.*[331] It adds, though, that it is *a subjective determination by an individual such as a judge or governor, or a group such as a … legislature of what is for the general good of all people.*[332] While this definition is not rigorous, it at least acknowledges a practical truth.[333] Walter Lippmann, in 1955, defined public interest as 'what men would choose if they saw directly, thought rationally, [and] acted disinterestedly and benevolently'.[334] Santoro and Kumar (2018) presented the public interest trilemma. They state: 'It is either a sum or an aggregation of individual non-competing interests; or an interest of the prevalent majority of a polity at one in time; or a common good that can be enjoyed only collectively.'[335] The public interest in this book is the recognition of what is best for the public, ensuring everyone's rights and protection.

When the legislator adopts a law that includes public interest, it is a signal to the judicial or executive discretion.[336] The sign indicates that decisions or measures should prioritise citizens' best interests, adopting a subjective approach. This may lead to arbitrary, inconsistent decisions, but judges can clarify the public-interest concept, thus limiting such inconsistencies.[337]

The concept of public interest has a long history.[338] Every country has its view of the public interest, which varies according to national law and legal culture. Analysing and understanding public interest is complex. It spans multiple sciences, including law, economics, management, philosophy, and politics. Within legal science, its meaning varies across different branches. For instance, the analysis of public interest in administrative law may differ from its analysis in regulatory theories.[339]

The Directive is laconic as to what the public interest means, and, as Lewis argued, the Directive 'is useful here in that it contains no separate test – the public interest is assumed if a breach of Union law is reported to a designated recipient in the manner specified in the relevant Articles'.[340] The same view is shared by Vandekerckhove, stating ' … disclosures relating to any of these could be regarded as 'public interest' and thus protected disclosures'.[341] While their opinions are respected in internal and authority reporting, this statement does not apply to

[331] SH Gifis, *Law Dictionary*, 4th edn (Barron's Educational Services, 1996).

[332] ibid.

[333] E Reksosh, 'Who Defines the Public Interest?' (2005) 2 *International Journal on Human Rights* 167, 170.

[334] W Lippmann, *The Public Philosophy* (Hamish Hamilton, 1955) 40.

[335] D Santoro and M Kumar, *Speaking Truth to Power – A Theory of Whistleblowing* (Springer, 2018) 70.

[336] Gifis (n 331).

[337] ibid.

[338] ER Boot, 'The Feasibility of a Public Interest Defense for Whistle-blowing' (2020) 39 *Law and Philosophy* 1, 7–8.

[339] M Bronwen and K Yeung, *An Introduction to Law and Regulation* (CUP, 2007) 16.

[340] Lewis (n 91) 18.

[341] W Vandekerckhove, 'Is It Freedom? The Coming About of the EU Directive on Whistleblower Protection' (2021) *Journal of Business Ethics* 1, 5.

public disclosures. Public interest cannot be taken for granted for whistleblowers who disclose publicly. National or EU judges should decide on the public interest in disclosure. Reporting a breach of EU law publicly does not automatically make it a matter of public interest.

Furthermore, the Directive fails to distinguish between national and European public interests. By referring to public interest, it is unclear whether the Directive intends for the meaning to have a national or European reach. The first understanding is that the notion of public interest in the Directive refers to each Member State's definition, based on its legal culture. Since the Directive has been transposed, related cases will soon reach the CJEU, potentially complicating public interest interpretation. Will EU judges focus on public interest like in national law, or expand it to include a new European public interest? The idea of the European public interest is not new, having been applied in another context, as evidenced by Regulation 1606/2002.[342] A key study found the European public interest is not defined in EU law.[343] The concept of European public interest, also called the public good or common interest, may reflect the interests of public institutions and private entities at the EU level.[344] To conclude, the notion of European public interest is flexible, with various meanings based on context.[345]

In Recital 3, the Directive states that a serious harm to the public interest is the creation of significant risks to society's welfare.[346] In the explanatory document for the proposed Directive on protecting whistleblowers, the European Commission analysed the concept of public interest through the Council of Europe's (CoE) perspective.[347] The CoE states that, while the notion of public interest should be understood globally as the 'well-being' or 'welfare' of society, in many areas this notion is similar across states; in other places, however, the same notion may be differently conceived and analysed. Therefore, the CoE abstains from defining 'public interest' and instead presents a non-exhaustive list of categories of content typically considered a subject of protected disclosures.[348] These standards, which are relevant to the public interest, involve violations of law and human rights, as well as risks to public health and safety and to the environment.[349] In addition, the list includes corruption, crime, legal and regulatory violations, abuse of power, public health and environmental risks, mismanagement, and cover-ups.[350]

[342] Regulation 1606/2002 of 19 July 2002 on the application of international accounting standards OJ L243/1, Art 3(2). In the English version of the Regulation, the term used is 'European public good', whereas in the French version '*intérêt public européen*'.

[343] C Hossfeld, Y Muller-Lagarde, D Alexander, M Pöschke and L Zevounou, 'L'intérêt public européen/ European Public Interest (2018) Rapport de recherche final, ANC, Autorité des normes comptables (hal-01862364).

[344] ibid 15.

[345] ibid.

[346] Directive 2019/1937, Recital 3.

[347] European Commission, Impact Assessment (n 101) 7.

[348] Council of Europe, Recommendation CM/Rec (2014)7, Protection of whistle-blowers, adopted by the Committee of Ministers, 30 April 2014, 7.

[349] ibid.

[350] ibid 24.

The European Court of Human Rights (ECtHR) has analysed the public-interest concept and established case-law on whistleblower protection under Article 10 of the European Convention on Human Rights (ECHR). The Strasbourg Court proceeds on a case-by-case basis, analysing what constitutes a matter of public interest.[351] The Court, citing its established case-law, notes that 'the interest which the public may have in particular information can sometimes be so strong as to override even a legally imposed duty of confidence'.[352] The Court has extensive case law on what constitutes public interest, covering various situations such as care for the elderly, abuses by authorities, private communications, violations of doctors' rules, criticism of public agents after a nuclear accident, and more.[353]

However, the notion of the public interest remains one that is and will be developed by the courts and is highly debated in the legal literature.[354] A case-by-case approach will clarify this notion. This can be explained by the specific nature of the public interest and the exclusivity of every problem. What is in the public interest evolves over time and in society. The transposition of the Directive and case-law from the European courts will clarify this notion. The debate continues, and the concept may become clearer in the future. Besides the European debate, there is also a national-level discussion.

Under French legislation on whistleblowers, the notion of public interest is still debated. The French State Council (Conseil d'Etat) issued a public report in 1998 on the general interest, which is relative to the public interest.[355] The report distinguished two conceptions of the public interest: the first, inspired by utilitarianism, in which the common interest is the sum of the interests of every individual; and the second, inspired by voluntarism, in which the general interest goes beyond the interests of individuals.[356] In this last conception, the public interest is the expression of the general will, and it is the concept that the French Republic adheres to.[357] In our society, individual interests often conflict, and the state and the courts are tasked with rediscovering the public interest.[358] Most importantly, every individual should set aside their interests when searching for the general interest. Precisely for whistleblowers, the courts will have the role of interpreting the public/general interest, for which, unfortunately, the case law is not abundant at the moment, as the French Law Sapin II is new.[359]

351 *Guja v Moldova* App no 14277/04 (ECtHR, 12 February 2008) para 74.
352 ibid 4.
353 *Mamère v France* App no 12697/03 (ECtHR, 7 November 2006).
354 B Bozeman, *Public Values and Public Interest* (Georgetown University Press, 2007) ch 1.
355 Conseil d'Etat, 'Réflexions sur l'intérêt général – Rapport public 1999' (1998) www.conseil-etat.fr/Decisions-Avis-Publications/Etudes-Publications/Rapports-Etudes/Reflexions-sur-l-interet-general-Rapport-public-1999 accessed 15 May 2025.
356 ibid.
357 ibid.
358 ibid.
359 E Daoud and S Sfoggia, 'Lanceurs d'alerte et enterprises: les enjeux de la loi Sapin II' [2017] *AJ Pénal Dalloz* 71, 72.

In Luxembourg, public interest and whistleblowing have been analysed in the context of the Luxleaks case. In the first instance, the Court did not provide any protection for the two whistleblowers under Article 10 ECHR.[360] In the appeal launched by the two accused whistleblowers, the Court of Appeal found that Article 10 ECHR can be applied and examined if the two whistleblowers may be protected under it.[361] One of the criteria is the public interest in the information given to the public. The Court of Appeal highlighted that the facts disclosed by Antoine Deltour sparked a public debate, leading to EU legislative initiatives in tax law.[362]

The Court of Appeal found that Antoine Deltour and Raphael Hälet met the public-interest criterion by being the first to raise the issue publicly, sparking intense debate over tax rulings. The Luxembourg Court of Appeal considered both national and European public interests, including the interests of the Luxembourg public and reactions from European institutions. This highlights the complexity of the concept of public interest, which is difficult to define.

The reporting person should weigh the facts and assess whether there is a risk of irreversible damage or an emergency needing immediate action. The public disclosure involves subjective aspects, as the concepts are not clearly defined at either the European or the national level. Judges will likely need to clarify these concepts to aid the reporting process.

C. Avoiding the 'Evil': Limiting Public Disclosures

Informing the public is a brave move. Over the years, 'blowing the whistle' has shifted from activism to a more institutionalised process, with public disclosure at its core. In addition to national legislation in EU countries, the Directive also restricts public disclosures by imposing requirements that whistleblowers must meet before making a public disclosure. In addition, public disclosure is a last resort for whistleblowers, except when they can disclose directly to the public after reporting to authorities or internally. Understanding the reasons for restricting disclosures is important.

The first reason is balancing the right to freedom of expression with employers' interests.[363] Public disclosures should be protected, respecting democratic principles such as accountability, transparency, and freedoms, including media freedom

[360] TA Lux, 29 Juin 2016, n° 1981/2016.

[361] CA Luxembourg, 15 Mars 2017, n° 117/17 X.

[362] ibid point 3 *les causes justificatives*, b) *le fait justificatif du lanceur d'alerte*, where it was stressed that '*Ces révélations ont été, et sont encore, au coeur de l'actualité européenne et la Commission européenne a fait de la lutte contre la fraude et l'évasion fiscale une priorité absolue. Celle-ci a notamment présenté, suite aux révélations LuxLeaks, un paquet de mesures contre l'évasion fiscale et un paquet de mesures sur la transparence fiscale, ainsi qu'un plan d'action pour une fiscalité des entreprises équitable et efficace dans l'Union européenne et le 18 mars 2015 une proposition de directive modificative sur l'échange obligatoire d'informations dans le domaine fiscal.*'

[363] Directive 2019/1937, Recital 34.

and expression. This must balance employers' interests in managing and protecting their business interests.[364]

The right to freedom of expression and information is enshrined in national constitutional traditions, as well as in Article 11 of the Charter of Fundamental Rights of the European Union and Article 10 ECHR.[365] The balance between the right to freedom of expression and the employer's interests is one of the criteria the ECtHR has adopted to protect whistleblowers.[366] The presence of this balance is evident not only at the European level but also in national legislation and case law. This balance of interests inspired the French legislature to design its disclosure channels. Reporting, inspired by freedom of expression, should be done in conformity with the duty of discretion and loyalty; it should be proportional. For these reasons, the Law Sapin II outlines the steps employees should follow, with application measures adopted by decrees or other legal acts.[367]

In the same vein, Irish legislation allows public disclosures under specific conditions. Section 10 provides for disclosure to other recipients under strict conditions.[368] The Act appears to aim to limit public access to whistleblowing information.[369] Finally, this balance was apparent in the 'Luxleaks' case. The Luxembourg Court of Appeal, applying the ECtHR criteria, struck a balance between the right to freedom of expression and the employer's interests at stake in granting or denying protection to whistleblowers.[370]

Aside from balancing interests, limiting public disclosures improves internal and authority reporting, which are better equipped to handle reports than the public. The Directive allows whistleblowers to report internally or to authorities, leaving the choice to them. This choice aims to *ensure that the information reaches those who can contribute to the early and effective resolution of risks to the public interest, as well as prevent unjustified reputational damages from public disclosures.*[371] Promoting internal and authority reporting enhances whistleblowing effectiveness, favouring quick, efficient action over public disclosure, which should be a last resort. Greater clarity is needed on the exceptions that allow whistleblowers to report directly to the public without using internal channels.

[364] ibid.

[365] Charter of Fundamental Rights of the European Union [2012] OJ C326/391, Art 11 and Convention for the Protection of Human Rights and Fundamental Freedoms (European Convention on Human Rights, as amended) (ECHR) Art 10.

[366] *Guja v Moldova* (n 351) para 76.

[367] Décret n° 2017-564 du 19 Avril 2017 relatif aux procédures de recueil des signalements émis par les lanceurs d'alerte au sein des personnes morales de droit public ou de droit privé ou des administrations de l'Etat, JORF n° 0093 du 20 Avril 2017.

[368] Protected Disclosures Act 2014, number 14 of 2014, s 10.

[369] M Kinsley, 'Protected Disclosures Bill 2013' (2014) 32 *Irish Law Times* 4.

[370] CA Luxembourg, 15 Mars 2017, n° 117/17 X.

[371] European Commission, Impact Assessment, (n 101) 34. See also Council of Europe, Resolution 1729, adopted 29 April 2010, Arts 6.1.2, 6.2.3.

7

Elements of Protection for Whistleblowers

A 2020 study for 'Protect: Silence in the City 2' showed that 70 per cent of financial workers who blew the whistle faced victimisation, dismissal, or neglect, or felt forced to resign afterwards.[1] These employees reported giving their names but faced retaliation and job loss. The issue is whether employees are motivated to report when statistics show a high risk of being 'punished' and losing all benefits, and the answer appears to be negative. The whistleblower will not risk their career or personal life without proper protection mechanisms.[2]

Whistleblower studies show potential whistleblowers face significant risks and obstacles.[3] First, whistleblowers may face termination or duress, often resulting in job loss. If they keep working, they encounter other challenges.[4] They may be marginalised, given trivial tasks – humiliating for their rank – and harassed in hostile workplaces. Alford notices that whistleblowers who stay with their employer may suffer an 'endless chain of abasement'.[5] Employers may also retaliate against whistleblowers by forcing them to undergo 'psychiatric fitness-for-duty examinations'.[6]

Suffering for whistleblowers does not stop with quitting their job. Studies have shown that they will have limited re-employment opportunities.[7] The stigma of whistleblowing makes them less attractive to hire and leads them to be regarded as disloyal.[8] As a result, whistleblowers often struggle to find new jobs after leaving to

[1] Protect: Silence in the City 2 (2020) protect-advice.org.uk/silence-in-the-city-2/ accessed 15 May 2025.

[2] FD Lipman, *Whistleblowers – Incentives, Disincentives, and Protection Strategies* (Wiley, 2012) 118.

[3] CF Alford, 'Whistle-blower Narratives: The Experience of Choiceless Choice' (2007) 74(1) *Social Research* 223–48; A Dyck, A Morse and L Zingales, 'Who Blows the Whistle on Corporate Fraud?' (2010) 65 *The Journal of Finance* 2213–53; KR Sawyer, J Johnson and M Holub, 'The Necessary Illegitimacy of the Whistleblower' (2010) 29 *Business and Professional Ethics Journal* 85–107.

[4] B van Rooij and AD Fine, 'Preventing Corporate Crime Within: Compliance Management, Whistleblowing, and Internal Monitoring' in ML Rorie (ed), *The Handbook of White-Collar Crime* (Wiley Blackwell, 2020) 235.

[5] Alford (n 3) 230.

[6] G Liyanarachchi and C Newdick, 'The Impact of Moral Reasoning and Retaliation on Whistle-blowing: New Zealand Evidence' (2009) 89(1) *Journal of Business Ethics* 37, 41.

[7] ibid 40.

[8] RD Fincher, 'Mediating Whistleblower Disputes: Integrating the Emotional and Legal Challenges' (2009) 64(1) *Dispute Resolution Journal* 62–70.

avoid retaliation. This incurs financial, personal, and social costs.[9] First, losing their job and being unable to find a new one results in a loss of income. If whistleblowers enter legal battles, they struggle to pay legal fees and survive. Second, social stigma may ostracise them, and stress about the future can affect their well-being.

Whistleblowers face risks beyond work. Blowing the whistle may expose you to liability, whether civil, administrative, or criminal. Under the liability provisions, the whistleblower may owe damages to their employer or the state. The other scenario of liability – the most common – is criminal liability for the whistleblower due to breaches of secrecy or confidentiality rules, document theft, trespassing, or other offences.[10] The key question is whether whistleblowing status can be a defence against criminal liability.[11]

Legislation in many countries and the EU seeks to protect whistleblowers from retaliation and liability. The legislation aims to protect whistleblowers from reprisals and legal liability, enabling them to report safely. Towards this end, several support measures, such as assistance or legal aid, are adopted to improve their protection. In addition, penalties exist for employers who try to impede employee reporting. Apart from protecting whistleblowers, legislation aims to protect third parties, such as colleagues or family members, who may be victimised alongside whistleblowers.

Besides the protections and support measures, there are other ways to alleviate whistleblowers' suffering. Anonymity and financial rewards are controversial aspects of whistleblower protections that are missing in much legislation.[12] Anonymity is an essential aspect of whistleblowers' protection, as they can report without letting anyone know who is behind the report. Nevertheless, anonymity raises several legal and ethical issues that will be addressed in detail below. Similarly, in some jurisdictions, such as the US, whistleblowers can receive financial rewards under specific rules. As with anonymity, monetary rewards are controversial, are not present in much legislation, and will be scrutinised below.

The EU Directive on protecting whistleblowers aims to safeguard whistleblowers. The Directive provides strong anti-retaliation protections and rights for whistleblowers, shielding them from liability.[13] These protections and rights

[9] van Rooij and Fine (n 4) 235.

[10] U Turksen, 'The Criminalisation and Protection of Whistleblowers in the EU's Counter-Financial Crime Framework' in K Ligeti and S Tosza (eds), White Collar Crime: A Comparative Perspective (Hart Publishing, 2019) 333.

[11] M Spencer and J Spencer, 'When it all Goes Bad: Criminal Remedies' in AJ Brown, D Lewis, R Moberly and W Vandekerckhove (eds), *International Handbook on Whistleblowing Research* (Edward Elgar, 2014) 424–26.

[12] TM Marcum, J Young and ET Kirner, 'Blowing the Whistle in the Digital Age: Are You Really Anonymous? The Perils and Pitfalls of Anonymity in Whistleblowing Law' (2020) 17(1) *DePaul Business and Commercial Law Journal* 1, 5. H Fleischer and KU Schmolke, Financial Incentives for Whistleblowers in European Capital Markets Law? Legal Policy Considerations on the Reform of the Market Abuse Regime, ECGI Law WP No 189/2012 (2012), 10, ssrn.com/abstract=2124678 accessed 15 May 2025.

[13] D Lewis, 'The EU Directive on the Protection of Whistleblowers: A Missed Opportunity to Establish International Best Practices?' (2020) 9(1) *E-Journal of International and Comparative Labour Studies* 1, 14–16.

are essential for employees to come forward and report. Though the Directive covers protections against retaliation, liabilities, and measures, it remains silent on anonymity and financial rewards. The focus of this part is on the protection offered by the Directive, analysing its strengths and weaknesses. References to other legislation will be made to provide insights that may be useful for the EU legal framework in the future.

In Europe and the US, the financial system's survival triggers changes to, or the enactment of, new whistleblowing laws. Whistleblowing is viewed as an effective enforcement tool and, secondarily, as an employee protection mechanism.[14] The whistleblower acts as a private enforcement tool to enforce legal rules. As a complement to the enforcement function of whistleblowing, protection is offered. As a result, the primary focus is on protecting the market, rather than the whistleblower. The Directive provides significant protection to whistleblowers under labour, civil, criminal, or administrative law. It should be seen if that protection is sufficient in practice.

I. Risks and Perils for the Whistleblower: Retaliation and Liabilities

A. Retaliation against the Employee who Blows the Whistle

Protection from retaliation is an incentive for whistleblowers to report.[15] In this regard, protection from retaliation is the price paid for providing information, whether to the employer, the relevant authorities, or the public. Weaknesses in anti-retaliation protections may discourage whistleblowers from reporting. The whistleblower may face retaliation from managers, colleagues and other implicated parties.[16] A tentative definition of retaliation is 'undesirable action against a whistleblower in response to reporting wrongdoing internally or externally'.[17]

The situation is not ideal for the whistleblower in the banking and financial sector. Areas that have been regulated for a long time might accept reports without retaliating against whistleblowers. That is not always true. A study by Protect, a British charity aiding whistleblowers, showed nearly 70 per cent of City whistleblowers face 'victimisation, ignoring, or retaliation dismissed'.[18] The European

[14] John Coffee Jr. describes it as a form of outsourcing. See more: JC Coffee Jr., *Corporate Crime and Punishment – the Crisis of Underenforcement* (Berrett-Koehler Publishers, 2020) 488. See also D Kafteranis, 'A New Enforcement Tool: A Directive to Protect Whistle-blowers' (2020) 41 *Business Law Review* 50.

[15] R Vaughn, *The Successes and Failures of Whistle-blower Laws* (Edward Elgar, 2012) 125.

[16] K Kenny, *Whistleblowing – Towards a New Theory* (Harvard University Press, 2019) 19.

[17] MT Rehg, MP Miceli, JP Near and JR Van Scotter, 'Antecedents and Outcomes of Retaliation Against Whisteblowers: Gender Differences and Power Relationships' (2008) 19(2) *Organization Science, INFORMS* 221, 222.

[18] Protect (n 1).

Commission noted this as well in its Impact Assessment for the Directive, highlighting protection issues. It identified three factors undermining reporting: fear of retaliation, poor protection at national and EU levels, and ineffective implementation due to low awareness and social-cultural issues.[19]

During the Open Public Consultation (OPC), launched by the European Commission before the proposal was presented, most responses to the question of why workers do not report wrongdoing focused on the legal and financial consequences. Furthermore, respondents viewed retaliation against whistleblowers as the key factor in safeguarding them, and other relevant studies support these findings. For instance, Transparency International France found in 2015 that almost 39 per cent of employees do not report wrongdoing out of fear of retaliation.[20] Several disasters show that whistleblowers are not reporting because they fear retaliation. For example, the UK's 1998 rail crash, which killed 35 and injured 484, was investigated, revealing an inspector had noticed the loose wiring. Still, he did not want to report it because he did not desire to 'rock the boat'.[21]

This fear of retaliation is justified. Surveys and disasters show that whistleblowers avoid reporting due to fears of reprisal. In the first Global Business Ethics Survey, which included over 10,000 workers across 13 countries, 33 per cent reported experiencing misconduct. Of these, 59 per cent reported it, but 36 per cent experienced repercussions.[22] Retaliation can lead to contract termination, loss of business, income, blacklisting, reputation damage, and other consequences. Several 'famous' whistleblowing cases in banking and finance have demonstrated the consequences of retaliation. For example, Michael Woodford, the former president of Olympus, wrote a book about his experience and the retaliation he encountered from his company and industry afterwards.[23] In a meeting at Oxford, Michael explained his financial losses and his fear for his and his family's future.[24]

Another example is Jonathan Sugarman, who reported illegal liquidity breaches at UniCredit in Dublin. He resigned from his position and has been unable to find a job since.[25] The European Commission's Impact Assessment prior to the Directive's adoption noted insufficient protection at both national and EU levels.[26] A minority

[19] European Commission Staff Working Document, Impact Assessment accompanying the document of the proposal for a Directive of the European Parliament and of the Council on the protection of persons reporting on breaches of Union law [2018] COM(2018) 218 final, 10.

[20] Transparency International, "Lanceurs d'alerte': quelle perception de la part des salariés?' (2015) transparency-france.org/wp-content/uploads/2016/04/R%C3%A9sultats-sondage-Harris- Interactive.pdf accessed 15 May 2025.

[21] A Hidden, QC, 'Investigation into the Clapham Junction Railway Accident' (1989) www.railwaysarchive.co.uk/documents/DoT_Hidden001.pdf accessed 15 May 2025.

[22] Global Business Ethic Survey, 'Measuring Risk and Promoting Workplace Integrity' (ECI, 2016) www.boeingsuppliers.com/2016_Global_Ethics_Survey_Report.pdf accessed 15 May 2025. The Global Business Ethic Survey is industry-financed.

[23] M Woodford, *Exposure* (Penguin, 2012).

[24] The meeting was held in the Brasenose College, University of Oxford in November 2019. Special thanks to the Principal of the College, John Bowers.

[25] Kenny (n 16) 150–51.

[26] European Commission, Impact Assessment (n 19) 12.

of Member States had adopted a comprehensive legal framework. In contrast, the majority of Member States had only sectoral provisions on whistleblowers' protection, such as in banking and financial services. The EU legislation was incomplete. Due to piecemeal laws and fear of retaliation, the European Commission proposed the Directive, which includes measures to address retaliation.

B. Risk of Liabilities for Blowing the Whistle

As whistleblowing is a *sui generis* field of law and cannot be classified into one category alone, such as civil law, criminal law, or administrative law, this means the whistleblower may face different or combined types of liability when reporting. Over the last decade, several scandals, such as Luxleaks and Swissleaks, have been reported by whistleblowers who faced criminalisation as a direct result of their whistleblowing.[27] Thus, in several jurisdictions, the whistleblower can be held criminally liable for breaches of criminal law.

More specifically, whistleblowers may face criminal charges for breaking secrecy laws.[28] Secrecy laws exist in areas like banking, finance, and national security. Secrecy in the banking and financial sector often carries criminal sanctions for those who breach it. In addition, whistleblowing in the banking and financial sector may involve acts or omissions that may expose whistleblowers to criminal liability.[29] Those offences may be theft, electronic fraud or trespassing.

Once the whistleblower is held liable, the question is whether a defence or immunity is available.[30] The whistleblower should report wrongdoing, but they may commit criminal offences. For instance, the whistleblower should take certain documents (theft), access computers (electronic fraud), enter offices illegally (trespassing), or reveal secrets (breach of secrecy rules). These acts are necessary to gather evidence for reporting but may also incur criminal liability. The matter of a criminal law defence arises. First, an excuse is not desirable.[31] If the whistleblower invokes an excuse, they concede that their acts were wrong but seek to avoid responsibility. The acts reported were not bad or immoral but necessary, which should justify the committed offences.[32]

The whistleblower needs a defence to use in front of a criminal court in order not to be held criminally liable. The defence justifies its actions as necessary to

[27] Turksen (n 10) 333.

[28] Spencer and Spencer (n 11) 423.

[29] C Harding, 'The Role of Whistleblowing and Leniency in Detecting and Preventing Economic and Financial Crime: A Game of Give and Take?' in K Ligeti and V Franssen (eds), *Challenges in the Field of Economic and Financial Crime in Europe and the US* (Bloomsbury Publishing, 2017) 101.

[30] ibid 103.

[31] ER Boot, 'The Feasibility of a Public Interest Defense for Whistleblowing' (2020) 39 *Law and Philosophy* 1, 18.

[32] 'Justifications are based on the saving of a prevailing interest and revolve therefore around the weighting of interests under proportionality.' For more extensive analysis: JH Blomsma, *Mens Rea and Defences in European Criminal Law* (Maastricth University, 2012) 531.

report, but its design and features are challenging. A first possible defence may be based on the public interest.[33] The need to inform and protect the public can be used as a defence for whistleblowers facing criminal charges. Another type of defence may be the whistleblower's status.[34] Being recognised as a whistleblower, thus fulfilling all relevant legal requirements, can constitute a defence against criminal charges arising from blowing the whistle. This type of defence is the one the Directive envisages and will be analysed in detail below.

II. The Protection of the Whistleblower as Designed by the Directive

A. The Directive's Anti-Retaliation Protection

The need to protect whistleblowers from retaliation is a central point of the Directive. As Recital 1 clearly states, potential whistleblowers are often discouraged from reporting because of fear of retaliation; for this reason, it is essential to provide balanced and adequate protection at the EU level.[35] Recital 87 states that reporting persons should be protected against retaliation from their employer, customer, or colleagues, including those in other organisations they contact during work. That is a strong statement for the protection that should be offered in different anti-retaliation situations. Recital 88 highlights this strong statement, noting that when retaliation *occurs undeterred and unpunished, it has a chilling effect on potential whistleblowers.*

Chapter VI of the Directive sets out protective measures for whistleblowers, which are satisfactory but have some issues. Regarding retaliation and other protections, the Directive effectively captures the anti-retaliatory practices that whistleblowers faced over the years within the legal framework.

First, Article 19 requires Member States to prohibit any form of retaliation against whistleblowers, third parties, and facilitators. The whistleblower is at the centre of the anti-retaliation protection. When an employee blows the whistle, they are often subjected to a hostile work environment. Employers will try to retaliate against whistleblowers, and these efforts can take different forms. The Directive lists 15 possible types of retaliation. The list of retaliation includes suspension, layoff, dismissal, demotion, transfer, change of work location, wage reduction, altered hours, withholding of training, negative performance or references, disciplinary

[33] Boot (n 31) 18–27.

[34] D Kafteranis, 'From Obscurity to Limelight: The Whistle-blowers' Protection under EU Law' in V Mitsilegas and SJ Wortman (eds), *Whistleblowing, Transparency and Criminal Law: A Comparative Perspective* (Brill, 2023).

[35] European Parliament and European Council Directive 2019/1937/EU of 23 October 2019 on the protection of persons, who report breaches of Union law [2019] OJ L305/17, Recital 1.

actions, reprimands, penalties, coercion, intimidation, harassment, and others, as set out in Article 19 of the Directive.

The list is not exhaustive, allowing Member States to adopt other types of retaliation. The extensive list of potential retaliation acts as a crucial safeguard for whistleblowers.[36] It covers many situations, leaving little room for additional measures that the Directive omits. The European Parliament, during negotiations, highlighted in particular damage to reputation on social media and psychiatric or medical issues.[37] These situations are in Article 19. It is encouraging that the Directive protects against both direct and indirect retaliation by employers towards whistleblowers.[38] The Directive considers not only the employer responsible for reprisals but also others linked to the whistleblower, including customers, service recipients, colleagues, and managers within or outside the organisation.

In addition, the Directive aims to protect not only whistleblowers but also third parties and facilitators from employer retaliation. Often, whistleblowers receive some help from third parties or others in reporting. These parties may have a working relationship with the whistleblower and employer, risking retaliation for their help. The Directive shields persons, including whistleblowers, from reprisals. Member States must also prohibit and punish attempts at or threats of retaliation under national law.[39]

Another essential element of anti-retaliation protection is the burden of proof. The Directive requires whistleblowers to prove that they were engaged in protected speech when retaliated against. There is no need for the whistleblower to demonstrate a nexus, or retaliatory connection, between whistleblowing and retaliation.[40] Recital 93 acknowledges that whistleblowers struggle to prove a link between their reports and retribution, while employers or retaliators often have more resources to justify their actions as unrelated. Therefore, the EU legislator relaxed the requirements for whistleblowers, shifting the burden of proof to the employer and giving them an advantage in retaliation cases before courts or tribunals.

Finally, employment tribunal adjudication can be difficult, expensive and ineffective for providing a solution.[41] If a whistleblower's employer issue arises,

[36] V Magner, 'Avant-propos' (2019) 4 *RAE-LAE* 677.

[37] E Andreis, 'Towards Common Minimum Standards for Whistleblower Protection across the EU' (2019) 4(2) *European Papers* 575, 582.

[38] JT Stappers, 'EU Whistleblower Protection Directive: Europe on Whistleblowing' (2021) 22 *ERA Forum* 87, 98.

[39] V Abazi, 'Whistleblowing in the European Union' (2021) 58 *Common Market Law Review* 813, 831.

[40] D Tom, 'Assessment of European Union Whistleblower Directive' (Government Accountability Project, 2020) wordpress-350926-1087337.cloudwaysapps.com/blog/assessment-of-european-union-whistleblower-directive/ accessed 15 May 2025.

[41] A Day, 'To Mediate or Adjudicate? An Alternative for Resolving Whistleblower Disputes at the Hanford Nuclear Site' (2013) 11(2) *Seattle Journal for Social Justice* 617, 635; D Lewis, 'Resolving Whistleblowing Disputes in the Public Interest: Is Tribunal Adjudication the Best that can be Offered?' (2013) 42(1) *Industrial Law Journal* 35, 36. Other methods can be arbitration or conciliation. Lewis provides an extensive analysis of all the possible methods of alternative dispute resolution between whistleblowers and employers. The author shares his views.

they should take it to an employment tribunal, which may be ineffective and complicated for resolving whistleblowing disputes.[42] First, employment tribunals do not have the power to investigate disclosures nor to order rectification where wrongdoing is established.[43] An employment tribunal focuses only on the labour dispute between the employer and the whistleblower, excluding wrongdoing. This is a disadvantage, especially when whistleblowers seek acknowledgement of misconduct. Second, employment tribunal adjudication entails high costs and fees, delays, fear, and stress, putting whistleblowers in a precarious financial and personal situation.[44] An optimal solution to employment tribunal adjudication issues is alternative dispute resolution.

Alternative methods should be considered, but the Directive lacks provisions for them. Besides going to the Employment Tribunal, the employer and whistleblower should be able to resolve issues through mediation and other alternative dispute resolution mechanisms.[45] Bringing a claim to an employment tribunal is time-consuming and costly and prolongs disputes. Mediation can be more effective, enabling parties to discuss issues openly. In addition, mediation can be quicker, cheaper, private, and effective for whistleblowers. The Directive's lack of mention of alternative dispute resolution mechanisms is a disadvantage for whistleblowers' protection. Member States or the European Commission may address this in future reviews.

B. Liabilities and the Confusing Wording of the Directive

Under Article 21 of the Directive, the issue of liabilities is analysed. Paragraph 2 of Article 21 outlines the conditions for protection against liability. If a whistleblower reports or makes a public disclosure, they must meet the conditions specified in the Directive. In that case, they should not incur any liability related to the report or the public disclosure. The condition the whistleblower must fulfil is that they have reasonable grounds to believe that the report or public disclosure was essential to reveal a breach. Any superfluous information reported by the whistleblower 'without having such reasonable grounds' will be dismissed, and any protection offered under the Directive will be forfeited. In addition, the whistleblower will not be protected from liability if their report involves classified information, national security, or legal, medical, or criminal process details.

From the above, it is clear that the whistleblower cannot incur any liability if they have reasonable grounds to believe that the reporting was necessary to reveal

[42] Lewis (n 41) 36; L Kierans, 'Whistleblowing Litigation and Legislation in Ireland: Are There Lessons to be Learned?' (2023) *Industrial Law Journal*, 1.

[43] ibid.

[44] M Peters, Ken Seeds and Carrie Harding, *Findings from the Survey of Employment Tribunal Applications 2008*, Employment Relations Research Series (BIS, 2010) 107.

[45] Lewis (n 41) 36.

a breach. The definition of what constitutes 'reasonable grounds' is a delicate matter. The basic dilemma with the 'reasonable grounds' requirement is whether a normal citizen would have thought this was a breach or whether a professional in the same position would have thought there was a breach.[46] If the whistleblower lawfully obtains or acquires access to necessary information or the related documents, then they enjoy immunity from liability.[47] This applies in two scenarios. First, when a whistleblower reports documents they have lawful access to, they are immune from liability. Second, if they copy or remove documents from their organisation in breach of contractual duties, they should not be liable. Therefore, a whistleblower is immune if they use documents they are lawfully entitled to, provided they relate to their work.

In addition, the whistleblower should not face civil, administrative, or labour liability when obtaining the necessary information as discussed above. Suppose a whistleblower obtains information by accessing emails. In that case, if they access documents that they typically cannot access, take photos of organisation buildings, or enter restricted locations, they should be liable under civil, administrative, or labour law. The situation differs from the criminal liability scene.[48]

Articles 21(6) and 23 specify that whistleblowers can receive full compensation and interim relief, pending legal penalties, in cases of confidentiality breaches and dismissals, respectively. In the preamble of the Directive, more information on remedies in the event of dismissal can be found. Under Recital 94, the whistleblower should be reinstated to their workplace and compensated for actual and future losses, including economic and intangible losses (such as suffering or pain). Recital 95 notices that reparation or compensation should not be dissuasive and discourage potential whistleblowers. Of particular interest is to notice that 'providing for compensation as an alternative to reinstatement in the event of dismissal might give rise to a systematic practice, in particular by larger organisations, thus having a dissuasive effect on future whistleblowers'.

Recital 95 references the Principles of the European Pillar of Social Rights, especially Principle 7, which states, 'before any dismissal, workers have the right to be informed of the reasons and be granted a reasonable period of notice. They have the right to access to effective and impartial dispute resolution and, in case of unjustified dismissal, a right to redress, including adequate compensation.' Thus, the Directive proposes remedies for whistleblowers, but Member States decide which to offer – generic or specific – and whether interim relief is available. Most proposed remedies are in the Directive's preamble, giving Member States more discretion since the preamble is not binding like the Articles.

[46] Tom Devine, who is a leading expert in whistleblowing research, suggests that the reasonable belief should be analysed in light of what a person with equivalent knowledge, training and experience would agree. He demands that this definition should be transposed in all national laws. See also Devine (n 40).

[47] Directive 2019/1937, Recital 92.

[48] Lewis (n 13) 14.

C. The Imperfect Shield against Criminal Liability in the Interplay between European and National Levels

If a whistleblower accesses information through criminal acts such as trespassing or hacking, their liability should be governed by national criminal law. This exception does not apply when the breach involves violations protected under Article 21(7) of the Directive. Under Article 21(7), whistleblowers are protected in legal cases involving defamation, copyright breach, secrecy, data protection, trade secrets, or labour law claims. Their status serves as a defence against liability.

Whistleblowers often face criminal liability when blowing the whistle, as it involves breaching rules protected by criminal law. They may breach professional secrecy or be accused of stealing confidential documents. In many countries, violating these rules is criminally sanctioned. Whistleblowers need protection from criminal liability and a defence to avoid punishment.[49] Accepting whistleblower status provides a shield against criminal liability. It shows the accused respected whistleblowing rules and did what was necessary, which justifies their non-liability. The whistleblower is not excused, but their status justifies the breach of criminal law.

Under the Directive, the whistleblower must have reasonable grounds to believe that the report or disclosure reveals a breach. It only requires suspicion that the information relates to a violation, not proof. If the whistleblower reports any superfluous information without reasonable grounds, they will not be protected under the Directive. In addition, the whistleblower should demonstrate public interest, but proving it is difficult, which will rather discourage them than encourage reporting. Defining the public interest and its scope is delicate and may weaken the whistleblower.[50]

Furthermore, the Directive encourages Member States to shield whistleblowers from legal, contractual, or non-disclosure obligations that may obstruct reporting. More specifically, legal or contractual obligations, such as the duty of confidentiality or non-disclosure agreements, cannot deny protection or penalise whistleblowers for reporting information that falls within the scope of such clauses or contracts and is necessary to reveal a breach. Thus, the whistleblower may breach contractual duties if necessary for reporting wrongdoing.

When reporting or disclosing trade secrets publicly, whistleblowers must comply with the protection rules set out in Article 3(2) of Directive 2016/943.[51] These conditions are unfavourable to whistleblowers and may conflict with the Whistleblower Directive and the Trade Secrets Directive. Two reasons make reporting of trade secrets rather complex for the whistleblower. First, the whistleblower

[49] The creation of a defence is only appropriate if this is necessary to ensure lawful conduct and blameless defendants are not punished. See also Blomsma (n 32) 290.

[50] V Abazi, 'Trade Secrets and Whistleblower Protection in the European Union' (2016) 1(3) *European Papers* 1061, 1069.

[51] Directive 2016/943 on the protection of undisclosed know-how and business information against their unlawful acquisition, use and disclosure, 8 June 2016, OJL157/1.

must prove that the information revealed pertains to *misconduct, wrongdoing, or illegal activity*.[52] Second, the disclosure should be made in the public interest. Concerning the burden of proof, the requirement to prove that the information relates to misconduct, wrongdoing, or illegal activity makes it a rather tricky task for the whistleblower.[53]

Hence, apart from the protections offered to whistleblowers regarding criminal liability under Article 21(7), any other possible liability of whistleblowers arising from acts or omissions unrelated to the report or not necessary to reveal a breach will remain governed by EU and national rules. The Directive urges courts to evaluate acts or omissions based on all the facts of the case, considering necessity and proportionality to determine whistleblower liability. The criminal liability situation is complex and confusing for the whistleblower, and this complexity persists with the requirement of a self-standing criminal offence.

The self-standing criminal offence in Article 21(3) requires that the whistleblower does not commit any criminal offence under national law when they acquire or access the necessary information to report or make a public disclosure. If this acquisition or access to the information constitutes a self-standing criminal offence, the whistleblower's liability is governed by national law. In practice, whistleblowers should not commit a criminal offence, such as theft or trespass, when obtaining the necessary information. In famous cases of whistleblowing in Europe, such as Luxleaks, whistleblowers have faced criminal charges.[54] This requirement may be a weakness for whistleblowers. They need information to report, but uncertainty remains whether their act or omission is a criminal offence due to the vagueness of the concept.[55]

From the laconic provisions of the Directive, whistleblowers should access and acquire information strictly related to their work and should avoid taking other, unrelated information, as criminal liability may arise. For instance, the whistleblower should avoid using co-workers' emails or accessing restricted areas. Not granting criminal immunity makes their actions a criminal offence, as they can be charged when obtaining information. Even if they avoid civil, administrative, or labour law liability, their criminal liability remains a significant concern.

The rise of digitalisation in workplaces causes confusion.[56] Access to workplace information is easier, possibly leading to whistleblowers being charged

[52] Directive on trade secrets, Art 5(b).

[53] Abazi (n 50) 1068.

[54] See to that end the Luxleaks case, where the two whistleblowers were accused of theft and breach of professional secrecy; TA Lux, 29 Juin 2016, n° 1981/2016; CA Luxembourg, 15 Mars 2017, n° 117/17 X; CSJ, cass., 11 Janvier 2018, n° 3911; CSJ, cass., 11 Janvier 2018, n° 3912.

[55] N Veronika and C Naomi, 'Whistleblowing in the European Union: A New Directive to Protect Citizens, Democracy and Rule of Law' (2019), 4, Blueprint for Free Speech static1.squarespace.com/static/5e249291de6f0056c7b1099b/t/5ed119f3deae375165af97b4/1616776389329/EU_NEW_DIRECTIVE_ANALYSIS_V5_ONLINE.pdf accessed 15 May 2025.

[56] R Bosua, S Milton, S Dreyfus and R Lederman, 'Going Public: Researching External Whistleblowing in a New Media Age' in AJ Brown, D Lewis, R Moberly and W Vandekerckhove (eds), *International Research Handbook on Whistleblowing* (Routledge, 2014) 250.

for accessing digital information without permission or understanding it.[57] An optimal solution is for the Directive to explicitly state that computer hacking for personal gain is prohibited. Limiting the scope to computer hacking, with more details in the Directive, will help the reporting person understand the related risks. Special attention should be given to acts or omissions unnecessary for reporting.

The Directive aims to establish a proportional safety net under which whistleblowers will access and report only necessary information. In future cases, judges should assess whether a whistleblower's actions are proportionate to their reporting goal. The whistleblower should act or omit only when necessary to report. In addition, the proportionality here means that the whistleblower should provide the amount of information which is required to make their report valid. They should not report information unrelated to the wrongdoing. Thus, the proportionality test will assess whether the whistleblower's actions or omissions are proportionate to the report made, whether the whistleblower exceeded what was necessary, and whether protection should be granted.[58]

Unfortunately, the proportionality test for a self-standing criminal offence is unclear. Logically, the Directive aims to prevent abusive reporting with a proportionality check, but its approach may confuse rather than clarify. The wording of the Directive, as it stands, can only confuse and complicate whistleblowing. The fear of criminal liability, without clear rules, will be an obstacle; it creates a chilling effect on whistleblowers and may undermine the Directive's purpose: to promote whistleblowing.

Furthermore, the Directive refers to the acquisition or access to information but not to the report or public disclosure. More specifically, a possible scenario is that a whistleblower will not be protected for how they obtained the information. Still, they may be protected when data is reported or disclosed publicly. From the wording of the Directive, such a scenario is not fictional. Still, it can become reality because the concept of a self-standing criminal offence concerns the acquisition or access to the information, not its report or public disclosure.

Consequently, the whistleblower will face criminal charges for the way they acquired or accessed the information but will be protected for the act of whistleblowing – the information they provided. It would not be ideal to punish, in criminal terms, a whistleblower who provided information proving a breach, simply because they acquired it 'illegally'. If the information relates to their workplace, in a general sense of the term 'workplace', the whistleblower should not incur criminal liability. What should matter is whether the information reveals a breach, not how the whistleblower accessed it.

[57] Council of Europe, Committee on Legal Affairs and Human Rights, 'Report on Improving the Protection of Whistle-blowers all over Europe', Doc. 14958, Sylvain Waserman, 30 August 2019, 15.

[58] 'First, proportionality is the most important aspect of defences. It captures and balances all factors into one normative end argument on the wrongfulness of the act or the blameworthiness of the defendant. This normative condition is flexible, because it consider many aspects, including the manner and degree in which the other criteria of a defence have been fulfilled', as stated by Blomsma (n 32) 531.

The intersection of the self-standing criminal offence with the whistleblowers' criminal immunity is an interesting relationship. By committing a criminal offence in reporting, the whistleblower will not be protected under the Directive, as they do not fulfil the requirement of a self-standing criminal offence. The waiver of criminal immunity will not apply, and the whistleblower will not be protected when most needed, especially during the acquisition of information. The criminal offence that the whistleblower will commit will almost always be related to the access or acquisition of the information. Therefore, it appears that the protection against criminal charges is an empty promise for whistleblowers under the Directive. Potential criminal immunity burdens whistleblowers and is hard to respect. The Directive's wording lacks clear protection from charges and complicates the issue of criminalising whistleblowers.

Another interesting aspect is the principles of mandatory and discretionary prosecution.[59] Depending on the tradition, the prosecutor may choose whether to prosecute (discretionary) or must prosecute every known offence (mandatory). The principle of discretionary prosecution is common in common law, where prosecutors have broad discretion to decide whether to prosecute.[60] Under the principle of discretionary prosecution, the whistleblower may be protected from criminal liability if the prosecutor decides not to prosecute them, because their acts were necessary to report and thus justified. On the other hand, the principle of mandatory prosecution is common in civil law, where prosecutors must prosecute any offence they become aware of. In that scenario, the whistleblower needs strong protection against criminal liability to shield against the prosecutor's charges.

The Directive seeks to justify whistleblower actions in criminal law, which falls under the general part of criminal law, where the Union usually lacks explicit competence. The fragility of this is apparent in the Directive's wording and the laconic details provided. Member States can develop this concept in their national criminal law, but the Directive leaves gaps. Also, it is doubtful if the Union had the competence to create a new criminal law defence affecting Member States' constitutional and criminal law traditions.[61]

The EU is in a delicate position regarding the creation of a defence. Following the Lisbon Treaty, the EU obtained significant legislative powers in the field of

[59] Systems of prosecution are either closer to the legality or opportunity principle. This is related to the discretion that the prosecutor has over the decision to prosecute and the permission to take into account facts which are different from the evidence of the case. G Mansfield and J Peay, *The Director of Public Prosecutions: Principles and Practices for the Crown Prosecutor* (Tavistock Publications, 1987) 27. See also JH Langbein, 'Controlling Prosecutorial Discretion in Germany' (1974) *41 University of Chicago Law Review* 439, 440.

[60] States, such as the UK, Ireland and the US, adhere to the opportunity principle where prosecutors have the opportunity to decide whether to prosecute or not based not only on the evidence provided but also to other factors. As a result, not every offence where there is evidence of guilt will be prosecuted as there may be other reasons which suggest inaction. See A Sanders, 'Introduction' in A Sanders (ed), *Prosecution in Common Law Jurisdictions* (Dartmouth, 1996) xi. See also M McConville and G Wilson (eds), *The Handbook of the Criminal Justice Process* (OUP, 2002).

[61] P Faraguna, 'Taking Constitutional Identities Away from the Courts' (2016) 41 *Brooklyn Journal of International Law* 492.

criminal law. These powers relate to establishing minimum rules for defining criminal offences and sanctions in serious cross-border crimes, and to harmonising criminal law to ensure the effective implementation of Union policies.[62] The creation of a criminal defence by the EU is not within its competencies. Criminal defences are part of criminal law's general part, not the substantive part.[63] Thus, the EU's ability to establish a defence in this area is unclear.

Indeed, adequate protection for whistleblowers should shield them from potential criminal liability arising from their reporting. The need to shield whistleblowers from criminal liability requires an EU criminal defence in the Directive. Since the Directive aims to protect whistleblowers, it would be helpful to shield them from criminal liability. The EU has expanded its powers into a new field to protect whistleblowers. Nevertheless, this extension should have been carried out correctly, with the EU respecting its powers and the criminal traditions of Member States. A different EU legal act under Articles 83(1) or 83(2) TFEU to protect whistleblowers would have been better, respecting the competences of the EU and the Member States.

Engaging in criminal law measures is a complex process, and the EU is often hesitant to pursue it. Criminal law is a core part of national law and sovereignty. The EU's success in adopting criminal law measures under certain conditions is already admirable. Extending these powers to other parts of criminal law is a method widely used by the EU. In the whistleblower protection scenario, the EU has exercised criminal law powers without a proper legal basis. The Directive's defence for whistleblowers has a weak foundation and may be ineffective. The EU should have avoided criminal protection for whistleblowers in this way. Still, it should have aimed to intervene by respecting its legal limits and conditions.[64] The final adoption of the criminal law measures in the Directive shows the EU's reluctance to deeply engage in criminal law, revealing a superficial approach.

Whistleblowers play a crucial role in disclosing financial and white-collar crimes.[65] Most whistleblowers in this sector take personal and professional risks to report breaches. The professionals in this high-risk sector need not only protection against reprisals but also strong, effective protection against criminalisation. Apart from blowing the whistle, these professionals have other reporting duties, such as in the context of money laundering, and they risk meaningful sanctions if they fail to comply.[66] A lack of adequate protection against

[62] Consolidated version of the Treaty on the functioning of the European Union [2012] OJ C326/47, Arts 83(1) and 83(2).

[63] 'The defences in this legal research do not negate the offence charged, but one of the two implied elements of criminal liability wrongfulness or blameworthiness. They are general because in principle, they can be raised to any offence charged', as noted by Blomsma (n 32) 526.

[64] Kafteranis (n 34).

[65] P Gottschalk, *Whistleblowing – White Collar Fraud Signal Detection* (Cambridge Scholars Publishing, 2018) 70.

[66] European Parliament and European Council Directive 2015/849/EU of 20 May 2015 on the prevention of the use of the financial system for the purposes of money laundering or terrorist financing, amending Regulation No 648/2012/EU, and repealing Directive 2005/60/EC and Commission Directive 2006/70/EC (Text with EEA relevance) [2015] OJ L141/73, Art 61.

reprisals and criminalisation may undermine the success of the Directive. The Member States should transpose the Directive in a way that ensures clear criminal liability without making it a sword hanging over whistleblowers' heads.[67] In such a sector, the legislator should protect whistleblowers when they report a potential breach, even if it is ultimately not a breach. Whistleblowers should be given a safe space, and the focus should be on the information reported, not on the whistleblower.

D. Measures to Support the Whistleblower

Under Article 20 of the Directive, Member States are required to implement a set of support measures. This set of measures should be available to the whistleblower, as defined in Article 4 of the Directive. First, whistleblowers should have freely accessible, comprehensive, and independent public information and advice. The information and advice should address the procedures and remedies available to protect them against retaliation, as well as the rights the whistleblower enjoys under the Directive (and the national legislation transposing it). As already noted, procedures and whistleblowing laws are complex, which may discourage reporters who are unsure how to report or whether they are protected.

Therefore, the first measure of support is of an informative nature. The whistleblower should have access to free, relevant, accurate, and confidential advice on any whistleblowing question. The whistleblower's questions depend on their reporting channel and whether the information is protected by whistleblowing laws or other procedures, including signposting. Providing this information ensures the whistleblower reports correctly without breaching legislation and that the data arrives on time to detect or prevent wrongdoing.

Furthermore, Member States should ensure competent authorities first assist whistleblowers before involving other authorities. The Directive only provides one example: certification of their entitlement to protection. Therefore, it leaves a wide margin of discretion to the national competent authorities to decide on the assistance and its form. The certificate example is important because it will serve as a shield that whistleblowers can present to authorities responsible for their protection.[68]

[67] The Luxembourg law on the protection of whistleblowers, transposing the Directive, states that whistleblowers should not be prosecuted for their actions when making a report. Nevertheless, there is an exception: when the whistleblower commits a self-standing criminal offence when obtaining the necessary information, then they may be criminally liable. As a result, the whistleblower risks to be criminally liable due to the way they acquired the information and, in that scenario, the defence of being a whistleblower will not be able to protect them.

[68] France has enacted this system. The certificate is granted by the Défenseur des droits under strict conditions. For more information: www.defenseurdesdroits.fr/le-lanceur-dalerte-une-definition-precise-pour-beneficier-dun-statut-protecteur-696 accessed 15 May 2025.

As a measure of support, the Directive requires Member States to provide legal aid to whistleblowers in criminal and civil cases.[69] Although the whistleblower can recover legal fees at the end of legal proceedings, they might not be able to pay them at the beginning, especially if they are unemployed or blacklisted. The rights of the accused in criminal proceedings have recently been a focus in the EU, which has offered significant protections. Legal aid should also be available to whistleblowers, as required by national law, in subsequent proceedings and for legal advice or assistance. The support requires the whistleblower to face charges and need legal counsel. While important, legal aid is not always effective in the Member States.

First, payment schemes are unsatisfactory for lawyers, and legal aid is not available to all who request it. Strict criteria apply to qualify. Especially for whistleblowers in the financial sector, it is unlikely that their revenues will justify legal aid. This may be an illusion, as financial-sector whistleblowers often lack the funds for lengthy legal battles.[70] Second, legal assistance can be delayed, harming urgent cases that need immediate help. It is ineffective for whistleblowers who often need urgent legal aid. A solution is to establish a dedicated fund offering financial assistance to them.[71] If a Member State establishes a public authority to support whistleblowers, creating a fund will enhance protection by providing concrete support. This fund, financed by sanctions on banks and financial institutions, should aid whistleblowers facing any proceedings.

Moreover, the Directive encourages Member States to offer financial and other support, including psychological assistance, to whistleblowers. Member States can extend support to include legal counselling, provided by the state or civil society organisations with specific obligations and rights. First, the information they receive should remain confidential. Member States should ensure civil society organisations do not suffer retaliation for assisting whistleblowers. Retaliation, such as economic restrictions or blacklisting, could disrupt the organisation's activities.[72]

Legal counselling or support may be provided by a state authority that works with whistleblowers. The Directive invites Member States to establish *an information centre or a single, identified, independent administrative authority* that can support whistleblowers. The Directive does not require Member States to establish

[69] European Parliament and European Council Directive 2016/1919 on legal aid for suspects and accused persons in criminal proceedings and for requested persons in European warrant proceedings [2016] OJ L297/1; European Parliament and European Council Directive 2008/52/EC on certain aspects of mediation in civil and commercial matter [2008] OJ L136/1.

[70] Woodford (n 23) 204.

[71] The SEC has created, in 2010, the Investor Protection Fund which is financed by the monetary sanctions imposed following a tip from a whistleblower. The fund provides financial rewards to successful whistleblowers. The idea of a fund in order to financially assist whistleblowers in the EU may get inspiration from the SEC fund. More information: Securities and Exchange Commission, 'Annual Report on Whistleblower Program' (2010) 5, www.sec.gov/files/whistleblower_report_to_congress.pdf accessed 15 May 2025.

[72] Lewis (n 13) 16.

such an authority but encourages it. Such an authority at the national level is crucial support for whistleblowers.[73] Allowing whistleblowers to seek advice from authorities reassures them and encourages reporting.

Member States should decide if this authority should only assist the whistleblower or also investigate and sanction the involved organisation. For instance, the Luxembourg Whistleblowing Office (Office des Signalements) has mostly an advisory role with limited investigative powers.[74] A drawback of creating such an authority will be the cost, as it will need to be well-resourced. Many states may struggle to establish and fund a new administrative authority. However, a viable solution would be to finance such an authority through the monetary sanctions imposed following a whistleblower's report. This will create sustainable funding for the authority and relieve the state of an additional cost.

A support measure missing from the Directive is raising awareness.[75] The European Parliament's 2016 Resolution highlights the role of public authorities, civil society, and trade unions in supporting whistleblowers and raising awareness about protection laws.[76] More specifically, the European Parliament called for 'a website to be launched where useful information on the protection of whistleblowers should be provided, and through which complaints can be submitted; stresses that this website should be easily accessible to the public and should keep their data anonymous'. The CoE has also advocated for developing public awareness by promoting national laws on whistleblowing *widely, aiming to create positive attitudes among the public and professions and to facilitate the disclosure of information in cases where the public interest is at stake.*[77]

Raising awareness is crucial for informing potential whistleblowers about their rights and duties and promoting social and cultural change in public perception. If the law encourages whistleblowing by informing citizens what to do, it creates a positive image and builds trust in the concept. Simultaneously, trust in the government is restored when it promotes whistleblowing, informs citizens, and respects whistleblowers, showing good intentions.

[73] Record Project, Public Procurement Transparency and Integrity, 'Guide to EU Directive on Whistle-blowers Protection – Key Elements relevant to Public Procurement' (2019) 11, www.access-info.org/wp-content/uploads/ML-2-Whistleblower.pdf accessed 15 May 2025.

[74] Guichet.lu, 'Office des signalements' (18 November 2024) guichet.public.lu/fr/citoyens/organismes/organismes_citoyens/ministere-justice/office-signalements.html accessed 15 May 2025.

[75] Lewis (n 13) 23. The European Commission has started to provide funding under the CERV programme to NGOs and other related parties in order to promote whistleblowing and raise awareness. One such project is the BRIGHT project www.edhec.edu/en/research-and-faculty/departments/management-and-humanities/bright-project

[76] European Parliament, Resolution of 24 October 2017 on legitimate measures to protect whistle-blowers acting in the public interest when disclosing the confidential information of companies and public bodies [2016] (2016/2224(INI)), para 53.

[77] Council of Europe Committee of Ministers, 'Recommendation CM/Rec(2014)7, Protection of Whistle-blowers' (adopted by the Committee of Ministers at the 1198th meeting on 30 April 2014) para 27.

E. Rights for the Alleged Wrongdoers and the Persons Associated with

The Directive grants whistleblowers certain rights and aims to ensure certain rights for the accused and their associates. Article 22's title is 'Measures for the protection of persons concerned'. At first, it is unclear who these persons are. Still, Article 5(10) provides the definition, according to which a 'concerned person' is a 'natural or legal person who is referred to in the report or public disclosure as a person to whom the breach is attributed or with whom that person is associated'. Interestingly, the definition includes both natural and legal persons, with significant rights attributed to them. Member States should ensure protective measures are available to alleged wrongdoers and their associates.

Member States should guarantee the right to an effective remedy, the right to a fair trial, the presumption of innocence and the rights of defence, including the right to be heard and the right to access their file. The Directive does not specify in which context these rights should be enjoyed. Still, it is clear that these rights should be guaranteed in all judicial proceedings, regardless of their nature – whether civil, administrative, or criminal. These rights come from the Charter of Fundamental Rights and EU legal acts on defence rights.

Interestingly, the Directive on protecting whistleblowers grants these rights to both individuals and legal entities. The Charter contains no provision indicating which Article applies to legal entities.[78] The Court of Justice of the European Union (CJEU) lacks a clear approach to assigning rights to companies under Union law. While the Directive's provision is welcome for granting the accused certain rights, the confusion about which rights are offered to companies is unacceptable. Due to the ambiguity of this provision at the Union level, it would have been wise to reformulate it or draw inspiration from the rights that legal entities enjoy under EU competition law.

The European Commission has enforcement powers in competition law.[79] Regulation 1/2003 grants the European Commission investigative and decision-making powers.[80] The European Commission's actions target companies that are entitled to certain procedural rights.[81] Some of these rights include the privilege against self-incrimination, the right to be heard, access to the file, adequate judicial

[78] P Oliver, 'Companies and their fundamental Rights: A Comparative Perspective' (2015) 46 *International and Comparative Law Quarterly* 661, 680. As the authors highlight, 'Exceptionally, Articles 42 to 44 of the Charter (on the rights to access to documents, to submit a complaint to the Ombudsman and to petition the European Parliament, respectively) expressly confer rights on them; but these are hardly the most important rights.'

[79] TFEU, Arts 101 and 102.

[80] European Parliament and European Council Regulation (EC) 1/2003 of 16 December 2002 on the implementation of the rules on competition laid down in Articles 81 and 82 of the Treaty [2003] OJ L1/1.

[81] WPJ Wouter, 'Fundamental Procedural Rights and Effective Enforcement of Articles 101 and 102 TFEU in the European Competition Network' (2020) 43(1) *World Competition* 5, 8.

process, and respect for the *ne bis in idem principle*.[82] The list shows that legal entities have certain rights under EU competition law, which may have inspired the Whistleblower Directive.

The last measure for protecting 'persons concerned' is to protect their identities.[83] This protection has two parts. First, the identity should be safeguarded during investigations from reports or disclosures. Second, their identity should be protected, as whistleblowers are under Articles 12, 17, and 18 of the Directive. The wording of the Directive is interesting. It does not refer to anonymity, as the Directive neither analyses nor demands anonymity,[84] nor confidentiality; instead, it requires the protection of identity. This protection relates more to privacy than anonymity. The provision indicates that some individuals will know the identity, so it needs to be safeguarded. Conversely, in anonymity, no one should know the identity.

F. Penalties for Those Impeding Whistleblowing

The Directive discourages retaliation against reporting persons by obliging Member States to penalise such actions.[85] Member States should set effective, proportionate penalties to deter those blocking whistleblowers, including criminal, civil, or administrative sanctions. These are necessary for enforcing whistleblower protection rules. Article 23 specifies the situations in which these penalties apply.[86] Examining these cases helps identify who should worry about penalties, the behaviours to sanction, and the types of penalties (civil, administrative, or criminal).

First, penalties should apply to those who impede reporting, retaliate against persons in Article 4, bring vexatious proceedings, or breach the confidentiality of reporting persons, as in Article 16. Because whistleblowing under the Directive is workplace-related, obstructive behaviour towards the whistleblower should originate in the workplace. This includes not only their direct manager but also anyone involved in behaviour impeding the whistleblower from reporting. The Directive targets individuals, including contractors or subcontractors, who obstruct whistleblowing in the workplace, whether directly or indirectly, regardless of whether they are colleagues. Nevertheless, no further penalties are specified for other obligations imposed by the Directive, as the establishment of internal reporting schemes and the follow-up of reports.[87]

[82] Case C-603/13 P *Galp Energia Espana and Others v Commission* [2016] ECLI:EU:C:2016:38, paras 71 to 77; Case C-238/99 P *Limburgse Vinyl Maatschappij and Others v* Commission [2002] ECR I-08375, paras 59 to 68.

[83] Directive 2019/1937, Art 22(2).

[84] Lewis (n 13) 21.

[85] Directive 2019/1937, Recital 102.

[86] S Detraz, 'Les sanctions relatives à la violation des règles sur la protection des lanceurs d'alertes selon la Directive' (2019) 4 *RAE-LAE* 713.

[87] Lewis (n 13) 23.

Regarding liability, Member States are free to choose whether to provide for civil, administrative, or criminal liability in their national legislation when transposing the Directive. For instance, the Irish Public Disclosures Act (PDA) 2014, in section 13, provides a right of action in tort to a whistleblower who was retaliated against by the person who caused them detriment because of the disclosure made.[88] The Irish legislator has chosen civil law liability, unlike some states that prefer criminal liability.

The Canadian Criminal Code, section 425.1, imposes a maximum sentence of up to five years' imprisonment for employers who retaliate against a whistleblower.[89] Under the Canadian Criminal Code, only external whistleblower reports are protected; internal reports are not, and retaliation against internal reporters is not a crime.[90] This shows Canadian legislation favours external whistleblowing. Similarly, Australia's Public Interest Disclosure Act 2013 makes retaliation against whistleblowers a criminal offence with up to two years' imprisonment.[91]

Despite criminal liability for individuals who retaliate against whistleblowers in Canada and Australia, neither law has resulted in any reported cases to date.[92] On the one hand, criminal prosecutions against those who retaliate against whistleblowers are desirable for their deterrent effect on potential offenders and their symbolic impact on employers' behaviour. The imposition of criminal liability establishes an ethical space where retaliation against whistleblowers cannot be tolerated. Still, on the contrary, they should be proportionally punished under criminal law. Criminal liability deters employers and others from retaliating against whistleblowers, as they fear potential criminal penalties.

On the other hand, criminal liability may not help whistleblowers; it could worsen the situation. Employers rarely commit outright crimes, such as direct retaliation against whistleblowers; instead, they often use reputational attacks, marginalisation, or similar tactics.[93] These attacks may not meet the standard of criminal intent beyond a reasonable doubt, so criminal liability cannot be established. In addition, there is a risk of scapegoating for broader failures, especially vulnerable groups such as junior staff and employees from diverse backgrounds. Finally, if criminal liability is imposed on natural persons, it can also be applied to legal persons where permitted.

[88] Public Disclosures Act, n° 14 of 2014, s 13.

[89] Canadian Criminal Code, s 425.1

[90] P Bowal, 'Retaliation Against Whistleblowers is a Crime' (2011) *Lawnow* 28, 30.

[91] Australia's Public Interest Disclosure Act 2013, s 19.

[92] A Graig, 'Whistleblowers Need More Protection in a Post-Covid Workplace', *Financial Times* (London, 2020) www.ft.com/content/284f67a5-c221-443d-b525-258a3fc7ee66 accessed 15 May 2025.

[93] ibid. See, for instance, K Kate and F Marianna, 'Post-Disclosures Strategies – Transforming Whistleblower Experiences' (2019) www.whistleblowingimpact.org/wp-content/uploads/2019/06/19-Costs-of-Whistleblowing-ESRC-report.pdf accessed 15 May 2025.

G. Penalties Against Abusive Reports

The Directive mandates that Member States impose penalties for abusive reports, making anyone who knowingly discloses false information liable under national law.[94] Penalties should be given to whistleblowers who knowingly report or disclose false information. The Directive abolished the good faith requirement but does not accept reports made in bad faith. If a whistleblower knows the report is untrue, they cannot be considered a whistleblower.[95] To the contrary, they should be penalised for knowingly reporting false information. Under this provision, only the reporting persons are concerned, not others who may be related to them.[96] This provision is significant because it creates a safety net against the reporting of false information and discourages 'bad faith' whistleblowers due to the potential penalty.

The liability may be civil, administrative, or criminal. The damaged party should also be able to recover damages from the reporting or public disclosure.[97] Penalties for employees who report false information should be proportional so as not to have a dissuasive effect on potential whistleblowers. The Directive urges Member States to adopt a lenient approach, as strict penalties may deter whistleblowers. Imposing criminal liability is problematic because it is more severe than civil or administrative penalties.

Providing false information is related to defamation. Most Member States likely already have laws to punish the spread of false information. Apart from defamation, other offences include libel, slander, and false accusation.[98] Depending on the legal system, the offence may vary, but it aims to punish those spreading false information. The whistleblower should reasonably believe the report shows a breach was correct at reporting. It is good practice to require the complainant to prove the whistleblower knew the information was false when reporting it.[99]

H. Anonymity and Financial Rewards

Anonymity is vital for whistleblowers' protection. The concept of anonymity in whistleblowing is delicate and not present in several pieces of legislation. Allowing anonymous whistleblowing encourages more reports and offers better protection for whistleblowers. This highlights the positive aspect of anonymity. On the contrary, it is argued that anonymous reporting can lead to abuse, reduce

[94] Directive 2019/1937, Art 23(2).

[95] Detraz (n 86) 714.

[96] ibid 714 where it is clear that the others related to the reporting person can still benefit from the measures of protection of the Directive for third parties.

[97] Directive 2019/1937, Art 23(2).

[98] See the Belgian Criminal Code, Arts 443, 445 and 448.

[99] Lewis (n 13) 16.

whistleblowing reliability, and undermine its moral and ethical standing. Before exploring anonymity and the Directive, it is helpful to review the advantages and disadvantages of anonymity as analysed by whistleblowing scholars.

First, while some whistleblowing laws permit anonymous reporting, others do not, favouring confidentiality.[100] Practical concerns can be an obstacle to anonymous whistleblowing. For instance, if the whistleblower is anonymous, communicating with them to gather more information will be challenging.[101] Anonymity can be costly. The person receiving the report may require additional resources to verify its authenticity or to determine if it is abusive.[102] The lack of reliability in anonymous whistleblowing can reduce its usefulness, as anonymous reports may lead to more unreliable reports that would not have been received.

Anonymity may have practical consequences for whistleblowers, as allowing anonymous reports could lead to many being received. The whistleblower's report may get lost among many anonymous reports, and they could be misled into thinking the system keeps their anonymity, which may not be the case.[103] Naïve users of technology may develop a false sense of security, believing they can use the corporation's IT infrastructure without detection. For instance, if printed in-house, the corporation can identify internal printers by inspecting invisible watermarks. Finally, if a corporation designs anonymity outside the law, whistleblowers may lack protection, as the law might not recognise them due to their anonymity.

The credibility of whistleblowing may be compromised due to ethical or moral objections.[104] Anonymity is disapproved of, seen as bad manners because it undermines trust and threatens the team's solidarity. Elliston suggests that anonymous whistleblowing is simply a matter of poor etiquette. Limiting anonymous whistleblowing is not a moral or ethical issue but a matter of fair play and preventing abuse. Those accused will try to shift the focus to the claimant's truthfulness rather than the veracity of their claims. Personal motives do not determine the truthfulness of information; instead, the focus should be on the information itself, not the motives behind an anonymous report.

Anonymity has both negative and positive aspects. First, anonymity protects the weak party – the employee – who is unable to defend themselves against large, powerful corporations.[105] Often, whistleblowers face large, powerful institutions that can initiate and sustain legal action against them. The law cannot foresee these moves or always protect the whistleblower. If the accused wants to defend themselves before the court, justice should be granted. The law cannot deny the right to a trial. These trials often punish whistleblowers, who lack funds for legal fees. While the law offers interim relief and legal aid, it is often insufficient. Anonymity

[100] Vaughn (n 15) 309.
[101] Lipman (n 2) 120.
[102] Vaughn (n 15) 309.
[103] Marcum, Young and Kirner (n 12) 5.
[104] FA Elliston, 'Anonymity and Whistleblowing' (1982) 3(1) *Journal of Business Ethics* 167, 175.
[105] Vaughn (n 15) 310.

protects whistleblowers by keeping their identity secret and preventing legal action against them.[106]

Therefore, anonymity encourages reporting of wrongdoing and protects whistleblowers. This dilemma between anonymity and the right to a fair trial centres on information or motives. Does the law focus on the information received or the whistleblower's motives? The answer varies across legal systems, as reflected in organisations that support whistleblowing. For instance, the UK states it is sceptical of anonymity.[107] This refusal is based on common law principles like loyalty and confidentiality. Conversely, GAP supports anonymous disclosures as essential protection for whistleblowers.[108]

Financial rewards for whistleblowers are also controversial, with a history dating back to the thirteenth century in common law. Today, they are common in the US, especially in finance, but in the EU, they are more reserved; no Member State offers rewards. The next part discusses their history, use, pros and cons, and suggests the EU should reconsider adopting financial rewards.

I. Staying Anonymous: Does it Really Help the Whistleblower?

The question of anonymous whistleblowing arose in Europe after the implementation of the Sarbanes-Oxley Act (SOX) requirements for US companies. Their EU-based subsidiaries were to enact 'procedures for the receipt, retention, and treatment of complaints received by the issuer regarding accounting, internal accounting controls, or auditing matters and the confidential, anonymous submissions by employees of the issuer of concerns regarding questionable accounting or auditing matters'.[109] Nevertheless, implementing anonymous reporting involves

[106] The issue of anonymous witnesses and victims and the accused's right of defence is debated in the criminal procedural law extensively. The Strasbourg Court has rich case law on it. The Court has considered anonymity as a necessary measure which is usually justified by the need for protection and in order to avoid intimidation. While every citizen has a civic duty to testify, they can do it anonymously if there is an exposure to risks. See S Lonati, 'Anonymous Witness Evidence before the European Court of Human Rights: Is It Still Possible to Speak of 'Fair Trial''? (2018) 8(1) *European Criminal Law Review* 116, 122. From the whistleblower literature perspective, there is no analysis on it. One possible scenario is that while the right to confront accusers is available to criminal proceedings, it may not be obligatory when something is reported (as there is no certainty that a criminal trial will follow).

[107] Public Concern at Work, 'Whistleblowing: A Time for Change – A 5-year Review by Public Concern at Work' (2016) 5, s3-eu-west-1.amazonaws.com/public-concern-at-work/wp-content/uploads/images/2019/12/18171747/PCAW_5yr-review_Time-for-a-Change.pdf accessed 15 May 2025.

[108] The Project on Government Oversight, 'Government Accountability project and public employees for environmental responsibility, the Art of Anonymous Activism: Serving the Public while Surviving Public Service' (2002) 7, www.bmartin.cc/dissent/documents/rr/leaking-POGO.pdf accessed 15 May 2025.

[109] Sarbanes–Oxley Act of 2002 ('Public Company Accounting Reform and Investor Protection Act (in the Senate) and 'Corporate and Auditing Accountability, Responsibility, and Transparency Act') (Pub. L. 107–204, 116 Stat. 745, enacted July 30, 2002) s 301(4). See also I Kampourakis, 'Dialectics of Transparency and Secrecy in the Information Age: The Role of Whistleblowing Legislation in the Regulatory Governance of Markets and in National Security' (Dissertation submitted in partial fulfillment of the Requirements for the Degree of Doctor Iuris to the Department of Law of Freie Universität Berlin 2018) 120.

collecting, processing, and transferring personal data, including that of the accused. It conflicts with data protection, as the accused may not know the allegations or have a chance to defend themselves.[110]

The French Data Protection Authority (CNIL) refused McDonald's and Exide Technologies, both under SOX, permission to set up anonymous whistleblowing hotlines, citing data protection concerns. The Article 29 Working Party on Data Protection, in its opinion 1/2006, addressed the issue of anonymous whistleblowing and data protection.[111] Although anonymous whistleblowing was discouraged, it was recognised as important for protecting whistleblowers. The Article 29 Working Party recommended its use when necessary, ensuring personal data is processed fairly and lawfully.

Anonymity is only marginally regulated by the Directive, which neither prohibits nor promotes anonymous reporting. Member States decide on this principle. The Directive emphasises confidentiality, requiring Member States to protect whistleblower identities unless disclosure is necessary for an investigation, in which case the whistleblower must be informed. Confidentiality is the main element for protecting whistleblowers under the Directive. Reporting channels, internal or external, should be both confidential and secure.[112] Sanctions should be imposed if the confidentiality of the reporting persons is breached. The Directive favours protecting confidentiality, leaving anonymity, which is harder to regulate, mainly under Member States' control. Interestingly, confidentiality and anonymity are distinct principles often discussed in legal literature.

The contours of confidentiality and anonymity should be designed. A key issue for the two principles is the lack of precise definitions. Being anonymous means no one knows your identity, but staying fully anonymous is not possible since at least one person will know who you are. This person is the reporting person who knows they made a report. Experts have stated that 'anonymity is one polar value of a broad dimension of identifiability versus non-identifiability along a continuum from 'fully anonymous to fully identified'.[113] On the other hand, confidentiality occurs when at least one authorised person knows the reporter's identity but has sworn not to disclose it. Nevertheless, since one person knows the identity, any expectation of anonymity is futile. Therefore, anonymity can be ensured if no person can identify the reporting person.

[110] D Lewis, 'Whistleblowing and Data Protection Principles: Is the Road to Reconciliation Really that Rocky?' (2011) 2(1) *European Journal of Law and Technology* 1, 3.

[111] Article 29 Data Protection Working Party, 'Opinion 1/2006 on the application of EU data protection rules to internal whistleblowing schemes in the fields of accounting, internal accounting controls, auditing matters, fight against bribery, banking and financial crime' (2006) ec.europa.eu/justice/article-29/documentation/opinion-recommendation/files/2006/wp117_en.pdf accessed 15 May 2025.

[112] Directive 2019/1937, Recital 3.

[113] GT Marx, 'What's in a Name? Some Reflections on the Sociology of Anonymity' (1999) 15 *The Information Society* 99, 100; CR Scott, 'To Reveal or Not to Reveal—A Theoretical Model of Anonymous Communications' (1998) 8(4) *Common Theory* 381, 387.

Anonymity is a key element of whistleblower protection, according to law scholars.[114] The European Parliament's 2017 Resolution was more positive about anonymity. It stated that

> the option to report anonymously could encourage whistleblowers to share information which they would not share otherwise; stresses, in that regard, that clearly regulated means of reporting anonymously, to the national or European independent body responsible for collecting reports, verifying their credibility, following up on the response given and providing guidance to whistle-blowers, including in the digital environment, should be introduced, setting out exactly the cases in which the means of reporting anonymously apply; stresses that the identity of the whistleblower and any information allowing his or her identification should not be revealed without his or her consent; considers that any breach of anonymity should be subject to sanctions.[115]

The European Commission noted that whistleblowers' protection was inadequate and proposed legislation. Anonymity should have been part of the Directive's protection, as the Commission has already adopted rules requiring anonymous reporting and a whistleblower tool for cartel reports, which allow anonymous reports.

It is unusual that the European Commission did not require anonymous whistleblowing in the Directive despite existing anonymity provisions in EU law. First, EU law mandates anonymous channels for reporting money laundering and financing of terrorist activities.[116] Article 61 of the fourth AML Directive, now replaced by Article 14 of Regulation 2024/1624 and supplemented by Directive 2018/843 (fifth AML Directive), requires Member States to mandate relevant entities to establish internal reporting procedures with a specific, independent, and anonymous channel.[117] In 2017, the European Commission introduced a new tool for reporting cartels and anti-competitive practices.[118] This tool allows anonymous reporting of potential breaches of EU competition law. After Ukraine's invasion, the European Commission introduced a reporting tool for citizens to report EU sanctions violations anonymously.[119] Additionally, the European Commission has added an

[114] Marcum, Young and Kieran (n 12) 1.

[115] European Parliament, Resolution of 24 October 2017 (n 76) para 49.

[116] Directive 2015/849, Art 61(3).

[117] European Parliament and European Council Directive 2015/849/EU of 20 May 2015 on the prevention of the use of the financial system for the purposes of money laundering or terrorist financing, amending Regulation No 648/2012/EU, and repealing Directive 2005/60/EC and Commission Directive 2006/70/EC (Text with EEA relevance) [2015] OJ L141/73. European Parliament and European Council Regulation 2024/1624 of 31 May 2024 on the prevention of the use of the financial system for the purposes of money laundering or terrorist financing [2024] OJ L111. European Parliament and European Council Directive 2018/1673 of 23 October 2018 on combatting money laundering by criminal law [2018] OJ L284/22.

[118] European Commission, Anonymous Whistleblower Tool ec.europa.eu/competition/cartels/whistleblower/index.html accessed 15 May 2025.

[119] European Commission, 'EU sanctions whistleblower tool' finance.ec.europa.eu/eu-and-world/sanctions-restrictive-measures/overview-sanctions-and-related-resources/eu-sanctions-whistleblower-tool_en accessed 15 August 2025.

anonymous tool to report violations of the Digital Services Act.[120] Therefore, the EU law already has provisions and tools which allow anonymous reporting.

Despite anonymous reporting being present in other EU laws, the Directive lacks clarity on this issue. First, the Directive pertains to informant anonymity, distinct from whistleblowers.[121] Informants are individuals who provide information to authorities for a financial reward, with protected anonymity that differs from that of whistleblowers. The Directive distinguishes between them and views anonymity and rewards somewhat negatively. The Directive then leaves it to the Member States to decide on anonymity.[122] Whistleblower reports can be anonymous if authorised by law. The Directive requires protecting whistleblowers who report anonymously but are later identified and face retaliation. It creates confusion by leaving anonymity decisions to Member States while mandating protections for those whose identities are revealed. The Directive overlooks the importance of anonymity and adopts a confusing approach to it.

The issue of data protection and anonymity was raised with the adoption of the Directive, as it happened during the implementation of anonymous reporting schemes under SOX. The recent GDPR regulation agrees with the Article 29 Working Party's view on data processing. It states that 'personal data shall be processed lawfully, fairly and in a transparent manner in relation to the data subject' ('lawfulness, fairness and transparency').[123]

The European Data Protection Supervisor (EDPS) issued guidelines on processing personal data in whistleblowing procedures in 2019.[124] The EDPS stated that 'whistleblowing should not be anonymous'.[125] It added: 'whistleblowers should be invited to identify themselves not only to avoid abuse of the procedure but also to allow their effective protection against retaliation'.[126] The EDPS cannot grasp the realities of whistleblowing. Whistleblowers face many risks, and anonymity is vital for protection. Its goal is to prevent identity reveal and avoid retaliation.[127]

Personal data rules should be respected, but a balanced approach is needed. The recipients of a report must verify the report's authenticity, protect personal data, and act accordingly. A general ban on anonymous whistleblowing, as proposed by

[120] European Commission, 'Digital Services Act whistleblower tool' digital-services-act-whistleblower.integrityline.app/ accessed 15 May 2025.

[121] Directive 2019/1937, Recital 30.

[122] Directive 2019/1937, Art 6(2).

[123] European Parliament and European Council Regulation (EU) 2016/679 of 27 April 2016 on the protection of natural persons with regard to the processing of personal data and on the free movement of such data, and repealing Directive 95/46/EC (General Data Protection Regulation) [2016] OJ L119/1, Art 1(a).

[124] European Data Protection Supervisor, 'Guidelines on Processing Personal Information within a Whistleblowing Procedure' [2019] edps.europa.eu/data-protection/our-work/publications/guidelines/guidelines-processing-personal-information-within_en accessed 15 May 2025.

[125] ibid 6.

[126] ibid.

[127] T Douville, 'Directive (UE) 2019/1937 du 23 octobre 2019 sur la protection des personnes qui signalent des violations du droit de l'Union – aspects relatifs à la protection des données à caractère personnel' (2019) 4 *RAE-LAE* 709, 710.

the EDPS, would harm whistleblowers and the whistleblowing process as a whole. A possible solution is the US approach to anonymous reporting, where the SEC and CFTC have established procedures for whistleblowers to report anonymously.[128] These procedures are simple to implement and effective.[129]

The Directive or Member States can be inspired by the following steps and procedures to allow anonymous whistleblowing.[130] First, the whistleblower who desires to report anonymously should have an attorney. Second, the attorney verifies the whistleblower's identity and examines the allegation to ensure that it is not malicious or being reported for an improper purpose.[131] Third, if the information is correct, the attorney submits the report for the whistleblower and certifies, under oath, its veracity to the extent the attorney can verify it. The whistleblower signs a copy of the report, which stays with the attorney. The attorney then becomes the future contact for anyone involved in the investigation.

In addition, the competent authority handling the report must ensure the whistleblower's anonymity. First, no information relevant to the whistleblower may leave the competent authority. Second, documents that identify whistleblowers can be used either with the whistleblowers' express consent or by redacting the whistleblowers' names wherever they appear. Finally, the whistleblowers' and the attorney's identities should stay protected and known only to the competent authority. These procedures may benefit the EU by enhancing whistleblowers' anonymity while respecting the rights of the accused. Also, the lawyer representing the whistleblower must serve justice and be a key figure in respecting procedures. With EU anonymity following SOX, it may be time to consider effective, simple methods to organise anonymity.

In conclusion, anonymity is a significant component of whistleblower protection. Despite the European Parliament's wish to include anonymous reporting in the Directive,[132] the final text leaves the decision to the Member States, which should decide how to proceed. It is peculiar, though, that the EU has already adopted provisions on anonymous reporting and has even established its own channel for reporting breaches of competition law, cartels, and sanctions.[133] In addition, the Directive removes the good faith requirement for whistleblowers, emphasising that motives are irrelevant if the information is accurate. It shifts

[128] Securities Whistleblower Incentives and Protections, Rule 21F-9, 17 C.F.R. §165.4.

[129] SM Kohn, 'Memorandum – Implementation of the European Union Whistleblower Protection Directive (2019/1937)' (2020) 9–10, g7x5y3i9.rocketcdn.me/wp-content/uploads/2020/08/Kohn-EU-Directive-Implementation-Memo.pdf accessed 15 May 2025.

[130] ibid 10.

[131] ibid. As financial rewards are possible for a successful whistleblower, the US attorneys accept for free to examine the authenticity of the whistleblower's allegations. If the attorney believes that the whistleblower is correct and may have a financial reward, then the attorney takes the case based on a contingency fee basis.

[132] European Parliament, Resolution of 24 October 2017, paras 47 and 49.

[133] European Commission Implementing Directive (EU) 2015/2392 of 17 December 2015 on Regulation (EU) No 596/2014 of the European Parliament and of the Council as regards reporting to competent authorities of actual or potential infringements of that Regulation [2015] OJ L332/126.

focus from the whistleblower's motives to the information. Therefore, promoting anonymous whistleblowing via the Directive is ideal, as it is not an issue knowing the whistleblower if they report original information.

The shift from motives to information reflects a change in our focus. The epicentre of protection should be the whistleblower as a person, not as a means to an end. Anonymity is a crucial component of whistleblower protection, as it mitigates the fear of retaliation. Providing anonymity recognises that the whistleblower is at risk. This danger is softened by anonymity and the assurance that the whistleblower's identity will remain secret. A change of culture is not apparent. Anonymity should be awarded to protect whistleblowers, not because of the risk of revealing their identity. The whistleblower should not be in a position of fear but should be at the centre of the scene. Therefore, we want to allow anonymity to protect the reporting person who is concerned that they may face retaliation if they do not remain anonymous.

J. Financial Rewards or Not for the Whistleblower?

Another protection type is financial rewards for whistleblowers, subject to certain conditions and authorisation under the law. The whistleblower should be incentivised, and this incentive stems from the promise of protection. The financial reward is a controversial form of protection.[134] While providing financial rewards is controversial and delicate, it is by no means new. In ancient Athens (fifth-fourth centuries BC), citizens called 'sycophants' often denounced lawbreakers and were rewarded.[135] In Roman criminal law, '*delatores*' could bring accusations ('*accussator*'), testify ('*testis*'), or provide information ('index'), depending on the case. In this last case, there were provisions about financial rewards.[136]

The common law tradition is by far the most significant in the context of financial rewards, and it served as the basis for the US whistleblower financial rewards system. In the thirteenth and fourteenth centuries, *qui tam writs were* created in the UK. Under the *qui tam*, every subject of the King could bring a lawsuit on behalf of the King and would receive a financial reward from the monetary sanctions subsequently imposed.[137] The *qui tam writs* did not survive due to numerous abuses of the procedure during their creation, and they were subsequently abolished by the UK in 1951. Despite its failure in the UK, *qui tam writs* were better secured under the US system and inspired the first US Act, which provided for financial rewards.

[134] Vaughn (n 15) 125.

[135] F Panagopoulou-Koutnatzi, *The Institution of Whistleblowing: An Ethical-Constitutional Perspective* (Sakkoulas Publications, 2016) 18.

[136] SH Rutlsdge, *Imperial Inquisitions: Prosecutors and Informants from Tiberius to Domitian* (Routledge, 2001) 9.

[137] RJ Beck, 'The False Claims Act and the English Eradication of Qui Tam Legislation' (2000) 78(3) *North Carolina Law Review* 539, 567.

In 1863, the False Claims Act (FCA), also known as Lincoln's Law, was enacted.[138] The FCA was passed during the Civil War to combat fraud by federal contractors in government programmes. An individual could start the *qui tam* action and sue on behalf of the state. If successful, they would receive a significant portion of the recovered amount.[139] Before 1943, there were not many reported civil FCA decisions.[140] Important changes in 1943 reduced effectiveness and limited the use of the FCA.[141] Then, several events involving whistleblowers, such as John Gravitt and Robert Wityczak, led to the 1986 amendments to the FCA. The amendments included reinstatement, double damages, and attorney fees. Whistleblower rewards increased by 15 to 30 per cent, based on the decision and government involvement.

Qui tam procedures have influenced US law, enabling whistleblowers to report and receive rewards. Some of these areas include the public health system, finance, and tax. In finance, the US has implemented whistleblower incentives (bounty programme) under the Dodd-Frank Act of 2010.[142] The programme is effective and has helped detect breaches of financial market laws.[143] The Securities and Exchange Commission (SEC) has received tips from around the world, with the largest number originating from Germany and the UK, among *other countries*.[144]

Under the SEC's rules, the whistleblower can receive a financial reward of 10 to 30 per cent of the sums collected. In calculating the monetary reward, the SEC considers the importance of the information, the degree of assistance provided, the interest in deterring such violations, and other factors.[145] If the information is misleading or fraudulent, the whistleblower is not entitled to a reward. Under Dodd-Frank, the whistleblower cannot file a claim with the government if the SEC does not decide to investigate.[146]

The reference to Dodd-Frank and its bounty programme is not random but relevant to its influence in Europe. The Market Abuse Regulation (MAR) is similar to the Dodd-Frank Act, both enacted after the 2009 financial crisis to show scepticism toward self-regulation (internal whistleblowing). Despite this scepticism, neither act seeks to revert to a 'command and control system', leading to a new

[138] False Claims Act 1863 31 U.S.C. §§ 3729–33.

[139] S Hamer, 'Lincoln's Law: Constitutional and Policy Issues Posed by the Qui Tam Provisions of the False Claims Act' (1997) 6 *Kansas Journal of Law & Public Policy* 89, 90.

[140] For an extensive analysis of the litigation under the FCA, see: JB Helmer, *False Claims Act: Whistleblower Litigation*, 6th edn (Bloomberg, 2013).

[141] Vaughn (n 15) 128.

[142] Dodd-Frank Wall Street Reform and Consumer Protection Act (Pub. L. No. 111-203, § 929-Z, 124 Stat. 1376, 1871, 2010).

[143] Coffee Jr. (n 14) 487. Professor Coffee characterises the programme as 'dramatically successful'.

[144] US Securities and Exchange Commission, 'Annual Report to Congress, Whistleblower Program' (2023) www.sec.gov/files/fy23-annual-report.pdf accessed 15 May 2025.

[145] See s 922 of the Dodd-Frank Act that amended the Securities Exchange Act of 1934 (15 U.S.C. 78a et seq). This provision is found in s 21F (c) of the latter Act.

[146] R Moberly, 'Sarbanes-Oxley's Whistleblower Provisions: Ten Years Later' (2012) 64 *South Carolina Law Review* 1, 47.

approach that combines different methods.[147] The whistleblower's information is the focus of these methods. Dodd-Frank's influence led the EU to include financial rewards in the MAR.

MAR is one of two EU legal instruments providing financial incentives in the financial sector.[148] Precisely, under Article 32(4) MAR, Member States may provide financial rewards to persons who provide information about potential infringements. Nevertheless, MAR provisions on financial incentives are vague and contain general terms.[149] Financial incentives are optional for Member States and at their discretion. Article 32(4) mentions only incentives, without details on their design or employee duties, possibly reflecting Member States' reluctance to adopt them.[150] The MAR provision on financial incentives lacks details on their nature and scope. The economic incentive tied to reporting is problematic. Whistleblowers should report to national authorities. If the information is new, they may get a reward. But if the authority already knows, they will not receive one, risking a lot for little benefit.[151]

In addition, rewards cannot apply when a pre-existing duty to report exists. Under MAR, the whistleblower must report possible breaches. The instauration of a financial incentives regime may create self-regulatory mechanisms which would be problematic for financial institutions. Given the controversial character of financial incentives, no Member State adopted such a regime.[152]

The other legal EU instrument that has provisions on financial rewards is the 'Prospectus Regulation'.[153] Similar to MAR, the provisions on financial rewards in the Prospectus Regulation are general rather than specific. First, Member States are responsible for adopting financial rewards; thus, it is not an obligation but an invitation. Second, there are specific requirements that must be met for an employee to receive a reward. The information must pertain to an actual or potential breach of the Regulation and must be new.

In addition, the information provided by the whistleblower should lead to sanctions or measures for breaching the Prospectus provisions. Furthermore, financial rewards cannot be given if an employee is legally required to report information. MAR and the Prospectus Regulation have similar rules, and, to our knowledge, no Member State offers whistleblower rewards under either of these EU laws.

Member States are not open to financial rewards; rather, they are the opposite. A specific resistance exists, reflected in France and the UK (when part of the

[147] Kampourakis (n 109) 124.

[148] European Commission Implementing Directive (EU) 2015/2392, Art 32(4).

[149] JA Kammerer, 'Market Behaviour' in M Lehmann and C Kumpan (eds), *European Financial Services Law* (Beck – Hart – Nomos, 2019) 867.

[150] Fleischer and Schmolke (n 12) 10.

[151] Kammerer (n 149) 868.

[152] D Kafteranis, 'The Question of One Million Dollars: Financial Rewards or Not for the Whistleblowers' (2021) 36(4) *International Journal of Banking Law and Regulation* 160.

[153] European Parliament and European Council Regulation (EU) 2017/1129 of 14 June 2017 on the prospectus to be published when securities are offered to the public or admitted to trading on a regulated market, and repealing Directive 2003/71/EC [2017] OJ L168/12.

EU). In 2014, the FCA defended its decision not to implement financial rewards, explaining why a bounty scheme would fail.[154] First, enacting financial rewards may undermine internal reporting, as whistleblowers might prefer reporting to authorities for financial incentives rather than internally. Second, adopting financial rewards would be costly and complex for the financial authorities to administer, and the rewards would be limited to only a few successful whistleblowers. For these reasons, the UK, despite its history with *qui tam writs* and the common law tradition, has not yet adopted financial rewards.

France is another interesting example where financial rewards are not adopted, and they may not be adopted soon.[155] The first reason stems from the definition of a whistleblower as found in French Law Sapin II (as reformed by the law transposing the Directive, known as the Waserman Law), which is the 2016 anti-corruption law that introduced horizontal whistleblower protection into the French legal system.[156] Under Sapin II, a whistleblower (*lanceur d'alerte*) should report in a disinterested manner and in good faith (*de manière désintéressée et de bonne foi*). The disinterested manner, as defined in the whistleblower law, excludes the possibility of a financial reward in France. Reporting in anticipation of a monetary reward is not permitted under French law.

In addition, during the legislative procedure for adopting the Law Sapin II, a financial rewards issue arose before the French Constitutional Court (Conseil Constitutionnel). A law provision allowed the Defender of Rights (Défenseur des droits) – an independent administrative authority – to provide financial assistance to whistleblowers. When the French Constitutional Court reviewed this provision, it ruled it unconstitutional; the Court stated that the Defender of Rights cannot provide financial assistance, and that whistleblowers can only request protection of their rights and freedoms.[157]

The examples show that financial rewards are not regarded positively. The Directive did not influence the issue of financial rewards. The European Commission's Impact Assessment concluded that the majority of Member States have not adopted monetary reward systems because they are seen as shifting the purpose of reporting away from the public interest to the personal gain of whistleblowers, thereby making whistleblowing appear like a commercial transaction, which may discredit whistleblowers in general. Member States, though, can apply additional measures to promote whistleblowing beyond the ECtHR/CoE standards, such as offering rewards.

[154] Financial Conduct Authority & Prudential Regulation Authority for the Treasury Committee, 'Note for Financial Incentives for Whistleblowers' (2014) www.fca.org.uk/publication/financial- incentives-for-whistleblowers.pdf accessed 15 May 2025.

[155] V Magnier and Y Paclot, 'Un nouveau champ de protection pour les lanceurs d'alerte' (2019) 4 *RAE-LAE* 699, 701.

[156] Loi n° 2016-1691 du 9 décembre 2016 relative à la transparence, à la lutte contre la corruption et à la modernisation de la vie économique, Art 6 as modified by Loi n° 2022-401 du 21 Mars 2022 – known as Waserman Law.

[157] Conseil Constitutionel, Décision No 2016-741 DC du 8 Décembre 2016 www.conseil-constitutionnel.fr/decision/2016/2016741DC.htm accessed 15 May 2025.

The Directive is silent on financial rewards. Although the European Commission mentioned financial rewards in the Impact Assessment, neither the draft nor the final Directive texts referred to them. It is odd that the EU has used financial rewards in other legislation (MAR and Prospectus Regulation). Still, it did not introduce financial rewards during the negotiations of the Directive. The Directive does not clearly ban or encourage financial rewards. Member States can choose to implement them within their legal systems.

Under the Directive, the lack of a reward system is seen as reinforcing employee loyalty and the existing 'three-tier' model. In principle, a whistle-blower should initially report internally but may also report directly to the competent authorities. They may make a public disclosure only as a last resort. The matter under discussion would be easily resolved if it were regarded as lying within the discretion of the Member States. Yet, it becomes more complex when considering the relevant ECtHR case-law. A reward system might conflict with its case-law, since the ECtHR thinks that whistleblowing 'motivated by a personal grievance or a personal antagonism or the expectation of personal advantage, including pecuniary gain, would not justify an extreme level of protection'.[158]

Within the EU, an additional difficulty is determining which authority is competent to provide these rewards. In academia, the competence of the ECB or ESMA has been justly questioned.[159] As a further argument against them, it has been pointed out that, since Member States would typically have different rewards in place, an employee would seek to report misconduct to the country offering the highest reward. This possibility alone, though, does not suffice to reject the idea of financial rewards for whistleblowers. If multiple countries are involved in a scandal, an employee would likely report to the state offering the best compensation, assuming it is also the most extensive protection. Regardless of whether this notion proves true, such options greatly encourage valuable disclosures. Considering these factors, omitting financial rewards from the Whistleblowing Directive appears reasonable.

The Whistleblowing Directive is unclear regarding financial rewards. Indeed, the proposal for a Directive indicates that financial rewards are problematic in the EU, as reporting shifts from the public interest to personal gain. Therefore, it is unsurprising that the Directive aligns financial rewards with registered informants rather than whistleblowers. For the latter, specific requirements exist about anonymity and financial rewards. The assumption of the Directive's effort to create

[158] *Guja v Moldova* App no 14277/04 (ECtHR, 12 February 2008) para 77. According to the ECtHR, 'it is important to establish that, in making the disclosure, the individual acted in good faith and in the belief that the information was true, that it was in the public interest to disclose it and that no other, more discreet means of remedying the wrongdoing was available to him or her'.

[159] D Kafteranis, 'Rethinking Financial Rewards for Whistle-blowers under the Proposal for a Directive on the Protection of Whistle-blowers Reporting Breaches of EU Law' (2019) 2(1) *Nordic Journal of European Law* 38, 43–44.

two distinguished systems of reporting is not apparent.[160] Member States can adopt financial rewards, but until now no Member State has done so – an interesting fact given that there are EU provisions on financial rewards since the adoption of MAR.

The Directive's insistence on public interest and the demonisation of personal gain conflict with the abolition of individual motives. The Directive does not focus on the whistleblower's personal motives, but rather on the truthfulness of the information reported. Therefore, it would not be a problem if the whistleblower gained financially from their actions. In addition, referring to it as an individual gain creates a negative feeling. Why not say the whistleblower is compensated for financial losses or career damage? The banking and financial sector is challenging and rewarding, where whistleblowers can be stigmatised, blacklisted, and face economic losses. In a 2020 Protect report, 7 out of 10 whistleblowers in the City faced victimisation or dismissal.[161] The financial reward complements their protection and serves as a reward for providing accurate information.

Nevertheless, the lack of regulation on financial rewards in Europe is not surprising, as there is a different aura surrounding whistleblowers across the continent; social and political circumstances in certain Member States have created prejudice against informers of any kind.[162] First, financial profit from whistleblowing is closely tied to snitching,[163] particularly in the context of European legal culture.[164] The whistleblower is considered to have a civic duty to report, acting in the public interest rather than being motivated by the need for financial reward. In addition, EU Member States prioritise maintaining loyalty and trust in employer-employee relationships.[165] The whistleblower should safely report internally rather than to authorities, where a financial reward may be offered. Employers see the reward scheme as damaging to internal reporting systems.

This fear of catastrophe in internal reporting is justified, given the SEC's bounty scheme. When the bounty scheme was enacted, it was unclear if an internally reporting whistleblower who faced retaliation could seek protection under Dodd-Frank. This issue was not resolved until the Supreme Court intervened.[166]

[160] A Lachapelle, 'And thus Tax Whistleblowing was Born! Comment on the Directive on Whistleblowers in Tax Matters' (2020) 588 *Tijdschrift voor Fiscaal Recht* 798, 803.

[161] Protect (n 1).

[162] Andreis (n 37) 587. ('These measures must be balanced with the different socio-cultural context. The different propensity of the EU is determined by a legal tradition in which the reporting person does not necessarily have positive connotations.'); TM Dworkin, 'SOX and Whistleblowing' (2007) 105 *Michigan Law Review* 1757, 1774.

[163] ES Callahan and TM Dworkin, 'Do Good and Get Rich: Financial Incentives for Whistleblowing and the False Claims Act' (1992) 37 *Villanova Law Review* 273.

[164] JF Kerléo, 'Qu'est-ce qu'un lanceur d'alerte?' in M Disant and D Pollet-Panoussis (eds), *Les lanceurs d'alerte. Quelle protection juridique? Quelles limites?* (LGDJ, 2017) 20.

[165] Kafteranis (n 159) 42.

[166] *Berman v Neo@Ogilvy LLC* 801 F.3d 145, 147–148, [2015] (US Court of Appeals, Second Circuit), where the Second Circuit decided that the protections under Dodd-Frank apply to internal complaints by attributing the Chevron deference under which courts should refer to agency interpretations of statutes that mandate agency action unless they are not reasonable. *Asadi v G.E. Energy LLC* 720 F.3d 620, [2013] (US Court of Appeals, Fifth Circuit) [628–29], where it was decided that Dodd-Frank protection applies only to external reporting (to the SEC).

In *Digital Realty Tr., Inc. v Somers*, the Supreme Court agreed that 'an employee who did not report any securities-law violations to the SEC did not qualify as a whistleblower' as was the purpose of the Act.[167]

Dodd-Frank's wording is precise: the whistleblower must report to the SEC to be protected. The Supreme Court emphasised that, since Congress has addressed this issue, Chevron deference cannot be applied to the SEC's interpretation of internal and external reporting. The Supreme Court's ruling has created a challenging time for whistleblowers who report internally rather than to the SEC.[168] Additionally, the SEC reporting requirement challenges internal compliance by incentivising whistleblowers to report externally rather than internally.[169]

Furthermore, another fear of Europeans may be reliance on whistleblowers as private enforcement tools.[170] The whistleblower replaces the public authorities in the pre-investigation process. As Professor Coffee said, 'this is a form of outsourcing, and it was done largely because Congress was very dissatisfied with the SEC's long-running inability to detect Bernie Madoff's Ponzi scheme'.[171] There is a need to recognise the failure of public enforcement and value whistleblowers' role in detecting and reporting wrongdoing in the banking and financial sector.

By offering financial rewards, enforcement agencies outsource their work to private actors.[172] Traditionalists may find this unthinkable, but in the US, the SEC and agencies like the IRS offer financial rewards. Besides the negative considerations of rewards, there are some advantages and positive aspects to consider. First, financial rewards are a form of compensation for whistleblowers who were retaliated against. Financial institutions should compensate for damages caused by wrongdoing, including compensation for whistleblowers.[173] Returning whistleblowers to the ex ante position they would have found themselves in had they not filed a report hardly presents a strong inducement compared to the risk they undertake, namely of committing 'career suicide'.[174] Second, the whistleblower bounty scheme costs taxpayers nothing; the government profits by paying rewards from fines received for reporting.[175] The government benefits from sanctions since

[167] *Digital Realty Tr. Inc. v Somers* No 16-1276, 2018 WL 987345, [2018] (US Supreme Court).

[168] MK Ramirez, 'Whistling Past the Graveyard: Dodd-Frank Whistleblower Programs Dodge Bullets Fighting Financial Crime' (2019) 50 *Loyola University Chicago Law Journal* 617, 636.

[169] S Lombard, 'Regulatory Policies and Practices to Optimize Corporate Whistleblowing: A Comparative Analysis' in S Lombard, V Brand and J Austin (eds), *Corporate Whistleblowing Regulation* (Springer, 2020) 10–11. See also SR Sipe, CT Metrejean and TA Pearson, 'The SEC, The Courts and Whistleblowers: An Examination into The Strength of The Anti-Retaliation Provisions Of The Dodd-Frank Act As Defined By Recent Federal Court Decisions' (2014-15) 19 *Journal of Legal Studies in Business* 8 (concerns have been raised long before the US Supreme Court decision).

[170] Kafteranis (n 34) 50.

[171] Coffee Jr. (n 14) 488.

[172] ibid 486.

[173] Moberly (n 146) 48.

[174] ibid 49.

[175] Coffee Jr. (n 14) 512.

recovered funds aid citizens and society. Without detection, retrieval would not be possible.[176]

The analysis shows scepticism towards financial rewards. The EU may not always welcome US innovations and is influenced by moral and philosophical values that shape its views on financial rewards.[177] The US experience highlights the advantages of whistleblowing, including financial rewards. More specifically, research on the US bounty scheme under the Dodd-Frank Act found that reporting becomes more frequent when rewards are high enough to compensate for the risk of retaliation.[178] A higher notification rate in capital markets increases clearance of relevant crimes, boosting investor confidence and economic growth.[179] A different study shows that reducing public spending is beneficial; relying on whistleblowers is cheaper than assigning such matters to the police.[180]

Most European leaders and citizens feel uncomfortable with the introduction of financial rewards. Misconduct should be reported out of civic duty, not for money. It may be time for Europeans to reconsider their moral stance and consider the benefits to society. As the Directive was transposed, voices emerged calling on Member States to go beyond its requirements and introduce financial rewards. The benefits of offering monetary rewards should be highlighted to promote their use in the EU. Offering rewards would improve whistleblowing and address negative views. Publicising successes and providing rewards will promote a whistleblowing culture in Europe by ensuring laws are effective.

Financial rewards will also benefit European society and the economy. Fraudulently taken amounts of money will return to the EU and national governments, and these amounts of money will be reintroduced into the economy, which will be beneficial to EU citizens. Given the funds fraudulently taken in the US and recovered by the SEC through whistleblowers, a similar situation may occur in Europe, where wrongdoing often goes undetected. Despite the EU's positive image amid corruption and related cases, recent scandals have revealed that corruption is indeed present within the EU, particularly among politicians.

Given the Danske Bank money laundering scandal, the Volkswagen Dieselgate scandal, bribery cases involving Novartis and Siemens, and the Wirecard scandal in Germany, it is reasonable to argue that the EU is not immune to corruption.

[176] ibid. Professor Coffee has also proposed a system where corporations would enter into deferred prosecutions agreements and part of the fine they pay would be put in a whistleblowers' fund to finance future rewards. In addition, he insists that the US should create a common financial reward scheme as now financial rewards are given only by certain federal agencies.

[177] W Mark, 'The EU Campaign for Whistleblower Rewards: A New Idea for Old Europe' (2020) www.whistleblowersblog.org/2020/08/articles/features/the-eu-campaign-for-whistleblower-rewards-a-new-idea-for-old-europe/ accessed 15 May 2025.

[178] B Franke, H Moser and D Simons, 'A Carrot Without a Stick – Whistleblowing Rewards Under the Dodd-Frank Act' (2018) SSRN Working paper, papers.ssrn.com/sol3/papers.cfm?abstract_id=2822313 accessed 15 May 2025.

[179] Securities and Exchange Commission, Securities Whistleblower Incentives and Protections, Federal Register, Vol 76 Nos 113, 34356 and 34362.

[180] Y Givati, 'A Theory of Whistleblower Rewards' (2016) 45 *Journal of Legal Studies* 43.

Additionally, European whistleblowers regularly submit reports to the SEC, as shown in the 2023 SEC report on its whistleblower programme.[181] It would be optimal for the EU to consider the US success with financial rewards and decide on a similar scheme.[182]

The analysis shows that financial rewards for whistleblowers are perceived differently in the US and the EU. While monetary rewards have benefits, they also have drawbacks, making their adoption delicate. In this delicate matter, other factors need to be considered. If whistleblowing is a moral duty, could financial rewards be offered?[183] Whistleblowing is viewed as a control mechanism which ensures corporate checks and balances.[184] It describes a 'moral protest' in which responsible parties are informed of hidden wrongdoing that harms public well-being. Whistleblowing is seen as a rational process with steps to facilitate reporting.

Whistleblowing stems from moral decision-making, showing employees' sensitivity to ethical issues.[185] The whistleblower has ethical concerns about specific behaviours and practices and, by making an ethical decision, decides to report. The ethical decision-making process is positively related to whistleblowing.[186] The whistleblower decides to report out of a moral duty. The moral motives and intentions of whistleblowers often do not align with financial rewards. If the whistleblower reports for ethical reasons, offering a financial reward adds no value. Nevertheless, research from a law-and-economics perspective has shown that monetary incentives have increased whistleblowing in sectors where such rewards are available.

Dyck, Morse and Zingales conducted research on financial incentives as an invitation to whistleblowing.[187] An analysis of several US fraud cases across various sectors, in which whistleblowers reported them, reveals that employees disclosed the fraud in 41 per cent of healthcare industry cases (where *qui tam* suits are available and thus financial rewards). In contrast, employees revealed fraud in 14 per cent of cases in sectors without financial rewards. In addition, they have proved that frivolous suits are not more common in industries where monetary rewards are available.[188] To the contrary, the percentage of frivolous reports in the

[181] SEC, 2023 Annual Report to Congress www.sec.gov/files/fy23-annual-report.pdf accessed 15 May 2025.

[182] J Zuckerman and M Stock, 'Top 6 Reasons Why the SEC Whistleblower Program is Successful' (2020) The National Law Review www.natlawreview.com/article/top-6-reasons-why-sec-whistleblower-program-successful?amp accessed 15 May 2025.

[183] S Valentine and L Godkin, 'Moral Intensity, Ethical Decision Making, and Whistleblowing Intention' (2019) 98 *Journal of Business Research* 277, 277–78.

[184] RK Chiu, 'Ethical Judgment and Whistleblowing Intention: Examining the Moderating Role of Locus of Control' (2003) 43 *Journal of Business Ethics* 65–74.

[185] LL Watts and RM Buckley, 'A Dual-Processing Model of Moral Whistleblowing in Organizations' (2017) 146 *Journal of Business Ethics* 669, 669–70.

[186] Valentine and Godkin (n 183).

[187] Dyck, Morse and Zingales (n 3) 2246.

[188] For a more extensive analysis, see: RM Bowen, AC Call and S Rajgopal, 'Whistle-blowing: Target Firm Characteristics and Economic Consequences' (2010) 85(4) *The Accounting Review* 1239–71.

healthcare industry, where rewards are available, is lower than in other sectors.[189] As a result, from a law-and-economics perspective, offering financial rewards increases the number of whistleblowers who report.

By way of conclusion, the issue of financial rewards is a delicate matter, and legal culture, moral considerations and cross-benefit analysis should well balance any decision on them. The long-standing use of financial rewards in the US should serve as an indicator and inspiration for the EU. A copy-paste solution for financial rewards from the US to the EU should be avoided. If ever enacted in the EU, the discussion should bring together all countries and consider their legal traditions, cultures, and histories. The EU will need to adopt a solution that satisfies all its Member States to some extent, delivers effective results, and avoids replicating the US approach.

K. Transposing the Directive: non-regression clause

The Whistleblowing Directive is a minimum harmonisation measure. Member States should adhere to their minimum standards and may go beyond if they so desire. Under Article 25(2), the Directive urges Member States not to lower their existing protection levels in national law as a result of its implementation. This requirement is known as a 'non-regression' clause. Non-regression clauses are known in the area of EU social law.[190] Most of the EU social legislation contains a non-regression clause.[191] The purpose of the non-regression clauses is to specify that the implementation of the Directive concerned cannot constitute grounds for reducing the level of protection it offers.[192]

Non-regression clauses have been considered binding by the CJEU.[193] However, non-regression clauses differ from 'standstill', which can prevent any unfavourable changes in national legislation covered by a specific Directive. As a result, non-regression clauses do not have a direct effect. They can be overlooked under certain circumstances, allowing changes to national legislation that may undermine the protection offered by the Directive. The CJEU has a rich body of case law on non-regression clauses in EU social legislation, in which it lays down the conditions under which Member States are required to respect them.

[189] Dyck, Morse and Zingales (n 3) 2246.

[190] B Bercusson, *European Labour Law*, 2nd edn (Cambridge University Press, 2009) 51.

[191] Non-regression clauses are an integral part of a number of EU labour law Directives. See: The Part-Time Work Agreement and Directive (Directive 97/81, clause 6(2)), the Directive on Protecting Young People at Work (Directive 94/33, Art 16), the Parental Leave Agreement and Directive (Directive 96/34, clause 4(2)), the Race Directive (2000/43, Art 6(2)), the Framework Equal Treatment Directive (2000/78, Art 8(2)) and others. For more, see also: C Kilpatrick, 'The European Court of Justice and Labour Law in 2009' [2010] *Industrial Law Journal* 287, 292–93.

[192] S Peers, 'Non-regression Clauses: The Fig Leaf Has Fallen' (2010) 39 *Industrial Law Journal* 436.

[193] ibid 438. See also, Opinion of the AG Tizzano, Case 144/04 *Werner Mangold v Rüdiger Helm*, paras 58–59.

In the *Angelidaki* case,[194] which concerned the meaning of the non-regression clause in the fixed agreement, the Court found that reductions in workers' protection under fixed-term contracts are not strictly prohibited. To be banned, the national reduction in protection should first concern the implementation of the Directive in question and second, be related to the general level of security afforded to workers with a fixed-term contract.[195] More specifically, and given the other cases decided by the Court on this matter, the implementation means that the non-regression clauses apply not only when the Directive is first transposed, but also to all other national measures adopted afterwards that aim to ensure its transposition. These later rules may add to or amend national laws transposing the Directive. Then, about the requirement to affect the general level of protection, the Court stated, 'only a reduction on a scale likely to affect overall on national legislation relating to fixed-term employment contracts is liable to be covered by clause 8(3)'.[196]

In the case of the Directive, the situation of the non-regression clause is complicated. First, most Member States lacked whistleblowing laws before the Directive, while some had well-developed ones. For instance, France had whistleblowing laws; now, as it transposed the Directive, it decided to keep some of its previous rules and to go beyond the minimum requirements. In countries without legislation, such as Luxembourg, a new law was enacted to transpose the Directive.

The situation is more delicate regarding sectoral rules on whistleblowing in Member States, partly due to the transposition of other Directives in the banking and financial sectors. If Member States decide to transpose the Directive into a single piece of legislation, the question is whether those sectoral rules are part of that transposition. More specifically, the question is whether those sectoral rules should be modified upon transposition to respect the non-regression clause, or whether the Directive does not bind these rules. Thus, there is no obligation to respect the non-regression clause of the Directive on the protection of whistleblowers. Another interesting question is whether Member States will amend their labour law legislation to comply with the Directive's standards (if their standards are lower than the minimum standards set by the Directive). These interesting questions are not part of this book, but we may soon have case law on them as the Directive is transposed.

[194] Joined Cases C-378-380/07 *Kiriaki Angelidaki and Others v Organismos Nomarchiakis Autodioikisis Rethymnis* (C-378/07), *Charikleia Giannoudi v Dimos Geropotamou* (C-379/07) and *Georgios Karabousanos and Sofoklis Michopoulos v Dimos Geropotamou* (C-380/07) [2009] ECR I-3071.

[195] Kilpatrick (n 191) 293.

[196] Joined Cases (n 194) para 140.

CONCLUDING REMARKS

This book analysed the legal protection of whistleblowers in the EU banking and financial sector. To achieve this goal, we examined the international and US legal frameworks for the protection of whistleblowers, as well as the EU sectoral provisions and the EU Whistleblower Directive. The outcome of this analysis is that, despite significant improvements in the legal protection of whistleblowers in the EU banking and financial sector, the existing level of protection remains insufficient and risks undermining the efficacy of whistleblowing as a reporting tool. Many reasons militate in this direction. First, the protection focuses primarily on protecting the market and, secondarily, on the whistleblower as an individual who deserves dedicated protection. Second, the existing legal framework for protecting whistleblowers at the EU level, encompassing banking and financial sectoral provisions and the Directive, is complex and perplexing.

The present book treats the issue of whistleblowing in the EU banking and financial sector coherently by juxtaposing the sectoral provisions with the Directive. In addition, it presents whistleblowing in the US banking and financial sector, along with the international legal framework for protecting whistleblowers. This comparison aims to inform on the trends in the US that influence the EU approach and the international legal framework that inspires EU and national legislation. The conclusions drawn may inspire significant changes that will enhance the protection of whistleblowers.

Following a brief review of the key advancements made by the recent Directive, we will outline the main arguments demonstrating why the current protective shield falls short of providing a comprehensive and multifaceted legal framework that offers efficient protection.

I. Conclusion: An Important but Challenging Directive

The Directive on protecting whistleblowers advances legal recognition and safeguards for whistleblowers under EU law. It demonstrates that whistleblowers can be protected under EU legislation, paving the way for future progress and transforming the negative perception of whistleblowing into a positive and recognised concept.

After several years of inaction regarding whistleblowing, the EU has finally decided to prioritise it on its agenda. Despite US whistleblowing legislation dating back over two centuries and sporadic scandals that highlighted the existence of whistleblowers, the EU had not taken any comprehensive action beyond sectoral provisions to protect whistleblowers. In recent years, a shift in the EU's approach towards whistleblower protection has been observed, from sectoral measures to a broad legal framework. The European Parliament first called for an EU legal act on whistleblower protection. The European Commission responded to this demand by proposing the Directive. This Directive marks a significant shift, ensuring that whistleblowers receive consistent protection across all areas of EU interest.

The adoption of the Directive is an event worth celebrating; from the limelight to the light, whistleblowers are now part of the EU legal framework. They have a reference point – the Directive – and standard minimum protections are available across all Member States. The Directive establishes common minimum standards accessible to whistleblowers in every Member State. Additionally, potential case law before national courts and the CJEU will evolve legislation and develop a cohesive EU legal framework for whistleblower protection. The Directive marks the start of a legal journey for whistleblowers within the EU.

II. Challenges Ahead

Despite its significance, the Directive presents challenges for the EU banking and financial sector. The choice of the EU to protect the whistleblower, primarily as an enforcement tool and, secondly, as a component of the exercise of their right to the freedom of expression, demonstrates a desire to protect the information leading to the detection of market wrongdoings and, in the second place, the right to free speech. The ultimate purpose of the Directive is to protect the internal market. The whistleblower gains value and protection only if the information they provide is of significant importance. The focus on the market, rather than on the whistleblower, is reflected in the choice of Article 114 TFEU as the primary legal basis and the exclusion of Article 153 TFEU, which concerns the protection of employees' health and safety.[1] Alternatively, the European Commission's promise to review Article 153 TFEU as a possible legal basis for the Directive's review underscores the EU's confusion over which legal basis to choose: protecting the internal market or safeguarding whistleblowers.[2]

Protecting the market is a significant issue, and we cannot deny that whistleblowers should be allies in that. Nevertheless, whistleblowing should also be connected to freedom of expression. The delicate balance of public and private interests reflects the need to protect the market or the right to freedom of expression. The whistleblower stands in the middle, and their protection depends on the interpretation of the rationale behind the whistleblowing legislation. For the

[1] Consolidated version of the Treaty on the functioning of the European Union, OJEU C 326.

[2] Directive, Art 27(3). The Commission has delayed the initial review that should have happened in 2025. For more details: ec.europa.eu/info/law/better-regulation/have-your-say/initiatives/14468-Whistleblower-Protection-Directive-evaluation_en accessed 15 May 2025.

EU, this is to be seen; future CJEU case law will shed light. The European Court of Human Rights (ECtHR) has highlighted the fragility of this balance and the uncertainty surrounding whistleblower protection. In the first instance decision of *Halet v Luxembourg*, the protection of private interests prevailed over free speech and public interest.[3]

Under the Directive, the enforcement perspective of whistleblowers aligns with the 'instrumental' or 'managerial' conception of whistleblowing, in which whistleblowers serve as regulatory intermediaries.[4] Whistleblowing is instrumentalised to serve the needs of authorities by providing them with information about rule breaches. As a regulatory intermediary, the whistleblower provides information either to the authorities or internally to their employer, but there are strict limitations on informing the public.

The EU legislation on the protection of whistleblowers presents challenges that may undermine its aim: protecting whistleblowers. These challenges are grouped in five main groups: (1) sectoral provisions in the EU banking and financial legislation and the co-existence with the Directive, creating a confusing and complex EU legal framework that may discourage, instead of encourage, the whistleblower; (2) the multi-level enforcement in the EU banking and financial sector; (3) the missed opportunity to establish an EU agency on whistleblowing; (4) the missing components of whistleblowers' protection: anonymity and financial rewards; and (5) a possible clash between the Directive and the ECtHR approach.

A. EU Banking and Financial Sector: The (Problematic) Co-Existence of Sectoral Provisions and the Directive

Whistleblowing legislation in the EU primarily resulted from the legal obligations imposed on US companies in Europe under the Sarbanes-Oxley Act (SOX).[5] The need for US companies operating in Europe to comply with SOX rules on whistleblowing shaped the path towards EU whistleblowing legislation. Next to SOX, the Dodd-Frank Act has also influenced EU legislation on whistleblowing, notably the Market Abuse Regulation (MAR), which is inspired by its provisions.[6]

The sectoral provisions were adopted before the Directive, stemming from the financial crises and the partial unification of the EU's banking and financial system. Sectoral provisions on whistleblowing exist in the SSM Regulation and

[3] *Halet v Luxembourg* App no 21884/18 (ECtHR, 11 May 2021).

[4] I Kampourakis, 'Whistleblowers as Regulatory Intermediaries: Instrumental and Reflexive Considerations in Decentralizing Regulation' [2020] *Regulation & Governance* 1.

[5] 18 U.S.C. § 1514A. See also Conseil d'État, *Le droit d'alerte: signaler, traiter, protéger* (2016) 23.

[6] Dodd-Frank Wall Street Reform and Consumer Protection Act, Pub. L. No. 111-203, 124 Stat. 1376 (2010) (codified as amended in scattered sections of 5, 7, 12, 15, 26, 28, 31, 42 U.S.C. (2012)). See European Parliament and European Council Regulation (EU) 596/2014 of 16 April 2014 on market abuse (market abuse regulation) and repealing Directive 2003/6/EC and Commission Directives 2003/124/EC, 2003/125/EC and 2004/72/EC [2014] OJ L173/1.

Framework Regulation, in the UCITS Directive, in Directive 2014/65 on statutory audits of annual accounts and consolidated accounts, in the MiFID II Directive, in the CSDR Regulation, in the RPIIPs Regulation, in the SFTR Regulation, in the IDD Directive, in the IOPR Directive, in the Prospectus Regulation and in the AML legislation, inter alia.

The EU banking and financial sector includes several sector-specific provisions on whistleblower protection that were already adopted before the Directive. When combined with the Directive's provisions, these provisions create a complex and confusing EU legal framework that is more likely to discourage than encourage whistleblowers.[7] The complexity stems from the fact that sectoral provisions have different reporting requirements than the Directive, and the protection they offer is often uncertain.

Given the complex aspects of sectoral whistleblowing provisions in the EU banking and financial area, one would have expected the advent of the Directive to provide a solution. The ECB's whistleblowing provisions can provide a good example of this antithesis. For instance, the Directive does not examine the whistleblower's good faith, whereas the ECB highlights this element in its legal framework and in the online information it provides. The ECB also goes further, stating that if a report is not made in good faith, it may lead to criminal proceedings in the relevant Member State.

To the contrary, the Directive does not clarify matters but complicates the situation.[8] According to Article 3(1) of the Directive, these sectoral provisions take precedence over the Directive and should be treated as *lex specialis*. In contrast, the Directive is a horizontal general legal framework. In practice, employees in the banking and financial sector should first seek protection under the sectoral provisions. Only if this is not possible should they seek protection under the Directive's provisions. This situation adds a layer of confusion and complexity for the whistleblower. The EU should reconsider this coexistence and render the sectoral provisions void, thereby promoting a single legal instrument for the protection of whistleblowers: the Directive.

Another complexity about sectoral provisions and the Directive is the distinction between a duty to report and a right to blow the whistle. The EU legislation fails to discern whether whistleblowing is a right or a duty. The EU Directive regards whistleblowing as a right, allowing individuals to blow the whistle or not without facing consequences for non-compliance. On the other hand, some sectoral EU

[7] E Feldman, 'Whistleblower Protection' (2011) 25 *Annual Review of Irish Law* 5, where she criticised that the whistleblowing provisions of the 2011 Criminal Justice Act (Ireland) were not clear and precise. As a result, it would be difficult for whistleblowers, without a legal background, to understand the meaning and purpose of these provisions. In a similar way, an employee without a legal background will not be able to discern between Union and national laws. Feldman highlighted in several discussions I had with her that the coexistence of sectoral provisions with the horizontal legislation on the protection of whistleblowers is confusing rather than enlightening for whistleblowers.

[8] D Kafteranis, 'Sectoral Provisions and the Directive on the Protection of Whistle-blowers: No to a Complex Relationship' (Oxford Business Law Blog, 4 June 2020) www.law.ox.ac.uk/business-law-blog/blog/2020/06/sectoral-provisions-and-directive-protection-whistle-blowers-no accessed 15 May 2025.

provisions on whistleblowing in the banking and financial sector appear to view whistleblowing as a duty, obliging individuals to report specific types of wrongdoing without choice.

If the whistleblower does not report under these provisions, they may face civil or criminal sanctions for failure to report. These specific whistleblowing provisions are annexed to the Directive and constitute *lex specialis*, having priority over the Directive's provisions. This confusing relationship between duty and right, as well as between the Directive and the sectoral provisions, cannot possibly encourage whistleblowing but seems to render it more burdensome. A clear distinction should be made between the right to blow the whistle and the duty to report. A clear distinction would prevent whistleblowers from being mistakenly drawn into legal battles when they fail to report, believing it is a whistleblowing matter rather than a legal duty.

B. Multi-Level Enforcement and Whistleblowers' Survival

The whistleblower serves as a private enforcement tool, supplementing public authorities and providing them with the information needed to detect and investigate white-collar crimes and address enforcement failures. The failure of public enforcement is evident, as it lacks the capacity, resources, and means to detect wrongdoing. The European Commission confirms the enforcement character of whistleblowing, but a segment of legal academia and traditionalists strongly rejects this idea.[9]

The whistleblower, as a private enforcement tool, is contrary to the concept of public enforcement. Traditionally, enforcement of rules has been the responsibility of public authorities, rather than employees. Proponents of public enforcement are hesitant to accept its failure, as demonstrated by scandals revealed by whistleblowers. Being reluctant to report, they cannot welcome the concept of private enforcement in which public authorities outsource enforcement to whistleblowers. The whistleblower has a twofold purpose: to protect the market, but they also need to be protected in a meaningful way.

Following the 2009 financial crisis, the European banking union has harmonised, to a certain extent, banking supervision and the ECB's enforcement powers at the national and EU levels. On the other hand, the financial markets have not been harmonised to the same degree as the EU banking sector, and ESMA does not possess the same powers as the ECB but has a somewhat limited role. Banking and financial supervision is already a complex task at the national level, so the EU's interference somewhat complicates rather than simplifies matters. This

[9] European Commission Staff Working Document, Impact Assessment accompanying the document of the proposal for a Directive of the European Parliament and of the Council on the protection of persons reporting on breaches of Union law [2018] COM(2018) 218 final, 3. See also J Coffee Jr., *Corporate Crime and Punishment* (Berrett-Koehler, 2020) 487.

complex system of banking and financial supervision does not leave whistleblowing untouched.

The creation of the whistleblower as an enforcement tool for EU rules and the regulatory character of the whistleblower as an intermediary are constrained by the multi-level enforcement and governance of the EU banking and financial sector. The whistleblower must report, but the process becomes an adventure in which a skilled puzzle-solver may have a chance to reach the right channel for reporting and be protected. The extent of the ECB's powers in the banking sector is unclear to the whistleblower. While the ECB can accept reports, there are doubts about how the ECB can handle the case and what protection should be offered to the reporting person. The ESMA faces a similar situation, where the treatment of the report and the protection of the whistleblower are even less comprehensible, given the ESMA's limited power in the financial sector.

C. Structural Changes in the Procedure: The Need for an EU Office on the Protection of Whistleblowers

The creation of Whistleblower Offices at both the national and EU levels is a solution that facilitates reporting and protects whistleblowers. The matter was discussed during negotiations on the Directive by the European Parliament and its Committees, but it fell into obscurity after the Directive was adopted.[10] These Offices are needed to coordinate whistleblowing at the national and EU levels, offering advice and guidance to whistleblowers and fostering cooperation between Member States and European Institutions when the report affects two or more Member States. Apart from advice and guidance, these Offices may be required to investigate the reports submitted. If they investigate reports, the Offices may be able to self-fund their activities through the monetary sanctions imposed.

Indeed, the creation of a new European body is not always the best option, given the plethora of new EU institutions created over the last few years and the principle of the attribution of competences. A new EU body will create confusion regarding competencies and jurisdiction, as existing EU bodies have powers over whistleblowers. Nevertheless, the creation of an EU Whistleblowing Office will alleviate the burden of whistleblowing. Legislation regarding whistleblowing is quite technical, and even lawyers may not fully understand the procedure. Considering that whistleblowers are not always lawyers or employees specialised

[10] European Parliament Resolution of 24 October 2017 on legitimate measures to protect whistle-blowers acting in the public interest when disclosing the confidential information of companies and public bodies (2016/2224(INI)) www.europarl.europa.eu/sides/getDoc.do?type=TA&language=EN&reference=P8-TA-2017-0402 accessed 15 May 2025, para 55. See also Opinion of the Committee on the Environment, Public Health and Food Safety for the Committee on Legal Affairs on the Proposal for a Directive of the European Parliament and of the Council on the protection of persons reporting on breaches of Union law, September 2018, p 3.

in these fields, the majority will feel lost when blowing the whistle. This uncertainty and insecurity justify the creation of an EU Whistleblowing Office.

The Offices at the national level should be Independent Administrative Authorities with special status if investigations are permitted under their powers. The Offices should ensure that whistleblowers are advised correctly on how, where, and what to report. They can coordinate actions taken in response to reports and also investigate them. The Offices are beneficial timewise as well. From a report to an investigation, valuable time is lost, which in the banking and financial sector can be disastrous. Rapid steps are needed to receive, check, and follow up on a report to tackle wrongdoing. If these Offices are not adequately established, whistleblowers may be confused about where to report, reminding us of the Kafkaesque nightmares of maladministration. The creation of offices in certain Member States, such as France and Luxembourg, demonstrates their usefulness. In contrast, other offices, such as in Slovakia, have faced political issues due to the sensitivity of whistleblowing concerning political corruption.

At the EU level, another solution may be to attribute the responsibilities of creating and coordinating the EU Whistleblowers Office to the European Ombudsman. In the 2017 Resolution, the European Parliament had proposed that the European Ombudsman take responsibility for establishing the Office.[11] The choice of the European Ombudsman as the responsible institution to develop the Whistleblowers Office is not arbitrary. The Ombudsman has a positive impact on society, enhancing people's trust in institutions and governments.[12] At the European level, attributing responsibility for creating an EU Whistleblower Office to the European Ombudsman would have a positive connotation for the public and whistleblowing.

D. Future Solutions: Anonymity and Financial Rewards

The failure to protect the whistleblower in a meaningful way is reflected in the absence of anonymity and financial rewards as components of whistleblowers' protection under the Directive. This statement does not cancel the other layers of protection offered under the Directive. Still, it aims to emphasise the importance of anonymity and financial rewards in providing more effective protection for whistleblowers. The whistleblower wants to stay anonymous in several instances to protect their identity and avoid negative consequences for their personal and professional life. In addition, financial rewards are essential to incentivise whistleblowers and compensate them for the information they provide.

[11] European Parliament, Resolution of 24 October 2017 on legitimate measures to protect whistle-blowers acting in the public interest when disclosing the confidential information of companies and public bodies [2016] (2016/2224(INI)) para 55.

[12] N Creutzfeldt, 'Trusting the Middle-Man: Impact and Legitimacy of Ombudsmen in Europe' (Project report – University of Westminster, 2016) www.law.ox.ac.uk/sites/files/oxlaw/ombuds_project_report_nc_2.pdf accessed 15 May 2025.

The US system of anonymity and financial rewards can be a source of inspiration for the EU. In the US, whistleblowers can remain anonymous, but a lawyer will be responsible for verifying their identity and representing them before the authorities. Financial rewards are given only if the information provided leads to a serious investigation and the discovery of serious wrongdoing. The US mechanisms have been in place for a long time, seem adequate, and sufficiently protect successful whistleblowers.

In the EU, anonymity and financial rewards are viewed with suspicion, possibly because of their extensive use under US law. If anonymity is a concern, the word can be replaced with the phrase 'protection of the identity of the whistleblower'. If financial rewards create negative feelings, the phrase can be replaced by monetary compensation or aid. There is an emerging need for the EU to consider these two components of whistleblower protection, as they present significant advantages.

E. A Possible Clash between the Directive and the ECtHR Approach

The adoption of the EU Directive may change the Strasbourg Court's approach or create two distinct European systems of whistleblower protection, as the *Halet v Luxembourg* saga indicates.[13] The EU Directive drew inspiration from the CoE texts and the case law of the Strasbourg Court.[14] The Parliamentary Assembly of the CoE welcomed the EU Directive in its Resolution 2300 (2019).[15] The Resolution invited CoE Member States to transpose the Directive into their national legal systems and, if necessary, go beyond its requirements by, for instance, creating independent authorities responsible for protecting whistleblowers.[16] In a careful analysis of the Strasbourg criteria alongside the provisions of the EU Directive, several clashes emerge that may become problematic in the near future.

First, the ECtHR, in its case law, focuses on the whistleblower's good faith. Recent cases show a move away from the good-faith requirement toward a reasonable-belief test.[17] It should be noted, though, that the Court proceeds to a case-by-case analysis, and, consequently, the requirement of good faith may become more focused on personal motives rather than the facts. Despite a slight

[13] D Kafteranis and R Brockhaus, 'Time to Reconsider Strasbourg's Whistleblower Case Law' (2020) European Law Blog, available at: europeanlawblog.eu/2020/09/21/time-to-reconsider-strasbourgs-whistleblower-case-law/ accessed 15 May 2025.

D Kafteranis and S Andreadakis, 'A New Perspective on the Protection of Whistleblowers Under ECHR: Halet v Luxembourg' (2023) 68(1) *Studies in Logic, Grammar and Rhetoric* 611.

[14] European Commission, Impact Assessment (n 9) 47.

[15] Council of Europe Parliamentary Assembly, 'Resolution 2300 (2019), Improving the Protection of Whistle-blowers all over Europe', (adopted by the Parliamentary Assembly at the 30th sitting on 1 October 2019).

[16] ibid.

[17] *Soares v Portugal* App no 79972/12 (ECtHR, 21 June 2016) para 46.

shift in the Court's case law, it has not altered its stance – for instance, by stating that the whistleblower's good faith should no longer be a requirement.

This is a controversial point in the Directive: the whistleblower should have only reasonable grounds to report, and no good faith is required.[18] Under the Directive, the personal motives are not checked. Another clash that may arise between the Strasbourg case law and the EU Directive concerns the authenticity of the information provided. The Strasbourg Court is clear in its case law that whistleblowers should provide authentic information and verify the veracity of their reports. On the contrary, the Directive allows the whistleblower to report even when they have reasonable suspicions of possible wrongdoing. On this point, it is clear that there are two different approaches, with the Strasbourg Court appearing to adopt a more restrictive approach than the Directive. The application of the Directive will provide more information on what constitutes reasonable suspicions and how national jurisdictions and the CJEU will assess them.

A second clashing point between the two approaches to the protection of whistleblowers is the proportionality check between the damage caused to the employer and the public interest in the information, as applied by the ECtHR. This proportionality check represents one of the six established criteria of the Strasbourg Court.[19] Under the Directive, this is not required. There is no proportionality check regarding the damage the employer suffered from the disclosure. A final point at which a clash is observed is the necessity of public interest, specifically whether the disclosed information serves it.[20] The Strasbourg Court places great emphasis on the public interest and on measures to determine the extent to which the public should be informed about reported matters. Under the Directive, the public interest is not required. The only exception is in cases of public disclosures, where the whistleblower must demonstrate a public interest.[21] Internal reporting, or reporting to the authorities, under the Directive, does not involve any check of public interest.

In the first decision in *Halet v Luxembourg*, the different approach between the ECtHR and the Directive became apparent. Although the Strasbourg Court referred to the newly adopted Directive in its presentation of the legal framework,[22] it did not consider it in its final assessment. This point was highlighted by the two dissenting judges of the decision.[23] Mr Halet was found guilty, as the Court found that it caused greater harm to his employer, PwC, than the public's interest in knowing the information. The Court said that the information Mr Halet presented was neither new, unknown, nor vital.[24] Thus, in the delicate balance of private and public interests, the Strasbourg Court decided in favour of the employer.

[18] European Parliament and European Council Directive 2019/1937/EU of 23 October 2019 on the protection of persons who report breaches of Union law [2019] OJ L305/17, Art 6(1)(a).
[19] *Guja v Moldova* App no 14277/04 (ECtHR, 12 February 2008) para 90.
[20] ibid para 80.
[21] Directive 2019/1937, Art 15(1)(b)(i).
[22] *Halet v Luxembourg*, paras 50–51.
[23] ibid p 32.
[24] ibid paras 104–106.

Under the Directive, as mentioned above, there is a balance between private and public interests. The Directive protects the whistleblower as long as the conditions for their protection are met under the Directive, and there is no requirement that the information reported be new, unknown, or vital. Under the Directive, the whistleblower must have reasonable grounds or even suspicion that wrongdoing is occurring.

When Mr Halet referred his case to the Strasbourg Court, the Directive was under negotiation. For Mr Halet, it would have been better to refer his case to the CJEU, but this was, of course, impossible at the time of his referral. If we speculate, the CJEU's decision would probably have been different, or at least, the CJEU would not have examined the criteria controlled by the Strasbourg Court. The first decision in *Halet v Luxembourg* gives a taste of the contradictions we may have shortly between the two European courts and the protection they offer to whistleblowers.

The possibility of two different approaches from the ECtHR and the EU to the requirements for protecting whistleblowers may create confusion and legal uncertainty for whistleblowers. One suggestion would be for the Strasbourg Court to reconsider its case law and align it with the wording of the Directive to ensure a uniform level of protection across the EU. The EU and the ECtHR shall maintain a respectful relationship, marked by harmony and co-operation. This relationship is informal. It is based on the presumption of equivalent protection as expressed in the *Bosporus* case.[25] In light of this mutual respect, the Strasbourg Court may reconsider its case law and adopt the level of protection as introduced by the Directive. A well-balanced approach might be a viable solution for whistleblowers.

A certain level of coordination between the two supranational European orders might intervene at the moment of the national implementation of the Directive. The duty for Member States to respect ECtHR's case law, as well as when transposing the Directive, might lead to an inevitable increase in guarantees. First and foremost, the Member States should take this occasion to broaden the material scope to encompass every breach of law. An EU national who blows the whistle but is not protected under the Directive may argue before national or EU courts that they should be protected under Article 53 CFR, and under Article 10 ECHR and that they should enjoy protection as a whistleblower under Article 11 CFR.[26] Both Article 53 ECHR and Article 53 CFR can be characterised as 'reflecting normative levers' that enhance the protection of freedom of expression in the CoE and the EU to a higher level.

[25] *Bosphorus hava yollari turizm ve ticaret anonim şirketi v Ireland* App no 45036/98 (ECtHR, 30 June 2005).

[26] Charter of Fundamental Rights of the European Union [2012] OJ C326/391, Arts 11 and 53.

BIBLIOGRAPHY

Council of Europe Official Documents and Publications

Council of Europe Civil Law Convention on Corruption, ETS No 174, 1 November 2003

Council of Europe Criminal Law Convention on Corruption, Eur. T.S. No. 173, 27 January 1999

Council of Europe Committee of Ministers, 'Reply to Recommendation 2162 (2019) on Improving the Protection of Whistle-blowers all over Europe' (Adopted by the Committee of Ministers on 29 April 2020 at the 1374th meeting of the Ministers' Deputies)

Council of Europe, Committee on Legal Affairs and Human Rights, 'The Protection of Whistle-blowers', Doc. 12006, Pieter Omtzigt, 14 September 2009

Council of Europe, Committee on Legal Affairs and Human Rights, 'Report on Improving the Protection of Whistle-blowers all over Europe', Doc. 14958, Sylvain Waserman, 30 August 2019

Council of Europe, Congress of Local and Regional Authorities, 'Report CG36(2019)14final on the Protection of Whistle-blower – Challenges and Opportunities for Local and Regional Government', 3 April 2019

Convention for the Protection of Human Rights and Fundamental Freedoms (European Convention on Human Rights, as amended) (ECHR) year

Council of Europe, European Committee on Legal Co-operation, 'Protecting Whistleblowers' (2020) www.coe.int/en/web/cdcj/activities/protecting-whistleblowers accessed 15 May 2025

Council of Europe Parliamentary Assembly, Recommendation 1916 (2010), 'Protection of Whistle-blowers', (adopted by the Parliamentary Assembly at the 17th sitting on 29 April 2010)

Council of Europe Parliamentary Assembly, 'Resolution 1729 (2010), Protection of Whistle-blower's (adopted by the Parliamentary Assembly at the 17th sitting on 29 April 2010)

Stephenson Paul and Levi Michael, 'The Protection of Whistle-blowers A Study on the Feasibility of a Legal Instrument on the Protection of Employees who Make Disclosures in the Public Interest, Council of Europe, CDCJ(2012)9FIN.

Council of Europe, 'Protection of Whistleblowers: A Brief Guide for Implementing a National Framework' (2016) rm.coe.int/16806fffbc accessed 15 May 2021

Council of Europe Committee of Ministers, 'Recommendation CM/Rec(2014)7, Protection of Whistle-blowers' (adopted by the Committee of Ministers at the 1198th meeting on 30 April 2014)

Council of Europe Parliamentary Assembly, 'Recommendation 2073 (2015), Improving the Protection of Whistle-blowers' (adopted by the Parliamentary Assembly at the 21st sitting on 23 June 2015)

Council of Europe Parliamentary Assembly, 'Recommendation 2162 (2019), Improving the Protection of Whistle-blowers all over Europe' (adopted by the Parliamentary Assembly at the 30th sitting on 1 October 2019)

Council of Europe Parliamentary Assembly, Resolution 2060 (2015), 'Improving the Protection of Whistle-blowers' (adopted by the Parliamentary Assembly at the 21st sitting on 23 June 2015)

Council of Europe Parliamentary Assembly, 'Resolution 2300 (2019), Improving the Protection of Whistle-blowers all over Europe', (adopted by the Parliamentary Assembly at the 30th sitting on 1 October 2019)

EU Official Publications

Decision (EU) 2016/456 of the European Central Bank of 4 March 2016 concerning the terms and conditions for European Anti-Fraud Office investigations of the ECB, in relation to the prevention of fraud, corruption and any other illegal activities affecting the financial interests of the Union (ECB/2016/3) [2016] OJ L79/34
Decision of the European Central Bank of 20 October 2020 amending the European Central Bank Staff Rules as regards the introduction of a whistleblowing tool and enhancements to the whistle-blower protection (ECB/2020/NP37)
European Commission Notice on Immunity from fines and reduction of fines in the cartel cases (2006/C 298/11)
European Commission, Public consultation on whistleblower protection, DG Justice and Consumers [2017] ec.europa.eu/newsroom/just/item-detail.cfm?item_id=54254 accessed 15 May 2025
European Commission's analysis of the Member States' legislative framework, Annex 6 ec.europa.eu/info/sites/info/files/1-11_annexes.pdf accessed 15 May 2021
European Commission Proposal for a Regulation on insider dealing manipulation (market abuse) [2011] COM(2011) 651 final eur-lex.europa.eu/legal-content/EN/TXT/?uri=celex%3A52011PC0651 accessed 15 May 2025
European Council, Opinion of the legal service on the legal basis for the proposal for a directive on the protection of persons reporting on breaches of Union law [2018] JUR_14620/18
European Council, Proposal for a Directive on the protection of persons reporting breaches of Union law: progress report [2019] eur-lex.europa.eu/legal-content/EN/TXT/?uri=COM%3A2018%3A0218%3AFIN accessed 15 May 2025
European Council, Proposal for a Regulation on insider dealing and market manipulation (market abuse) – Presidency compromise [2012] 10198/12 db.eurocrim.org/db/en/doc/1744.pdf accessed 15 May 2025
European Banking Authority, Mandate of the Standing Committee on anti-money laundering and countering terrorist financing (AMLSC) [2020] EBA/DC/2020/309 www.eba.europa.eu/sites/default/documents/files/document_library/About%20Us/Legal%20Framework/Updated%20Files%2026022019/854476/2020%2001%2022%20BoS%20ESAs%20Review%20-%20AMLSC%20mandate.pdf accessed 15 May 2025
European Central Bank, Administrative Circular 1/2006 on internal administrative inquiries [2006]
European Central Bank. Guide to Banking Supervision [2014] www.bankingsupervision.europa.eu/ecb/pub/pdf/ssmguidebankingsupervision201411.en.pdf accessed 15 May 2025
European Central Bank, Information on the use of the breach reporting mechanism (BRM), www.bankingsupervision.europa.eu/banking/breach/form/shared/pdf/BRM_important_legal_information.pdf accessed 15 May 2021
European Central Bank, Letter from Danièle Nouy to Mr Sven Giegold regarding whistle-blower protection at the ECB (2017) www.bankingsupervision.europa.eu/ecb/pub/pdf/ssm.meplet-ter170630.en.pdf?f508ce662d57696b218f9f355ea2e5aa accessed 15 May 2025
European Central Bank, 'ECB Annual Report on supervisory activities 2024' (2024) www.banking-supervision.europa.eu/press/other-publications/annual-report/html/ssm.ar2024~700cba1314.en.html accessed 15 May 2025
European Court of Auditors, Opinion no 4/2018 of 9 November 2018 concerning the Proposal for a Directive of the European Parliament and of the Council on the protection of persons reporting on breaches of Union law [2018]
European Data Protection Supervisor, Guidelines on processing personal information within a whistleblowing procedure [2019]
European and Social Committee, Opinion on the proposal for a Directive on the protection of persons reporting breaches of Union law [2018] SOC/593
European Commission, Anonymous Whistleblower Tool ec.europa.eu/competition/cartels/whistle-blower/index.html accessed 15 May 2021

European Commission Staff Working Document, Impact Assessment accompanying the document of the proposal for a Directive of the European Parliament and of the Council on the protection of persons reporting on breaches of Union law [2018] COM(2018) 218 final

European Commission Communication COM(2018) 214 on strengthening whistleblower protection at EU level [2018]

European Commission Proposal for a Directive of the European Parliament and of the Council on the protections of persons reporting on breaches of Union law: 2018/0106 (COD) [2018]

European Commission, Reinforcing sanctioning regimes in the financial services sector [2010] SEC(2010) 1946 final

European Parliament Committee on Constitutional Affairs, Opinion on legitimate measures to protect whistle-blowers acting in the public interest when disclosing the confidential information of companies and public bodies [2017]

European Securities and Markets Authority Final Report – guidelines on certain aspects of the MiFID compliance function requirements [2012]

European Ombudsman Decision closing her own-initiative inquiry OI/1/2014/PMC concerning whistleblowing [2015]

European Parliament Directorate General for Internal Policies, Policy Department for Budgetary Affairs, In-analysis for the CONT Committee on the Future Cooperation between OLAF and the European Public Prosecutor's Office [2017] PE 603.789

ESMA www.esma.europa.eu/whistleblowers-corner accessed 15 May 2025

European Parliament Committee on Constitutional Affairs, Opinion for the Committee on Legal Affairs on the proposal for a Directive on the protection of persons reporting on breaches of Union law [2018] C8-0159/2018

European Parliament Committee on Economic and Monetary Affairs, Opinion for the Committee on Legal Affairs on the Proposal for a Directive on the protection of persons reporting on breaches of Union law [2018] C8-0159/2018

European Economic and Social Committee, Opinion on the Communication from the Commission to the European Parliament, the Council and the European Economic and Social Committee Strengthening whistleblower protection at EU level (COM (2018) 214 final) and on the Proposal for a Directive on the protection of persons reporting breaches of Union law [2019] (COM (2018) 218 final) C 62/155

European Parliament Committee on the Environment, Public Health and Food Safety for the Committee on Legal Affairs, Opinion on the Proposal for a Directive on the protection of persons reporting on breaches of Union law [2018] C8-0159/2018

European Parliament Committee on Legal Affairs, Opinion on the legal basis for the proposal for a directive on the protection of persons reporting on breaches of Union law [2018] JURI_AL(2018)629554

European Parliament Committee on Legal Affairs, Opinion on the legal basis for the proposal for a directive on the protection of persons reporting on breaches of Union law [2019] JURI_AL(2019)637335

European Parliament, Explanatory Statement on the Draft European Parliament Legislative Resolution on the proposal for a directive on the protection of persons reporting on breaches of Union law [2018] C8-0159/2018

European Parliament Committee on Legal Affairs, Report on the proposal for a Directive on the protection of persons reporting on breaches of Union law [2018] A8-0398/2018

European Parliament, Resolution of 15 December 2011 on the mid-term review of the European strategy 2007-2012 on health and safety at work [2011] P7_TA(2011)0589

European Parliament, Resolution of 23 October 2013 on organised crime, corruption, and money laundering [2013] P7_TA(2013)0444

European Parliament, Resolution of 25 November 2015 on tax rulings and other measures similar in nature or effect [2015] P8_TA(2015)0408

European Parliament, Resolution of 16 December 2015 on bringing transparency, coordination and convergence to corporate tax policies in the Union [2015] P8_TA(2015)0457

European Parliament, Resolution of 6 July 2016 on tax rulings and other measures similar in nature of effect [2016] P8_TA(2016)0310
European Parliament, Resolution of 24 October 2017 on legitimate measures to protect whistle-blowers acting in the public interest when disclosing the confidential information of companies and public bodies [2016] (2016/2224(INI))
European Parliament, Rules of Procedure [2017]
European Securities and Markets Authority, Final Report ESMA's technical advice on possible delegated acts concerning the Market Abuse Regulation [2015] ESMA/2015/224
Explanatory Memorandum of the Proposal for a Regulation on Market Abuse
European Central Bank, Important legal information before using the whistleblowing platform [2021] www.bankingsupervision.europa.eu/banking/breach/form/html/BRM_important_legal_information.en.html accessed 15 May 2025
European Commission, Occupational pension funds – rules governing the activities and supervision of institutions for occupational retirement provision ec.europa.eu/info/business-economy-euro/banking-and-finance/insurance-and-pensions/occupational-pension-funds_en#documents accessed 15 May 2025
European Commission Proposal for a Directive on insurance mediation (recast) [2012] COM(2012) 360 final
European Commission, Anti-money laundering and counter terrorist financing ec.europa.eu/info/policies/justice-and-fundamental-rights/criminal-justice/anti-money-laundering-and-counter-terrorist-financing_en accessed 15 May 2025
European Commission Communication, EU law: Better results though better application [2017] OJ C18/10

French Official Publications

Conseil d'État, *Le droit d'alerte: signaler, traiter, protéger* (2016)
Conseil d'État, rapport public, *L'intérêt général*, ED n° 50 (1999)
CNIL, Déliberation relative à une demande d'autorisation de MacDonald's France pour la mise en œuvre d'un dispositif d'intégrité professionnelle, n° 2005-110 (2005)
François Pillet, Rapport rélatif à la transparence, à la lutte contre la corruption et à la modernisation de la vie économique pour le Sénat, 22 Juin 2016, N° 712
Sénat, Rapport fait sur la proposition de directive sur la protection des personnes dénoncent les infractions au droit de l'Union N° 638 (2018)

Luxembourg Official Publications

Chambre des Salariés, 'Protection des lanceurs d'alerte' (2018) www.csl.lu/bibliotheque/publications/268723fee5.pdf accessed 15 May 2025
CCSF, www.cssf.lu/fileadmin/files/Lois_reglements/Circulaires/Hors_blanchiment_terrorisme/cssf04_155.pdf accessed 15 May 2025

Irish Official Publications

Government Reform Unit, Department of Public Expenditure and Reform, Protected Disclosures Bill 2013 – Regulatory Impact Analysis, July 2013

Report of The Commission Of Investigation into The Banking Sector In Ireland, Misjudging Risk: Causes Of The Systemic Banking Crisis In Ireland (2011)
The Final Report of the Tribunal of Inquiry into Certain Planning Matters and Payments – The Mahon Tribunal (2012) 2644 www.planningtribunal.ie/images/finalReport.pdf accessed 15 May 2025

Swedish Official Publications

The Swedish Parliament, Opinion on the application of the Principles of Subsidiarity and Proportionality (Proposal for a Directive of the European Parliament and of the Council on the protection of persons reporting on breaches of Union law) June 2018

UK Official Publications

Anthony Hidden, QC, 'Investigation into the Clapham Junction railway accident' (1989) www.railwaysarchive.co.uk/documents/DoT_Hidden001.pdf accessed 15 May 2021
European Scrutiny Committee, 'Whistleblowing and Breaches of EU Law' (2019) publications.parliament.uk/pa/cm201719/cmselect/cmeuleg/301-lxx/30104.htm accessed 15 May 2025
Secretary of State for Health, *Shipman Inquiry 5th Report* (Cm 6394, 2004)

US Official Publications

Appointment of Members of the Merit Systems Protection Board, 5 U.S.C. § 1201 (1989) www.govinfo.gov/app/details/USCODE-2010-title5/USCODE-2010-title5-partII-chap12-subchapI-sec1201 accessed 15 May 2025
Banks and Banking 12 U.S.Code Title 12 www.govinfo.gov/app/details/USCODE-2011-title12/USCODE-2011-title12-toc accessed 15 May 2025
Criteria for Determining Amount of Award, 17 C.F.R. § 240.21F-6 (2018)
Expenses of Detection of Underpayments and Fraud, etc., 26 U.S.C. § 7623(a); Treas. Reg. § 301.7623-l(a), (c) (as amended 1998)
Filing of Retaliation Complaints, 29 C.F.R. § 1980.103
Retaliating Against a Witness, Victim, or an Informant, 18 U.S.C. § 1513(e)
Securities and Exchange Commission, Securities Whistleblower Incentives and Protections, Federal Register, Vol. 76 no. 113
Securities and Exchange Commission, 'Annual Report on Whistleblower Program' (2010) < www.sec.gov/files/whistleblower_report_to_congress.pdf accessed 15 May 2021
Securities and Exchange Commission, 2023 Annual Report to Congress – Whistleblower Program – (2023) www.sec.gov/files/fy23-annual-report.pdf accessed 15 May 2025
Securities and Exchange Commission, 'Proposed Rules for Implementing the Whistleblower Provisions of Section 21F of the Securities Exchange Act of 1934, 17 CFR Parts 240 and 249' (2010) Release No. 34-63237; File No. S7-33-10 www.sec.gov/rules/proposed/2010/34-63237.pdf accessed 15 May 2025
Securities and Exchange Commission, 'Whistleblowers Incentive and Protections Final Rules' (2011) 229 [Release No. 34-64545; File No. S7-33-10] www.sec.gov/rules/final/2011/34-64545.pdf accessed 15 May 2021
Securities Whistleblower Incentives and Protection, 15 U.S.C. § 78u-6(h)(1)(B)(iii) (2010)

Senate Report n° 107-46, The Madrid Protocol Implementation Act (2002) www.congress.gov/congressional-report/107th-congress/senate-report/46/1?overview=closed accessed 15 May 2025

Senate Report n° 111-176, The Restoring American Financial Stability Act (2010) www.congress.gov/congressional-report/111th-congress/senate-report/176/1 accessed 15 May 2025

US Office of Special Counsel, osc.gov/Pages/about.aspx accessed 15 May 2021

US Securities and Exchange Commission, 'SEC awards 450,000 dollars to whistle-blower' (2020) www.sec.gov/news/press-release/2020-75 accessed 15 May 2025

US Sentencing Guidelines Manual § 8A1.2 cmt. 3(k) (U.S. Sentencing Comm'N 2003)

US Sentencing Guidelines Manual § 8B2.1(b)(5)(C) (U.S. Sentencing Comm'N 2016)

US Securities and Exchange Commission, '2019 Annual Report to Congress – Whistleblower Program' (2019) www.sec.gov/files/sec-2019-annual%20report-whistleblower%20program.pdf accessed 15 May 2025

US Securities and Exchange Commission, 'Annual Report to Congress, Whistleblower Program' (2020) www.sec.gov/files/2020%20Annual%20Report_0.pdf accessed 15 May 2025

US Securities and Exchange Commission, 'SEC announces million-dollar whistleblower award to compliance officer' (2015) www.sec.gov/news/pressrelease/2015-73.html accessed 15 May 2025

US Senate Permanent Subcommittee on Investigations, 'Tax Haven Banks and US Tax Compliance' (2008)

Whistleblower Protection Enhancement Act of 2012, Pub. L. No. 112-199, 126 Stat. 1465 (2012)

White MJ, 'SEC Chair White Offers A New Model for Enforcement' (2016) www.sec.gov/news/speech/chair-white-speech-new-york-university-111816.html accessed 15 May 2025

Secondary Sources

Books

Allegrezza Silvia, A (ed), *The Enforcement Dimension of the Single Supervisory Mechanism* (Wolter Kluwer Italia, 2020)

Ambros, K, *European Criminal Law* (CUP, 2018)

Andersen, S, *The Enforcement of EU Law* (OUP, 2012)

Ashworth, A and Redmayne, M, *The Criminal Process*, 3rd edn (OUP, 2005)

Bercusson, B, *European Labour Law*, 2nd edn (CUP, 2009)

Birkenfeld, RC, *Lucifer's Banker: The Untold Story of how I Destroyed Swiss Bank Secrecy* (Greenleaf Book Group Press, 2016)

Blomsma, JH, *Mens Rea and Defences in European Criminal Law* (Maastricht University Press, 2012)

Bodig, M, *Legal Doctrinal Scholarship – Legal Theory and the Inner Workings of a Doctrinal Discipline* (Edward Elgar, 2021)

Bok, S, Secrets: *On the Ethics of Concealment and Revelation* (Vintage Publishing, 1989)

Bozeman, B, *Public Values and Public Interest* (Georgetown University Press, 2007)

Bronwen, M and Yeung, K, *An Introduction to Law and Regulation* (CUP, 2007)

Brownlie, I, *Principles of Public International Law* (OUP, 2008)

Cassese, A, *International Law*, 2nd edn (OUP 2005)

Chaltiel Terral, F, *Les lanceurs d'alerte* (Dalloz éd., 2018)

Coffee Jr., JC, *Corporate Crime and Punishment – The Crisis of Underenforcement* (Berrett-Koehler Publishers, 2020)

Craig, P and de Burca, G, *EU Law –Texts, Cases and Materials*, 6th edn (OUP, 2015)

Cryer, R, Hervey, T, Sokhi-Bulley, B and Bohn, A, *Research Methodologies in EU and International Law* (Hart Publishing, 2011)

Damian, C, Davies, G and Monti, G, *European Union Law* (OUP 2010)

De George, RT, *Business Ethics*, 1st edn (Collier Macmillan Publishers, 1982)
Devers, G, *La Protection du Lanceur d'Alerte par la jurisprudence* (Tim Buctu editions, 2015)
Engel, A, *The Choice of Legal Basis for Acts of the European Union* (Springer, 2018)
Eric, B, *The Ethics of Whistleblowing* (Routledge, 2019)
Ferguson, G, *Global Corruption – Law, Theory and Practice*, 3rd edn, vol 1 (UVIC Press, 2008)
Financial Crisis Inquiry Commission, *The Financial Crisis Inquiry Report: Final Report of the National Commission on the Causes of the Financial and Economic Crisis* (Public Affairs edn, 2011)
Garner, BA (ed), *Black's Law Dictionary* (Thomson Reuters, 2009)
Gifis, SH, *Law Dictionary*, 4th edn (Barron's Educational Services, 1996)
Gottschalk, P, *Whistleblowing – White Collar Fraud Signal Detection* (Cambridge Scholars Publishing, 2018)
Haentjens, M and de Gioia-Carabellese, P, *European Banking and Financial Law* (Routledge, 2015)
Harris, D, O'Boyle, M, Bates, E and Buckley, C, *Law of the European Convention on Human Rights* (OUP, 2014)
Helmer, JB, *False Claims Act: Whistleblower Litigation*, 6th edn (Bloomberg, 2013)
Kerr, A and Kierans, L, *Protected Disclosures Act 2014*, 2nd edn (Round Hall Press, 2024)
Kenny, K, *Whistleblowing – Towards a New Theory* (Harvard University Press, 2019)
Klip, A, *European Criminal Law. An Integrative Approach*, 3rd edn (CUP, 2016)
Knell, A, *Corporate Governance: A Practical Implementation Guide for Unlisted Companies* (CIMA Publishing, 2006)
Kohn, SM, *The New Whistleblower's Handbook – A Step by Step Guide to Doing What's Right and Protecting Yourself* (Lyons Press, 2017)
Lasagni, G, *Banking Supervision and Criminal Investigation – Comparing the EU and US Experiences* (Springer, 2019)
Lewis, J, Bowers QC, J, Fodder, M and Mitchell, J, *Whistle-blowing: Law and Practice* (OUP, 2017)
Lipman, FD, *Whistleblowers – Incentives, Disincentives, and Protection Strategies* (Wiley, 2012)
Lippmann, W, *The Public Philosophy* (Hamish Hamilton, 1955)
Malinauskaite, J, *Harmonisation of EU Competition Law Enforcement* (Springer, 2020)
Mansfield, G and Peay, J, *The Director of Public Prosecutions: Principles and Practices for the Crown Prosecutor* (Tavistock Publications, 1987)
Mitsilegas, V, *EU Criminal Law* (Hart Publishing, 2009)
______, *EU Criminal Law After Lisbon. Rights, Trust and the Transformation of Justice in Europe* (Hart Publishing, 2016)
Moloney, N, *EU Securities and Financial Markets Regulation*, 3rd edn (OUP, 2014)
Nader, R, Petkas, P and Blackwell, K, *Whistle Blowing* (Grossman Publishers, 1972)
Panagopoulou-Koutnatzi, F, *The Institution of Whistleblowing: An Ethical-Constitutional Perspective* (Sakkoulas Publications, 2016)
Peterson, JC and Farell, D, *Whistleblowing – Ethical and Legal Issues in Expressing Dissent* (Kendall/Hunt Publishing Company, 1986)
Rose, C, *International Anti-Corruption Norms* (OUP, 2015)
Rutledge, SH, *Imperial Inquisitions: Prosecutors and Informants from Tiberius to Domitian* (Routledge, 2001)
Santoro, D and Kumar, M, *Speaking Truth to Power – A Theory of Whistleblowing* (Springer, 2018)
Schabas, WA, *The European Convention on Human Rights – A Commentary* (OUP, 2015)
Schulman, JF, Modesitt, N and Westman, DP, *Whistleblowing: The Law of Retaliatory Discharge*, 3rd edn (Bloomburg BNA, 2016)
Snyder, F, *New Dimensions in European Community Law* (Weidenfeld and Nicholson, 1990)
Stanger, A, *Whistleblowers* (Yale University Press, 2019)
Thüsing, G and Forst, G (eds), *Whistle-blowing A Comparative Study* (Springer, 2016)
Vandekerckhove, W, *Whistleblowing and Organizational Social Responsibility: A Global Assessment* (Ashgate, 2006)
Vaughn, R, *The Successes and Failures of Whistle-blower Laws* (Edward Elgar, 2012)

Weatherill, S, *The Internal Market as a Legal Concept* (OUP, 2017)
White, CAR and Ovey, C, *Jacobs, White & Ovey: The European Convention on Human Rights* (OUP, 2010)
Woodford, M, *Exposure* (Penguin, 2012)

Chapters in Edited Collections

Aguilera, RV, Goyer, M and Kabbach de Castro Luiz, R, 'Regulation and Comparative Corporate Governance' in M Wright, D Siegel, K Keasey and I Filatotchev (eds), *The Oxford Handbook of Corporate Governance* (OUP, 2013)
Allegrezza, S, 'Judicial Review as a Fundamental Right: Article 47 of the Charter' in S Allegrezza and V Covolo (eds), *Effective Defence Rights in Criminal Proceedings – A European and Comparative Study on Judicial Matters* (Wolters Kluwer, 2018)
Austin, J, 'To Reward or Not to Reward: A Cross-Jurisdictional Comparison of the Reasons Why Securities Regulators Have Adopted or Rejected Policies to Pay Whistleblowers' in S Lombard, Vivienne Brand and Janet Austin (eds.), *Corporate Whistleblowing Regulation* (Springer, 2020)
Banisar, D, 'Whistleblowing: International Standards and Developments' in IE Sandoval (ed), *Contemporary Debates on Corruption and Transparency: Rethinking State, Market, and Society* (World Bank, Institute for Social Research, UNAM, 2011)
Bittle, S and Hébert, J, 'Controlling Corporate Crimes in Times of De-regulation and Re-regulation' in ML Rorie (ed), *The Handbook of White-Collar Crime* (Wiley, 2020)
Blay-Grabarvzyk, K, 'Le statut incertain des lanceurs d'alerte' in M Disant and D Pollet-Panousis (eds), *Les lanceurs d'alerte* (LGDJ, 2017)
Bell, J, 'Legal Research and the Distinctiveness of Comparative Law' in M Van Hoecke (ed), *Methodologies of Legal Research* (Hart Publishing, 2011)
Bok, S, 'Whistle-Blowing and Professional Responsibilities'. Reprinted in Callahan, J. C. (ed), *Ethical Issues in Professional Life* (Oxford University Press,1988)
Borsjé, P and van Meerten, H, 'A European Pensions Union: Towards a Strengthening of the European Pension Systems' in F Pennings and G Vonk (eds), *Research Handbook on European Social Security Law* (Edward Elgar, 2015)
Bosua, R, Milton, S, Dreyfus, S and Lederman, R, 'Going Public: Researching External Whistleblowing in a New Media Age' in AJ Brown, D Lewis, R Moberly and W Vandekerckhove (eds), *International Handbook on Whistleblowing Research* (Edward Elgar, 2014)
Boyne, SM, 'Financial Incentives and Truth-Telling: The Growth of Whistle-blowing Legislation in the United States' in G Thüsing and G Forst (eds), *Whistleblowing – a Comparative Study* (Springer, 2016)
Busch, D and Ferrarini, G, 'Who's afraid of MiFID II?' in D Busch and G Ferrarini (eds), *Regulation of the EU Financial Markets* (OUP, 2016)
Buy, F, 'Lanceurs d'alerte et secrets d'affaires. Que fait-on des accords de confidentialité?' in M Disant and D Pollet-Panousis (eds), *Les lanceurs d'alerte* (LGDJ, 2017)
Chalmers, D, 'The Democratic Ambiguity of EU Law Making and its Enemies' in A Arnull and D Chalmers (eds), *The Oxford Handbook of European Union Law* (OUP, 2015)
Davies, ACL, Bogg, A and Costello, C, 'The Role of the Court of Justice in Labour Law' in A Bogg, C Castello and ACL Davies, *Research Handbook on EU Labour Law* (Edward Elgar, 2016)
Deckert, K and Sweeney, M, 'Whistleblowing: National Report for France' in G Thusing and G Forst (eds), *Whistleblowing – A Comparative Study* (Springer, 2016)
Deu, TA and U Lisa, 'The Right of Access to a Lawyer under Directive 2013/48/EU' in S Allegrezza and V Covolo (eds), *Effective Defence Rights in Criminal Proceedings – A European and Comparative Study on Judicial Matters* (Wolters Kluwer, 2018)

Devine, T, 'International Best Practices for Whistleblower Statutes' in D Lewis and W Vandekerckhove (eds), *Developments in Whistleblowing Research* (International Whistleblowing Research Network, 2015)
du Laing, B, 'Promises and Pitfalls of Interdisciplinary Legal Research: The Case of Evolutionary Analysis in Law' in M Van Hoecke (ed), *Methodologies of Legal Research* (Hart Publishing, 2011)
Fasterling, B, 'Whistleblower Protection: A Comparative Law Perspective' in AJ Brown, D Lewis, R Moberly and W Vandekerckhove (eds), *International Handbook on Whistleblowing Research* (Edward Elgar, 2014)
Faunce, T, Crow, K, Nikolic, T and Morgan Jr, FM, 'Because They Have Evidence: Globalizing Financial Incentives for Corporate Fraud Whistleblowers' in AJ Brown, D Lewis, R Moberly and W Vandekerckhove (eds), *International Handbook on Whistleblowing Research* (Edward Elgar, 2014)
Feldman, E, 'Whistleblower Protection' in R Byrne and W Binchy (eds), *Annual Review of Irish Law* (Thomson, 2011)
Foegle, J-P, 'Le lanceur d'alerte dans l'Union Européenne: démocratie, management, vulnérabilité' in M Disant and D Pollet-Panousis (eds), *Les lanceurs d'alerte* (LGDJ, 2017)
Gerhards, S and Rothenhofer, K, 'Packaged Retail and Insurance-based Investment Products Regulation (PRIIP)' in M Lehmann and C Kumpan (eds), *European Financial Services Law* (Beck – Hart – Nomos, 2019)
Gortsos, CV, 'European Banking Union Within the System of European Banking and Monetary Law' in MP Chiti and V Santoro (eds), *The Palgrave Handbook of European Banking Union Law* (Palgrave Macmillan, 2019)
_____ 'Public Enforcement of MiFID II?' in D Busch and G Ferrarini (eds), *Regulation of the EU Financial Markets* (OUP, 2016)
Hage, J, 'The Method of a Truly Normative Legal Science' in M Van Hoecke (ed), *Methodologies of Legal Research* (Hart Publishing, 2011)
Harding, C, 'The Role of Whistleblowing and Leniency in Detecting and Preventing Economic and Financial Crime: A Game of Give and Take?' in K Ligeti and V Franssen (eds), *Challenges in the Field of Economic and Financial Crime in Europe and the US* (Bloomsbury Publishing, 2017)
Hendrickx, F, 'Completing Economic and Social Integration: Towards Labour Law for the United States of Europe' in N Countouris and M Freedland (eds), *Resocialising Europe in a Time of Crisis* (CUP 2013)
Henkel, C, 'Whistleblower Rights and Protection Under U.S. Law in the Private Sector' in M Disant and D Pollet-Panousis (eds), *Les lanceurs d'alerte* (LGDJ, 2017)
Hoffman, HCH, 'General Principles of EU Law and EU Administrative Law' in C Barnard and S Peers (eds), *European Union Law* (OUP, 2020)
Kafteranis, D, 'From Obscurity to Limelight: The Whistle-blowers' Protection under EU Law' in V Mitsilegas and SJ Wortman (eds), *Whistleblowing, Transparency and Criminal Law: A Comparative Perspective* (Brill forthcoming)
Kammerer, JA, 'Market Behaviour' in M Lehmann and C Kumpan (eds), *European Financial Services Law* (Beck – Hart – Nomos, 2019)
_____ 'Title VI Competent Authorities' in M Lehmann and C Kumpan (eds), *European Financial Services Law* (Beck – Hart – Nomos, 2019)
Kellerbauer, M, 'Article 102' in M Kekkerbauer, M Klamert and J Tomkin (eds), *The EU Treaties and the Charter of Fundamental Rights – A Commentary* (OUP, 2019)
Kellerbauer, M and Martin, D, 'Article 45' in M Kekkerbauer, M Klamert and J Tomkin (eds), *The EU Treaties and the Charter of Fundamental Rights – A Commentary* (OUP, 2019)
Kellerbauer, M and Klamert, M, 'Article 352' in M Kellerbauer, M Klamert and J Tomkin (eds), *Commentary on the EU Treaties and the Charter of Fundamental Rights* (OUP, 2019)
Kerléo, J-F, 'Qu'est-ce qu'un lanceur d'alerte ?' in M Disant and D Pollet-Panoussis (eds), *Les lanceurs d'alerte* (LGDJ, 2017)
Kumpan, C and Grutze, R, 'Credit Rating Agency Regulation' in M Lehmann and C Kumpan (eds), *European Financial Services Law* (Beck – Hart – Nomos, 2019)

Lehmann, M and Kumpan, C (eds), *European Financial Services Law* (Beck – Hart – Nomos, 2019)
Lewis, D, 'Introduction' in D Lewis (ed), *A Global Approach to Public Interest Disclosures: What Can We Learn from Existing Whistleblowing Legislation and Research?* (Edward Elgar, 2010)
Lewis, D, Brown, AJ and Moberly, R, 'Whistleblowing, its Importance and the State of the Research' in AJ Brown, D Lewis, R Moberly and W Vandekerckhove (eds), *International Handbook on Whistleblowing Research* (Edward Elgar, 2014)
Lobel, O, 'New Governance as Regulatory Governance' in D Levi-Faur (ed), *The Oxford Handbook of Governance* (OUP, 2012)
lõhmus, U, 'European Criminal Law: Can a General Part be developed through Case Law?' in A Klip (ed), *Substantive Criminal Law of the European Union* (OUP, 2011)
Lombard, S, 'Regulatory Policies and Practices to Optimize Corporate Whistleblowing: A Comparative Analysis' in S Lombard, V Brand and J Austin (eds), *Corporate Whistleblowing Regulation* (Springer, 2020)
Lucantoni, P, 'Securities Clearing and Settlement – European Markets Infrastructure Regulation' in M Lehmann and C Kumpan (eds), *European Financial Services Law* (Beck – Hart – Nomos, 2019)
Lui, A and Turksen, U, 'Vulnerabilities, Obstacles and Risks in Reporting Financial Crimes' in N Ryder and L Pasculli (eds), *Corruption, Integrity and the Law: Global Regulatory Challenges* (Taylor & Francis Group, 2020)
Manfred, Z, 'Criminal Sanctions to be Imposed on Individuals as Enforcement Instruments in European Competition Law' in C-D Ehlermann and I Atanasiu (eds.), *European Competition Law Annual 2001: Effective Private Enforcement of EC Antitrust Law* (Hart Publishing, 2003)
McConville, M and Wilson, G (eds), *The Handbook of the Criminal Justice Process* (OUP, 2002)
McConville, M and Chui, HW, 'Introduction and Overview' in M McConville and WH Chui (eds), *Research Methods for Law* (Edinburgh University Press, 2007)
Mendes, J, 'The EU Administrative Institutions, Their Law, and Legal Scholarship' in P Cane et al (eds), *The Oxford Handbook of Comparative Administrative Law* (OUP, 2021)
Miceli, MP, Dreyfus, S and Near, JP, 'Outsiders 'Whistle-blowers': Conceptualising and Distinguishing 'Bell-Ringing' Behaviour' in AJ Brown, D Lewis, R Moberly and W Vandekerckhove (eds), *International Handbook on Whistleblowing Research* (Edward Elgar, 2014)
Miller, GP, 'The Compliance Function: An Overview' in JN Gordon and W-G Ringe (eds), *The Oxford Handbook of Corporate Law and Governance* (OUP, 2018)
Mitsilegas, V, 'EU Criminal Law Competence after Lisbon: From Securitised to Functional Criminalisation' in DA Arcarazo and CC Murphy (eds), *EU Security and Justice law* (Hart Publishing, 2014)
Moberly, R, 'To Persons or Organisations that May be Able to Effect Action: Whistle-blowing Recipients' in AJ Brown, D Lewis, R Moberly and W Vandekerckhove (eds), *International Handbook on Whistleblowing Research* (Edward Elgar, 2014)
Mulbert, PO and W Alexander, 'CRD IV Framework for Banks' Corporate Governance' in D Busch and G Ferrarini (eds), *European Banking Union* (OUP, 2020)
Parker, C and Lehmann, NV, 'Compliance: 14 questions' in P Drahos (ed), *Regulation Theory – Foundations and Applications* (ANU, 2017)
Pender, K, Cherkasova, S and Yamaoka-Enkerlin, A, 'Compliance and Whistleblowing: How Technology Will Replace, Empower and Change Whistleblowers' in J Madir (ed), *Fintech – Law and Regulation* (Edward Elgar, 2019)
Sanders, A, 'Introduction' in A Sanders (ed), *Prosecution in Common Law Jurisdictions* (Dartmouth, 1996)
Schutze, R, 'EU Competences – Existence and Exercise' in A Arnull and D Chalmers (eds), *The Oxford Handbook of European Union Law* (OUP, 2015)
Spencer, M and Spencer, J, 'When it All Goes Bad: Criminal Remedies' in AJ Brown, D Lewis, R Moberly and W Vandekerckhove (eds), *International Handbook on Whistleblowing Research* (Edward Elgar, 2014)
Syrpis, P, 'The EU and National Systems of Labour Law' in A Arnull and D Chalmers (eds), *The Oxford Handbook of European Union Law* (OUP, 2015)

Tridimas, T, 'Abuse of Rights in EU Law: Some Reflections with Particular Reference to Financial law' in R de la Feria and S Vogenauer (eds), *Prohibition of Abuse of Law: A New General Principle of EU Law?* (Hart Publishing, 2011)
Turksen, U, 'The Criminalisation and Protection of Whistleblowers in the EU's Counter-Financial Crime Framework' in K Ligeti and S Tosza (eds), White Collar Crime: A Comparative Perspective (Hart Publishing, 2019)
van Hoecke, M, 'Legal Doctrine: Which Method(s) for What Kind of Discipline?' in M Van Hoecke (ed), *Methodologies of Legal Research* (Hart Publishing, 2011)
Van Hulle, K, 'Risk Disclosure in the European Insurance Industry: Implications for Occupational Pension Funds' in OS Mitchell, R Maurer, and JM Orszag (eds), *Retirement System Risk Management – Implications of the New Regulatory Order* (OUP, 2016)
van Rooij, B and Fine, AD, 'Preventing Corporate Crime Within: Compliance Management, Whistleblowing, and Internal Monitoring' in ML Rorie (ed), *The Handbook of White-Collar Crime* (Wiley Blackwell, 2020)
Vandekerchove, W, 'European Whistleblower Protection' in D Lewis (ed), *A Global Approach to Public Interest Disclosures: What can we Learn from Existing Whistleblowing Legislation and Research?* (Edward Elgar, 2010)
Vandekerckove, W, Uys, T, Rehg, MT and Brown, AJ, 'Understandings of Whistleblowing: Dilemmas of Societal Culture' in AJ Brown, D Lewis, R Moberly and W Vandekerckhove (eds), *International Handbook on Whistleblowing Research* (Edward Elgar, 2014)
Vanderkerckhove, W, Brown, AJ and Tsahuridu, E, 'Managerial Responsiveness to Whistleblowing: Expanding the Research Horizon' in AJ Brown, D Lewis, R Moberly and W Vandekerckhove (eds), *International Handbook on Whistleblowing Research* (Edward Elgar, 2014)
Vogenauer, S, 'The Prohibition of Abuse of Law: An Emerging General Principle of EU law' in R de la Feria and S Vogenauer (eds), *Prohibition of Abuse of Law: A New General Principle of EU Law?* (Hart Publishing, 2011)
Wattel, PJ, 'Introduction' in PJ Wattel, O Marres and H Vermeulen (eds), *European Tax Law* (Wolters Kluwer, 2018)
Westerman, PC, 'Open or Autonomous? The Debate on Legal Methodology as a Reflection of the Debate on Law' in M Van Hoecke (ed), *Methodologies of Legal Research* (Hart Publishing, 2011)
Wilson, G, 'Comparative Legal Scholarship' in M McConville and WH Chui (eds), *Research Methods for Law* (Edinburgh University Press, 2007)
Windsor, D, 'Capitalism' in LM Salinger (ed), *Encyclopaedia of White-Collar and Corporate Crime*, 2nd edn (SAGE, 2013)
Wundenberg, M, 'Compliance in Wertpa-pierfirmen' in Veil (ed), *Europäisches Kapitalmarktrecht* (Mohr Siebeck, 2014)
Wyatt, D, 'Community Competence to Regulate the Internal Market' in M Dougan and S Currie (eds), *50 Year of the European Treaties: Looking Back and Thinking Forward* (Hart Publishing, 2009)
Zetzsche, D and Nast, D, 'Funds' in M Lehmann and C Kumpan (eds), *European Financial Services Law* (Beck – Hart – Nomos, 2019)

Articles

Abazi, V, 'The European Union Whistleblower Directive: A Game Changer for Whistleblowing Protection?' [2020] *Industrial Law Journal* 1
_____ 'Trade Secrets and Whistleblower Protection in the European Union' (2016) 1(3) *European Papers* 1061
_____ 'Whistleblowing in the European Union' (2021) 58 *Common Market Law Review* 813
Alford, CF, 'Whistle-blower Narratives: The Experience of Choiceless Choice' (2007) 74(1) *Social Research* 223

Alibert, J and Foegle, J-P, 'Première victoire d'un lanceur d'alerte en référé sous l'empire de la loi 'Sapin II" [2019] *La Revue des droits de l'homme*, journals.openedition.org/revdh/6313 accessed 15 May 2021

Andreadakis, S, 'Enhancing Whistleblower Protection: It's All About the Culture' (2019) 30(6) *European Business Law Review* 859

Andreadakis, S and Kafteranis, D, 'Internal Whistleblowing in the US after Digital Realty Trust v Somers: Any Lessons to be Learnt from Europe?' (2025) 54(2) *Industrial Law Journal* 357

Andreis, E, 'Towards Common Minimum Standards for Whistleblower Protection across the EU' (2019) 4(2) *European Papers* 575

Ashton, J, '15 Years of Whistleblowing Protection under the Public Interest Disclosure Act 1998: Are We Still Shooting the Messenger?' (2015) 44(1) *Industrial Law Journal* 29

Barnett, T, 'A Preliminary Investigation of the Relationship Between Selected Organizational Characteristics and External Whistleblowing by Employees' (1992) 11 *Journal of Business Ethics* 949

Barrière, F, 'Les lanceurs d'alerte' [2017] *Revue des sociétés* 191

Beck, RJ, 'The False Claims Act and the English Eradication of Qui Tam Legislation' (2000) 78(3) *North Carolina Law Review* 539

Beller, R, 'Whistleblower Protection Legislation of the East and West: Can It Really Reduce Corporate Fraud and Improve Corporate Governance? A Study of the Successes and Failures of Whistleblower Protection Legislation in the US and China (2010) 7 *New York University Journal of Law & Business* 873

Berkebile, C, 'The Puzzle of Whistleblower Protection Legislation: Assembling the Piecemeal' (2018) 28 *Indiana International & Comparative Law Review* 1

Berkowitz, AD, Tusk, CM, Downes, IJ and David, CS, 'Whistleblowing' (2011) 16(4) *Employee Relations Law Journal* 15

Bieber, R and Maiani, F, 'Enhancing Centralised Enforcement of EU Law: Pandora's Toolbox?' (2014) 51 *Common Market Law Review* 1057

Boot, ER, 'The Feasibility of a Public Interest Defense for Whistle-blowing' (2020) 39 *Law and Philosophy* 1

Bowal, P, 'Retaliation Against Whistleblowers is a Crime' [2011] *Lawnow* 28

Bowen, RM, Call, AC and Rajgopal, S, 'Whistle-blowing: Target Firm Characteristics and Economic Consequences' (2010) 85(4) *The Accounting Review* 1239

Bradley, C, 'Breaking Up is hard to do: The Interconnection Problem in Financial Markets and Financial Regulation: A European (Banking) Union Perspective' (2014) 49 *Texas International Law Journal* 271

Brand, V, 'Corporate Whistleblowing, Smart Regulation and Regtech: The Coming of the Whistlebot?' (2020) 43(3) *University of New South Wales Law Journal* (advance) 1

Bucy, PH, 'Information as a Commodity in the Regulatory World' [2002] *Houston Law Review* 946

Caillier, JG, 'Public Service Motivation and Decisions to Report Wrongdoing in U.S. Federal Agencies: Is this Relationship Mediated by the Seriousness of the Wrongdoing' [2016] *American Review of Public Administration* 1

Callahan, ES and Morehead Dworkin, T, 'Do Good and Get Rich: Financial Incentives for Whistleblowing and the False Claims Act' (1992) 37 *Villanova Law Review* 273

_____ 'The State of State Whistleblower Protection' (2000) 38 *American Business Law Journal* 99

_____ 'Who Blows the Whistle to the Media, and Why: Organisational Characteristics of Media Whistle-blowers' (1994) 96 *American Business Law Journal* 151

Cameron, I, 'European Court of Human Rights: April 2007-April 2008' (2008) 14(4) *European Public Law* 468

Cardilli, MC, 'Regulation Without Borders: The Impact of Sarbanes-Oxley on European Companies' (2003) 27(2) *Fordham International Law Journal* 786

Cary, WL, 'Federalism and Corporate Law: Reflections upon Delaware' (1974) 83 *Yale Law Journal* 663

Centonze, AL, 'The Irish Banking Crisis' (2014) 5(2) *Review of Business and Finance Studies* 85

Chiu, RK, 'Ethical Judgment and Whistleblowing Intention: Examining the Moderating Role of Locus of Control' (2003) 43 *Journal of Business Ethics* 65

Colneric, N, 'Does the Case Law of the European Court of Human Rights Show that the Convention States of the European Convention on Human Rights Must Prescribe Priority of Internal Whistle-blowing as a Rule?' (2018) 6 *Soziales Recht* 232

Daoud, E and Sfoggia, S, 'Lanceurs d'alerte et enterprises: les enjeux de la loi Sapin II' [2017] *AJ Pénal Dalloz* 71

Davies, G, 'Democracy and Legitimacy in the Shadow of Purposive Competence' (2015) 21(1) *European Law Journal* 2

Day, Angela, 'To Mediate or Adjudicate? An Alternative for Resolving Whistleblower Disputes at the Hanford Nuclear Site' (2013) 11(2) *Seattle Journal for Social Justice* 617

de la Feria, R, 'Prohibition of abuse of (Community) Law: The Creation of a New General Principle of EC Law through Tax' (2008) 45 *Common Market Law Review* 395

Del Mundo Carmina, FS, 'How Countries Seek to Strengthen Anti-Money Laundering Laws in Response to the Panama Papers, and the Ethical Implications of Incentivizing Whistleblowers' (2019) 40 *Northwestern Journal of International Law and Business* 87

Delmas, C, 'The Civic Duty to Report Crime and Corruption' (2014) 9(1) *Les ateliers de l'**éthique*** 50

Doron, I and Apter, I, 'The Debate Around the Need for an International Convention on the Rights of Older Persons' (2010) 50 *The Gerontologist*

Douville, T, 'Directive (UE) 2019/1937 du 23 octobre 2019 sur la protection des personnes qui signalent des violations du droit de l'Union – Aspects relatifs à la protection des données à caractère personnel' (2019) 4 *R.A.E-L.E.A.* 709

Dyck, A, Adair, M and Luigi, Z, 'Who Blows the Whistle on Corporate Fraud?' (2010) 65 *Journal of Finance* 2213

Dyens, S, 'Le bénéfice de la protection due au lanceur d'alerte est conditionné au respect de la procédure d'alerte' [2018] *AJ Collectivités Territoriales* 404

Earle, BH and Madek, GA, 'The Mirage of Whistleblower Protection Under Sarbanes-Oxley: A Proposal for Change' (2007) 44 *American Business Law Journal* 1

Elliston, FA, 'Anonymity and Whistleblowing' (1982) 3(1) *Journal of Business Ethics* 167

Faraguna, P, 'Taking Constitutional Identities Away from the Courts' (2016) 41 *Brooklyn Journal of International Law* 492

Fasterling, B and Lewis, D, 'Leaks, Legislation and Freedom of Speech: How Can the Law Effectively Promote Public-Interest Whistleblowing' (2014) 153 *International Labour Review* 71

Filler, RH and Markham, JW, 'Whistleblowers—A Case Study in The Regulatory Cycle For Financial Services' (2018) 12 *Brooklyn Journal of Corporate, Financial & Commercial Law* 337

Fincher, RD, 'Mediating Whistleblower Disputes: Integrating the Emotional and Legal Challenges' (2009) 64(1) *Dispute Resolution Journal* 62

Fischer, J, Harshman, E, Gillespie, W and Ordower, H, 'Privatizing Regulation: Whistleblowing and Bounty Hunting in the Financial Services Industries' (2000) 1 *Dickinson Journal of International Law* 117

Fleischer, H and Schmolke, KU, 'Financial Incentives for Whistleblowers in European Capital Markets Law? Legal Policy Considerations on the Reform of the Market Abuse Regime' (2012) ECGI Law WP No 189/2012, ssrn.com/abstract=2124678 accessed 15 May 2021

Foegle, J-P, 'Un renforcement en demi-teinte du statut du lanceur d'alerte dans l'Europe des droits de l'homme' (2015) La Revue des droits de l'homme, Actualités Droits-Libertés 1, revdh.revues.org/1073 accessed 15 May 2021

Freeman Engstrom, D, 'Harnessing the Private Attorney General: Evidence from Qui Tam Litigation' (2012) 112 *Columbia Law Review* 1244

Georgiadou, G, 'The European Commission's Proposal for Strengthening Whistleblower Protection' (2018) 3 *EUCRIM* 166

Giubboni, S, 'Being a Worker in EU law' (2018) 9(3) *European Labour Law Journal* 223

Givati, Y, 'A Theory of Whistleblower Rewards' (2016) 45 *Journal of Legal Studies* 43

Givati, Y, 'Of Snitches and Riches: Optimal IRS and SEC Whistleblower Rewards' (2018) 55 *Harvard Journal on Legislation* 106

Gordon, A, 'Public Interest and the Three Dimensions of Judicial Review' (2013) 64(2) *Northern Ireland Legal Quarterly* 125

Greenberger, M, 'The Extraterritorial Provisions of the Dodd-Frank Act Protect US Taxpayers from Worldwide Bailouts' (2012) 80(4) *UMKC Law Review* 1

Greer, S, 'The Exceptions to Article 8 to 11 of the European Convention on Human Rights' (1997) 15 Human Rights Files, Council of Europe Publishing 9

Hamer, S, 'Lincoln's Law: Constitutional and Policy Issues Posed by the Qui Tam Provisions of the False Claims Act' (1997) 6 *Kansas Journal of Law & Public Policy* 89

Herlin-Karnell, E, 'Annotation, Case Comment Case C-301/06, Ireland v. Parliament and Council' (2009) 46 *Common Market Law Review* 1667

Hoedt-Rasmussen, I and Voorhoof, D, 'Whistleblowing for Sustainable Democracy' (2018) 36(1) *Netherlands Quarterly of Human Rights* 3

Hoffman, MW and Schwartz, MS, 'The Morality of Whistleblowing: A Commentary on Richard T. De George' (2014) 124(4) *Journal of Business Ethics* 771

Hossfeld, C, Muller-Lagarde, Y, Alexandre, D, Poschke, M and Zevounou, L, 'L'intérêt public européen/European public interest: Rapport de recherche final' (2018) ANC – Rapport de recherche – Autorité des normes comptables 1

Humphreys, D, 'The Elusive Quest for a Global Forests Convention' (2005) 14 *Review of European Community & International Environmental Law* 1

Hyde, J, 'The Protected Disclosures Act 2014: An Overview' (2014) 11 *Irish Employment Law Journal* 2

Jubb, PB, 'Whistleblowing: A Restrictive Definition and Interpretation' (1999) 21 *Journal of Business Ethics* 77

Junod, V, 'La Liberté d'Expression du Whistleblower' (2009) 77 *Revue Trimestrielle des droits de l'homme* 238

_____ 'Lancer l'alerte: quoi de neuf depuis "Guja"?: (Cour eur. dr. h., "Bucur et Toma c. Roumanie", 8 janvier 2013)' (2014) 98 *Revue trimestrielle des droits de l'homme* 459

_____ 'A New Enforcement Tool: a Directive to Protect Whistle-blowers' (2020) 41 *Business Law Review* 50

_____ 'Can Artificial Intelligence Replace Whistle-blowers in the Business Sector?' (2019) 3(2) *International Journal of Technology Policy and Law* 160

_____ 'Reporting to the Boss or the Authorities: The Ongoing Dilemma of the Whistle-blower' [2018] *Cambridge Law Review* 10

_____ 'Rethinking Financial Rewards for Whistle-blowers under the Proposal for a Directive on the Protection of Whistle-blowers Reporting Breaches of EU Law' (2019) 2(1) *Nordic Journal of European Law* 38

_____ 'The Future of the Whistle-blowing Directive: Criticising its Legal Bases' [2021] *Queen Mary Law Journal*

_____ 'The Question of One Million Dollars: Financial Rewards or Not for the Whistle-blowers' (2021) 36 (4) *International Journal of Banking Law and Regulation* 160

_____ 'The Role of the European Parliament in the Adoption of the Directive on the Protection of Whistle-blowers' (2020) 4 *Revue des affaires européennes* 903

_____ 'What to Expect from the Directive on the Protection of Whistle-blowers?' (2021) 32(5) *European Business Law Review* 979–89

Kafteranis, D and Andreadakis, S, 'A New Perspective on the Protection of Whistleblowers under ECHR: Halet v Luxembourg' (2023) 68(1) *Studies in Logic, Grammar and Rhetoric* 611–27

Kafteranis, D et al., 'The Citizens' Role in combatting Economic Crimes: Insights from Tax Offences, Money Laundering, and Sanctions Evasion' [2025] *European Law Journal* 1–24

Kampourakis, I, 'Whistleblowers as Regulatory Intermediaries: Instrumental and Reflexive Considerations in Decentralizing Regulation' [2020] *Regulation & Governance* 1

Kenny, K, 'Censored: Whistleblowers and Impossible Speech' (2017) 71 *Human Relations* 16

Kenny, K, Fotaki, M and Scriver, S, 'Mental Health as a Weapon: Whistleblower Retaliation and Normative Violence' (2019) 160(3) *Journal of Business Ethics* 801
Kierans, L, 'Whistleblowing Litigation and Legislation in Ireland: Are There Lessons to be Learned?' [2023] *Industrial Law Journal*, 1.
Kilpatrick, C, 'The European Court of Justice and Labour Law in 2009' [2010] *Industrial Law Journal* 287
King, ME, 'Blowing the Whistle on the Dodd-Frank Amendments: The Case Against the New Amendments to Whistleblower Protection in Section 806 of Sarbanes-Oxley' (2011) 48 *American Criminal Law Review* 1457
King, SM, Chilton, BS and Roberts. GE, 'Reflections on Defining the Public Interest' (2010) 41(8) *Administration & Society* 954
Kinsley, M, 'Protected Disclosures Bill 2013' (2014) 32 *Irish Law Times* 1
Kountouris, N, 'The Concept of 'Worker' in European Labour Law: Fragmentation, Autonomy and Scope' [2017] *Industrial Law Journal* 1
Kreiner Ramirez, M, 'Whistling Past the Graveyard: Dodd-Frank Whistleblower Programs Dodge Bullets Fighting Financial Crime' (2019) 50 *Loyola University Chicago Law Journal* 617
Kwon, MM, 'Whistling Dixie About the IRS Whistleblower Program Thanks to the IRC Confidentiality Restriction' (2010) 29 *Virginia Tax Review* 447
Lachapelle, A, 'And thus Tax Whistleblowing was Born! Comment on the Directive on Whistleblowers in Tax Matters' (2020) 588 *T.F.R* 798
Langbein, JH, 'Controlling Prosecutorial Discretion in Germany' (1974) 41 *University of Chicago Law Review* 439
Leczykiewicz, D, 'Prohibition of Abusive Practices as a General Principle of EU Law' (2019) 56 *Common Market Law Review* 703
Leifer, SC, 'Protecting Whistleblower Protections in the Dodd-Frank Act' (2014) 113 *Michigan Law Review* 121
Lenoir, N, 'Les lanceurs d'alerte – Une innovation française venue d'Outre-Atlantique' (2015) 42 *La Semaine Juridique – Entreprise et Affaires* 38
Lewis, D, 'Is a Public Interest Test for Workplace Whistle-blowing in Society's Interest?' (2015) 57(2) *International Journal of Law and Management* 147
_____ 'Resolving Whistleblowing Disputes in the Public Interest: Is Tribunal Adjudication the Best that Can Be Offered?' (2013) 42(1) *Industrial Law Journal* 35
_____ 'The Council of Europe Resolution and Recommendation on the Protection of Whistleblower' (2010) 39(4) *Industrial Law Journal* 432
_____ 'The EU Directive on the Protection of Whistleblowers: A Missed Opportunity to Establish International Best Practices?' (2020) 9(1) *E-Journal of International and Comparative Labour Studies* 1
_____ 'Whistleblowing and Data Protection Principles: Is the Road to Reconciliation Really that Rocky?' (2011) 2(1) *European Journal of Law and Technology* 1
Liyanarachchi, G and Newdick, C, 'The Impact of Moral Reasoning and Retaliation on Whistleblowing: New Zealand Evidence' (2009) 89(1) *Journal of Business Ethics* 37
Lonati, S, 'Anonymous Witness Evidence before the European Court of Human Rights: Is It Still Possible to Speak of "Fair Trial"?' (2018) 8(1) *European Criminal Law Review* 116
Looseveld, S, 'EU Financial Supervisory Powers, Whistleblowing and Self-reporting' (2019) 34(9) *Journal of International Banking law and Regulation* 317
Loyens, K and Vandekerckove, W, 'Whistleblowing from an International Perspective: A Comparative Analysis of Institutional Arrangements' (2018) 8 *Administrative Sciences* 30
Luchtman, M and Vervaele, J, 'Enforcing the Market Abuse Regime: Towards an Integrated Model of Criminal and Administrative Law Enforcement in the European Union?' (2014) 5(2) *New Journal of European Criminal Law* 196
Magner, V and Paclot, Y, 'Un nouveau champ de protection pour les lanceurs d'alerte' (2019) 4 *RAE-LAE* 699
Magner, V, 'Avant-propos' (2019) 4 *RAE-LAE* 677

Marcum, TM, Young, J and Kirner, ET, 'Blowing the Whistle in the Digital Age: Are You Really Anonymous? The Perils and Pitfalls of Anonymity in Whistleblowing Law' (2020) 17(1) *DePaul Business and Commercial Law Journal* 1
Marguénaud, J-P and Mouly, J, 'La protection européenne des salariés lanceurs d'alerte par la Cour de Cassation: un troublant exemple d'improvisation' [2016] *Recueil Dalloz* 1741
Marx, GT, 'What's in a Name? Some Reflections on the Sociology of Anonymity' (1999) 15 *The Information Society* 99
Matt Hu, SW, 'Fine-Tuning the Tax Whistleblower Statute: Why Qui-tam is not a Solution' (2014) 99 *Minnesota Law Review* 783
Maublanc, J-P, 'Réévaluation de l'abus de droit à la lumière de la jurisprudence communautaire sur les pratiques abusives' [2007] *Revue du Marché commun et de l'Union européenne* 267
McAllister, BJ, 'The Impact of the Dodd-Frank Whistle-blower Provisions on FCPA Enforcement and Modern Corporate Compliance Programs' (2017) 14 *Berkley Business Law Journal* 45
Mendelsohn, J, 'Calling the Boss or Calling the Press: A Comparison of British and American Responses to Internal and External Whistle-blowing' (2009) 8 *Global Studies Law Review* 723
Menegatti, E, 'Taking EU Labour Law Beyond the Employment Contract: The Role Played by the European Court of Justice' (2020) 11(1) *European Labour Law Journal* 26
Miceli, MP and Near, JP, 'Retaliation Against Whistleblowers: Predictors and Effects (1986) 71(1) *Journal of Applied Psychology* 137
Moberly, RE, 'Confidentiality and Whistleblowing' (2018) 96 *North Carolina Law Review* 751
_____ 'Sarbanes-Oxley's Structural Model to Encourage Corporate Whistleblowers' (2006) 83 *Brigham Young University Law Review* 1107
_____ 'Sarbanes-Oxley's Whistleblower Provisions: Ten Years Later' (2012) 64 *South Carolina Law Review* 1
_____ 'Unfulfilled Expectations: An Empirical Analysis of Why Sarbanes-Oxley Whistleblowers Rarely Win' (2007) 49 *William & Mary Law Review* 65
Moberly, RE, Thomas, JA and Zuckerman, J, 'De Facto Gag Clauses: The Legality of Employment Agreements That Undermine Dodd-Frank's Whistleblower Provisions' 30(1) *Journal of Labor and Employment Law* 87
Morehead Dworkin, T, 'SOX and Whistleblowing' (2007) 105 *Michigan Law Review* 1757
_____ 'Whistleblowing, MNCs, and Peace' (2002) 35 *Vanderbilt Journal of Transnational Law* 457
Morehead Dworkin, T and Brown, AJ, 'The Money or the Media? Lessons from Contrasting Developments in US and Australian Whistleblowing Laws' (2013) 11(2) *Seattle Journal for Social Justice* 653
Morehead Dworkin, T and Near, MP, 'Whistleblowing Statutes: Are They Working?' (1987) 25 *American Business Law Journal* 241
Nanavati, J, 'The IRS Whistleblower Regulations' [2018] *CPA Journal* 67
Neal, M, 'Securities Whistleblowing under Dodd-Frank: Neglecting the Power of "Enterprising Privateers" in Favor of the "Slow-Going Public Vessel"' (2012) 15 *Lewis & Clark Law Review* 1107
Near, JP and Miceli, MP, 'Organizational Dissidence: The Case of Whistle-Blowing' (1985) 4 *Journal of Business Ethics* 1
Nunziato, MC, 'Aiding and Abetting, a Madoff Family Affair: Why Secondary Actors Should be Held Accountable for Securities Fraud Through the Restoration of the Private Right of Action for Aiding and Abetting Liability Under the Federal Securities Laws' (2010) 73 *Albany Law Review* 603
O' Brien, C, 'Social Blind Spots and Monocular Policy Making: the ECJ's Migrant Worker Problem' (2009) 46 *Common Market Law Review* 1107
Oberg, J, 'The Legal Basis for EU Criminal Law Harmonisation: A Question of Federalism?' (2018) 43(3) *European Law Review* 366
Odudu, O and Bailey, D, 'The Single Economic Entity Doctrine in EU Competition Law' (2014) 51 *Common Market Law Review* 1721
Oelrich, S, 'Making Regulation Fit by Taking Irrationality into Account: The Case of the Whistleblower' (2019) 12 *Business Research* 175

Oliver, P, 'Companies and their fundamental Rights: A Comparative Perspective' (2015) 46 *International and Comparative Law Quarterly* 661
Osborne, S, 'Dodd-Frank Whistleblower Provision: Determining Who Qualifies as a Whistleblower' (2017) 41 *Delaware Journal of Corporate Law* 908
Ouwerkerk, JW, 'Criminalization Powers of the European Union and the Risks of Cherry-Picking between Various Legal Bases: The Case for a Single Legal Framework for EU-Level Criminalization; (2017) 23 *Columbia Journal of European Law* 503
Pacella, JM, 'Cybersecurity Threat: Compliance and the Role of Whistleblowers' (2016) 11 *Brooklyn Journal of Corporate, Financial & Commercial Law* 39
Pailler, P, 'Le nouveau statut de lanceur d'alerte' [2017] *Revue du droit bancaire et financier* 1
Papandrea, M-R, 'Leaker Traitor Whistleblower Spy: National Security Leaks and First Amendment' (2014) 94 *Boston University Law Review* 449
Park, H, Blenkisopp, J, Oktem, KM and Ugur, O, 'Cultural Orientation and Attitudes toward Different Forms of Whistle-blowing: A Comparison of South Korea, Turkey, and the U.K.' (2008) 82(4) *Journal of Business Ethics* 929
Peers, S, 'Non-regression Clauses: The Fig Leaf Has Fallen' (2010) 39 *Industrial Law Journal* 436
Portier, P, 'Les canaux de signalement interne et externe selon le droit européen, une avancée par rapport à la loi Sapin 2 ?' (2019) 4 *RAE-LAE* 705
Portuese, A, Gough, O and Tanega, J, 'The Principle of Legal Certainty as a Principle of Economic Efficiency' (2014) 44 *European Journal of Law and Economics* 131
Racho, T, 'La possibilité d'un encadrement juridique des lanceurs d'alerte par l'Union Européenne' (2016) 10 *Revue des Droits de l'Homme* 1
Rapp, GC, 'Four Signal Moments in Whistleblower Law: 1983-2013' (2013) 30(2) *Hofstra Labor and Employment Law Journal* 1
Reeder, M, 'Proceeding Legally: Clarifying the SEC/Dodd-Frank Whistleblower Incentives' (2017) 7 *Harvard Business and Law Review* 269
Rehg, MT, Miceli, MP, Near, JP and Van Scotter, JR, 'Antecedents and Outcomes of Retaliation Against Whistleblowers: Gender Differences and Power Relationships' (2008) 19(2) *Organization Science, INFORMS* 221
Reksosh, E, 'Who Defines the Public Interest?' (2005) 2 *International Journal on Human Rights* 167
Rettig, CP, 'The IRS Whistleblower Program: Making Money the Old-Fashioned Way!' [2012] *Journal of Tax Practice & Procedure* 21
Reynolds, S, 'Comparative Legal Analysis: From the Prevalent Methodology to a Necessary Prerequisite' (2016) 23 *Maastricht Journal of European and Comparative Law* 366
Rubinstein, K, 'Internal Whistleblowing and Sarbanes-Oxley Section 806: Balancing the Interests of Employee and Employer' (2007) 52 *New York Law School Law Review* 637
Sawyer, KR, Johnson, J, and Holub, M, 'The Necessary Illegitimacy of the Whistleblower' (2010) 29 *Business and Professional Ethics Journal* 85
Scholten, M, 'Mind the Trend! Enforcemet of EU Law has been Moving to 'Brussels' (2017) 24(9) *Journal of European Public Policy* 1348
Scott, CR, 'To Reveal or Not to Reveal—A Theoretical Model of Anonymous Communications' (1998) 8(4) *Communication Theory* 381
Shu-Acquaye, F, 'Dodd-Frank Wall Street Reform and Consumer Protection Act: The Evolution of Whistleblower Protections, Employment Contracts and Mandatory Arbitration Agreements' (2017) 15 *DePaul Business & Commercial Law Journal* 127
Sinzdak, G, 'An Analysis of Current Whistle-blower Laws: Defending a More Flexible Approach to Reporting Requirements' (2008) 96(6) *California Law Review* 1633
Sipe, SR, Metrejean, CT and Pearson, TA, 'The SEC, The Courts and Whistleblowers: An Examination Into The Strength of The Anti-Retaliation Provisions Of The Dodd-Frank Act As Defined By Recent Federal Court Decisions' (2014-15) 19 *Journal of Legal Studies in Business* 8
Skivenes, M and Trygstad, SC, 'When Whistle-Blowing Works: The Norwegian Case' (2010) 63(7) *Human Relations* 1071

Soltes, K, 'Facilitating Appropriate Whistleblowing: Examining Various Approaches to What Constitutes "Fact" to Trigger Protection under Article 33 of the United Nations Convention against Corruption' (2012) 27(4) *American University International Law Review* 925
Sophie, L, 'Moralisation de la vie publique: le Conseil de l'Europe et la lutte contre la corruption' [2013] *Constitutions* 461
Sordino, M-C, 'Lanceur d'alerte et droit pénal : entre méfiance et protection?' [2017] *Revue des sociétés* 206
Stappers Tadeusz, J, 'EU Whistleblower Protection Directive: Europe on Whistleblowing' (2021) 22 *ERA Forum* 87
Stéphane, D, 'Les sanctions relatives à la violation des règles sur la protection des lanceurs d'alertes selon la Directive' (2019) 4 *RAE-LAE* 713
Stolowy, N, Paugam, L and Londero, A, 'The Whistleblower: An Important Person in Corporate Life? An Answer from Comparative Law' (2019) 3 *Journal of Business Law* 167
Strasser, F, 'When the Big Whistle Blows . . .' [1989] *National Law Journal* 43
Sylvia, C and Stabile, E, 'Rethinking Compliance: The Role of Whistleblowers' (2016) 84 *University of Cincinnati Law Review* 451
Tridimas, T, 'Terrorism and the ECJ: Empowerment and Democracy in the EC Legal Order' (2009) 34(1) *European Law Review* 103
Uys, T and Smit, R, "Resilience and Whistleblowers: Coping with the Consequences" (2016) 47(4) *South African Review of Sociology* 60
Valentine, S and Godkin, L, 'Moral Intensity, Ethical Decision Making, and Whistleblowing Intention' (2019) 98 *Journal of Business Research* 277
Vallet-Pamart, J, 'Genèse de la directive protégeant les lanceurs d'alerte' (2019) 4 *RAE-LAE* 681
van Meerbeeck, J, 'The Principle of Legal Certainty in the Case-Law of the European Court of Justice: From Certainty to Trust' (2016) 41(2) *European Law Review* 275
van Waeyenberge, A and Davies, Z, 'The Whistleblower Directive (2019/1937): A Satisfactory but Incomplete System (2021) 12(1) *European Journal of Risk Regulation* 236
Vandekerckhove, W, 'Is It Freedom? The Coming About of the EU Directive on Whistleblower Protection' [2021] Journal of Business Ethics 1
_____ 'Freedom of Expression as the "Broken Promise" of Whistleblower Protection' (2016) 10 *Revue des droits de l'homme* (online), journals.openedition.org/revdh/2680?lang=en accessed 15 May 2025
Vaughn, RG, 'America's First Comprehensive Statute Protecting Corporate Whistleblowers' (2005) 57 *Administrative Law Review* 1
Veil, R, 'Enforcement of Capital Markets Law in Europe – Observations from a Civil Law Country' (2010) 11 *European Business Organization Law Review* 409
Ventry Jr., DJ, 'Whistleblowers and Qui Tam for Tax' (2008) 61 *TAXLAW* 357
Vervaele, JAE, 'European Criminal Justice in the European and Global Context' (2019) 10(1) *New Journal of European Criminal Law* 7
Voorhoof, D, 'Freedom of Expression under the European Human Rights System' (2010) 2 *Inter-American and European Human Rights Journal* 3
Watts, LL and Buckley, RM, 'A Dual-Processing Model of Moral Whistleblowing in Organizations' (2017) 146 *Journal of Business Ethics* 669
Whelan, P, 'Contemplating the Future: Personal Criminal Sanctions for Infringement of EC Competition Law' (2008) 19 King's Law Journal 364
White, S, 'A Matter of Life or Death – Whistleblowing Legislation in the EU' (2018) 3 *EUCRIM* 171
Wilson, S, 'The New Market Abuse Regulation and Directive on Criminal Sanctions for Market Abuse: European Capital Markets Law and New Global Trends in Financial Crime Enforcement' (2015) 16 *ERA Forum* 427
Wouter, WPJ, 'Fundamental Procedural Rights and Effective Enforcement of Articles 101 and 102 TFEU in the European Competition Network' (2020) 43(1) *World Competition* 5
Yeoh, P 'Whistleblowing: Motivations, Corporate Self-Regulation, and the Law' [2014] *International Journal of Law & Management* 459

Newspaper and Magazine Articles

BBC, 'Daphne Caruana Galizia murder: Suspect pleads guilty' (23 February 2021) < www.bbc.com/news/world-europe-56172454 accessed 15 May 2025

BBC, 'FinCEN Files: All you need to know about the document leak' (21 September 2020) < www.bbc.com/news/uk-54226107 accessed 15 May 2025

Brunsden, J, 'LuxLeaks: Luxembourg's response to an international tax scandal' *Financial Times* (23 June 2017) www.ft.com/content/de228b90-3632-11e7-99bd-13beb0903fa3 accessed 15 May 2025

Burke Kennedy, E, 'Overview: What is the Mahon tribunal?' (2012) *The Irish Times* < www.irishtimes.com/news/overview-what-is-the-mahon-tribunal-1.705457 accessed 15 May 2025

Curley, S, 'Danske Bank: the story of Europe's biggest money laundering scandal' *Times Malta* (23 October 2018) timesofmalta.com/articles/view/danske-bank-the-story-of-europes-biggest-money-laundering-scandal.692375 accessed 15 May 2025

Deloitte (interview with Keith Darcy and Maureen Mohlenkamp), 'Whistleblower Programs: Who should be in charge?' *The Wall Street Journal* (14 April 2015) deloitte.wsj.com/riskandcompliance/2015/04/14/whistleblower-programs-who-should-be-in-charge/ accessed 15 May 2025

Garside, J, 'Panama Papers: European parliament opens inquiry' *The Guardian* (27 September 2016) www.theguardian.com/world/2016/sep/27/panama-papers-inquiry-opens-at-european-parliament accessed 15 May 2025

Graig, A, 'Whistleblowers need more protection in a post-Covid workplace', *Financial Times* (London, 2020) www.ft.com/content/284f67a5-c221-443d-b525-258a3fc7ee66 accessed 15 May 2025

Irwin-Hunt, A, 'Luxembourg tries to shed 'tax heaven' label', *Financial Times* (15 September 2020) www.ft.com/content/ebfea57b-ce1c-4e1d-8b08-640d1a87ff99 accessed 15 May 2025

Loftus, P, 'Johnson & Johnson Ordered to Pay $327 Million' *The Wall Street Journal* (4 June 2011) www.wsj.com/articles/SB10001424052702303745304576364621661093868 accessed 15 May 2025

Marriage, M, 'Esma and the invisible whistleblower hotline', *Financial Times* (18 December 2016) www.ft.com/content/59162a1e-c3a6-11e6-9bca-2b93a6856354 accessed 15 May 2025

Morse, J and Bower, A, 'The Party Crasher' *TIME* (2002-2003)

Nader, R, 'Editorial:A Code for Professional Integrity', *The New York Times* (15 January 1971) 43

Pasztor, A, 'Northrop Agrees to Pay $325 Million to Settle Suit', *The Wall Street Journal* (Los Angeles, 3 April 2009) B1

Radden Keefe, P, 'The bank robber – the computer technician who exposed a Swiss bank's darkest secrets' (2016) *The New Yorker* < www.newyorker.com/magazine/2016/05/30/herve-falcianis-great-swiss-bank-heist accessed 15 May 2025

Reinicke, C, 'Who is Harry Markopoulos? The famed Madoff whistleblower could make millions after publishing a report accusing GE of fraud', *Business Insider* (16 August 2019) markets.businessinsider.com/news/stocks/harry-markopolos-madoff-whistleblower-accounting-expert-who-is-he-2019-8-1028453215 accessed 15 May 2025

Ryntjes, D, 'US regulators offer rewards to corporate whistleblowers in Europe', *DW Business* (Washington, 18 August 2010) www.dw.com/en/us-regulators-offer-rewards-to-corporate-whistleblowers-in-europe/a-5917709 accessed 15 May 2025

Steinbuch, Y, 'Chinese doctor who worked with late whistleblower dead from coronavirus', *New York Post* (3 March 2020) nypost.com/2020/03/03/chinese-doctor-who-worked-with-late-whistleblower-dead-from-coronavirus/amp/ accessed 15 May 2025

Thomas, JA, 'Policing the Banks is an Inside Job', *The New York Times* (30 September 2016) www.nytimes.com/2016/10/01/opinion/policing-the-banks-is-an-inside-job.html?_r=0 accessed 15 May 2025

TIME, 'Person of the Year: The Whistleblowers 2002' content.time.com/time/specials/packages/article/0,28804,2019712_2019710_2019677,00.html accessed 15 May 2025

Tufekci, Z, 'Wikileaks Put Women in Turkey in Danger, for No Reason' *Huffpost* (25 July 2016, updated 6 December 2017) www.huffpost.com/entry/wikileaks-erdogan-emails_b_11158792?guccounter=1 accessed 15 May 2025

Woodward, A and Pickrell, R, 'Whistleblower doctor Li Wenliang, who was censored after sounding the alarm about the coronavirus, has died in Wuhan', *Business Insider* (6 February 2020) www.businessinsider.com/coronavirus-whistleblower-doctor-li-wenliang-in-critical-condition-2020-2?r=US&IR=T accessed 15 May 2025

Transparency International Publications

Terracol, M, 'Are EU Governments Taking Whistleblower Protection Seriously?' Transparency International and Whistleblowing International Network (2021) images.transparencycdn.org/images/2021_EU-Governments-Whistleblower-Protection_English_12052021.pdf accessed 15 May 2025

Transparency International, 'Building on the EU Directive for Whistleblower Protection' (2019) www.transparency.org/whatwedo/publication/building_on_the_eu_directive_for_whistleblower_protection accessed 15 May 2025

Transparency International. 'A Best Practice Guide for Whistleblowing Legislation' (2018) www.transparency.org/whatwedo/publication/best_practice_guide_for_whistleblowing_legislation accessed 15 May 2025

Transparency International, 'Whistleblower Protection in the EU : Analysis of and Recommendations on the Proposed EU Directive' (2018) www.transparency.org/whatwedo/publication/whistleblower_protection_in_the_eu_analysis_of_and_recommendations accessed 15 May 2025

Transparency International, 'The Business Case for 'Speaking Up': How Internal Reporting Mechanisms Strengthen Private-Sector Organisations' (2017) www.transparency.org/whatwedo/publication/business_case_for_speaking_up accessed 15 May 2025

Transparency International, 'Two sides of the same coin? Independence and accountability of the European Central Bank' (2017) transparency.eu/resource/two-sides-of-the-same-coin-independence-and-accountability-of-the-european-central-bank/ accessed 15 May 2025

Transparency International, '"Lanceurs d'alerte": quelle perception de la part des salariés?' (2015) transparency-france.org/wp-content/uploads/2016/04/R%C3%A9sultats-sondage-HarrisInteractive.pdf accessed 15 May 2025

Reports

Article 29 Data Protection Working Party, 'Opinion 1/2006 on the application of EU data protection rules to internal whistleblowing schemes in the fields of accounting, internal accounting controls, auditing matters, fight against bribery, banking and financial crime' (2006) ec.europa.eu/justice/article-29/documentation/opinion-recommendation/files/2006/wp117_en.pdf accessed 15 May 2025

Blueprint for Free Speech, 'Factsheet on the Draft law of the Republic of Germany for better protection of whistleblowers and for the implementation of the Directive on the protection of persons reporting breaches of Union law' (2020) static1.squarespace.com/static/5e249291de6f0056c7b1099b/t/605ca1d69bc3860571bf08de/1616683492728/EN+Factsheet+German+Law.pdf accessed 15 May 2025

Broeders, D and Prenio, J, 'Innovative Technology in Financial Supervision (suptech) – The Experience of Early Users' (2018) FSI Insights on Policy Implementation No 9 www.bis.org/fsi/publ/insights9.pdf accessed 15 May 2025

Clarke, B and Hardiman, N, 'Crisis in the Irish Banking System' (2012) Geary WP2012/03 researchrepository.ucd.ie/bitstream/10197/4925/1/Clarke_and_Hardiman%2c_Crisis_in_the_Irish_banking_system._2012.pdf accessed 15 May 2025

Creutzfeldt, N, 'Trusting the Middle-Man: Impact and Legitimacy of Ombudsmen in Europe' (Project report – University of Westminster, 2016) www.law.ox.ac.uk/sites/files/oxlaw/ombuds_project_report_nc_2.pdf accessed 15 May 2025

Defenseur des droits (2024) Biennial Report on the protection of whistleblowers in France 2022-2023

Devine, T and Walden, S, 'International Best Practices for Whistleblower Policies' (2013) Government Accountability Project www.whistleblower.org/sites/default/files/pictures/Best_Practices_Document_for_websit e_March_13_2013.pdf accessed 15 May 2025

European Commission, 'Report from the Commission to the European Parliament and the Council on the implementation and application of Directive (EU) 2019/1937 on the protection of persons who report breaches of Union law' COM(2024) 269 final, 3 July 2024

Financial Conduct Authority & Prudential Regulation Authority for the Treasury Committee, 'Note for Financial Incentives for Whistleblowers' (2014) www.fca.org.uk/publication/financialincentives-for-whistleblowers.pdf accessed 15 May 2025

Gerdemann, S, 'Position Paper on the National Implementation of the Directive for the Protection of Persons Reporting on Breaches of Union Law'(2020) Whistleblower Netzwerk and Transparency International Deutschland www.whistleblower-net.de/wp-content/uploads/2020/05/Paper-National-Implementation-WBD.pdf accessed 15 May 2025

Global Business Ethic Survey, 'Measuring Risk and Promoting Workplace Integrity' (ECI, 2016) www.boeingsuppliers.com/2016_Global_Ethics_Survey_Report.pdf accessed 15 May 2025

Hossfeld, C, Muller-Lagarde, Y, Alexander, D, Pöschke, M and Zevounou, L, 'L'intérêt public européen/ European Public Interest (Rapport de recherche final, ANC, Autorité des normes comptables, 2018, hal-01862364)

Institute of International Finance, 'Deploying Regtech against financial crime' (2017) www.iif.com/portals/0/Files/private/32370132_aml_final_id.pdf accessed 15 May 2025

Kenny, K and Fotaki, M, 'Post-Disclosures Strategies – Transforming Whistleblower Experiences' (2019) www.whistleblowingimpact.org/wp-content/uploads/2019/06/19-Costs-of-Whistleblowing-ESRC-report.pdf accessed 15 May 2025

Nad, V and Colvin, N, 'Whistleblowing in the European Union: a New Directive to Protect Citizens, Democracy and Rule of law' (2019) Blueprint for Free Speech static1.squarespace.com/static/5e249291de6f0056c7b1099b/t/5ed119f3deae375165af97b4/1616776389329/EU_NEW_DIRECTIVE_ANALYSIS_V5_ONLINE.pdf accessed 15 May 2025

Nyberg, P, 'Commission of Investigation into the Banking Sector in Ireland, Dublin' (2011) merrionstreet.ie/en/news-room/releases/commission-of-investigation-into-the-banking-sector.38671.shortcut.html accessed 15 May 2025

Peters, M, Seeds, K, and Harding, C, 'Findings from the Survey of Employment Tribunal Applications 2008' Employment Relations Research Series (BIS 2010) assets.publishing.service.gov.uk/government/uploads/system/uploads/attachment_data/file/144018/10-756-findings-from-seta-2008.pdf accessed 15 May 2025

Protect, 'Silence in the City 2' (2020) protect-advice.org.uk/silence-in-the-city-2/ accessed 15 May 2025

Public Concern at Work, 'Whistleblowing: A Time for Change – A 5-year Review by Public Content at Work' (2016)

Securities and Exchange Commission, 'Assessment of the SEC's Bounty Program' (2010) Report No. 474 www.sec.gov/files/474.pdf accessed 15 May 2025

The Project on Government Oversight, 'Government Accountability project and public employees for environmental responsibility, the Art of Anonymous Activism: Serving the Public while Surviving Public Service' (2002) www.bmartin.cc/dissent/documents/rr/leaking-POGO.pdf accessed 15 May 2025

Wolff, H-J, 'Normenkontrolle und Gesetzesbegriff in der attischen Demokratie' (1970) extrait des Sitzungsberichte der Heidelberger Akademie der Wissenschaften

Online Sources

Bather, A and Kelly, M, 'Whistleblowing: The Advantages of Self-regulation' (2005) 82 Working Paper Series, Department of Accounting, University of Waikato, researchcommons.waikato.ac.nz/handle/10289/1683 accessed 15 May 2025

Blanchard, OJ, 'The Crisis: Basic Mechanisms, and Appropriate Policies' (2008) MIT Department of Economics, Working Paper N° 09-01 papers.ssrn.com/sol3/papers.cfm?abstract_id=1324280 accessed 15 May 2025

Brockhaus, R and Kafteranis, D, 'No more Piecemeal Tactics: Call for a comprehensive implementation of EU's Whistleblowing Directive' (VerBlog, 10 July 2020) dx.doi.org/10.17176/20200710-235503-0 accessed 15 May 2025

Campbell, T, 'Workplace Free Speech as Human Rights' (2002) Centre for Applied Philosophy and Public Ethics www.yumpu.com/en/document/view/34268179/workplace-free-speech-as-a-human-right-cappe-centre-for accessed 15 May 2025

Devine, T, 'Assessment of European Union Whistleblower Directive' (Government Accountability Project, 17 April 2019) www.whistleblower.org/blog/assessment-of-european-union-whistleblower-directive/ accessed 15 May 2025

_____ 'Assessment of European Union Whistleblower Directive' (Government Accountability Project, 2020) wordpress-350926-1087337.cloudwaysapps.com/blog/assessment-of-european-union-whistleblower-directive/ accessed 15 May 2025

Esposito, M, 'The European Financial Crisis – Analysis and a Novel Intervention' (2014) Harvard University scholar.harvard.edu/files/markesposito/files/eurocrisis.pdf accessed 15 May 2025

Fazzari, R, 'Offshore Trove Exposes Trump-Russia links and Piggy Banks of the Wealthiest 1 Percent' (International Consortium of Investigative Journalists, 5 November 2017) www.icij.org/investigations/paradise-papers/paradise-papers-exposes-donald-trump-russia-links-and-piggy-banks-of-the-wealthiest-1-percent/ accessed 15 May 2025

Feinstein, S and Devine, T, 'A Comparative Analysis of US v EU Whistleblower Law' (Government Accountability Project, 2019) whistleblower.org/blog/a-comparative-analysis-of-u-s-v-e-u-whistleblower-law/ accessed 15 May 2025

Filoromo, M and Arbitman, Z, 'Can compliance officers be whistleblowers' (Corporate Compliance Insights, 14 March 2019) www.corporatecomplianceinsights.com/can-compliance-officers-be-whistleblowers/ accessed 15 May 2025

Franke, B, Moser, H and Simons, D, 'A Carrot Without a Stick – Whistleblowing Rewards Under the Dodd-Frank Act' (2018) SSRN Working paper, papers.ssrn.com/sol3/papers.cfm?abstract_id=2822313 accessed 15 May 2025

Globaleaks, www.globaleaks.org accessed 15 May 2025

Goel, A, 'Algorithmic Bias: Challenges and Solutions' (MS&E 238 Blog, 4 August 2017) mse238blog.stanford.edu/2017/08/adeesh/algorithmic-bias-challenges-and-solutions/ accessed 15 May 2025

Gottlieb, C, 'New EU Directive strengthens protection of whistleblowers' (Alert Memorandum, 22 October 2019) www.clearygottlieb.com/-/media/files/alert-memos-2019/new-eu-directive-strengthens-protection-of-whistleblowers.pdf accessed 15 May 2025

Greenberg, A, 'How reporters pulled off the Panama Papers, the biggest leak in whistleblower history' (*Wired*, 4 April 2016) www.wired.com/2016/04/reporters-pulled-off-panama-papers-biggest-leak-whistleblower-history/ accessed 15 May 2025

Haigh, R and Bowal, P, 'Whistleblowing and Freedom of Conscience: Towards a New Legal Analysis' (2012) Comparative Research in Law & Political Economy, Research Paper No. 1974982, digitalcommons.osgoode.yorku.ca/cgi/viewcontent.cgi?article=1315&context=clpe accessed 15 May 2025

Handley, A, 'New EU whistleblowing Directive – what UK financial services firms need to know' (Hogan Lovells Publications, 11 December 2019) www.hoganlovells.com/en/publications/new-eu-whistleblowing-directive-what-uk-financial-services-firms-need-to-know accessed 15 May 2025

Kafteranis, D, 'Protection of Whistleblowers in the European Union: The Promising Parliament Resolution and the Challenge for the European Commission' (Oxford Business Law Blog, 14

December 2017) www.law.ox.ac.uk/business-law-blog/blog/2017/12/protection-whistleblowers-european-union-promising-parliament accessed 15 May 2025
_____ 'Sectoral Provisions and the Directive on the Protection of Whistle-blowers: No to a Complex Relationship' (Oxford Business Law Blog, 4 June 2020) www.law.ox.ac.uk/business-law-blog/blog/2020/06/sectoral-provisions-and-directive-protection-whistle-blowers-no accessed 15 May 2025
_____ 'The Pilatus Bank Scandal: Time to Reconsider Banking Supervision, Anti-money Laundering and Whistle-blower's Protection in the EU' (European Law Blog, 5 December 2018) europeanlawblog.eu/2018/12/05/the-pilatus-bank-scandal-time-to-reconsider-banking-supervision-anti-money-laundering-and-whistle-blowers-protection-in-the-eu/ accessed 15 May 2025
Keenan, A, 'The EU's Whistleblowing Directive' (Orrick Finance, 9 December 2019) blogs.orrick.com/financial/2019/12/09/the-eus-whistleblowing-directive/ accessed 15 May 2025
Kostyack, B, 'Illicit Cash Act Contains Anti-Money Laundering Provisions for International Whistleblower Rewards (Whistleblower Network News, 26 February 2020) whistleblowersblog.org/2020/02/articles/whistleblower-news/illicit-cash-act-contains-anti-money-laundering-provisions-for-international-whistleblower-rewards/ accessed 15 May 2025
Mario Draghi letter to Sven Giegold (European Central Bank, 26 September 2019) www.ecb.europa.eu/pub/pdf/other/ecb.mepletter190927_Giegold~bdb5d44333.en.pdf accessed 15 May 2025
Pantazatou, K, 'The New Directive on Whistleblowers' Protection: Any Impact on Taxation?' (Kluwer International Tax Blog, 22 May 2019) kluwertaxblog.com/2019/05/22/the-newdirective-on-whistleblowers-protection-any-impact-on-taxation/ accessed 15 May 2025
US Department of Justice Civil Division, 'Statistics' (2013) www.justice.gov/civil/docs_forms/C-FRAUDS_FCA_Statistics.pdf> accessed 15 May 2025
Webber, SJ and Davis-Nozemack, K, 'Lost Opportunities: The Underuse of Tax Whistleblowers' (2015) Accounting Faculty Publications, Paper 53 ecommons.udayton.edu/acc_fac_pub/53/ accessed 15 May 2025

Other Material

Basel Committee on Banking Supervision, 'Compliance and the Compliance Function in Banks' (2005) www.bis.org/publ/bcbs113.pdf accessed 15 May 2025
Bernie Madoff Biography www.biography.com/crime-figure/bernard-madoff accessed 15 May 2025
Casey, KL, 'Statement by SEC Commissioner: Adoption of Rules for Implementing the Whistleblower Provisions of Section 21F of the Securities Exchange Act of 1934' (2011) www.sec.gov/news/speech/2011/spch052511klc-item2.htm accessed 15 May 2025
International Consortium of Investigative Journalists (ICIJ), 'Luxleaks Investigation' www.icij.org/investigations/luxembourg-leaks/ accessed 15 May 2025
International Consortium of Investigative Journalists (ICIJ), 'The Panama Papers: Exposing the Rogue Offshore Finance Industry' www.icij.org/investigations/panama-papers/ accessed 15 May 2025
Kohn, SM, 'Letter to the President of the European Parliament in relation to the Proposal for a Directive of the European Parliament and of the Council on the Protection of Person reporting breaches of Union law' (2019) www.whistleblowers.org/wp-content/uploads/2019/02/EU-WB-Directive-Letter-2.7.19.pdf accessed 15 May 2025
_____ 'Memorandum – Implementation of the European Union Whistleblower Protection Directive (2019/1937)' (2020) g7x5y3i9.rocketcdn.me/wp-content/uploads/2020/08/Kohn-EU-Directive-Implementation-Memo.pdf accessed 15 May 2025
_____ 'The AML Whistleblower Program: A New Era for Money-Laundering Enforcement' (International Banker, 7 March 2024) internationalbanker.com/banking/the-aml-whistleblower-program-a-new-era-for-money-laundering-enforcement/ accessed 15 May 2025

Paredes, TA, 'Statement at Open Meeting to Adopt Final Rules for Implementing the Whistle-blower Provisions of Section 21F of the Securities Exchange Act of 1934' (2011) www.sec.gov/news/speech/2011/spch052511tap-item2.htm accessed 15 May 2025

Record Project, Public Procurement Transparency and Integrity, 'Guide to EU Directive on Whistle-blowers Protection – Key Elements relevant to Public Procurement' (2019) www.access-info.org/wp-content/uploads/ML-2-Whistleblower.pdf accessed 15 May 2025

Scaturro, R, 'Defining Whistleblowing' (2018) IACA Research & Science www.iaca.int/images/Research/Research_paper_05_Ruggero_Scaturro_final.pdf accessed 15 May 2025

Searle, N, 'EU Directive on Institutions for Occupational Retirement Provisions (IORP II)' (2016) The National Law Review www.natlawreview.com/article/eu-directive-institutions-occupational-retirement-provision-iorp-ii?amp accessed 15 May 2025

US Securities and Exchange Commission, 'SEC announces $300,000 whistleblower award to audit and compliance professional who reported company's wrongdoing' www.sec.gov/news/press-release/2014-180 accessed 15 May 2025

Warner, MR, 'Senators Introduce Legislation to Improve Corporate Transparency and Combat Money Laundering, Terrorist Financing' (2019) Press Release, www.warner.senate.gov/public/index.cfm/2019/9/date accessed 15 May 2025

Worth, M, 'The EU Campaign for Whistleblower Rewards: A New Idea for Old Europe' (2020) www.whistleblowersblog.org/2020/08/articles/features/the-eu-campaign-for-whistleblower-rewards-a-new-idea-for-old-europe/ accessed 15 May 2025

Zuckerman, J and Stock, M, 'Top 6 Reasons Why the SEC Whistleblower Program is Successful' (2020) The National Law Review www.natlawreview.com/article/top-6-reasons-why-sec-whistle-blower-program-successful?amp accessed 15 May 2025

ILO Official Documents and Publications

ILO, Law and practice on protecting whistle-blowers in the public and financial services sector (2019) www.ilo.org/wcmsp5/groups/public/---ed_dialogue/---sector/documents/publication/wcms_718048.pdf accessed 15 May 2025

ILO, Thesaurus (2005) www.ilo.org/inform/online-information-resources/terminology/thesaurus/lang--en/index.htm accessed 15 May 2025

Theses

Kampourakis, I, 'Dialectics of Transparency and Secrecy in the Information Age: The Role of Whistleblowing Legislation in the Regulatory Governance of Markets and in National Security' (Dissertation submitted in partial fulfillment of the Requirements for the Degree of Doctor Iuris to the Department of Law of Freie Universität Berlin 2018)

INDEX